THE NEW CAMBRIDGE C
SAMUEL BECK

In the past decade, there has been an unprecedented upsurge of interest in Samuel Beckett's works. *The New Cambridge Companion to Samuel Beckett* offers an accessible and engrossing introduction to a key set of issues animating the field of Beckett studies today. This *Companion* considers Beckett's lasting significance by addressing a host of relevant topics. Written by a team of renowned scholars, this volume presents a continuum in Beckett studies ranging from theoretical approaches to performance studies and from manuscript research to the study of bilingualism, intertextuality, late modernism, history, philosophy, ethics, body and mind. The emphasis on burgeoning critical approaches aids the reader's understanding of recent developments in Beckett studies while prompting further exploration, assisted by the guide to further reading.

Dirk Van Hulle is Professor of English Literature at the University of Antwerp. With Mark Nixon, he is co-director of the Beckett Digital Manuscript Project (BDMP), author of *Samuel Beckett's Library* and editor-in-chief of the *Journal of Beckett Studies*. Van Hulle is the author of *Textual Awareness, Manuscript Genetics: Joyce's Know-How, Beckett's Nohow* and *The Making of Samuel Beckett's 'Stirrings Still' and 'what is the word'*. His most recent publication is *Modern Manuscripts: The Extended Mind and Creative Undoing*.

A complete list of books in the series is at the back of this book

THE NEW CAMBRIDGE
COMPANION TO
SAMUEL BECKETT

THE NEW CAMBRIDGE COMPANION TO
SAMUEL BECKETT

EDITED BY
DIRK VAN HULLE
University of Antwerp

CAMBRIDGE
UNIVERSITY PRESS

32 Avenue of the Americas, New York, NY 10013-2473, USA

Cambridge University Press is part of the University of Cambridge.

It furthers the University's mission by disseminating knowledge in the pursuit of education, learning and research at the highest international levels of excellence.

www.cambridge.org
Information on this title: www.cambridge.org/9781107427815

© Cambridge University Press 2015

This publication is in copyright. Subject to statutory exception and to the provisions of relevant collective licensing agreements, no reproduction of any part may take place without the written permission of Cambridge University Press.

First published 2015

Printed in Great Britain by Clays Ltd, St Ives plc

A catalog record for this publication is available from the British Library.

Library of Congress Cataloging in Publication Data
The New Cambridge Companion to Samuel Beckett / edited by
Dirk Van Hulle, University of Antwerp.
  pages   cm. – (Cambridge companions to literature)
 ISBN 978-1-107-07519-1 (hardback) – ISBN 978-1-107-42781-5 (paperback)
 1. Beckett, Samuel, 1906–1989 – Criticism and interpretation.   I. Hulle, Dirk van, editor.
PR6003.E282Z781726 2015
848′.91409–dc23   2014025983

ISBN 978-1-107-07519-1 Hardback
ISBN 978-1-107-42781-5 Paperback

Cambridge University Press has no responsibility for the persistence or accuracy of URLs for external or third-party Internet Web sites referred to in this publication and does not guarantee that any content on such Web sites is, or will remain, accurate or appropriate.

CONTENTS

Notes on Contributors	*page* ix
Acknowledgements	xiii
List of Abbreviations	xv
Introduction: A Beckett Continuum	xvii
DIRK VAN HULLE	
Chronology of Beckett's Writings	xxvii

PART I   CANON

1. Early Beckett: 'The One Looking Through His Fingers'   3
   JOHN PILLING

2. *Molloy*, *Malone Dies*, *The Unnamable*: The Novel Reshaped   19
   ANGELA MOORJANI

3. Still Stirrings: Beckett's Prose from *Texts for Nothing* to *Stirrings Still*   33
   PETER BOXALL

4. *Waiting for Godot* and Beckett's Cultural Impact   48
   RÓNÁN MCDONALD

5. *Endgame* and Shorter Plays: Religious, Political and Other Readings   60
   EMILIE MORIN

6. Ruptures of the Visual: Beckett as Critic and Poet   73
   MARK NIXON

PART II   POETICS

7. Beckett and Late Modernism   89
   SHANE WELLER

CONTENTS

8 Beckett's Intertexts 103
   ANTHONY UHLMANN

9 Bilingual Beckett: Beyond the Linguistic Turn 114
   SAM SLOTE

10 Samuel Beckett and the 'Idea' of Theatre: Performance through Artaud and Deleuze 126
   S. E. GONTARSKI

PART III TOPICS

11 Samuel Beckett with, in, and around Philosophy 145
   PETER FIFIELD

12 Love and Lobsters: Beckett's Meta-Ethics 158
   JEAN-MICHEL RABATÉ

13 Beckett, Body and Mind 170
   ULRIKA MAUDE

14 'Humanity in Ruins': Beckett and History 185
   SEÁN KENNEDY

   Works Cited 201
   Index 221

NOTES ON CONTRIBUTORS

PETER BOXALL is Professor of English at the University of Sussex. His books include *Don DeLillo: The Possibiity of Fiction* (2006), *Since Beckett* (2009) and *Twenty-First Century Fiction* (2013). He is co-editor of volume 7 of *The Oxford History of the Novel*, editor of *1001 Books* and editor of *Textual Practice*. *The Value of the Novel* is forthcoming with Cambridge University Press, and he is currently working on a monograph entitled *The Prosthetic Imagination: A History of the Novel as Artificial Life*.

PETER FIFIELD is Junior Research Fellow in English at St John's College, Oxford. He is the author of *Late Modernist Style in Samuel Beckett and Emmanuel Levinas* (2013) and editor of *Samuel Beckett: Debts and Legacies* (2013) and a special issue of *Modernism/modernity* on Beckett and the archive (2011). His current book project examines physiological illness in modernist writing, including the work of D. H. Lawrence, Virginia Woolf and Ford Madox Ford.

S. E. GONTARSKI is Robert O. Lawton Distinguished Professor of English at Florida State University. He has written widely on modernist literature, cultural studies and philosophy. His most recent books are two in the series "Understanding Philosophy, Understanding Modernism," which he also co-edits: *Understanding Bergson, Understanding Modernism* (2013) and *Understanding Deleuze, Understanding Modernism* (2014), both edited with Paul Ardoin and Laci Mattison. He has also recently edited *The Beckett Critical Reader: Archives, Theories, and Translations* (2012) and *The Edinburgh Companion to Samuel Beckett and the Arts* (2014).

SEÁN KENNEDY is Associate Professor of English and Associate Dean (Research and Outreach) at Saint Mary's University, Halifax, Nova Scotia. He has published widely on Samuel Beckett, including *Beckett and Ireland* (Cambridge University Press, 2010). He is also the founder of the Queering Ireland conference organisation.

NOTES ON CONTRIBUTORS

ULRIKA MAUDE is Senior Lecturer in Modernism and Twentieth-Century Literature at the University of Bristol. She is the author of *Beckett, Technology and the Body* (Cambridge University Press, 2009) and editor of *Beckett and Phenomenology* (2009, with Matthew Feldman), *The Cambridge Companion to the Body in Literature* (2015, with David Hillman) and the *Bloomsbury Companion to Modernist Literature* (2015, with Mark Nixon). She has published essays and articles on modernism, perception and theories of embodiment, and she is currently finishing a monograph on Beckett and medicine. She is a member of the editorial board of the *Journal of Beckett Studies*.

PROFESSOR RÓNÁN MCDONALD is the director of the Global Irish Studies Centre, University of New South Wales. He was the director of the Beckett International Foundation, University of Reading, from 2004 to 2010. He has research interests in Irish modernism and the value of the humanities. His books include *Tragedy and Irish Literature* (2002), *The Cambridge Introduction to Samuel Beckett* (2007) and *The Death of the Critic* (2008).

ANGELA MOORJANI is Professor Emerita of French and Intercultural Studies at the University of Maryland, Baltimore County. She has published widely on Beckett's fiction and theatre and is co–editor-in-chief of *Samuel Beckett Today / Aujourd'hui*. Her books and essays on repetition and mourning in literature and the arts fuse psychoanalysis and pragmatics with feminist thought. She has recently been investigating French cultural ghosts in Beckett's œuvre.

EMILIE MORIN is Lecturer in the Department of English and Related Literature at the University of York. Her research focuses on modern and contemporary British and Irish literature, theatre history and European modernism. She has published essays on various facets of Beckett's work and is the author of *Samuel Beckett and the Problem of Irishness* (2009) and co-editor of *Theatre and Ghosts: Materiality, Performance and Modernity* (2014) and *Theatre and Human Rights after 1945: Things Unspeakable* (forthcoming).

MARK NIXON is Associate Professor in Modern Literature at the University of Reading, where he is also the director of the Beckett International Foundation. With Dirk Van Hulle, he is editor-in-chief of the *Journal of Beckett Studies* and co-director of the Beckett Digital Manuscript Project. He is also an editor of *Samuel Beckett Today / Aujourd'hui* and the current president of the Samuel Beckett Society. He has published widely on Beckett's work; recent books include *Samuel Beckett's Library*, written with Dirk Van Hulle (Cambridge University Press, 2013) and the critical edition of Beckett's short story "Echo's Bones" (2014).

JOHN PILLING is Emeritus Professor of English and European Literature at the University of Reading and has been director of the Beckett International Foundation and editor of the *Journal of Beckett Studies*. He is the author and/

or editor of several critical studies on Beckett, collections of essays and editions (notably the *Collected Poems*, with the late Seán Lawlor), most recently the first full-length monograph on *More Pricks Than Kicks*. He is collaborating on forthcoming editions of the six *Murphy* notebooks and the "Whoroscope" Notebook, and writing *Shadows as Solid Things: Four Nouvelles and Three Novels*.

JEAN-MICHEL RABATÉ, Professor of English and Comparative Literature at the University of Pennsylvania since 1992, is a curator of Slought Foundation, an editor of the *Journal of Modern Literature* and a Fellow of the American Academy of Arts and Sciences. He has authored or edited more than thirty books on modernism, psychoanalysis and philosophy. Recent and forthcoming books include *Crimes of the Future* (2014), *An Introduction to Literature and Psychoanalysis* (2014), *A Companion to 1922* (2015) and *The Value of Samuel Beckett* (forthcoming).

SAM SLOTE is Associate Professor in the School of English at Trinity College Dublin and co-director of the Samuel Beckett Summer School. His most recent book is *Joyce's Nietzschean Ethics* (2013). In addition to Joyce and Beckett, he has written on Virginia Woolf, Vladimir Nabokov, Raymond Queneau, Dante, Mallarmé and Elvis.

ANTHONY UHLMANN is Director of the Writing and Society Research Centre at the University of Western Sydney. He is the author of *Beckett and Poststructuralism* and *Samuel Beckett and the Philosophical Image* and editor of *Beckett in Context*. He was the editor of the *Journal of Beckett Studies* from 2008 to 2013. His most recent book is *Thinking in Literature: Joyce, Woolf, Nabokov*.

DIRK VAN HULLE is Professor of English Literature at the University of Antwerp (Centre for Manuscript Genetics). With Mark Nixon, he is co-director of the Beckett Digital Manuscript Project, editor-in-chief of the *Journal of Beckett Studies* and co-author of *Samuel Beckett's Library* (Cambridge University Press, 2013). His publications include *Textual Awareness* (2004); *Manuscript Genetics: Joyce's Know-How, Beckett's Nohow* (2008); *Modern Manuscripts: The Extended Mind and Creative Undoing* (2014) and (with Shane Weller) *The Making of Samuel Beckett's "L'Innommable" / "The Unnamable"* (2014).

SHANE WELLER is Professor of Comparative Literature and co-director of the Centre for Modern European Literature at the University of Kent. His publications include *A Taste for the Negative: Beckett and Nihilism* (2005); *Beckett, Literature, and the Ethics of Alterity* (2006); *Literature, Philosophy, Nihilism: The Uncanniest of Guests* (2008); *Modernism and Nihilism* (2011) and (with Dirk Van Hulle) *The Making of Samuel Beckett's "L'Innommable" / "The Unnamable"* (2014).

ACKNOWLEDGEMENTS

My first debt of gratitude is to John Pilling, whose friendship and rigorous scholarship have been an inspirational model for many years. It is a great honour to tread in his footsteps and edit the successor to his first edition of *The New Cambridge Companion to Samuel Beckett*. I would also like to thank Ray Ryan for entrusting me with this task of composing the second edition of the companion to Beckett studies for a new generation of students, and Edward Beckett for his unremitting support of Beckett scholarship.

I wish to thank all the contributors to this volume for their inspired essays, their professionalism and the great collaboration. I also owe a debt of gratitude to Steven Connor, Andrew Gibson, James Knowlson and Geert Lernout for their invaluable feedback at different stages in the genesis of this project. And especially with regard to the last stages in this process, I would like to thank Olga Beloborodova, Wout Dillen, and especially Pim Verhulst and Pim Verheyen for all their help with the chronology and copyediting of this companion. Knowing how rare the name of the character 'Pim' in Beckett's *Comment c'est* is, it is almost unbelievable that there are two young Beckettians at the University of Antwerp called Pim and that this volume would not have been the same without their help, but that is 'how it is'.

ABBREVIATIONS

Works by Samuel Beckett

ATF   *All That Fall and Other Plays for Radio and Screen*, Preface and Notes by Everett Frost (London: Faber & Faber, 2009).

BDMP1   *Stirrings Still / Soubresauts and Comment dire / what is the word*: a digital genetic edition (The Beckett Digital Manuscript Project, module 1), ed. by Dirk Van Hulle and Vincent Neyt (Brussels: University Press Antwerp, 2011), <http://www.beckettarchive.org>.

BDMP2   *L'Innommable / The Unnamable*: a digital genetic edition (The Beckett Digital Manuscript Project, module 2), ed. by Dirk Van Hulle, Shane Weller and Vincent Neyt (Brussels: University Press Antwerp, 2013), <http://www.beckettarchive.org>.

CDW   *The Complete Dramatic Works* (London: Faber & Faber, 1986).

CIWS   *Company / Ill Seen Ill Said / Worstward Ho / Stirrings Still*, ed. by Dirk Van Hulle (London: Faber & Faber, 2009).

CP   *Collected Poems*, ed. by Seán Lawlor and John Pilling (London: Faber & Faber, 2012).

CSP   *The Complete Short Prose, 1929–1989*, ed. by S. E. Gontarski (New York: Grove Press, 1995).

Dis   *Disjecta: Miscellaneous Writings and a Dramatic Fragment*, ed. by Ruby Cohn (London: John Calder, 1983).

DN   *Beckett's 'Dream' Notebook*, ed. by John Pilling (Reading: Beckett International Foundation, 1999). Note: Citations from this book refer to item rather than page number.

Dream   *Dream of Fair to Middling Women* (Dublin: Black Cat Press, 1992).

E   *Endgame*, Preface by Rónán McDonald (London: Faber & Faber, 2009).

ECEF   *The Expelled / The Calmative / The End / First Love*, ed. by Christopher Ricks (London: Faber & Faber, 2009).

HD   *Happy Days*, Preface by James Knowlson (London: Faber & Faber, 2010).

HII   *How It Is*, ed. by Magessa O'Reilly (London: Faber & Faber, 2009).

ABBREVIATIONS

KLT	*Krapp's Last Tape and Other Shorter Plays*, ed. by S. E. Gontarski (London: Faber & Faber, 2009).
LSB I	*The Letters of Samuel Beckett, vol. I, 1929–1940*, ed. by Martha Dow Fehsenfeld and Lois More Overbeck (Cambridge: Cambridge University Press, 2009).
LSB II	*The Letters of Samuel Beckett, vol. II, 1941–1956*, ed. by George Craig, Martha Dow Fehsenfeld, Dan Gunn, and Lois More Overbeck (Cambridge: Cambridge University Press, 2011).
MC	*Mercier and Camier*, ed. by Seán Kennedy (London: Faber & Faber, 2010).
MD	*Malone Dies*, ed. by Peter Boxall (London: Faber & Faber, 2010).
Mo	*Molloy*, ed. by Shane Weller (London: Faber & Faber, 2009).
MPTK	*More Pricks Than Kicks*, ed. by Cassandra Nelson (London: Faber & Faber, 2010).
Mu	*Murphy*, ed. by J. C. C. Mays (London: Faber & Faber, 2009).
PTD	*Proust and Three Dialogues with Georges Duthuit* (London: John Calder, 1965).
SP	*Selected Poems 1930–1989*, ed. by David Wheatley (London: Faber & Faber, 2009).
TFN	*Texts for Nothing and Other Shorter Prose 1950–1976*, ed. by Mark Nixon (London: Faber & Faber, 2010).
Un	*The Unnamable*, ed. by Steven Connor (London: Faber & Faber, 2010).
W	*Watt*, ed. by Chris Ackerley (London: Faber & Faber, 2009).
WFG	*Waiting for Godot: A Tragicomedy in Two Acts*, Preface by Mary Bryden (London: Faber & Faber, 2010).

Samuel Beckett – Archival and Other Material

GD	'German Diaries' (6 notebooks), Beckett International Foundation, The University of Reading.
WN	'Whoroscope' Notebook, Beckett International Foundation, The University of Reading, UoR MS3000.

Library Archives

HRC	Harry Ransom Humanities Research Center, The University of Texas at Austin.
JEK	James and Elizabeth Knowlson Collection, The University of Reading.
TCD	Department of Manuscripts, Trinity College Dublin Library.
UoR	Beckett International Foundation, The University of Reading.

DIRK VAN HULLE

INTRODUCTION: A BECKETT CONTINUUM

Beckett seems to hit a nerve at this moment in time. The increasing interest in his works in the past two decades is marked by at least two important trends. On the one hand, Beckett's status as a challenging writer has stimulated critics and philosophers such as Deleuze and Badiou to write key interpretations that have in their turn become objects of further critical investigation within Beckett studies and literary theory, leading to an intellectually vibrant field of study. On the other hand, the interest in Beckett has been reinforced by a historicist trend, focussing for instance on Beckett's Irish background, and by the invigorating effect of newly discovered archival material. In the past fifteen years and especially since the publication of James Knowlson's biography (1996) and John Pilling's *Beckett before Godot* (1997), several scholars have drawn attention to an impressive amount of archive material that had not been taken into account before. Notable examples are the Dante notes (Ferrini 2003; Caselli 2005a); the TCD manuscripts (Frost and Maxwell 2006); the notes on Arnold Geulincx (Uhlmann et al. 2006; Tucker 2012; Frost 2012); Beckett's interwar notes on philosophy and psychology (Feldman 2006b); his students' notes on the lectures at Trinity College, Dublin (Le Juez 2007); and the 'German Diaries' (Nixon 2011). The publication of Beckett's letters (2009–) made a wealth of new information widely available, and so did the BDMP (2011–).

All this new material has had a considerable impact on the perception of the Beckett canon, to such a degree that S. E. Gontarski coined the phrase 'the grey canon' (Gontarski 2006) to denote all the writings by Beckett (notes, letters, diaries, criticism, self-translations, abandoned works) that provide us with a new context to interpret his published works. There are evidently numerous ways to approach both the Beckett canon and the 'grey' canon, depending on whether or to what extent one wishes to take this newly available contextual information into account. These are methodological questions any student of literature will be confronted with at some point, and for which the intellectual energy in Beckett studies currently provides an excellent paradigm. This new edition of *The New Cambridge Companion to Samuel Beckett* aims to guide students and interested readers through Beckett criticism the way John Pilling's excellent first edition (1994) did for a different period in Beckett studies. The primary goal is to offer an accessible and stimulating introduction to a key set of issues animating the field of Beckett studies today, and to address the central question of why Beckett matters now.

In recent years, Beckett criticism has sometimes tended to present itself in terms of two camps, with respectively historicist and theoretical interests. I think we have moved beyond that black-and-white antithesis. For instance, an expert in literary theory such as Anthony Uhlmann (author of *Beckett and Poststructuralism*) can at the same time be the scholar who made Beckett's notes on Arnold Geulincx available in the 2006 translation of Geulincx's *Ethics*. As the contributors to this volume show, what makes Beckett studies so vibrant today is the interaction among different approaches, ranging from theory to contextual, historical and archival research. This mutually beneficial interaction, resulting in a critical continuum, is the overarching rationale of this book.

A Critical Continuum

The practice of Beckett criticism in the last few years shows that an exchange of ideas between various approaches is mutually enriching. Historicist and more theoretical interests are in many ways complementary and their interaction is marked not just by polite respect, but by an appreciation of the benefits of working together. Instead of dividing Beckett studies into dichotomies, the notion of a continuum is perhaps more accurate and more productive. In the 1980s and 1990s, Beckett studies may indeed have been somewhat dominated by what Jean-Michel Rabaté refers to as 'capital-T Theory' (Rabaté 2011b, 700). Gradually, this preoccupation with such thinkers as Kristeva, Derrida, Cixous, Foucault and Lacan shifted to other concerns. After the critical construction of a 'universal' Beckett in the second half of the previous century (emphasizing an ahistorical view of the human condition), students of his work have become increasingly aware of the importance of the 'demented particulars' (*Mu* 11). The current appreciation of the dialectics between what Pascale Casanova called 'Beckett, l'abstracteur' and the Beckett of the particulars contributes in a considerable way to the unprecedented upsurge of interest in Beckett's works, especially during and following the Beckett Centenary in 2006.

The interplay between these concrete and abstract aspects of Beckett's work is certainly not only an academic matter; it relates to the content and intrinsic qualities of Beckett's works and poetics of 'stripping away'. In times of social or economic crisis, Beckett's works apparently find increased resonance, possibly because of his concern with ethics and ascesis. As Fintan O'Toole noted during the 2013 Beckett Summer School,[1] one of the reasons why Beckett matters today has to do with the unsentimentalized, humorous persistence of his characters – in spite of themselves, in spite of the world, in spite of death. Beckett addresses the big questions, not unlike the protagonist in his favourite poem by Walther von der Vogelweide, sitting on a stone and pondering the basic ethical question of 'wie man zer welte solte leben' ['how one should live in the world'] (Vogelweide 1994, 72). To an era marked by overabundant irrelevance, Beckett's antithetical stringency offers a counterbalance, which makes him a figure of our time.

To understand his method of 'stripping away', it is important to be aware of the particulars, without which there would be nothing to strip away in the first place. On the one hand, this implies an enhanced attention to the historical circumstances, including the impact of Beckett's Irish background and of the Second World War, which 'deeply scoured his imagination' (McDonald 2009, xiv). On the other hand, this renewed attention to the particulars chimes with contemporary concerns. For instance, Beckett's sustained examination of the embodied mind and the mental mechanisms to deal with the particulars dovetails with the recent 'cognitive turn' in several disciplines within the humanities, notably in narrative theory. Thus, for instance in 'Re-Minding Modernism', David Herman reads 'Beckett's late-modernist or proto-postmodernist novel *Murphy*' as an enactment of an 'anti-Cartesian model of the mind', because the strict division between body and mind, 'the pure Cartesianism to which he had aspired is tantamount to a debilitating solipsism' (Herman 2011, 267–8). When after Murphy's death his ashes end up on the floor of a pub, it is therefore significant that his mind and body are freely mixed and distributed among the particulars, swept away by daybreak 'with the sand, the beer, the butts, the glass, the matches, the spits, the vomit' (*Mu* 171).

The way Beckett deals with the particulars is a matter of both form and content, which are inextricably bound up in his work. So in order to examine why Beckett matters today, this companion not only gives an introduction to the Beckett canon (Part I, with three essays on Samuel Beckett's prose, two essays on his drama and one essay on the poetry and criticism), but also opens up more space to accommodate different shades of critical perspective on artistic practice/form (Part II) and content (Part III).

Part I (*Canon*) starts with Beckett's fiction. John Pilling (Chapter 1) makes use of notes such as the *Murphy* notebooks, which have only recently become publicly available (2013), to discuss Beckett's early works, from his first stories to *Murphy* and *Watt*. Angela Moorjani (Chapter 2) analyses Beckett's reshaping of the novel in *Molloy*, *Malone Dies* and *The Unnamable*, taking into account the changes in critical approaches to the trilogy from the earliest reception to the most recent scholarship. Peter Boxall (Chapter 3) investigates the development of Beckett's prose after *The Unnamable*, carefully reflecting on the dangers of implicit periodization, which – for pragmatic reasons – is not always avoidable.

With regard to Beckett's dramatic works, Rónán McDonald (Chapter 4) takes Beckett's most famous play, *Waiting for Godot*, as an adequate starting point for an analysis of the cultural impact of his work, in terms of both theatrical performance and the continued impact in a broader cultural sense. For, ever since the initial bafflement that characterized its early reception, the piece has inspired philosophers and artists alike, and has become so iconic that it has even been parodied in children's programmes such as *Sesame Street*. Emilie Morin (Chapter 5) discusses religious, political and other readings of Beckett's *Endgame* and shorter plays, taking into account the tension between authorial control and the fluidity of the texts due to Beckett's revisions, as well as issues of censorship and bowdlerization (such as the Lord Chamberlain's objection to the line about God in *Endgame* – 'The bastard! He doesn't exist!', *CDW* 119). The plays and their reception are an adequate corpus and starting point for an evaluation of developments in Beckett criticism, from 'humanist' to 'existentialist' interpretations, from Adorno's 'Versuch, das *Endspiel* zu verstehen' to Deleuze's 'L'Épuisé' and beyond.

Focusing on Beckett's criticism and poetry, Mark Nixon (Chapter 6) studies a lesser known but no less important aspect of Beckett's canon, building on Lawrence E. Harvey's pioneering book on this topic. Harvey's study, however, dates from 1970. It took more than four decades before the first critical edition of Beckett's poetry was published (Beckett 2012). As to the critical writings, Beckett's literary analyses and his capacity as an art critic are increasingly being revalued. Chapter 6 therefore focuses on Beckett's interest in the visual arts as evidenced for instance in the 'German Diaries' and in his correspondence with Georges Duthuit.

Part II (*Poetics*) zooms in on Beckett and late modernism, Beckett's intertexts, his bilingual writings and the performative aspects of his work. A few decades ago, the question of whether Beckett was a modernist or a postmodernist was the subject of long debates, notably since Brian McHale's discussion of Beckett as a 'late modernist' in *Constructing Postmodernism* (1992, 28) and the publication of Anthony Cronin's biography, *The Last Modernist*. Instead of resurrecting these old debates, Shane Weller (Chapter 7) explores a new view on Beckett as an exponent of late modernism. Taking into account the broader field of modernism studies, this chapter describes what this late modernism entails, examines how it manifests itself and attempts to define Beckett's place in literary history.

Anthony Uhlmann (Chapter 8) discusses the vastness of the intertextual complex surrounding Beckett's texts, each of which is – in Roland Barthes's terms – a tissue of past citations. This aspect of Beckett's work is especially interesting when the incorporation of passages from a variety of historical sources is deliberately fragmentary as in *Happy Days*. Winnie's 'something something', filling the gaps in the partially remembered quotes (as in the reference to Thomas Gray, 'something something laughing wild amid severest woe'), emphasizes the ambiguity of both the presence of this body of knowledge and its phantom limbs (*CDW* 150; Gray 2013). As Chapter 8 shows, intertextual research is not a matter of 'source hunting' or of looking for 'influences', but of examining the condition of the Beckettian text and of enhancing readers' appreciation of the complex interplay and tensions between the authority of writers and thinkers of the past (such as Dante, Shakespeare, Racine) and Beckett's experimental, innovative texts.

The multilingual nature of Beckett's reading is directly relevant to an appreciation of his works' bilingualism (Sardin 2002; Montini 2007; Mooney 2011; Slote 2011) and the linguistic scepticism that informs them. The recently published second volume of the letters contains a very open statement by Beckett about his reading of Fritz Mauthner's *Beiträge zu einer Kritik der Sprache*, which had greatly impressed him ('qui m'a très fortement impressionné'; *LSB II* 462). The role of language was central in Beckett criticism in the 1980s and 1990s, for instance in studies such as Steven Connor's chapter on self-translation in *Samuel Beckett: Repetition, Theory and Text*. This role has been reassessed in the past decade, notably by Steven Connor himself in the preface to his edition of *The Unnamable* (Connor 2010, xx), referring to Alain Badiou's urge to move beyond 'language-centred poststructuralist criticism'. Sam Slote (Chapter 9) examines the changing role of language in both Beckett's writings and Beckett criticism.

One of the issues that keeps recurring in Beckett studies relates to the tension between Beckett's instructions as a director of his own plays and the performative future of his dramatic work. In more general terms, the question is whether 'avant-garde' is a historical label or a dynamic concept that requires constant updating. Whereas Chapters 4 and 5 deal mainly with the plays as texts and with their critical reception, S. E. Gontarski (Chapter 10) investigates the performative aspects – through Artaud and Deleuze – with an equal openness toward, on the one hand, Beckett's *Theatrical Notebooks* (1993c, d) and, on the other hand, current innovative performances.

Part III (*Topics*) focuses on the themes of philosophy, ethics, the embodied mind and history. The relationship between Beckett's work and philosophy is bidirectional: his long-standing interest in philosophy has left its traces for instance in his philosophy notes and in his personal library; conversely, the philosophical interest in Beckett is evidenced for instance in the works of Theodor Adorno, Alain Badiou, Simon Critchley, Gilles Deleuze or Martha Nussbaum. If the recent developments in Beckett studies can duly be called 'important and invigorating' (Gibson 2011, 926), this is to a large extent due to an open view on philosophical and historical approaches as being mutually complementary – a view that may even be paradigmatic of a more general trend in literary studies (combining archival and theoretical approaches). Peter Fifield (Chapter 11) therefore regards both Beckett's interest in philosophy and philosophers' interest in Beckett from complementary perspectives.

Beckett's fascination with philosophy is related to his obvious interest in ethics, which manifests itself for instance in the copy of Spinoza's *Ethics* in his library (Van Hulle and Nixon 2013, 132–3) or his extensive notes on Geulincx's *Ethica*. Jean-Michel Rabaté (Chapter 12) investigates the relevance of Beckett's ethics or 'meta-ethics', founded on ignorance and impotence, characterized by a reluctance to act as the committed intellectual, but also by 'a spirit of obstinate ethical perseverance facing barbarism' (Rabaté 2010, 104).

In several ways, Beckett's work can be regarded as an 'inquiry into the human mind' (to borrow the title of a work by Thomas Reid, used by Beckett during the composition of *L'Innommable*). Many of his writings are concerned with consciousness and perception. In the past, this aspect of his works was usually discussed from the perspective of philosophy and/or psychology (see for instance Anzieu 1983). Psychology was only one of the many approaches to cognition, and I believe Beckett's work prefigures many of the concerns that have only recently been grouped under the label '4e cognition' (encompassing the *e*mbedded, *e*mbodied, *e*nactive and *e*xtended mind). An interesting new avenue of research relates these issues to brain science, including contemporary concepts of mental disorder.[2] What is innovative about these approaches is the renewed attention to embodiment. From this perspective, Ulrika Maude (Chapter 13) studies the interaction between body and mind as reflected in Beckett's notes on Samuel Johnson – including both his interest in Johnson's intellectual accomplishments and his remarkably detailed attention to the lexicographer's physical afflictions.

In Chapter 14, Seán Kennedy nuances Beckett's own statement that he had 'no sense of history' (qtd. in McNaughton 2005, 106) and approaches the question of why Beckett matters today from a historical perspective. While

Adorno suggested that it would be barbaric to write poetry after Auschwitz, this was 'precisely the point at which Beckett's creative powers were finally and fully engaged', according to Kennedy. One of the case studies is a discussion of the bowler hat in Beckett's writings. This historicizing approach illustrates what Andrew Gibson has called 'a new phase' in Beckett studies: 'A young generation of scholars have abandoned the theoretical turn that dominated work on Beckett from the late 1980s onwards' (Gibson 2011, 926). What Kennedy's essay also shows, however, is that a historicizing approach does not imply a foreclosure of other approaches.

In one form or another, all the chapters thus illustrate how the Beckettian particulars function within a theoretical discourse; how they relate to a critical framework; and how they can be conducive to various critical approaches and their mutually beneficial interaction, which marks the intellectual dynamism of Beckett studies today.

A Continuum of Multiple Canons

As a tribute and respectful reference to Ruby Cohn's *A Beckett Canon*, the introduction to this companion is called 'A Beckett Continuum', not only because of the critical continuum described in the previous section, but also because Beckett's work can be seen as a continuum. As Peter Boxall notes in Chapter 3, it is difficult not to succumb to the neatness of parcelling Beckett's work into a beginning, a middle and an end, which would reduce his individual writings to symptoms or emanations of a particular historical condition or a 'phase' in Beckett's developing poetics. The challenge is to recognize the ways in which his works were partially shaped by the logic of historical conditions, and at the same time to acknowledge their resistance to that logic. So, even though it has pragmatic advantages to faintly distinguish an early, middle and late period (as in the first three chapters on Beckett's prose), the notion of a continuum problematizes the idea of a solid 'œuvre' with neatly identifiable phases and clear turning points. In his letters – for instance to Jacoba van Velde – Beckett seldom spoke of his work in terms of his œuvre but rather in terms of his *travail*. Each of his writings can function as an autonomous work, but also as part of an ongoing 'work' or *travail*. His writings have the same 'negative capability' as the word 'still' in the middle of Keats's 'Ode to a Grecian Urn', depicting both the action of dancing figures on the Grecian urn and the stillness of their fixation in a work of art: 'For ever warm and *still* to be enjoy'd, / For ever panting, and for ever young' (Keats 1988, 345). This form of 'being in uncertainties' applies to Beckett's works both on a micro level (as in Belacqua's appreciation of Dante's 'superb pun' on the word 'pietà' in the story 'Dante and the Lobster', *MPTK* 11) and on a macro level (as in Beckett's conscious decision to let his œuvre/*travail* end in the middle of a sentence, *CIWS* 135).

Instead of presenting a list of works and a separate chronology, it therefore seemed more appropriate to combine the two in a Chronology of Beckett's Writings. The column on the left lists the works in the order in which they were written (which sometimes differs from the order of their publication). If the year of publication differs from the year of writing, the year of publication is indicated in parentheses. The start of the writing process determines the order of the works, no matter in which language they were written. The English titles are in roman, the French titles in bold typeface (with one exception: the poem 'Cascando' was not translated into French, but into German as 'Mancando'). This way, a few patterns emerge at a glance. For instance, until fairly recently it was generally assumed that Beckett's so-called revelation at the end of the Second World War coincided more or less with his decision to write in French, which was not the case, as James Knowlson, John Pilling and others have pointed out. The survey shows how many poems Beckett had already written in French in 1937–8. Another pattern that emerges is that self-translation only became more or less systematic from the 1950s onwards; and that from the late 1950s onwards, his plays tended to be originally composed in English whereas there is a slight tendency towards writing prose texts in French first and subsequently translating them into English (although this is by no means a general rule).

The self-translations are indicated in the column on the right (again with the year of publication in brackets). The titles of poems are in quotation marks; reviews are in grey typeface and other prose texts in italics. In order not to overshoot the mark, the survey does not enumerate all the separate 'textes pour rien' and 'fizzles', only their collective publications as *Textes pour rien* (1955) and *Texts for Nothing* (1967), *Foirades* (1973) and *Fizzles* (1976), which Beckett started writing in the 1950s and 1960s. The published reviews and essays are mentioned as separate publications. Some reviews and essays (such as 'Les deux besoins' and 'Le Concentrisme or Jean du Chas' remained unpublished until they were included in the collection *Disjecta* in 1983.

Inevitably, the survey cannot take all the subtleties into account. For instance: the survey indicates the four texts known as 'Faux départs' as a French title, although one of the texts is actually written in English; the poem 'something there' should perhaps be regarded as an adaptation rather than a translation of 'hors crâne'; even though the story 'Dante and the Lobster' was published separately in *This Quarter* (December 1932), it is

INTRODUCTION

not listed separately, but as part of the collection *More Pricks than Kicks* (1934), also including the stories 'Fingal', 'Ding-Dong', 'A Wet Night', 'Love and Lethe', 'Walking Out', 'What a Misfortune', 'The Smeraldina's Billet Doux', 'Yellow' and 'Draff'; the story 'Echo's Bones' (originally meant to be included in the same collection) was published posthumously, edited and annotated by Mark Nixon (2014); the dramatic text *Fragment de théâtre* (1974), translated by Beckett as *Rough for Theatre I* (1976), was preceded by an early English version, called 'The Gloaming'; translations of other writers' work have not been included, even though in some cases (for instance 'Long after Chamfort') one could argue that the translation deserves to be treated as a Beckett creation in its own right.

The aim of presenting the original works and the self-translations in separate columns is to show that there is a sort of mirror canon or self-translation canon next to what Ruby Cohn called *A Beckett Canon*. And the combination of this canon with its mirror canon results in 'a Beckett continuum' if it is completed with Beckett's unpublished canon (see Nixon 2014), including 'Lightning Calculation' (1935); 'Match nul ou L'Amour paisible' (1938), the 'Petit Sot' poems (1938–9), 'Au bout de ces années perdues' (1951–2), 'Hourrah je me suis repris' (1952), 'On le tortura bien' (1952), 'Ici personne ne vient jamais' (1952), 'Coups de gong'/'Espace souterrain' (1952), 'Mime du rêveur A' (1956), 'J. M. Mime' (1963), 'Petit Odéon' fragments (1967–8), 'Chien anagramme de niche' (before 1969), 'Film-Vidéo Cassette project' (1972), 'Long Observation of the Ray' (1975–6), 'Epilogue' (1981), 'Last Soliloquy' (1981), 'Mongrel Mime' (1983?), 'On my way' (1983?) and 'Bare Room' (1984). This unpublished canon, together with the published canon, the self-translation canon and the manuscripts that are becoming digitally available in the ongoing Beckett Digital Manuscript Project, constitute a Beckett continuum that accords with the most Beckettian of all possible words: 'on', the word that fully encompasses the creative power of its negativity, 'no', going on by means of epanorthosis and 'aporia pure and simple', proceeding 'by affirmations and negations invalidated as uttered' (*Un* 1), as in the last line of *The Unnamable* – 'I can't go on, I'll go on' – or the first lines of *Worstward Ho* and the last part of *Stirrings Still* – 'On' and 'So on'.

NOTES

1 Round table 'Beckett's Impact and Relevance Today', with Daniela Caselli, Peter Fifield, J. C. C. Mays, Mark Nixon, Fintan O'Toole and H. Porter Abbott; chair: Dirk Van Hulle.
2 Adam Piette gave an impetus in this direction by focusing on the neurological aspect of early neuropsychology and the recognizable syndromes that feature

for instance in *Murphy*. In 2008, Elizabeth Barry guest edited a volume of the *Journal of Beckett Studies*, introducing new relations between the disciplines of neuroscience, psychoanalysis and literary studies, which 'have opened up some of the most suggestive avenues in Beckett criticism to be seen for some time', marking 'a new threshold in Beckett studies' (Barry 2008, 3). Beckett's works were analysed against the background of neurological disorders such as Cotard's syndrome (Fifield 2008), aphasic symptoms (Salisbury 2008) and Tourette's (Maude 2008).

CHRONOLOGY OF BECKETT'S WRITINGS

Originals	Translations
1929 'Dante ... Bruno. Vico .. Joyce' *Assumption* *Che Sciagura* 'For Future Reference' (1930) 'Return to the Vestry' (1930) 1930 'Casket of Pralinen for a Daughter of a Dissipated Mandarin' (1931) 'Miserere oh colon'/'Text 3' (1931) 'Hell Crane to Starling' (1931) 'Whoroscope' 'At last I find' (2012) 'From the Only Poet to a Shining Whore' *Proust* (1931) 'Tristesse Janale' (2012) *Le Concentrisme or Jean du Chas* (1983) 1931 *The Possessed* 'Yoke of Liberty'/'Moly' 'Alba' (1935) 'Enueg II' (1935) 'Enueg I' (1935) 'Ce n'est au pélican'/'Text 2' (2012) *Sedendo et Quiescendo* (1932) *More Pricks than Kicks* (1934) 1932 'Dortmunder' (1935) 'Text'/'Text 1' 'Sanies II' (1935) 'Spring Song' (2012) *Dream of Fair to Middling Women* (1992)	

Originals	Translations
'Calvary by Night' (1970)	
'Home Olga' (1934)	
'Serena I' (1935)	
'Serena II' (1935)	
1933	
'Sanies I' (1935)	
'Malacoda' (1935)	
'Serena III' (1935)	
Echo's Bones (2014)	
'Echo's Bones' (1935)	
1934	
'Da Tagte Es' (1935)	
'The Vulture' (1935)	
'Seats of Honour' (2012)	
'Gnome'	
'Up he went' (2009)	
Schwabenstreich	
Proust in Pieces	
Poems by Rainer Maria Rilke	
Humanistic Quietism	
A Case in a Thousand	
Recent Irish Poetry	
Pappini's Dante	
Ex Cathezra	
The Essential and the Incidental	
Censorship in the Saorstat	
1935	
Murphy (1938)	*Murphy* (1947)
1936	
An Imaginative Work!	
'Cascando'	'Mancando' (2012)
1937	
'Ooftish' (1938)	
Intercessions by Dennis Devlin (1938)	
'Dieppe' (1961)	'Dieppe' (1945)
1938	
'they come' (1946)	'elles viennent' (1968)
'Ascension' (1946)	
'La Mouche' (1946)	
'musique de l'indifférence' (1946)	
Les deux besoins (1983)	
'à elle l'acte calme' (1946)	
'être là sans mâchoires sans dents' (1946)	
'bois seul' (1946)	
'ainsi a-t-on beau' (1946)	

Originals	Translations
'Rue de Vaugirard' (1946)	
'Arènes de Lutèce' (1946)	
'jusque dans la caverne' (1946)	
1940	
Human Wishes (1983)	
1941	
Watt (1953)	*Watt* (1968)
1945	
'Saint-Lô' (1946)	
MacGreevy on Yeats	
La Peinture des van Velde ou le monde et le pantalon	
1946	
'Antipepsis' (1997)	
La Fin (1955)	*The End* (1954)
Mercier et Camier (1970)	*Mercier and Camier* (1974)
The Capital of the Ruins (1986)	
L'Expulsé (1946)	*The Expelled* (1962)
Premier Amour (1970)	*First Love* (1973)
Le Calmant (1955)	*The Calmative* (1967)
1947	
Eleutheria (1995)	
'bon bon il est un pays' (1955)	
Peintres de l'empêchement (1948)	
'je voudrais que mon amour meure' (1948)	'I would like my love to die' (1948)
'je suis ce cours de sable qui glisse' (1948)	'My way is in the sand flowing' (1948)
'que ferais-je sans ce monde' (1948)	'What would I do without this world' (1948)
'Mort de A.D.' (1955)	
'vive morte ma seule saison' (1955)	
Molloy (1951)	*Molloy* (1955)
1948	
Malone meurt (1951)	*Malone Dies* (1956)
En attendant Godot (1952)	*Waiting for Godot* (1954)
1949	
Three Dialogues with Georges Duthuit	
1950	
L'Innommable (1953)	*The Unnamable* (1958)
1951	
Textes pour rien (1955)	*Texts for Nothing* (1967)
1952	
Henri-Hayden, homme-peintre (1955)	

Originals	Translations
1954	
Hommage à Jack B. Yeats	*Homage to Jack B. Yeats* (1971)
Foirades (1973)	*Fizzles* (1976)
1955	
From an Abandoned Work (1956)	*D'un ouvrage abandonné* (1967)
Fin de partie (1957)	*Endgame* (1958)
1956	
Acte sans paroles I (1957)	*Act Without Words I* (1958)
All That Fall (1957)	*Tous ceux qui tombent* (1957)
Fragment de théâtre I (1974)	*Rough for Theatre I* (1976)
1957	
Embers (1959)	*Cendres* (1959)
1958	
Krapp's Last Tape	*La Dernière bande* (1959)
Fragment de théâtre II (1976)	*Rough for Theatre II* (1976)
Act Without Words II (1959)	*Acte sans paroles II* (1959)
Pochade radiophonique (1975)	*Rough for Radio II* (1976)
Comment c'est (1961)	*How It Is* (1964)
1959	
L'Image	
1960	
Happy Days (1961)	*Oh les beaux jours* (1963)
1961	
Words and Music (1962)	*Paroles et musique* (1966)
Esquisse radiophonique (1973)	*Rough for Radio I* (1976)
Cascando (1963)	*Cascando* (1963)
1962	
Play (1964)	*Comédie* (1964)
1963	
Film (1967)	*Film* (1972)
1964	
Faux départs (1965)	
All Strange Away (1976)	
1965	
Come and Go (1967)	*Va et vient* (1966)
Imagination morte imaginez	*Imagination Dead Imagine*
Eh Joe (1967)	*Dis Joe* (1966)
Assez (1966)	*Enough* (1967)
1966	
Breath (1969)	*Souffle* (1971)
Bing	*Ping* (1967)

Originals	Translations
1967 *Pour Avigdor Arikha* (1976)	*For Avigdor Arikha* (1976)
1969 *Sans*	*Lessness* (1970)
1970 *Le Dépeupleur* *Abandonné* (1972)	*The Lost Ones* (1972)
1972 *Not I* (1973) *Sounds* (1978)	*Pas moi* (1975)
1973 *Still 3* (1978) *As the Story Was Told*	
1974 'hors crâne' (1976) 'dread nay' (1977) *La Falaise* (1975) *That Time* (1976)	'something there' (1975) *Cette fois* (1978)
1975 *Footfalls* (1976) *Ghost Trio* (1976)	*Pas* (1977)
1976 *Company* (1980) 'Roundelay' 'thither' (1977) *neither* (1977) *... but the clouds ...* (1977) 'mirlitonnades' (1978)	*Compagnie* (1980)
1977 'The Downs' (1989) 'one dead of night' (2012) *A Piece of Monologue* (1979)	*Solo* (1982)
1979 *Un Soir* (1980)	*One Evening* (1980)
1980 *Rockaby* (1981) *Ohio Impromptu* (1981) *Mal vu mal dit* (1981)	*Berceuse* (1982) *Impromptu d'Ohio* (1982) *Ill Seen Ill Said* (1981)
1981 *The Way* *Quad* (1984) *Ceiling* (1985)	*Plafond* (1985)

Originals	Translations
Worstward Ho (1983)	
1982	
Catastrophe	*Catastrophe*
Nacht und Träume (1984)	
1983	
Quoi où	*What Where* (1986)
Stirrings Still (1989)	*Soubresauts* (1989)
1984	
'Brief Dream' (1989)	
1987	
'il ne sait plus' (2012)	
'ochone' (2012)	
'Là'/'go where never before' (1990)	
1989	
'Le médecin' (2012)	
'Comment dire'	'what is the word'

Compiled by Pim Verhulst

PART I
Canon

I

JOHN PILLING

Early Beckett
'The One Looking Through His Fingers'

'Where would I go, if I could go, who would I be, if I could be, what would I say, if I had a voice, who says this, saying it's me?'[1]

Being Seen

Given what Beckett was to say on the subject of fame, after he had acquired it in the mid-1950s – that success and failure had never mattered much to him – it seems safe to suppose that none of the early difficulties he experienced in finding a publisher for his first substantial fiction (*Dream of Fair to Middling Women*) would have been very much softened by a more sympathetic hearing than he was to receive; he was inured to failure before he could reasonably expect to succeed. But at the same time rejection left a lasting mark on a personality ill-equipped to cope with it, blest or cursed as he was with a personality already well on the way to being either unable or unwilling to constitute itself as a 'synthesis' (*Dream* 118) of the numerous disparate and warring elements which he could not control. In middle age Beckett remembered one of the many earlier versions of himself – a poet with only a few poems to his credit, and with only one published collection[2] – as 'a very young man with nothing to say and the itch to make' (Harvey 1970, 273); yet for the best part of thirty years – 'both in public and in private, under duress, through faintness of heart, through weakness of mind' (*PTD* 123) – he had been seeking to leave some trace of having been, since he could not easily or without irony claim that he was 'Getting known' (*KLT* 10). It was clear to Beckett that 'the prospect of self-extension' (*Dis* 19) had to be more than just a simple antithetical matter ('nothing so simple as antithetical', *Dream* 137). But he was quite unclear as to how to transcend the merely negative and destructive impulses intrinsic to his psyche, and thereby avoid each 'forced move' on the way to ultimate defeat and a resigned handshake across the board. It was early borne in on Beckett that, since even 'At his simplest he was trine' (*Dream* 120), 'images of extreme complexity' (*MC* 150) would inevitably be generated in the absence of any limitations imposed by considerations of purpose and utility. Indeed, with almost complete confidence (as 'Mr Beckett' says of his creature 'Bel', short for 'Belacqua'), we can say of the young Beckett that 'various though he was, he epitomised nothing' (*Dream* 126).

Dream, for all its deficiencies and in spite of its recurrent assaults on conventional narrative pieties, reflects this variety very satisfactorily, albeit without ever suggesting that any point of repose will be easily achieved; what is naturally enough proving impossible to deliver by design is clearly not going to occur by accident. As Beckett had in fact anticipated before he had even begun the novel – in his book-length essay *Proust* (written over some three weeks in the late summer of 1930 and published in the spring of 1931) – the 'perpetual exfoliation of personality' could never amount to a 'total soul', which he could only envisage as a chimera possessing a 'fictitious value' (*PTD* 25, 41). A 'lost reality' and a 'lost self' were, apparently in mutual ignorance of each other, actively combining to frustrate any possibility of a 'composite of perceiver and perceived' – as it was to be described in the first of the *Three Dialogues with Georges Duthuit* (*PTD* 101) – ever being established. Beckett was alive to the practical aspect that, whenever and wherever artifice could be brought into the mix, a 'precise value can be assigned' (*Dream* 119); but the imprecise fly in the ointment remained the fact that 'nothing is less like me than me' (*Dream* 77). Once we realise that almost exactly the same phrase occurs in the first paragraph of Diderot's great dialogue *Le neveu de Rameau,* namely 'nothing is less like him than himself' (1976, 34), it begins to look as if even this self-cancelling admission has no option but to participate in a wilderness of distorting mirrors.

Dream leaves no turn, even the many which it has itself created, unstoned, largely because its 'ramshackle' structure (139) cannot help but upset the applecart. But Beckett *in propria persona*, without a Belacqua to steer by, as it were, is almost equally a being in need of *re*-construction, a spectral figure made up of alternatives hedged round by qualifications. In Beckett's appointments diary for 1967, for example, he jotted down a fragment of Italian poetry from the lead poem in Camillo Sbarbaro, *Pianissimo*, published in 1914 (compare *Dream* 30: 'pianissimissima'):

> Nel deserto
> io guardo con asciutti occhi me stesso
> [In the desert
> I look at myself with dry eyes] (Sbarbaro 1993, 169)

It was at about this time that Beckett liked to take brief holidays in Sbarbaro's native Liguria, and no doubt the dry eyes of the desert seemed in some ways apt on discovering that the poet had died in October 1967. But an agenda more personal to Beckett was active even here, for this quotation is part of a dialogue of self and soul stretching back across the decades to a Beckett *not* in Italy, but in Germany, and looking at pictures the better to be able to look at himself. Here is Beckett in Berlin, in the bleak winter of 1936, looking at a famously enigmatic Brueghel canvas (*Dutch Proverbs*), and introjecting the experience as a kind of knife wound:

> I am the pretty young man, shall I never learn to cease thinking of myself as young, as [in] Brueghel's 'Proverbs', *der durch die Finger sieht* [the one looking out through his fingers]. *Was sehe ich durch die Finger* [What do I see through these fingers?]. *Mich, übergehenden Augen* [Myself, in floods of tears]. (GD entry for 18 December 1936; amended quotation from Nixon 2011, 152)

And here, some ten weeks later, in Dresden, is what looks like a dry run for the *nine* 'irreconcilable' images of *Mercier and Camier* (qtd. in Nixon 2011, 150), with not a canvas in sight, but with an infinite regress threatening to create an exceptionally complex image:

> When I take off my glasses and bring my nose as close to the mirror as my nose permits, then I see myself in my right eye, or alternatively my reflection's left eye, half profile left, and inversely. If I squint to the left I am full face in left eye, and inversely. But to be full face at once in the mirror and in my eye, that seems an optical impossibility. But it is not necessary after all to take off my glasses. By keeping them [on] I see myself 3 times at once, in the mirror, in my glasses and in my eyes.[3]

'Am I as much as … being seen?', M asks himself some twenty-five years on: a question hardly requiring an answer in the circumstances in which he finds himself (the play *Play*), since neither W1 nor W2 can even hear him, let alone *see* him (*KLT* 64).

Catching the Eye

It was out of these self-staged regresses that the young Beckett emerged, or that the proxy prepared to speak for him spoke. Hence the succession of striking openings – in essay, poem, book review or fiction alike:

> The danger is in the neatness of identifications ('Dante … Bruno. Vico .. Joyce', *Dis* 19)
>
> He could have shouted and could not ('Assumption', *CSP* 3)
>
> The Proustian equation is never simple (*PTD* 11)
>
> Exeo in a spasm ('Enueg I', *CP* 6)

> Behold Belacqua an overfed child (*Dream* 1)
>
> All poetry [...] is prayer ('Humanistic Quietism', reviewing *Poems* by Thomas MacGreevy in *The Bookman*, June 1934, *Dis* 68)
>
> It was morning and Belacqua was stuck in the canti of the moon[4] ('Dante and the Lobster', *MPTK* 3)

As the revision of 'Dante and the Lobster' indicates, these special effects had to be worked for. But the best surviving evidence of how hard Beckett worked at them, as well as the best actual example of how effective they can be, is to be found in the first of the six manuscript notebooks in which Beckett wrote what became his first published novel (*Murphy*, 1938), where after nearly a dozen attempts at an opening sentence he came up with: 'The sun shone, having no alternative, on the nothing new' (*Mu* 3). Here, at least, the 'pretty' young man – more often than not now the 'tired' young man (see GD entry for 19 December 1936) for whom 'the fatiguing lust of self-emotion' (*Dream* 24) had proved such a tormenting thorn in the flesh – could forget himself for a moment, by finding himself a pretty good sentence to set the ball rolling, even if his sense of himself *as himself*, beyond any alternative existence in the more or less distorting mirrors of words or pigment, could never hope to be very secure in the subjunctive domain of fiction.

At one level, Beckett of course knew himself much too well, which meant that his multiplying self-images tended to pursue each other endlessly in a series of echoes, initially as echoes of others for the most part, but even more tellingly echoes of himself by way of 'that most necessary, wholesome and monotonous plagiarism – the plagiarism of oneself' (*PTD* 33). At another level, he knew himself hardly at all, a factor which perhaps adds an extra poignancy to the detail jotted down in the *'Dream' Notebook* from the third book of Ovid's *Metamorphoses* ('He'll live to be old, said Tiresias, if he never know himself (*si se non noverit*)'),[5] which is of course precisely the opposite of what actually happens to the Narcissus so besotted with himself that poor Echo can only waste and pine. Beckett's sallies into classical literature are few and far between, but Narcissus and Echo served him exceptionally well as a narrative constellation emblematic of his own spiritual condition, and indeed proved much more useful to him in the long run than the ragbag of doublets – Damon and Phythias, Pylades and Orestes, Nisus and Euryalus, Theseus and Pirithous – that he had found in a cluster in the third book of Robert Burton's *The Anatomy of Melancholy* (*DN* 813).

It was not so much the ragbag as the tag, the 'precious margaret' (*Dream* 48), that prompted Beckett to think in terms of catching the eye with a well-shaped phrase ('the sparkle') or a compelling image, as in a number of his very early poems. For example:

> stoo*pi*ng to the *prone*
> who must s*oon* take *up* their life and walk ('The Vulture', CP 5; emphasis added)

Or:

> a*nd* the mi*nd* a*nn*ulle*d*
> *w*recked in *w*ind ('Enueg I', CP 6; emphasis added)

Or, from the same poem:

> a *slu*sh of vigilant *gu*lls in the grey *spew* of the *sew*er (CP 8; emphasis added)[6]

Once read, they are difficult to forget, irrespective of how well one understands them. But details can only become patterns within interactive and organised structures, and these are not often found in Beckett's early poems. This was a perhaps inevitable consequence of his determination to demonstrate that poetry is not, or ought not to be, a narrative art, even when a poem like 'Enueg I' suggests that the severity of this position permits exceptions. But if one tries, for example, to reintroduce narrative back into the four lines of 'Da Tagte Es':

> red*eem* the surrogate *g*oodbyes
> the sh*eet* a*stream* in your hand
> who ha*v*e no more for the land
> and the *g*lass unmis*t*ed ab*ov*e your eyes (CP 22; emphasis added)

the whole fragile delicacy of it evaporates; you have to supply your own story, your own 'aspirin' (see Harmon 1998, 24) if you want the poem to have the 'precise value' which it is seeking to do without.

We should not then, under the circumstances, be overly surprised that Beckett's hostility to narrative (as normally understood) left him dissatisfied by the writing of short stories. Yet it was here, however, in a medium which he could never really think of as much more than a commodity, that he was at least ready to compromise. Rather than conjuring brilliant beginnings he could favour memorable *dénouements*: a lobster about to be boiled ('Dante and the Lobster'), a suicide pact that fizzles out ('Love and Lethe'), a marriage ill-begun and about to go west ('What a Misfortune'), a minor operation gone disastrously wrong ('Yellow'). He was quite often fully prepared to equip these items with a 'punch line' to send them on their way:

> It is a quick death, God help us all. / It is not. ('Dante and the Lobster', MPTK 14)

> In the words of one competent to sing of the matter [Ronsard], l'Amour et la Mort – caesura – *n'est qu'une mesme chose*. / May their night be full of music at all events. ('Love and Lethe', *MPTK* 91)
>
> 'Gone west', he said. / They went further. ('What a Misfortune', *MPTK* 140)
>
> By Christ! he did die! / They had clean forgotten to auscultate him! ('Yellow', *MPTK* 164)

And equally rough treatment could be meted out to a succession of quirkily individual, if oddly negligible, characters who could be whistled up and whispered down almost in the same breath: 'She saw her life as a series of staircase jests' (of Ruby Tough in 'Love and Lethe') comes at us out of the blue, just as if it were itself a member of the category it designates,[7] but cunningly positioned at the end of a paragraph precisely so that it cannot *not* be seen, much like a poet weighting the end of a line (compare: 'How like an epitaph it read, with the terrible sigh in the end-pause of each line' in 'What a Misfortune', *MPTK* 116). Unwanted 'attention', by contrast, is occasioned, especially in a medium like the short story – a genre in which there is rarely room for the kind of complexity which a novelist could take several paragraphs to explore – when Beckett is either writing in a tired and rather slipshod manner, or simply trying too hard to introduce a complexity to stimulate the mind – 'It is a tiring style', he had said of Proust, 'but it does not tire the mind' (*PTD* 88) – rather than hoping to catch the eye:

> The Smeraldina, far far away[8] with the corpse and her own spiritual equivalent in the bone-yard by the sea,[9] was dwelling at length on how she would shortly gratify the former, even as it, while still unfinished, had that of Lucy, and blot the latter for ever from her memory. ('Draff', *MPTK* 180)

You can read this sentence several times and still be left without much sense of what is being said, probably because the one corpse (not to mention the one 'spiritual equivalent') Beckett would have liked to blot forever from his own memory at this time was precisely the one he could not forget: his father's, dead after two massive heart attacks in June 1933. In the event, or rather in the aftermath of the event, all that Beckett was prepared to do to help the reader of 'Draff' at this point was to add a footnote ('A most foully false analogy'), when arguably what is really 'false' here is not the analogy in itself – however hostile Beckett strives to be to 'analogymongers'[10] – but rather the motive or corpus of motives that has led him to conceal his own deeply emotional involvement. The difficulty of negotiating between having nothing to say and having no way of saying something that you are reluctant to deal with openly has not been successfully resolved in this understandably delicate, but ultimately unsatisfactory, instance. There was a price to be paid for looking out through the fingers whilst keeping one's gloves on.

Multiplications of Tissue

Early Beckett hinges – except when undergoing 'break down'[11] – on the unusual but potentially productive premise that in telling yourself you have nothing to say you are effectively giving yourself free rein to say anything you like.[12] Better still, you can say it in any number of ways, each of which can be easily abandoned and taken up again. So it was that, with *Murphy* effectively finished, Beckett was in a position to tell his friend MacGreevy: 'I could do more work on it but do not intend to' (*LSB I* 345). It was as if he could always tell himself that he had had 'nothing' in mind to begin with. But even this could not satisfy a radical scepticism which was always finding an exception to every rule, especially when there were no rules that seemed capable of being stated, despite recurrent invocations of an aesthetic of 'statement'.[13] From early on content to think of himself as 'a postpicassian with a pen in his fist' (*Dream* 46) – as clear a statement of Beckett's onanistic and viciously circular aesthetic as could reasonably be wished for – Beckett could never in fact long remain at ease with 'categories' without 'transelement[ing]' them (*Dream* 35).[14] There was always another way of looking out to find a way of looking back in; it was a case of being 'doomed to a literature of saving clauses' (*Dream* 46), because literature itself was precisely such a clause. There had to be something more than what came to seem like the merely optional or *'facultatif'* products of the pen in the hand availing itself of the optional stops along the way, as distinct from what could be retrospectively assessed as scheduled stops or designated ports of call (*LSB I* 133). It was precisely in this search for something essential or 'necessary' that Beckett tried to devise a nondoctrinal doctrine of 'need' as seen most clearly in 1937–8 in the programmatic essay 'Les Deux Besoins' and in the semi-programmatic 'review' of Denis Devlin's first collection of poems, *Intercessions*.[15] By way of theoretically privileging this notion of 'need' Beckett could hope to keep his premises and his conclusions wrapped indissolubly around one another, and create in his best 'infundibuliform' manner. Whether, with or without this substitute for a doctrine, such an outcome would naturally have occurred of its own accord can only be guessed at. But for so long as it served to keep Beckett active, the doctrine could be continually varied to suit any impulse apparently offering a creative opportunity.

The young Beckett stuck in the uncertain ruts of impending middle age could remember when he had been something of a rising star in the academic firmament of Dublin's Trinity College:

> He is a university man, of course, said Mrs Nixon.
> I should think it highly probable, said Mr Nixon. (W 17)

He had, in the eyes of his peers, if not in his own estimation, possessed an exceptional mind, at once plastic and absorbent, both alert to angles,[16] especially those not ordinarily available to vision, and desperately self-involved. As has been seen, however, it was a mind inevitably sometimes at the mercy of the right kind of stimulus and the right kind of response. When it was furnished with sufficient (but not excessive) personal input, as for example in the 1931 poem 'Alba' or the 1936 poem 'Cascando', Beckett seems easily enough to transcend himself, as if he were capable of genuine metamorphoses rather than endlessly narcissistic echoes in a self-defeating vortex. But with too much personal input a carefully prepared firework simply fails to ignite (there are several in the 1929–30 poem 'Casket of Pralinen …'), and when Beckett is too long 'held up' by what he knows to be 'the absurdest difficulties of detail' (Beckett 1936) he loses hold on what is salient, as anyone might. These difficulties are perhaps best seen in the *Murphy* notebooks, now thankfully (after seventy-five years exclusively in private hands) available for public scrutiny. In late January 1936 Beckett lamented to MacGreevy that 'all the sense and impulse [of *Murphy*] seem to have collapsed' (*LSB I* 306), and by mid-April things were not much improved. One does not need to read much between the lines of chapter 8 of *Murphy*, either as published or as it comes under revision and critique in the notebooks, to see that it was precisely the 'multiplication of tissue' operative there which was imperilling the *performative* aspects of the novel, its *brio* and *bravura*. As in the very different situation of a gallery and a hotel mirror in Nazi Germany, multiplication was bringing Beckett close to the impotence of self-division. As a failsafe against complete collapse, Beckett can, however, be seen, very late in the day, not just making plans as to how best to proceed – the refining fire of 'spontaneous combustion' having signally and significantly failed to serve his purposes (*LSB I* 134) – but actually putting his essentially simple plot (self-evidently the least of his concerns) under pressure to deliver the goods, or something like them, with the tempo and the direction of the narrative under distinctly better control in the wind-up to the conclusion of the novel, almost as if the sheer desire or need to get the thing finished was the finally enabling factor.

Murphy very impressively makes its rhetorical filigree more memorable than its homespun plot of pursuit and flight, asylum and exile, the merest pretext for embellishment:

Early Beckett

> Celia spent every penny she earned and Murphy earned no pennies. (*Mu* 14)
>
> When body odour and volubility meet, then there is no remedy. (45)
>
> So far as the prophetic status of the celestial bodies was concerned Murphy had become an out-and-out preterist. (115)
>
> Cooper experienced none of the famous difficulty[17] in serving two employers. [...]. [He] was the perfect size for the servant so long as he kept off the bottle and he moved incorruptible[18] between his corruptors with the beautiful indifference of a shuttle,[19] without infamy and without praise.[20] (123)

More sustained are passages which look as if they might almost have emerged from close readings of a manual on how to paint genre scenes:

> Bounding the grey pavement, stretching away on either hand beneath the grey spans of steps, the areas made a fosse of darkness. The spikes of the railings were a fine saw edge, spurting light. (*Mu* 83)
>
> [Murphy's] figure so excited the derision of a group of boys playing football in the road that they stopped their game. She watched him multiplied in their burlesque long after her own eyes could see him no more. (90)[21]
>
> The leaves began to lift and scatter, the higher branches to complain, the sky broke and curdled over flecks of skim blue, the pine of smoke toppled into the east[22] and vanished, the pond was suddenly a little panic[23] of grey and white, of water and gulls and sails. (173)

These are scenes – they are certainly something that *someone* must have seen – in a fairly conventional novel with a surprisingly large canvas, a novel peopled with interesting characters in well-documented social settings, as if the conventional 'Realist' contract were still operative.[24] But Beckett had told the world in his *Proust* book back in 1931 that the 'old pact' was 'out of date' (*PTD* 22). This is why some of the life of even the immensely accomplished *Murphy* drains away when effectively that 'old pact' reasserts itself, as when the narrator is reduced to conveying information rather than shining as a phrasemaker,[25] or when he feels obliged to opt for the lower slopes of reportage rather than stage-managing the splendidly 'antic' dialogues. These exchanges are perhaps not wholly unlike what the actors of *En attendant Godot* were to be given some twelve years later, but in *Murphy* they are more obviously designed immediately to impress an audience, and consequently less long-lasting in what they leave behind.

Murphy is at its best when its narrator calls the shots, or on the occasions when Beckett generates cunning interlacements which imply that the narrator is not just carrying out some humdrum second-order activity, but actually playing verbal harmonics on his material as he distributes it across space and time. And of course space and time are here (if nowhere else in Beckett) so meticulously recorded that as indices of authenticity they, too, begin to look bogus.[26] Indeed, the problem is not confined to these flagged-up specifics: the spatial poise which can be found at the level of the sentence, or over the short distance of a paragraph, operating at its best within an elapsed time inherent in and specific to the very act of reading, is not always matched by the way in which Beckett places larger masses of narrative in juxtaposition with one with another.

This was a 'conventional' aspect which he not unnaturally elected to abandon altogether in writing *Watt* at the beginning of 'the fiendish forties'.[27] Yet perhaps the most remarkable property of *Murphy* is the way Beckett – in psychotherapy in London, and still in mourning over the death of his father – for the most part remains sufficiently controlled to just about keep at bay the very real pain he was suffering. This remains the case, and in some ways defines the dominant *modus operandi*, even when we 'lose' the protagonist of the novel (in its penultimate chapter, the twelfth of the thirteen) as he gets 'swept away with the sand, the beer, the butts, the glass, the matches, the spits, the vomit' from the floor of a saloon bar (*Mu* 171). For the abiding impression Murphy leaves – he cannot be allowed to be there at the end – is of an 'unheroic'[28] and nontragic figure, who has been kept contextualised in a cocktail of high spirits, flair, by the application of a modicum of hard-headed wisdom. One feels that Rimbaud, for one – ever alert to his more visionary moments biting the dust – would have applauded the way the rather hectic flights of fancy gradually give way to a levelling, a rude awakening cunningly anticipated by the telephone call which interrupts Murphy's ecstasies in chapter 1. In the final chapter we are left with the kites in the park failing and falling from the sky, and with the pitiful figure of Mr Kelly catapulting himself out of his chair. Mr Kelly is here making the same 'error' at the end that Murphy made at the beginning, Beckett having conceived of the two characters as differential aspects of his own sole self[29]: going out, rather than staying in.[30] The last few pages of *Murphy* are written with exceptional care and finesse, and read almost as if Beckett knew he would never be doing this kind of thing again, but was nevertheless quite pleased to have done it this well. A reader feels he might be entitled to a pat on the back for having got this far, and as if the narrator were waving farewell both to his characters and to us. There was never to be quite so perfect a demonstration of 'fly[ing] them almost out of sight' (*LSB I* 274) – the characters as well as their kites – from this point on.

Starting All Over Again

On at least one of some six visits to Germany between 1928 and the mid-1930s Beckett had obviously spent 'a very dark night in Altona' (*Dream* 133), probably in its red-light district. But dark as those nights may have been, they were not as dark as the nights ahead of him during the tough German winter of 1936–7, with Beckett having chosen of his own volition to contend with bombastic Nazis (Goebbels on the radio), and ravaged by a succession of unpleasant bodily ills and a gradually dwindling pocketbook,[31] with the only compensation a swollen record of diary entries in which he could at least delude himself that they were not 'self-communion'. Creatively, all that came out of this were some materials for the postwar *nouvelles* and (perhaps) the art gallery remembered by voice C in the 1975 play *That Time* as a refuge from the weather. But Germany broke the recurrent stranglehold of reverting shamefacedly back to Ireland and home, and in its way it was what *That Time* was to see as a 'turning point'.[32] In the meantime the rejection slips for *Murphy* were mounting up, with Beckett for once rallying to his own cause, if only in letters or from the privacy of his diary: 'It is impossible to controvert *Murphy* as construction'.[33]

With both Dublin and London proving impossible on Beckett's return from Germany, by late September 1937 Beckett had decided that his best (and possibly his last) chance of some peace of mind was in Paris, which had once been a 'happy land' ('Sanies II', *CP* 14). There, in a creative move which initially he found it difficult to maintain, Beckett switched to French, with poems once again his preferred medium. What Arsene, in his supposedly 'short statement' in *Watt*, would later dismiss as 'the whole bloody business starting all over again' (*W* 31, 39) was starting all over again, and in very straitened circumstances. But in 1940 France fell, the Becketts had to flee incognito from Paris (they had been members of a penetrated Resistance cell), followed – for the best part of the next three years – by hard labour working in the fields around Roussillon by day, and trying for the most part unsuccessfully to write the novel *Watt* by night, proof of a kind perhaps that 'the only way one can speak of nothing is to speak of it as though it were something' (*W* 64). In the process Beckett's English was put under such pressure that it almost vaporised, such that it made more sense to him by late 1946, with *Watt* still in its uncomfortable cocoon (where it was to remain until 1953), to tell his friend George Reavey: 'I do not think I shall write very much in English in the future' (*LSB II* 48).

Watt is such a confrontational book – it seems to be all foreground and no perspective – that you might be forgiven for thinking that Beckett had looked at too many paintings in Germany to be able to see anything very clearly. Yet to try to look behind or beyond the blizzards of words[34] in *Watt* is probably in itself a kind of category error in approaching a book refusing any label you care to attach to it: 'What was this pursuit of meaning, in this indifference to meaning?' (*W* 62). For most readers, in spite of the obstacles to negotiate, it is when *Watt* suddenly flickers into focus that it becomes memorable, whether in its opening *tableau vivant* (an anticipation of the many plays to come), or on the occasion of the visit of the Galls, or in the absurdities of Mr Nackybal in putative pursuit of the Mathematical Intuitions of the Visicelts. Or simply in wonderfully disruptive *volte-faces*:

> One wonders sometimes where Watt thought he was? In a culture park? (W 63)
>
> Or was Erskine out of his mind? And he himself Watt, was he not perhaps slightly deranged? And Mr Knott himself, was he quite right in his head? Were they not all three perhaps a little off the hooks?[35] (W 104)

Also liberally scattered throughout *Watt* (but especially in part III) are some of Beckett's most tender and moving scenes, with an odd kind of beauty in the writing, partly reminiscent of the park scenes in *Murphy*:

> But ah, when exceptionally the desired degrees of ventilation and radiance were united, in the little garden, then we were peers in peace, each in his own way, until the wind fell, the sun declined. (W 131)

What *Dream* would have intellectualised as 'recondite relations of emergal' (16) here seem like refreshing exceptions to the atomisation of the very idea that literature might, as Aristotle[36] had long ago proposed in the *Poetics*, be 'the imitation of an action'. More often, and for most readers probably too often for comfort, *Watt* seems like film music detached from the film it is a part of, overly devoted to proving 'by exhaustion'[37] that writing is nothing more than the *iteration* of an action.

Taking a Walk

Although *Watt* continually shifts its ground in a disconcertingly vertiginous manner – a combination of the hero's 'headlong tardigrade' (W 24) and the obstinate rigour of its shadowy narrator 'Sam' – it freed something in Beckett. To ensure his personal survival as a fugitive in wartime he had had to keep on the *qui vive*. With the liberation of France he began to emerge from an inner world congested with too many 'secret things' ('Enueg I'). A revised definition of the notion of 'need' from that which had coiled round itself in the assessment of Denis Devlin's *Intercessions* for the last issue of pre-war *transition* can just about be seen (even if it was never heard) in a text submitted for radio broadcast, 'The Capital of the Ruins', 1946 (Beckett 1999a, 17–28), which seems to have ended on the cutting-room floor. Such was also the fate of what followed *Watt* – *Mercier et Camier* (1946) – with its reimagined Watt making a kind of farewell appearance far too late for him to affect anything. Beckett was effectively yielding to one of the few 'forced move[s]' (*Dream* 43) he had left, having earlier coped more or less successfully with a mind more shield than sword in its creative manifestations. 'There is', he told the readers of the *Dublin Magazine* in August 1945, 'at least this to be said for mind, that it can dispel mind' (*Dis* 95).[38] This was the mind that had made anything resembling the so-called automatic writing of the Surrealists little more than 'bambochades' (*Dis* 126).[39] A better course offered itself in a model with its meaning radically relocated and revised from the role its author had intended:

> It makes me think of the painter in Cervantes who, when asked, 'What are you painting?', replied: 'What comes out of my brush.' (*Dis* 131)[40]

Separations not unnaturally remained in the forefront of the picture, like the two 'absolutely distinct' (we are assured) Van Velde brothers imagined in a *real* postwar Paris:

> They separate, more and more, the one from the other. They will separate, more and more, the one from the other. Like two men who, setting out from the Porte de Chatillon, will have walked, without knowing the way very well, with frequent halts to give themselves courage, one in the direction of the rue Champ-de-l'Alouette [the field of larks], the other in the direction of the Île des Cygnes [the isle of swans]. (*Dis* 124, my translation)[41]

In much the same way A and C will separate in Beckett's first great burst of postwar creativity (*Molloy*, 1947, published in French in 1951), just as Molloy and Moran will find themselves separated from one another in the same novel. But with separation goes 'the art of combining', 'l'art de combiner ou combinatoire', as the text 'Assez' puts it in a more openly combinatory manner (*TFN* 94; Beckett 1967, 36).

Looking out through the fingers had given way to going out on the road. 'There are times', Beckett had written in 1938 (in mild rebuttal of a famous 'tag' of Stendhal's), 'especially in Europe, when the road reflects better than the mirror' (*Dis* 55, my translation). By 1947, after a number of experimental *sorties* in the *nouvelles* of 1945 and 1946, theory had turned into practice. Asked how he could have come, and in the event had come, to write *Molloy*, Beckett replied: 'It was like taking a walk' (personal interview, Paris, 8 August 1969), although he had still not given up the view that one was a victim of all that one had written, looking back over it all, as if the road and the mirror could never quite meet.

NOTES

1 The opening utterance of the fourth of the *Texts for Nothing*, originally written in French in the summer of 1951.

2 *Echo's Bones and Other Precipitates*, 1935: 13 poems in a print run of 327 copies, more than 50 of them *hors commerce*.
3 GD entry for 1 March 1937; cf. *German Diaries*, edited by Mark Nixon (Frankfurt am Main: Suhrkamp, forthcoming).
4 In Dante's *Paradiso*, as subsequently confirmed. But the phrasing could easily conjure up for a literate reader Astolfo's visit to the moon in Ariosto's *Orlando Furioso*, excerpts from which were on Beckett's TCD undergraduate syllabus for Italian. This opening sentence was revised from the version first published in the last issue of the *émigré* magazine *This Quarter* in December 1932.
5 *DN* 156, item 1098. A line from later in the Ovid story (III, 463) is at the heart of the poem 'Malacoda' (1933–5), line 25 (*CP* 21).
6 Beckett had tried, or was trying, this phrasing out in *Dream* (157) at about the same time as he was writing 'Enueg I': November 1931.
7 No doubt the 'jests' are Beckett's, and probably part of a complex private joke especially if the 'staircase' here derives from a famous Marcel Duchamp painting (*Nude Descending a Staircase*), the painting which Beckett reinterprets towards the end of the spoof lecture 'Le Concentrisme' (1930; 'Décomposition des joyeux qui descendent en colimaçon', *Dis* 42). Later in 'Love and Lethe' – a story almost certainly written close to the death of Beckett's father – the storyteller casually, too casually perhaps, notes of Ruby Tough's mother: 'On the stairs she met Mr Tough descending. They passed' (*MPTK* 85). Compare Beckett's otherwise mysterious 'mémoire d'escalier' in a letter about the death of his father (2 July 1933; *LSB I* 165), written in the week after the fatal second heart attack of 26 June 1933.
8 Compare the first line of the 1932 poem 'Sanies II' (*CP* 14): 'a land which, like the green hill of a very well-known hymn, now seems far away'.
9 A travesty of the title, and by implication a refutation of the largely positive sentiments, of Paul Valéry's 'Le Cimetière marin' in the collection *Charmes, ou Poèmes* (1922).
10 *Dis* 19; and compare to Moran in part 2 of *Molloy*: 'so avid is the mind of the flimsiest analogy' (*Mo* 179).
11 Beckett broke down the word 'breakdown' into two units in a letter to MacGreevy (16 January [1936]) in which he was trying to explain why *Murphy* was not making much headway (*LSB I* 299).
12 Molloy believes 'I always say either too much or too little [...] never enough and always too much' (*Mo* 32).
13 See 'a statement of itself' in the 1931 poem 'Alba' (*CP* 10), and similar instances in *Dream* (26) and *LSB I* (134).
14 Adapting W. R. Inge on *Christian Mysticism* from *DN*, item 701.
15 *Dis* 56, 91. An idea still found as late as Harvey's monograph (1970, 248).
16 Compare the young man playing billiards in Jack B. Yeats's novel *The Charmed Life* (London: George Routledge & Sons, Ltd., 1938) 'trying to forget himself in angles, and failing' (91).
17 As in Carlo Goldoni's best-known comedy, *The Servant of Two Masters*, and Matthew 6:24, Luke 16:13.
18 An idea borrowed from Dante via line 6 of Beckett's poem 'Malacoda' (*CP* 21), begun in 1933 and subsequently worked on until late 1935.
19 Moran uses exactly the same image – but minus 'beautiful' – to characterise the way in which he imagines himself 'devouring' his page (*Mo* 138).

20 A translation of Dante (*Inferno* III, 36: *senza infamia e senza lode*), given (in the original Italian, but with no source indicated) on verso 6915 (provisional UoR numbering in MS 5517) for addition to the recto text in the fifth notebook towards *Murphy* (February 1936).
21 Compare the 'ring of guffawing boys' witnessing rutting dogs (*LSB I* 341), although the inspiration for this seems to have been a different sport (cricket) and a real-life friend or associate by the name of Hilliard (*LSB I* 279).
22 Because Beckett has misremembered where he first found the motif: *not* in Louis Laloy's book on Chinese music, which influenced the indented section of 'Alba' (*CP* 272), but – as the *'Dream' Notebook* shows (see items 238 and 499) – in the *Journal* (2 February 1904) of Jules Renard. Beckett had already used (or abused) the motif in *Dream* (52) and in the short story 'Walking Out' (first version 1931).
23 Compare 'Serena II', lines 35 and 37 (*CP* 19).
24 A bizarre *über*-'Realism', or perhaps a kind of *trompe l'oeil* in reverse, rules at the beginning of chapter 7 of *Murphy*, where the syntax reflects what is actually being said *behind* what is apparently being offered: 'The encounter, on which so much unhinges, between Murphy and Ticklepenny, took place on Friday, 11 October (though Murphy did not know that)' (*Mu* 73). What no reader other than Beckett could possibly have known was that the scene of Murphy meeting Ticklepenny had in fact been *written* on 11 October 1935 (a Friday)!
25 Compare *LSB I* 62: 'phrase-hunting in St Augustine'.
26 See John Bolin's claim that 'the convergences and divergences (Celia's delivery of the horoscope and Murphy's encounter with Ticklepenny excepted) have little or no effect on what actually happens in the end' (2013, 52), an outcome not addressed in, but obviously latent in a July 1936 letter on the preordained dénouement or 'necessary end' of the novel (*Dis* 102).
27 Letter to James Knowlson of 1 June 1971 (UoR JEK).
28 Beckett describes his character Murphy as 'the fundamental unheroic' in his German Diaries entry for 18 January 1937.
29 See *LSB I* 274 (letter of 8 September [1935]): 'My next old man, or old young man, not of the big world but of the little world [cf. *Mu* 112–13], must be a kite-flyer', both literally (Mr Kelly) and metaphorically (Murphy).
30 Compare 'Mercier and Camier did not remove from home, they had that great good fortune' (*MC* 3). See the seventeenth-century Dutch painter Gerard Dou (1615–75) 'who never left home' (GD entry for 17 March 1937).
31 'I am very tired & often feel like turning back, but back where?' (Letter of 9 January 1937 to MacGreevy, *LSB I* 421).
32 'that was a great word with you before they dried up altogether' (*KLT* 101).
33 From a GD entry for 18 January 1937. Compare *LSB II* 350ff., and 380ff., the latter especially.
34 This is surely a much more telling factor than Beckett's occasional 'lapses' into Gallicisms. But, as *Watt* tells us: 'Here is one who seems on the one hand reluctant to change his state, and on the other impatient to do so' (*W* 72).
35 Compare W2 in *Play* wondering 'Am I perhaps a little unhinged already?' (*KLT* 63). It is of course perfectly possible to controvert the construction of *Murphy*; see below and footnote 26.
36 The first *Watt* notebook (HRC) opens with a series of questions modelled on Aristotle, which are subsequently jettisoned.

37 Compare Beckett's footnote to lines 77–83 of *Whoroscope* (*CP* 244), *Proust* on 'exhaustive enumeration' (*PTD* 92), and Celia (in 'weary ellipsis') telling Murphy what to avoid (*Mu* 26).
38 In manuscript 'dispel' was originally 'delight' (manuscript of 'MacGreevy on Yeats', TCD), suggesting that Beckett had decisively *changed* his mind in the interim.
39 A French word meaning 'to lark about' or 'go on a spree', perhaps (as Jim Knowlson has suggested to me) as typified by the 'merry pranks' tirelessly and ultimately tediously engaged in by Till Eulenspiegel.
40 The painter 'Orbaneja' from Ubeda, used by Cervantes to critique inferior artistry of the kind that he found epitomised by Avellaneda's bandwagon attempt to compose a sequel to part I of *Don Quixote*, remembered dismissively *en passant* a few pages from the end of part II.
41 For the Isle of Swans compare *Ohio Impromptu* (*KLT* 137).

2

ANGELA MOORJANI

Molloy, Malone Dies, The Unnamable
The Novel Reshaped

Introduction

Composed in French between 1947 and 1950, Beckett's postwar trilogy has confounded readers ever since. The perplexity it occasions, no doubt anticipated by the writer in the Joycean manner, has prompted some critics to condemn any attempt to elucidate Beckett's paradoxical and aporetic texts as critical hubris. The author himself tendered a different approach in having Moran's bid to decipher the dance of his bees – a model of *Molloy*'s bewildering shape – dissolve into the rapturous awareness of uncertainty and the limits of understanding. Roland Barthes famously celebrated the pleasure of such indecipherable texts that place readers in a state of self-perdition, set adrift by the loss of their cultural anchors. In positioning his readers in the same paradoxical situations as his characters, Beckett weakens our power to obliterate his writing's otherness as, in his 1945 essay on the van Velde brothers, he claims viewers are capable of annihilating the otherness of a newly painted canvas by their humanizing gaze (Beckett 1989a, 10).

The notion of a dialogical encounter will guide my review of generations of critics who have grappled with the three novels in French and English. Because texts are necessarily reshaped or recontextualized by each new critical encounter, the many strong readings through time – clashing or not – make up an intertextual space of dialogue in which earlier and later voices respond to one another.

If encounters with Beckett's trilogy draw on such an extraordinary number of critical horizons and disciplines, these are suggested in tantalizing ways by the texts themselves. If some of these are 'red herrings', as Simon Critchley (2004, 168, 190) claims, agreeing with others who have drawn attention to Beckett's crafty ways of misleading readers, then following their scent has its own rewards in probing a writerly practice that makes a virtue of impasse, failure, and the aporetic method of discouraging reduction to the identical.

Early Response to the Trilogy: Existential Humanism or Literature of Silence?

As often told, Beckett's three novels made their appearance on a traumatized French literary scene, still reeling under the experience and testimonies of a war so brutal that the very concept of the human and the ethics of writing became matters of anguishing reappraisal. Whereas the existentialist or absurdist writers – Jean-Paul Sartre, Simone de Beauvoir, and Albert Camus, among others – sought renewal by adopting the values of the French Resistance by way of political commitment, solidarity, and the reembrace of humanism, other avant-garde writers, particularly Maurice Blanchot and Georges Bataille, in placing all human values in question, spoke of the 'constraint' of having to write in the face of nothingness. Theirs was a 'literature of silence', as Sartre (1947, 271–4) termed it in an article written in 1945, consisting of a radical critique of language, knowledge, and humanism. The immediate postwar appeal and fame of the existentialists and absurdists was bound to make its influence felt in Beckett criticism in the first decades, but the influence of the literature of silence would continue to inform avant-garde thinking and practice into the twenty-first century.

Advocating 'an art of a different order', at the time he was writing the trilogy, Beckett rewrote the Blanchotian 'constrained' to write by 'utter necessity' (Blanchot 2001, 3) with 'the *obligation* to express' in the face of the 'nothing to express' and the lack of means to express (*Dis* 139, 142; emphasis added).[1] To replace 'constraint' with 'obligation' is a matter of some import, but clearly by this programmatic pronouncement Beckett was aware of his affinity with the adepts of the literature of silence to whom he felt more drawn than the existentialists.

Six rejections by Parisian publishers vouch for the uneasiness evoked by the first novel of the trilogy. On publication in 1951 by the Éditions de Minuit, its director Jérôme Lindon assured *Molloy* of at least twenty-five reviews, many by influential writers and theorists, leaving an extraordinary record of its first reception in the intellectual milieu of the French capital.

Although the names Proust, Joyce, and Kafka appear repeatedly in their reviews, these early readers of the first novel of the trilogy also found much that moved it beyond the writings of the three iconic modernists and other experimental *romanciers*, Louis-Ferdinand Céline, Sartre, Camus, and Jean Genet among them. For most of the critics, if not all, *Molloy*, is situated on the outer limits of the fiction of the times. What was it about this novel that so impressed its first critics? For some, it was its unblinkered view of ruin, collapse, and bodily decay – in short, the powerful evocation of the disaster of being human. Some saw in this abject, scatological, and, in Gaëtan Picon's words, 'cruel epic of filth' a legacy of the war (qtd. in Pingaud 1963, 267–8). Theodor Adorno (2010b, 173; 1990, 380) would take up this view a decade later by focusing on the decomposition of the subject of *L'innommable* into filth and by designating Beckett's anti-art as the only tolerable response to the concentration camps. Commentators on the English translation of the three novels, first published 1955–58, would explore the import of war trauma at a much later date with the advent of historicizing approaches. The different receptions of the French and English versions of the three novels are obviously owed in part to changed historical, cultural, and scholarly contexts of reading.

Of the 1951 essays, Beckett (*LSB II* 441) preferred Georges Bataille's and Maurice Nadeau's, which emphasize the spectral and nonhuman condition of Beckett's antiheroes, a matter of much future speculation. For Bataille (1951, 388, 394–5), this *'absence* d'humanité' corresponds to a death by which we are shadowed in the disguise of an inhuman spectre. Commenting on the novel's mixture of the fantastic and the sordid, Bataille refers to Molloy as an *'informe* figure de l'*absence*' (389; emphasis in original), putting to use his theory of the *informe* (formless), which he links to waste, or the abject, and whose influence on postwar twentieth-century art cannot be overestimated.

In a surprising confluence with Beckett's 1937 view (*LSB I* 518–19), unpublished at the time, about of the 'veil' of language that is best rent and gashed and the use of words to disparage words in order 'to sense a whispering of [...] the silence underlying all', Bataille (1951, 387–8, 390) identifies the silence of *Molloy* with the ruin of a language-facade, punctured and torn to the point of meaninglessness; a literature that remains literary beyond the negation of sense; and a 'residue of being' outside language. The latter view would be frequently echoed, including by Alain Badiou (1992, 335–6), if without the ontological anxiety perceived by Bataille.[2]

The seriousness of these early readings did not preclude glosses on the trilogy's humour and 'violent irony' (Bataille 1951, 392). 'An ironic genius, subtle charmer, a humourist', for Nadeau (1963, 263), in Ruby Cohn's early tome on his 'comic gamut' (1962, 129), Beckett turns many of his comic devices in the trilogy to 'bitter use'. Fifty years later, in an excellent overview of theories of the comic relevant to Beckett's humour, Laura Salisbury (2012, 78) scrutinizes the conflictual rhythms of the trilogy's laughably f(l)ailing body occasioning an explosive indigestion of words.

Besides Bataille's discerning comments, there is much in the 1951 reviews on the subject of Beckett's language, the critics noting its abstractness, the impoverishing use of French, the learned negligence of his bewildering style, and, more generally, the dehumanizing use of language to say nothing or to cancel itself out. For *Molloy*'s early reviewers, then, decomposing bodies, the *informe*, and the nullity of language and meaning are so many signs of human-lessness.

If reading Beckett through the lens of existential humanism applies to some second-generation critics' investigations of authentic being and the quest for self, the label clearly does not fit the trilogy's earliest readers.[3]

Nihilism or Radical Otherness (*le dehors*)?

Of the smaller number of reviews garnered by *Malone meurt* (1951) and *L'innommable* (1953), Beckett (*LSB II* 441) expressed his preference for Nadeau's and Blanchot's. In his new piece, Nadeau (1952, 1273-4, 1279) highlights the both tragic and 'often humorous and jubilant' rage with which the trilogy's speakers welcome their unravelling humanity that brings them closer to the unreachable goals of nothing, silence, and ultimate reality. Small wonder that Beckett liked this essay, as in a letter to A. J. Leventhal of 3 February 1959, the author of *L'innommable* was to qualify his own work, in one of his many puns on 'nothing', as 'next next to nothing' (qtd. in Weller 2010c, 119).

Sharing his radical view of the writer's predicament, Beckett (*LSB II* 441), termed Blanchot's 1953 piece, 'la chose capitale' (the definitive thing). Blanchot's influential reading of the trilogy posits a heterogeneous space-time, with cyclical time in conflict with timelessness; physical spaces set against an abstract space; and embodied characters doubled by a subject without a subject (see Moorjani 1992, 178-81; Critchley 2004, 189). Demanding multiple viewpoints, such a nonhomogeneous space-time and subjectivity intimate the infinite coiled in the finite.

Blanchot (1953, 681-2, 684-5) probes literary space in *L'innommable* as an imaginary place in which writers fall into a radical exteriority to self. This *dehors*, between nonbeing and being, is likened to an endless dying or to a void having become a neuter, or impersonal, utterance, both penetrating and relentless, without beginning, without end, from which writers seek to escape in vain. For Blanchot, this unstoppable and blank utterance is not the opposite of silence, for silence murmurs endlessly within it (678). Finally, for him, the novel's subject without a name interposes 'a porous and dying' first person and a number of figural masks between himself and his dispossessed utterance (679, 681). Agreeing with Blanchot, critics have seen in *L'innommable* a performative enactment of the self-alienated subject's entrapment in the spectral space where writing erupts and wanes.

No doubt Schopenhauer's influential Upanishadic/Buddhist-inspired meditation on a spectral inner being immersed in the timelessness of a before- and after-life lurks behind Beckett and Blanchot's conception of the writing process, a view, moreover, shared by many modernists (see Moorjani 1996, 83–8). This ascetic conception helps us to understand the embedding by Beckett and Blanchot of such ghostly limbos in their fictions from the 1930s onward; Belacqua's 'darkened mind gone wombtomb' (*Dream* 45) comes to mind.

The influence Blanchot's theorization of literary space was to have on future thinkers – Michel Foucault, Roland Barthes, Jacques Derrida, Gilles Deleuze – and his influence on subsequent scholars filtered through poststructuralist theory help to explain the view of the trilogy from the 1950s to the present as a literary event reshaping the novel. One such study is Thomas Trezise's *Into the Breach* of 1990, in which, exploring the trilogy's affinity with Blanchot, Bataille, and Emmanuel Levinas, he argues – as others were to – that it also anticipates a Deleuze or a Derrida, particularly in its focus on dispossession involving the 'breach' of an outside within subjectivity and its questioning of the ends of literature and the human (Trezise 1990, 33, 120–1). For Trezise, the voice of the trilogy's narrators is a 'non-self-coincidental voice' of the without within subjectivity, which can be projected outward, but which, even when the narrators hear it from within, is not their own (138).

Blanchot's reading, however, is not without its detractors. Bruno Clément (1989), ignoring the two novelists' earlier parallel fictions and essays, attacks Blanchot's reading as ventriloquized by Beckett's text. Blanchot is further blamed for slighting Beckett's rhetorical craft (Clément 1989) and 'abstract' form (Casanova 1997), critical views that complement rather than contradict Blanchot's earlier insightful reading.

In a partial overlap with Blanchot's and Clément's views of the writing process in the trilogy, Porter Abbott (2008, 83–9) draws on the scientific/cognitive concept of 'emergent behaviour' to buttress the claim by writers that fictional worlds are dictated to them. Staging the moment of emergence of writing from outside the writer's control, Beckett's novels, Abbott maintains, also bear witness to later authorial shaping.

Meanwhile, in *Le voisin de zéro*, Hélène Cixous (2007) playfully explores Beckett's asymptotic 'next next to nothing' in terms of a lingering in zero's vicinity. Counter to a number of early Anglophone critics who taxed Beckett with French-inspired nihilism and despair (see Graver and Federman 1979, 74–5), thinkers increasingly came to concur on the trilogy's impossible nihilism, including (besides Nadeau and Cixous) Adorno, Badiou, Stanley Cavell, Critchley, Deleuze, and Derrida (see Weller 2005, 13–25.)

History, Trauma, Ethics, Politics

Trezise (1990, 147–9) links the voice in the breach of Beckett's trilogy to an ethics of intersubjectivity, the post-Holocaust ethical demand formulated by

Levinas for a relation to alterity that counters the ego's attempt to reduce otherness to itself. In confluence with deconstructive thought's turn to ethics and interactional pragmatics, a number of Beckett commentators, moreover, privilege Levinas's Saying as interruption of the Said as an ethical form of language fostering an openness to the other and to trauma (see Salisbury 2012, 174–7).

In Adorno's view, as increasingly noted by Beckett commentators, Beckett's writing is a form of social criticism by what it refuses or subtracts – that is, by its very negativity – so that more than social realism, it is a truly engaged form of literature (Adorno 1984, 353–4; Critchley 2004, 183). In-depth political readings of Beckett followed, beginning in the 1980s, from Peter Gidal's (1986) probing of Beckett's positioning of his interlocutors against identification with dominant ideologies and hierarchies, particularly the patriarchal,[4] to Alain Badiou who, in Andrew Gibson's summary (2002, 93–4, 102), derives Beckett's 'ethico-political aesthetic' from a fidelity to the possibility of the event – 'the mode in which the new enters the world' – which involves a breaking away from received knowledge by means of subtraction.

A sense of historical trauma, as we have seen, was connected with Beckett's trilogy from its first appearance. Later critics have recognized in the trilogy the signs of postwar and personal mourning and melancholy, a form of psychic encrypting whose memorial space of an exteriority in the ego converges with the space of writing.[5] In the present interweaving of history, trauma, and the archive in Beckett studies, commentators are evoking the numerous passages in the trilogy that refer, if obliquely, to World War II, the Holocaust and the testimonies of survivors of the camps, Beckett's work in the Resistance, and postwar conflicts.[6] Others are investigating what Beckett's trilogy can tell us about the impossibility of post-Holocaust witnessing and the ethics of the sayable and the unsayable (Garrison 2009; Jones 2011, 1–45). Reading *The Unnamable* in multiple contexts, Gary Adelman (2004, 77–84) finds voiced in it both the writer's plight Blanchot depicts in his 1953 essay and the trauma of the Holocaust survivor evoked in *L'écriture du désastre* (1980), in which Blanchot meditates not only on writing's entrenchment in disaster but on ethical/political obligation in the face of historical trauma.

At the same time, impelled by the historicizing trend in criticism and the interest in cultural space bound up with postcolonial identities, scholars increasingly recontextualized Beckett's postwar novels in relation to Irish history, landscape, and culture. For Seán Kennedy (2005, 22), Beckett situated himself obliquely to Irish cultural history by turning to French, an obliqueness also noted by earlier critics such as Vivian Mercier

(1977, 20–45). As Patrick Bixby (2009, 174) argues, Beckett's writing in the trilogy 'marks the haunting return of pastness and placedness in traces that cannot be completely elided even by the space-clearing gestures of his unwriting'. For Bixby, the three novels perturb both imperialist and nationalist narratives about Irish culture in their caricaturing of historical figures, topography, and place names, and their parodies of local cuisine, customs, and rituals (182–91). Still, Declan Kiberd's claim (1995, 535) that the voices in Beckett's works, after *Murphy*, are 'unambiguously Irish' is contradicted by the trilogy's two versions in an overlapping French and Hiberno-English: each language is palpable in the other, while interconnecting variously with the cultural archives of each and well beyond.[7]

But the archival material is far from exhausted. Even before the publication of the Beckett biographies, it was apparent to readers that the trilogy is riddled with traces of Beckett's personal past and the history of his readings and writings. The latter is complicated by the displacement of the enunciating centre into literary heteronyms – the trilogy's fictional writers – who paradoxically project in turn into homopseudonyms of the writer's name, such as Malone's Lemuel. 'Autography' is one critic's apt term for this convoluted form of self-(un)writing (Abbott 1996). Archival and historical research, trauma studies, and ethical and political analysis continue to be among the most productive forms of inquiry in Beckett criticism.

The Shape of an 'Art of a Different Order'

With the three novels Beckett engaged increasingly with the twentieth-century critique of representational form. Certain of the nonrepresentational techniques with which he experimented at the time have, after their adoption by the *nouveau roman* and postmodern fiction, lost some, if only some, of their power to perplex: confounding author, narrator, and character; self-cancelling fictions chronicling their own writing and unwriting; bewildering textual mirrors (*mise en abyme*); discontinuous spaces obscuring the borders between a before-life, an after-life, and the here and now; multiple meanings tendered and withdrawn; multiplication of voices; desubjectifying self-writing; misdirection, blockage, gaps, uncertainty, and aporia. At first publication, though, such shape-changing challenges to traditional forms of the novel caused critics to place the trilogy at the outer limits of fiction writing. Around the same time, Thomas Hogan (1954, 56, 58), an astute Irish critic of the French trilogy, detected the art of disconnectedness Beckett practised and defended in terms of an art of *empêchement* (blockage) and nonrelation between subject and object.[8]

In Beckett's 1948 article, 'Peintres de l'empêchement', at the very time he was calling for 'an art of a different order', one 'unresentful of its insuperable indigence' (*Dis* 141–2), he depicts, in the terms of the nonfigurative painterly experiments of the time, an infinite and blurred unveiling, one semi-transparent plane behind another, towards what cannot be unveiled (Beckett 1983, 136). Further qualified as an art of entombment and incarceration (136–7), such a blocked process recurs in *The Unnamable*'s 'fine impenetrable veils' (2006d, 294), 'caged beast born of caged beast' series (380), and 'endless chain' of talkers (349). Hugh Kenner (1961, 105–6) and David Hesla (1971, 181–3), among others, detected this process of infinite regress early on. Later critics associated it with Beckett's faltering multiplication of voices echoing fragmented voices heard imperfectly, fractured mirror images endlessly deflected. Drawing on post-structural theories, exegetes noted that the Beckettian infinite and paradoxical *mise en abyme*, with its multiplication of differences, fails to capture what is always effacing itself in a spectral *fort-da*. The lack of coincidence with the alien voice *dehors*, they maintain, effects a non-Cartesian break between consciousness and being. Moreover, in an often-noted inversion of the process of infinite regress, the speaker of *The Unnamable*, who invents the 'caricatures' of Beckett's previous novels (2006d, 309), is also invented by them, eclipsing narrative control. Finally, from the point of view of the trilogy's *en abyme* construction, in which embedded monologues (or polylogues in the case of *Molloy*) operate simultaneously in the mode of polyphonic writing, it is difficult to maintain that the first part of *Molloy* follows the second or that the end of *The Unnamable* circles back to the beginning of *Molloy* (Moorjani 1982, 40–3).[9]

Together with a nonrepresentational art, Beckett increasingly evoked the task of finding a new form that admits chaos without reducing it to form (see Driver 1961a, 23). In part privileging mathematics for this purpose, Beckett (*LSB II* 86), writing in 1948 to Georges Duthuit, expressed admiration for Antonello da Messina's 'victory over the reality of disorder' in the mathematically ordered space of his *Saint Sebastian*. For two early critics, Beckett's fictional procedures of infinite regress and 'next next to zero' manoeuvres in the trilogy correspond to the mathematical manipulations of an unreachable mathematical limit; the square root of two continuing endlessly; or an asymptotic curve approaching zero (Mercier 1959, 144–5; Kenner 1961, 105–6). Going a step further, content approaching zero multiplied by length approaching infinity is a mathematical equivalent of *The Unnamable*'s indeterminacy (Kishin Moorjani; pers. comm.). Still, even mathematics fails to escape Beckett's sardonic humour, as *Molloy*'s sucking stone and fart counting incidents remind us.

The order within disorder reversing to the disorder within order in *Molloy*'s diptych has been noted by exegetes. Anthony Uhlmann (1999, 58–64) analyses the interpenetration of the two in terms of a Deleuzian inclusive disjunction, whereas I discern in *Molloy*'s topology of 'period doubling' what mathematicians identify as the orderly approach to chaos: the narrator (1) of the preamble (written last), divides into the pseudocouple Molloy-Moran (2), who each split into A and B/C (4), who further divide (8), and so on (Moorjani 1992, 183).

Critics have studied Beckett's 'first dirty, then make clean' aesthetic (2006d, 294), whose various methods he sketched in the beginning pages of *The Unnamable*, in terms (among others) of 'decreation' (Cohn 1983, 12), 'narratricide' (Abbott 1996, 1–22), 'rhetorical epanorthosis' (Clément 1989, 180–7), aporia as a rhetorical impasse (Hill 1990, 63), deictic deviations and other post-structural undermining of language from within language, Cartesian methodological doubt or the Sceptical or phenomenological *epoche* (Hesla 1971, 85, 178–83; Badiou 1995, 19), and the oscillating *fort-da* game, a method of going on, without beginning, without ending, while leaving the door ever so slightly ajar.[10]

Thus in *Malone Dies*, in consonance with Freud's view of repetition in *Beyond the Pleasure Principle*, the repeated disappearance and reappearance of subject and object in Malone's *fort-da* play function to defer absence and death. Accordingly, identifying his dwindling Venus pencil with a murder weapon, Malone writes the writing self and written selves (of this and previous novels) into a violent end (the *fort* position).[11] Writing's involvement with death, its matricidal and patricidal phantasms, had already come to the fore in *Molloy*'s oedipal aggression by and against parental figures, but not without Eros coming into the picture. Writing's violence, with its personal, historical, and sacrificial implications, results in a call for an 'other of writing', beyond the death drive (Derrida 2001, 18–32), the unwriting, a being silent in writing, explored in the three novels' ascesis of a space removed from the realms of symbolic violence and cruel fictions.

Beckett's astute awareness of Europe's artistic and literary avant-gardes includes, of course, surrealism, with which he had close ties, and which despite his mockery of the group, had important implications for his aesthetic (Albright 2003, 8–28). Reading the emblematic knife-rest that repeatedly pops up in the trilogy as a Duchampian 'found object' has its rewards. Shared with the surrealists is the 'destruction' of subjectivity and objectivity (Sartre, qtd. in Albright 2003, 22); the reappearance (perhaps via the German Romantics) of the uncanny; and the transcription of myth and pre-cultural and dreamlike primary processes into enigmatic forms. Among the latter are discontinuous spaces blurring boundaries between the everyday and the imaginary.

To shape this chaotic material, Beckett adopted a modern version of the Dantean fourfold hermeneutics demanding contrapuntal readings in interconnecting contexts. Thus if it is intimated in *Molloy* that there are possibly four voices corresponding to Youdi – the inner imperatives of a superego spy; the instructions of a spymaster, with historical resonances; the commands of a laughable, hidden divinity; and in the context of writing, the obligation to write – each reading remains inconclusive in the modes of ironic myth, (post)modern allegory, or red herrings. Yet, as is often remarked, such clues nevertheless leave their marks. And added to these four voices is possibly a fifth (reminiscent of the five Molloys), the impersonal voice *dehors* fading into the in-between space of writing.

'Ironic myth' is Northrop Frye's term for the modern practice of myth, whose unheroic and self-deprecating distance from the heroic stories it echoes he detected in Kafka, Joyce, and Beckett, among others (Frye 1957, 40, 42; 1960, 442). If the trilogy's allegorical and mythical patterns appeared startling to many, not so to Frye who places ironic myth and modern allegory, with its intermittent character and uncertain meanings, among literary procedures that challenge realist representation (1957, 91, 132–40).

The lack of space constrains me to outline only briefly some of the major readings in the interlocking contexts. Critics from the 1960s to the 1990s uncovered an astonishing number of mythic and religious allusions in the trilogy, whereas more recent commentators have been reading *Molloy*, in particular, through the lens of modern or postmodern allegory. Besides radicalizing ironic myth to the point of near-obliteration, the author of the trilogy, they find, toyed with forms of allegory that leave meaning indeterminable.[12]

Psychoanalytic allegory in the trilogy is as ubiquitous and tantalizing as the mythic. To be sure, the two partially overlap so that, in a parody of detective novels, Beckett rescripts the intertwined Oedipus myth and complex in *Molloy* in two contrapuntal, dreamlike transformations, one of the other, only to erase them (Moorjani 1982, 108, 118). In an attempt to accommodate psychic catastrophe in his writing, Beckett's sly manipulation of Freudian, Jungian, Kleinian, and Rankian thought and mechanisms in the trilogy was evident to many (mostly Anglophone) critics from the 1950s to the 1990s. Their psychoanalytic readings were often met with consternation and rejection until the biographies and Beckett's notes on psychoanalysis revealed his therapy with Wilfred Bion in the mid-1930s and his extensive psychoanalytic culture. Parallels between Beckett's novels and the analytic situation followed, with renowned French analyst Didier Anzieu (1992) conjecturing that Beckett continued his sessions with Bion in the shape of a fictionalized self-analysis. Bion and other post-Kleinians, Jacques Lacan, Julia Kristeva, and other Lacanians, Nicolas Abraham, and Maria Torok are among the later psychoanalytic thinkers to whom exegetes have turned to analyse Beckett's trilogy.[13]

Needless to say, finding a form to accommodate disorder also functions in the political and historical realms. As Adorno (1984, 354, 362, 446) argues, engaged art, such as Beckett's, instead of emphasizing social content, 'must elevate social criticism to the level of form', a form shaped by social tensions and catastrophes, without mimicking them, so that in the postwar context 'form *per se* is a subversive protest'. We have seen to what extent Beckett uses deflected (displaced) textual manoeuvres to obliquely refer to traumatic historical events. Beckett's mingling of a spoken and at times obscene street idiom with a poetic register (more noticeably in the French) in the mode of Céline (Cohn 1962, 99–102) or J. M. Synge (Bowles 1958, 1011) is also a form of social protest, at least for Roland Barthes in his 1953 *Le degré zéro de l'écriture* (chapters 5–7).

In addition to the experimental forms contending with inner and outer disorder, the trilogy's otherworldly context has given rise to considerable critical speculation: Is Beckett a religious writer, despite textual and extra-textual denials, given the many biblical echoes and allusions to Christian, Gnostic, and apophatic discourses as well as to Eastern mysticism (via Schopenhauer)? Is he foremost a Protestant writer or perhaps a secular mystic, adopting in the trilogy the operations of a profane negative theology, emptying consciousness and language to experience silence and nothingness? Or are his otherworldly allusions, too, in the ironic mode? What remains difficult to contest is that the meditative turn taken by much of the trilogy is enmeshed in the millennia of spiritual traditions by which its author remains haunted.[14]

Along with the meditative mode, the poetic qualities of the trilogy have repeatedly attracted acclaim. Poetic rhythms and textual exploits, involving rhetorical tropes and witty language play, serve to foreground the methods of saying and unsaying to the detriment of the representational said. Accordingly, Beckett's 'cunning' literary strategies and poetic voice, Porter Abbott cautions (1973, 1, 137), must be balanced against his (ironic?) claim of incompetence.[15]

In a 1960 review of the trilogy, renowned British critic Frank Kermode accused Beckett of the imitative form fallacy, in which 'modern delinquency' is mimicked by a 'deliquescence of form' (qtd. in Graver and Federman 1979, 203–4). He must have only skimmed the three novels whose wild poetry, subversive form, and humorous stutterings are, as we have seen, shaped into an 'art of a new order', encompassing, but not imitating, the outer and inner catastrophes that in part occasioned the search for a form accommodating chaos.

Rethinking the Human and the 'Body's Long Madness'

Renewed critical interest since the 1980s in affect and the material body has led scholars to a focus on the abject and dwindling corporeality in the trilogy that for the first French critics placed the human in question. Thus, the twenty-first century vogue of the anti-*Bildungsroman* was, for some commentators, anticipated by the trilogy's reversal of the genre's upward mobility into a downward spiral into the supine posthumanity of Molloy, Malone, Sapo-Macmann, and Mahood.[16] As noted by critics, supine posture joins other forms of human dispossession in the three novels: homelessness and deficiencies of mind and body, the collapse of old age, the prelanguage and prebody images of early childhood, the indigent and nonconformist vagrancy of the Ancient Cynics, and a Gnostic fallen and aporetic existence.

The copious psychoanalytic and medical literature on the body in pieces and the body in pain has served critics to investigate pain and decomposing bodies in the entire Beckett corpus.[17] Indeed, a startling consequence of this attentiveness to the body is the trope of text as a corporeal construct. Following Julia Kristeva, who maintains that writing entails the surfacing into the body of the text of an abject prebody – a precultural flow of bodily waste related to a mourned archaic maternal object – critics have reconceived the trilogy in terms of the abject in the reenactment of its expulsion or failed birth (Hill 1990, 120) or countering 'borderline' feelings of failed birth with embodiment in words (Grossman 1998, 63–71). Other scholars are exploring the suffering subject within the framework of neuroscience, drawing, for example, on studies of aphasia and Tourette and Cotard's syndromes.[18]

Emphasis on the body in its interaction with the environment has yielded further fascinating new readings of *The Unnamable*. Drawing on the postcognitive concept of 'extended mind', in which the mind is distributed across the brain and body interrelating with the environment, Dirk Van Hulle (2012, 74–6) is exploring a model of consciousness contesting the modernist inward turn, whereas Elizabeth Effinger (2011, 376–8) analyses the speaker's amorphous corporeality in its mutual deformations with his environments in terms of the posthuman.

Further attention to the undercutting of anthropocentrism in the three novels is tied to the current reevaluation of the human-animal distinction and the ethical implications of animal suffering, a topic much in evidence in the trilogy (see Bryden 2013). In a quite different framework, recalling Descartes's body-machine, the focus of early critical attention by Hugh Kenner (1961, 117–32), and announcing the technologically extended 'transhuman', Yoshiki Tajiri (2007) investigates a number of supplements to the deficient body in the trilogy. For early and late readers of the trilogy, the 'body's long madness' (Beckett 2006c, 51) makes a mockery of human ascendency.

Endless Intertextuality

The focus of unending critical examination, the allusions in the trilogy to the realms of literature, philosophy, religion, mythology, psychoanalysis, history, autobiography, mathematics, the hard and social sciences, and the arts comprise an open-ended invitation to explore crosscurrents. Although Beckett more often than not kept his allusions in the trilogy hidden, an astonishing number was no secret to critics from the 1950s onward. The relatively recent access to Beckett's reading notebooks from the 1930s, his German diaries, the notes students took of his courses at Trinity College Dublin, his letters, and the contents of his personal library permits scholars to discover formerly ignored literary ghosts and to reassess Beckett's other debts and legacies. Of special value are the intertextual studies focusing on the crisscross between literature and the arts and literature and philosophy.[19] Among other ongoing explorations already noted, a promising turn is genetic criticism's examination of manuscript drafts of the three novels to shed light on the rescripting process leading to the published versions, as in the digital genetic edition of *L'Innommable/The Unnamable* (BDMP 2). Happily, the critical dialogue with the three novels is not about to come to an end.

NOTES

1 Beckett was most likely aware of Blanchot's 1943 statement at the time (see Beckett *LSB II* 216).
2 Owing to lack of space, I have translated most French texts into English and cited only the English version of the trilogy.
3 The 1951 French critics are cited extensively in Moorjani (2013, 102–7). An insightful phenomenological-existentialist reading is found in Hesla (1971, 167–205), along with references to critics of like persuasion.
4 Boxall (2004) provides a discerning overview of other feminist readings (and references) and investigates homoeroticism in the trilogy. See also Susan Mooney (2010).
5 Commentators who explore this psychoanalytic approach are discussed in Moorjani (2004, 185, 189 n. 36).

6 For a sampling, see Knowlson (1996, 337), Uhlmann (1999, 40–57), Touret (2006, 27–30), and Gibson (2010a, 119–27).
7 Sinéad Mooney (2011, 119–60) analyses the translated hybridity of the trilogy.
8 On Beckett's nonrepresentational art see, for instance, Dearlove (1982) and Casanova (1997).
9 Mercier (1959, 145) was perhaps the first to remark on the challenge posed to Descartes by the trilogy's voice off. On post-structural readings, including repetition in the trilogy, see Moorjani (1982), Connor (2007b [1988]), Hill (1990), Trezise (1990), Begam (1996), Katz (1999), Uhlmann (1999), Migernier (2006), and Szafraniec (2007).
10 See Moorjani (1982, 31–6, 51–3). Numerous critics have later commented on Beckett's use of the *fort-da*.
11 Begam (1996, 120–48) examines *Malone Dies* in the context of 'death of the author' theories.
12 For a partial list of mythic figures and the critical literature on myth and allegory in *Molloy*, see Moorjani (1982, 106–7) and Campbell (2012).
13 Details and references are found in Moorjani (2004).
14 Jacobsen and Mueller (1964, 49–50) and Hesla (1971, 63–5) explored these questions early on; Bryden (1998, ch. 2–4) provides a revealing discussion of the trilogy's biblical and Christian citations. For an impressive re-examination of Beckett's religious stance and an overview of commentaries in this area, see Connor (2007a).
15 A detailed semiotic analysis of the trilogy is found in Sherzer (1976).
16 See Bixby (2009, 191–9) and additional references to the *Bildungsroman* in Susan Mooney (2010).
17 See the issue *Samuel Beckett Today/Aujourd'hui* 10 (2000) devoted to affect; Moorjani (2004, 181–3); and Tanaka, Tajiri, and Tsushima (2012).
18 See the essays by Laura Salisbury, Ulrika Maude, and Peter Fifield in the *Journal of Beckett Studies* 17.1–2 (2008).
19 The chapters on intertextuality and philosophy in the present volume will help fill in what cannot be covered in this essay. See also the essays on various literatures in *Samuel Beckett in Context* (2013), edited by Anthony Uhlmann, and the bibliography of critical literature on the trilogy after 1970 in *Samuel Beckett Today/Aujourdhui* 26 (2014, 225–66), an issue devoted to the three novels.

3

PETER BOXALL

Still Stirrings

Beckett's Prose from *Texts for Nothing* to *Stirrings Still*

To discuss the development of Beckett's prose after *The Unnamable*, from *Texts for Nothing* to *Stirrings Still*, requires us to think about Beckett's work in terms of its historical and biographical contexts. It suggests, at the outset, that these works belong to a distinct phase in Beckett's writing, and assumes, more broadly, that the œuvre itself is one that passes through discrete periods, that follows a shaped trajectory.

Indeed, one can quickly sketch an outline of these phases that most of Beckett's readers would recognise. The early period, perhaps, stretches from *Dream of Fair to Middling Women* and *More Pricks than Kicks* to *Watt*. *Watt* might be thought of as a transitional novel, the work in which a mature voice starts to emerge, which flowers in Beckett's rich middle period, opened by the *Novellas*, and most beautifully realised in his trilogy of novels, *Molloy*, *Malone Dies*, and *The Unnamable*. This last, written first in French as *L'Innommable* and completed in December 1950, perhaps marks the end of the middle period. Beckett's writing, so the mythology goes, is brought to a shuddering halt in the final lines of the trilogy – 'you must go on, I can't go on, I'll go on' (*Un* 134). After this point, his work takes two directions. The first of these is opened by his 'turn' to the theatre. He starts to dabble in drama while writing his great middle-period prose works, finishing a draft of *Eleutheria* in February 1947, and then finishing *En attendant Godot* in 1949, after the completion of *Malone meurt*, and before starting on *L'Innommable*. These early plays might be thought of as a kind of apprenticeship in theatre, which allows him a respite from the abstraction of prose, after he reaches the deep and awful impasse at the end of *The Unnamable*. His theatrical works, from *Endgame*, through *Happy Days* and *Krapp's Last Tape*, to the late short pieces for television, offer Beckett a forum in which to extend the difficult thinking that had animated his prose, without succumbing to the aporetics that seemed to bring some kind of curtain down on his novelistic imagination. The second direction, and that which concerns us here, is that taken by his stunted prose, after the close of *The Unnamable*. First in *Texts for Nothing*, then in the bruisingly difficult and violent *How It Is*, Beckett crafts a kind of telegrammatic prose that struggles on joylessly, bereft of many of the pleasures or compensations of plot, character or comedy ('Thalia', the narrator of *How It Is* calls out plaintively to his comic muse, 'for pity's sake a leaf of thine ivy', *HII* 31). Even this anti-novelistic prose then gives way, after *How It is*, to the agonisingly brief texts of the 1960s and 1970s, scraps and fizzles of narrative, flickering on the very edge of nonexistence – a kind of borderline prose which is given an odd extension in *The Lost Ones*, the only longer prose work written during this time. This stretch of halting prose, strung in the lee of that catastrophic climax to *The Unnamable*, then ends with a final, wintry renaissance, in the appearance of a late trilogy of novellas: *Company*, *Ill Seen Ill Said*, and *Worstward Ho*. In these pieces, and particularly in *Company*, something like a novelistic urge returns, filtered through the sparse rhythms generated by the late prose – a bleakly nostalgic but unenchanted poetry which extends beyond the late novellas to colour his final, calmly irreconciled pieces: 'neither', 'what is the word' and *Stirrings Still*.

It is difficult, as I have said, to resist such narrative development when contemplating Beckett's œuvre, although one is conscious, even as one succumbs to its dangerous neatness, of its partial falsity. It is hard not to make a carefully folded ham sandwich of Beckett's work, to parcel it into a beginning, a middle and an end, even in the knowledge, as Hamm puts it, that the 'end is in the beginning' (*CDW* 126), that the œuvre insistently refuses to obey the terms of any trajectory, any story that takes us from the beginning, through the middle, to the end. It is difficult, too, once we have acknowledged this trajectory, with whatever reservations, to resist the idea that it is not confined to Beckett's development as an individual artist, but is part of a larger historical process, or unfolding. Beckett's passage – from the Joycean extravagance of his early, mannered work, through the comic agony of frenzied becoming in his middle period, to the bleached impossibility of his later prose – seems to be not simply the quirk of Beckett's individual imagination, but the expression of some cultural logic, in whose thrall the writing is caught. Drew Milne suggests this fundamental connection between the phases of Beckett's writing and the broader historical conditions of literary culture when he argues that 'more than any other writing of the second half of the twentieth century Samuel Beckett's writing embodies the fate of fiction' (1999, 93). The shift in Beckett's career from the early articulacy to the purgatorial impoverishment of the later work is a critical response to a more general impoverishment of the literary imagination in the wake of modernism, which has ushered in what Milne calls the 'ends of fiction'. 'The works he wrote from 1970 till his death', Milne suggests, 'find new and distinctive ways of reworking the ends of fiction reached in his earlier works' (93). The failure of the novelistic imagination that brought *The Unnamable* to a close was one which is produced not simply by Beckett's own exhaustion, but by the exhaustion of the culture at large – the exhaustion that it was the 'fate' of fiction itself to suffer. The inventiveness of the late works is thus shaped and limited by this experience of cultural termination; its frozen, static quality is to be seen as a symptomatic response to the depletion of the energy that fuelled the modernist avant-garde imagination. Beckett's later work has to eek itself out on the 'famished and slender means' of the literary imagination under the conditions brought about by 'capitalist relations of production' in the late twentieth century (Milne 1999, 94). With the emergence of the global culture industry, in which art forsakes its autonomy from the marketplace, 'Beckett's writing can offer little but an autopsy on the ends of fiction, a postmortem inquiry into abstracted formal conditions' (94).

To talk about a 'late phase' in Beckett's writing, then, to group these prose texts written after *The Unnamable* together as a body of works which belong to a distinct historical and biographical period, involves us in a kind of historical determinism. The works themselves lose some of their singularity, their freedom to stage themselves as individual acts of creation, becoming instead a symptom or manifestation of some kind of historical condition, or the working out of an aesthetic principle that shapes the œuvric development of Beckett's writing career. This, as I have said, might in a sense be inescapable, and might be a necessary element of the critical response to this work. But it is also paradoxical, because Beckett's writing, from the start, has been driven by a fascination with, and commitment to, the capacity for the creating mind to free itself from the historical and political forces which position and shape it. His work might be a particularly powerful critique of the historical conditions of the present, and this might encourage the tendency to read his work in a historically determined fashion; but it is also famously committed to ridding itself of any historical or geographical context. It is the most recognisable cliché of Beckett studies that his work comes from no specific place, and no specific time. It is perhaps this combination of historical articulacy with an insistent ahistoricism that makes him such a powerful critic of his time; as Milne argues, the embargo or 'taboo' on references to 'contemporary society' in Beckett's writing is an integral part of its dissidence, its 'determinate negation of the society it is mediated by' (1999, 93). But the challenge for a criticism that can gain access to this political and aesthetic power is to preserve at once his critical relationship with a specific political history, and the creative power of his negativity, his inventive refusal of the demands and limits of such history. An early tradition in Beckett criticism sees Beckett's writing as an interrogation of a universal human condition, and so tends to overlook or even to strenuously deny the historical specificity of his writing; but a more recent critical movement which is more articulate about his dissident political power – see for example the recent emergence of studies on Beckett's relationship with Irish politics, such as those by Declan Kiberd (1996) and Seán Kennedy (2010a) – tends to sacrifice his critical freedom, reading the emptiness and negativity of his work as a direct response to the historical conditions they disdain. To offer a critical assessment of the late works in particular, to understand the qualities that they share as a body of writing, requires us to read between these opposite imperatives; we have to understand how the prose after *The Unnamable* is shaped both by the stylistic logic of late aesthetics, and by the cultural logic of late capitalism. But we have also to understand how the texts themselves resist that logic, and move insistently beyond the historical and literary conditions that determine them.

To gain some kind of critical access to this balance in the later work between freedom and determinism, it is perhaps necessary to see the late prose in the context of Beckett's writing as a whole, and in the light of its recurrent fascination with the conditions that shape the movement of the creating mind. From *Dream of Fair to Middling Women* to *Stirrings Still*, Beckett's writing has tested the limits of the imagination in slipping free of the conditions which enable it, in extending itself beyond the historical and formal horizons which determine its possibility. His writing might be regarded as a long interrogation of the mobility of the literary imagination, its capacity, in one of Beckett's most important and recurrent words, to 'stir', to stray within and outside the horizons of the possible, or what he calls the 'plane of the feasible' (*PTD* 103). At the heart of his first, undisciplined novel, *Dream of Fair to Middling Women*, one can see the embryonic emergence of this concern, this attempt to understand how the literary tradition carries within itself a history of ahistoricity – how literary texts themselves work with and against the historical flows which carry them. The novel is shaped by a fascination with the play between the surface of the text – the written surface as that which it is possible to express – and that which lies beyond the text, the latent spaces between and outside the words, which do not themselves speak but which nevertheless make themselves felt, or leave some kind of trace. There are a series of metaphors that Beckett employs to articulate this play between the said and the unsaid. The narrator returns repeatedly to the figure of the rat scuttling behind the wallpaper in the German attic room in which he is living in the early chapters of the novel.

He can hear at night, he says 'the rats, galavanting and cataracting behind the wall-paper, slashing the close invisible plane with ghastlily muted slithers' (*Dream* 15), and this unseen movement of the rat, the 'first stir behind the paper, the first discrete slither' (15), comes to stand in for the stirrings of an unbound imagination. The unseen scratching of Beckett's rat, like the scratching and tearing of Charlotte Perkins Gilman's hidden woman behind the wallpaper in her 1892 story 'The Yellow Wallpaper', marks the movement of the text beyond its own historical boundaries. And this rat analogy, as it extends across the text, merges with another of Beckett's figures for the oscillating movement between the said and the unsaid, one which sees the relationship between the visible and the invisible in astronomical terms. Late in the novel, one of the characters remarks that 'the greatest triumph of human thought was the calculation of Neptune from the observed vagaries of the orbit of Uranus' (*Dream* 221). There is a beauty to be found, it is suggested here, in the way that an unseen heavenly body makes a legible mark on the seen universe; something compelling about the deduction of an unknown, undreamt thing, from the slight distortion it causes in the path of the known. As the narrator puts it, earlier in the novel, when gazing at the 'abstract density' of the 'night firmament', this coming together in the dark sky of the seen and the unseen mirrors the movement of the 'mind achieving creation' (16). If the sky is 'seen merely', Belacqua thinks, it appears as 'a depthless lining of [the] hemisphere', a 'crazy stipling of stars'; but if one is alert to the unseen that is threaded through the seen sky, the hidden orbits that pass silently through it, it becomes a figure for the 'passional movements of the mind charted in light and darkness' – for the 'passional intelligence' which 'tunnels, surely and blindly', through 'the interstellar coalsacks of its firmament in genesis'. 'The inviolable criterion of poetry and music', he thinks, 'is figured in the demented perforation of the night colander' (16). The night sky contains within it the unseen, 'incommunicable' elements of poetry and music, which withhold themselves, but which are nevertheless 'there', like an 'insistent, invisible rat, fidgeting behind the astral incoherence of the art surface' (16–7).

As these ideas surface in *Dream*, they remain rather inchoate, limited by the mannered, burlesque comic tone. But as his work matures, from *Dream* to *The Unnamable*, one can see an increasingly tight focus being brought to bear on the movement of the creating mind, and an increasingly powerful analysis of the ways that the resources of the literary tradition allow for the imagination not only to test and locate the limits of what it is possible to see and to say, but also to exceed those limits. The deduction of Neptune from the orbit of Uranus re-emerges several times in Beckett's writing, appearing again in *Murphy*, in the famous scene in which Mr Kelly flies his kite in

Hyde Park. As the novel draws to a close, exceptionally windy conditions allow Mr Kelly to fly his kite 'out of sight':

> Except for the sagging soar of line, undoubtedly superb so far as it went, there was nothing to be seen, for the kite had disappeared from view. Mr Kelly was enraptured. Now he could measure the distance from the unseen to the seen, now he was in a position to determine the point at which seen and unseen met. It would be an unscientific observation, so many and so fitful were the imponderables involved. But the pleasure accruing to Mr Kelly would be in no way inferior to that conferred (presumably) on Mr Adams by his beautiful deduction of Neptune from Uranus. (*Mu* 174)

Here, Beckett returns to the question of the influence of the unseen on the seen, but he does so in a much richer intertextual environment. The narrator likens the winding out of Mr Kelly's kite to the passage of historical time, to the unfolding of what he calls the 'historical process' (*Mu* 174). The releasing of a 'wild rush of line' as the kite soars, is equivalent, the narrator suggests, to the historical rush of the 'Industrial revolution' (174). But if the soaring kite suggests this historical linearity, the beauty of its flight stems not from its capacity to represent the linear onward progress of time, but from its sideways transgression of that fugitive boundary where the historical meets with the unhistorical. The disappearing kite locates that invisible border that separates the seen from the unseen, the known from the unknown, not at the far horizon of historical time, or at some notional 'end of history'. Rather, it is a limit that is always at work in history itself, intervening between historical processes that reveal themselves to us, and those that stay latent, that fuel the motor of passing time without themselves coming to appearance. And in marking this immanent limit, Mr Kelly's kite draws knowingly on the literary historical processes that have allowed us to bring such a limit into some kind of knowability. The vibrating relation here between the seen and the unseen might call to the abiding interest in Beckett's writing between the visible and the invisible, as part of both Dante's and Milton's 'cosmologies' – a concern with what Beckett narrators call 'darkness visible' that recurs insistently later in his œuvre (*CIWS* 11). But here, the capacity of Mr Kelly's kite to identify and cross this boundary is seen as part of the tradition of literary realism, and more specifically nineteenth-century literary realism. As Victor Sage (1977) has pointed out, the predominant reference in this passage is to Charles Dickens, and to the idiot savant in Dickens's novel *David Copperfield*, Mr Dick, who has a similar fascination with kites, attaching the pages of his 'memorial' to the sails of his kite, in the hope that he too might be able to take his narrative beyond his own horizons, might sail his insane chronicle (prototype perhaps both of Malone's and of Hamm's) past that point where seen and unseen meet. But if Dickens is the foremost reference here, the passage is redolent of that concern – running throughout nineteenth-century realism – with the capacity to coax the unseen elements of the culture out of hiding, to plumb those hidden forces that make historical time without yielding themselves to historical legibility. As George Eliot puts it in *Daniel Deronda*, it is the task of the literary realist not simply to say what is there, but to understand how what is perceptible is shaped and formed by what is not perceptible. 'Men', she says, 'like planets, have both a visible and an invisible history'. As the 'astronomer threads the darkness with strict deduction', she goes on, like Adams deducing the existence of Neptune from the orbit of Uranus, so the 'narrator of human actions, if he did his work with the same completeness, would have to thread the hidden pathways of feeling and thought which lead up to every moment of action' (Eliot 2009, 139).

It is this capacity for literary narrative to 'stir', like the fidgeting rat, from the field of the possible, to extend itself from what is seen and given to what is unseen and hidden, that Beckett's fiction sets out to test. As it moves from the slightly bent realism of *Dream* and *Murphy*, through the increasingly abstract realms of *Watt*, the *Nouvelles* and the trilogy, the prose becomes increasingly absorbed in this question, to the exclusion of the other elements of narrative fiction. The focus shifts gradually from the maintenance of a residual plot to an ever more intense examination of the conditions that allow for narrative to come about. Beckett's narrators find themselves increasingly recklessly destroying their narrative scenarios, in order to free themselves from their own appurtenances, from the domain of the seen, the possible and the feasible, into Eliot's 'hidden pathways' that it is the vocation both of the astronomer and of the novelist to 'thread'. As the narrator of *The Unnamable* puts it, we are no longer 'somewhere on a road, moving, between a beginning and an end, gaining ground, losing ground' (*Un* 25), but rather find ourselves in a narrative place that continually undoes itself, in order more fully to reveal the emptiness that lies behind the 'art surface', that place where the imagination stirs freely, without bounds. As Arsene puts it, in *Watt*, the prose moves insistently towards the 'sites of a stirring beyond coming and going', in which one might experience a 'being so light and free that it is as the being of nothing' (*W* 32). But if the passage from *Dream* to *The Unnamable* sees this tightening focus on the conditions of narrative invention – on the capacity of the creating mind to stir, like Mr Kelly's kite, from the field of the possible – what this period also sees, paradoxically enough, is a drastic narrowing of the literary horizon, a straitening of the gate. The literary imagination hypostatises, in Beckett's writing, as it is exposed to its own increasingly hungry gaze. As Beckett probes the resources of realism, and then of modernism, as he ransacks the funds of what Keats famously calls 'negative capability' (1966, 40–1), he finds that these resources are depleting before his eyes. The skymole capacity – to thread wormholes of silence and of hidden potential that underlie the surface of the visible in George Eliot, and then in James Joyce – withers and shrivels, as Beckett's narrators become increasingly desperate in their attempt to tear apart the art surface, or as Beckett puts it in one of his most famous letters, to 'drill one hole after another' (*LSB I* 518) into the language in which the text is written. What brings the narrator of *The Unnamable* to his shattering conclusion, to the blank impasse in which he can neither continue nor cease, is the final recognition of this terminal depletion, not only in Beckett's œuvre, but in the culture more generally. The novels of the trilogy oscillate between statement and denial, between revealed surface and hidden depth, vibrating at a higher and higher frequency in their bid at once to make narrative and to free themselves from its historical conditions of possibility, until finally sense disintegrates into a kind of feedback scream. The aporia with which *The Unnamable* closes marks the moment when the tense contradiction between saying and unsaying, the seen and the unseen, yields to a blank, inarticulate antinomy, a Munchian howl. As the narrator draws towards the close, it appears that the play between the visible and the invisible is finally drained of energy, no longer yielding intellectual creativity, or any kind of literary knowing. There is no longer a dialectical relation between these terms, but finally only the statement of a blank opposition that yields no thinking, and no beauty. We are in the world, and removed from it. We are in language, and banished from it. We must endlessly continue to speak, but we can never start. We are stranded, becalmed, the narrator of *The Unnamable* says, between the 'all of all and the all of nothing' (*Un* 105).

If the development of Beckett's prose is intimately linked to the 'fate of fiction', it is this articulation of the dwindling of the imagination that makes it so. When Beckett's prose continues to go on, in the wake of that awful aporia reached at the close of *The Unnamable*, it does so, in a sense, only by extending the narrator's recognition that it is unable to do so, that literature itself, in an adaptation of Adorno's famous formulation, has become in some sense 'impossible', 'barbaric' (1983, 34). From *Texts for Nothing* to *Stirrings Still*, the prose begins in the knowledge that it cannot begin, and ends in the knowledge that it cannot end; in the understanding, as the narrator of *The Lost Ones* puts it, that the 'beginning' is as 'unthinkable as the end' (*CSP* 212–13). 'Suddenly', the first of the *Texts for Nothing* begins, the first prose Beckett writes after the close of *The Unnamable*; 'Suddenly, no, at last, long last, I couldn't any more, I couldn't go on' (100). The fund of the unseen and the unsaid, it seems, the creative negativity that has driven not only Beckett's work, but that makes literary thinking itself possible, has been exhausted; as Gilles Deleuze puts it, Beckett's prose 'falls into an aporia' at the end of *The Unnamable*, as the narrator has 'exhausted the possible' (1998, 157). From the *Texts* and *How It Is*, through to the extreme short works of the later 1960s and 1970s – such as *Ping* and *Imagination Dead Imagine* – the fictional imagination persists only to demonstrate that the conditions that enable it have disappeared. There is no longer, in these texts, a hidden element which it is the goal of the texts to divine or to penetrate, no rat slithering and stirring behind the wallpaper. Rather, here, that which is hidden is brought out of hiding, presented before us in the glare of a kind of unlimited revealment. While the experience of duration and movement in Beckett's early and middle prose was generated by the dialectical tension between what is said and what is withheld, here we find ourselves projected into a textual environment in which there is no longer any productive relationship between these terms, in which, in Fredric Jameson's terms, the dialectic that drives literary thinking has 'stalled' (1994, xii).

The particular literary quality that is shared by all of Beckett's later prose, from *Texts for Nothing* to *Stirrings Still*, is produced in part by this sense that the invisible has been brought out of hiding. This is manifest in the landscapes of the texts themselves. The bright white spaces of *Ping*, of *Imagination Dead Imagine*, of *The Lost Ones* – these are spaces in which nothing is hidden, in which, as in *Ping*, 'all [is] known' (*CSP* 193), or, in *Worstward Ho*, 'All [is] seen' (*CIWS* 93), 'all [is] always to be seen', and 'Nothing [is] ever unseen' (*CIWS* 90–1). These spaces flicker on the very edge of perceptibility, precisely because there is nothing here that is not exposed to view, because all is 'white in the whiteness' (*CSP* 182). There is no play of light and dark, but the light itself is omnipresent. 'The light that makes all so white', the narrator of *Imagination Dead Imagine* says, comes from 'no visible source', as 'all shines with the same white shine' (182), just as the light in *The Lost Ones* 'appears to emanate from all sides and to permeate the entire space as though this were uniformly luminous down to its last particle of ambient air' (215). If these texts are an early response to the globalisation of capital, to the tendency for capitalism, in its late phase, to absorb its own margins, to produce an infinitely fungible, homogenous public sphere – reflected in a bureaucratised culture industry – then this hypervisibility is its most marked symptom. The rotunda of *Imagination Dead Imagine*, the cylinder of *The Lost Ones* – these are protoglobal spaces, pictures of the revealed totality, in which all forms of withdrawal, all forms of dissent, have been banished. This is Beckett's prevision of the electronic reach, in the twenty-first century, of the NSA. There is dimness here, of course, aplenty. There is a surplus of darkness, a veritable glut of gloom; but darkness here becomes difficult to distinguish from light, and does not enter into any kind of productive tension with it – or offer any kind of relief from its glare. Just as these texts respond to a situation in which 'all [is] known' (*CSP* 193), all is brought to light, we also find ourselves in a position in which nothing is known, 'all' is 'gone from mind' (200). Everything is doused in light, in the cylinder of *The Lost One*s, 'with the slight reserve that light is not the word' (215). Light itself sheds a kind of darkness here, knowledge disseminates a kind of ignorance. Where all is light, we find ourselves projected into a kind of universal dark; where all is known, we forsake the very conditions of knowledge. Seeing itself, in this dark light, becomes ill.

But if the shining landscapes of the late prose, aglow with visible darkness, are one way in which these texts manifest a kind of ultraexposure, it is also the case that the texts train a merciless light on the mechanics of their own narrative becoming. Perhaps the defining trait of these fictions, apart from their starkly exposed geographies, is their frantic refusal to leave any element of the narrating process unilluminated, their neurotic attempt to bring every turn of the creating mind into the field of the seen. They read, as John Pilling puts it, as 'exercises in openly fleshing out the skeleton of a fiction' (1979, 157). They offer pictures of the minimal conditions that are required for narration to occur, to give the starkest account of the way that these conditions work. In order for text to come about, the narrator of 'Text 13' proposes, we need a 'voice', and 'somewhere a kind of hearing', and also 'somewhere a hand', some kind of tool with which to 'leave a trace, of what is made, of what is said'. As the narrator puts it, you 'can't do with less' (*CSP* 152). All of these texts develop an extreme metafictional consciousness of these conditions, of these minima. 'I see the scene', the narrator of 'Text 5' says, of the process of his own narration: 'I see the scene, I see the hand' (*CSP* 119). The writing hand, shuttling back and forth on the paper, 'comes creeping out of the shadow, the shadow of my head, then scurries back' (119). But, just as the exposure of the landscapes themselves to omnipresent light produces a kind of darkness, so here does the revelation of the mechanics of narration not only make such mechanics visible, but also enshrouds them, or annuls them. The experience of reading these texts is defined above all by this extraordinarily rapid switching between revelation and concealment, or rather by the feeling that these urges, to reveal and conceal, become the same thing, when they are directed at the limit conditions which determine the process of writing itself. In order to reveal the fictional scenario in its fullness, these texts discover, you have also to reveal that they are fictions; but to do so returns the fictions themselves to the darkness of nonbeing, and reveals the nonexistence of the very narrative agent striving for revelation. There is some moment, these texts suggest, at which the creating mind invents the fictional scenario before us; some animating moment, as the narrator of *Worstward Ho* puts it, that is the 'germ of all' (*CIWS* 90). If we are to see everything, if 'nothing' is to remain 'unseen', then we must see this initial moment, it must be brought into the field of the visible. But the attempt so to do brushes against the impossible, as if a system is trying to incorporate its own outside, or a machine is trying to produce its own fuel. It leads to that full emptiness that is caused by the contemplation of infinity. To bring the creator out of hiding – to overcome that theological ban on seeing the moment of creation that is given its fullest poetic expression in John Milton's *Paradise Lost* – the creator has to become part of his or her own creation, the text must incorporate its own genesis, give birth to itself. As the narrator of *Company* puts it, he must become the 'deviser of the voice and of its hearer and of himself' (*CIWS* 20). *Company* and *Worstward Ho* are the texts that seek, most exhaustively, to account for this genesis, to include it among the elements that become knowable, to narrate the moment of their own becoming. The narrator of *Worstward Ho* seeks at once to invent a body and be that body, to bow the body down in subjection, and be the bowed subject; he seeks to 'bow it down' and 'be it bowed down' (*CIWS* 89). But at their very limits, these texts discover that the attempt to incorporate the moment of creation into the created field brings the very process of revelation into an identity with a kind of radical unknowing. To narrate, the narrator of *Worstward Ho* declares, is to put a fictional body in a fictional place. But to narrate the conditions of fictional narration is to reveal, at the selfsame moment, that the body and the place do not exist. 'Say a body', the narrator demands, 'Where none'. 'A place. Where none. For the body. To be in' (*CIWS* 81). To attempt this kind of revelation causes the fictional scenario to vibrate between exposure and erasure, to take fiction itself to the limits of its possibility where these things – creation and erasure – are somehow, terribly, the same.

It is this mania for exposure, then – this desperate attempt to produce world pictures in which nothing is left out, and in which the process of picture making is itself fully depicted – that is both the cause and the symptom of a general stalling of literary dialectics. Just as the omnipresence of light in the landscapes of these late texts leads to a peculiar universal darkness, so does the exposure of the intricate movement of literary creation have the effect at once of unearthing it and interring it. The very possibility of literary thinking is cancelled out by this determination to reveal what makes it possible. The literary mind continues to stir; as the title of one of Beckett's last prose pieces suggests, there are still stirrings even here, still a kind of movement. But the opposition between movement and stasis, that opposition between continuing to go on and ceasing to go on that brings

The Unnnamable to an aporia, has fallen, at this extremity, into a kind of stalled identity. There are still stirrings here, but these stirrings have gone still. Now, at the end of a writing career, and in the midst of a late historical exhaustion of dialectical thinking, one can no longer distinguish between continuation and termination, between the seen and the unseen, the latent and the revealed. If Beckett's works seem particularly articulate about the historical conditions of the late twentieth century, then it is perhaps because they give the most eloquent testimony to this evacuation of the categories that have driven political and cultural life through the history of modernity. These brief and agonising works give expression to a kind of eviscerated freedom – the freedom that we might associate with contemporary democracy, under global conditions. The subjects in these works, like the subjects of western democracies, are bound so tightly into a kind of administered being that they can no longer gain any purchase on the forces that compel them or bind them. The late prose pictures a kind of totalitarian democracy where freedom becomes difficult to distinguish from unfreedom, where forms of resistance to or withdrawal from the status quo lose traction, where privacy becomes a kind of public, where the movement of the dissident mind becomes difficult to distinguish from the stasis of the compliant. The stillness of these works (in both senses – their immobility and their tendency still to continue after their enabling conditions have disappeared) is the expression of a kind of deadened historical afterlife, the weakest of protests against the historical failure of protest, which draws its negativity only from a pale affirmation, its dissidence only from its deadpan depiction of a kind of compulsory obedience.

This view of Beckett's prose, this reading of what Beckett (1972, 3) has called the 'coincidence of contraries' – as his almost mute protest against the cultural assimilation of the dissident imagination, under the conditions of late capitalism –follows from the almost inescapable tendency to see his work in terms of a historical trajectory. The powerful coincidence of a general late historical melancholia with Beckett's own entry into a distinct late phase has created a critical context which has saturated these works, which has designated them, from the outset, as 'late' works. It is this designation, in turn, that has set the terms in which we have measured their capacity for dissidence, for invention – their ability to stir from the field of the possible. To see Beckett's late works as the increasingly static symptom of a narrowing capacity for literary invention, as I have done so far in this essay, is to see in these pieces the running out of historical energy; it is to see their radicalism, their creative power, as a direct function of their articulation of the end of invention, the end of creativity, the ends, as Milne puts it, of fiction. But, as I suggested at the outset of this essay, it is perhaps necessary to see these texts not only in terms of their status as late works, but also as singular pieces in themselves, each of which struggles to free itself from the historical forces that position it. In order to grasp the radicalism of these texts, to address the dissident power they harbour, it is perhaps necessary to read them both with and against their historical grain. Read with the historical grain, these works give expression to a kind of entropic decline, the contraction of the literary horizons, the freezing of creative energies; read against the grain, however, each of these texts opens fields of historical possibility, new formations that do not conform to a late historical cultural logic. Beckett's late works give expression to the depletion of historical forms, and in so doing offer a mute and inarticulate protest against such depletion; but they also refuse the logic of steady decline, opening pockets in the homogenised surface that belong not to a history that is passing, but rather gesture to a time that is still to come, a futurity yet to come to expression.

The difficulty of talking about this second movement in Beckett's late prose, though, is that it is almost indissociably bound up with the first. In Beckett's work after *The Unnamable* it is lateness, hypostasy, exhaustion that yields the experience of novelty, singularity and rebirth. These two movements, like so much in Beckett's late imagination, do not only oppose each other, but conspire with one another. As Edward Said puts it in his great study of late aesthetics, in the work of irreconciled artists such as Beckett we find 'lateness and newness' 'next to each other' (2007, 17). It is the pressure that Beckett puts on the known, his capacity to exhaust the historical forms available to him, that leads to the breaking open of the present, and the irruption of an unseen and unthought futurity into the space of the contemporary. In Deleuze's terms, it is the very movement towards completion that causes cracks to open in the surface of the known, opening new seams of invisibility. In the works after *The Unnnamable*, Deleuze argues, the tendency towards the 'exhaustion of the possible' leads to the discovery of new and previously unmapped fault lines – what he calls 'immanent limits that are ceaselessly displaced' – which open 'hiatuses, holes or tears' in the texts which 'suddenly widen in such a way as to receive something from the outside or from elsewhere' (1998, 158). In these texts, it is the very movement towards identity that leads to the persistence of disidentity, the pressure of homogeneity that opens a kind of heterogeneity, termination that yields a new beginning. As the narrator of 'Text 9' puts it, 'variety' is a species of 'monotony', rather than its antidote or counterpoison. 'What variety', he says, 'and at the same time what monotony, how varied it is and at the same time how, what's the word, how monotonous' (*CSP* 137). From the *Texts* through to *Stirrings Still*, it is the dedication to monotony – to the exploration of the contracting field of the selfsame, the homogenous – that leads to the discovery of a kind of variety. The more powerfully the texts insist on sameness, on solitude, on the boundedness of late being, the more insistently they discover difference, multiplicity, the stirring of the new. The first novella of the late 'trilogy', *Company*, like the late theatrical work *Ohio Impromptu*, dramatises the ineluctable movement towards solitude, the steady binding into solitary being. Both these works move relentlessly towards the recognition that 'you' are 'as you always were': 'Alone' (*CIWS* 42). Both works play out in miniature the historical process by which mobility and multiplicity contract towards stasis and solitude. But the discovery of both works is that the more fully one extrapolates this process, the more faithful one is to this experience of binding, the more powerfully one exceeds its constraints. The various elements that go into the making of narrative – the distinctions between first, second and third person in *Company*, and between 'reader' and 'listener' in *Ohio Impromptu* – congeal steadily towards that final revelation that 'you' are 'alone'; that the voice, the hearer, and the hand that are the necessarily diverse elements of composition in 'Text 5' belong in the end to the same bound entity, fabling to itself in the dark. As the vast multitude of crawling creators resolves into a single voice at the end of *How It Is*, so do all of these texts insist on the resolution of the many into the one. But the result of this concentration into homogeneity is the production of extraordinarily persistent forms of dissonance and difference that refuse to be bound, and that open up new tears in the word surface, a new 'play', as Andrew Gibson has put it, 'between binding and unbinding' (1999, 140).

This strange conjunction of the bound and the unbound reaches perhaps it is most intense expression in the late novella *Worstward Ho*. Here, radical abbreviation is a symptom of the narrowing of the historical, political and literary fields. In the frozen environment of this work, all qualities demonstrate their identity with their opposite, as dialectics becomes squashed into a painful stasis, and contradiction moves so rapidly as to become a kind of failed reconciliation. Success and failure become indistinguishable – for this text to succeed it would have to 'fail better' (*CIWS* 81) – and the difference between continuing and ceasing, which was so powerful and aporetic at the end of *The Unnamable* is deleted, by the grace of abbreviation. 'From now', the narrator says midway through his journey to the 'worst', he will no longer differentiate between continuing and turning back. From now, 'back is on'. 'No more from now now back and now back on. From now back alone' (98). When 'back' and 'on' have become the same thing, there is no need continually to employ these oppositional terms; as in George Orwell's 'Newspeak', a quality and its opposite can be designated by the same term. But if this contraction spells a kind of ultimate stasis, if this is the means by which this text might arrive at the worst, then the extraordinary effect of abbreviation in this text is that it carries within it those differences that it seeks to expel, as a kind of flaw or fault line that opens onto an elsewhere. The very process by which the narrator declares that 'back' is 'on' produces a kind of surplus that has no language with which to describe itself, but which is preserved in the abbreviated word surface, as that which has been abbreviated. As the narrator himself puts it, the 'flaw' in this text is its 'want of flaw' (*CIWS* 101). The smoothness of the abbreviated surface is shot through with seams of darkness, which is where that invisibility that George Eliot sees as the fuel of the creating mind is preserved.

It is this capacity to give a kind of expression to a fugitive darkness that is preserved in the midst of a compulsory enlightenment that makes Beckett a 'contemporary', in the sense that Giorgio Agamben gives to that term. For Agamben, a contemporary is not one who is well adjusted to the current time, who is happily in step with it, but one who is able to divine those flaws in the surface that have no existing language to describe them, and that require of us the invention of a new way of seeing if they are to come to visibility. 'The contemporary', Agamben writes, 'is the one whose eyes are struck by the beam of darkness that comes from his own time' (2011, 14); the one who can see the 'invisible light that is the darkness of the present' (18–9). Beckett's late prose belongs, in a sense, to a historical period that is passing or past, as it belongs to an œuvre which is moving towards completion; but if this is the case, it is also true that these works, perhaps more powerfully than any other written in the late twentieth century, suggest the emergence of a new contemporaneity, a new set of historical possibilities and fault lines, that belong to a period that is only now coming to thought. If we are seeing now what Alain Badiou (2012) has recently called the 'rebirth of history', if the turn of the millennium heralds the arrival of new world historical dynamics, then Beckett's precise and painstaking forms of seeing, his testing of the limits of the visible under a dying regime, become a guide to the future.

4

RÓNÁN MCDONALD

Waiting for Godot and Beckett's Cultural Impact

Capturing 'cultural impact' is only partly served by empirical methods. The expanding ripples created by *Waiting for Godot*, and Becket's other works, go in many directions and are not always visible. We can confidently declare that this is the play which catapulted Samuel Beckett from relative obscurity to international notoriety and, onwards, to his current position as an icon of twentieth-century literature and theatre. It is clear that, after Beckett, world drama changes. He revealed possibilities for the medium that had not hitherto been reckoned with, in particular the dramatic power of inaction, silence, and waiting. Many leading playwrights, including Harold Pinter, Tom Stoppard, and Václav Havel, have acknowledged his influence, but the impact goes far beyond those who write in conscious imitation of his example. His mature novels, though less of a direct influence on future practitioners than his drama, are venerated as masterpieces of twentieth-century prose, profoundly registering the intellectual and cultural crises of late modernity in scrupulously wrought and cadenced sentences. His impact on visual artists and film-makers is immense, as is his legacy among twentieth-century philosophers, from Theodor Adorno to Alain Badiou. *Waiting for Godot* remains the single work with which his name is, still, most closely associated. It remains perhaps the most well-known play of the twentieth century, and not just by theatre goers. 'Godot' has entered the language as a figure of nonarrival, a ready metaphor as likely to pop up in discussion of a bus timetable as of intellectual drama. He is now the stuff of journalistic rhetoric and political oratory, of linguistic coins like 'Big Brother' or 'Scrooge', circulating outside their literary origins.

Part of the reason for the play's permeability into a wider culture is its sparseness – the instantly recognisable stage setting. Beckett's bare tree and derelict tramps have often featured in newspaper cartoons and satirical sketches, even featuring in a skit on Sesame Street, entitled 'Waiting for Elmo' ('A modern masterpiece. A play so modern, and so brilliant, it makes absolutely no sense to anybody'). The visual imprint of much of Beckett's drama is one of its most striking qualities: two old people in dustbins, a middle-aged woman dressed in finery buried up to her waist in sand, a desperate old man crouched over a tape recorder, a man and two women in urns. Because of their searing visual simplicity these images circulate within the cultural store in a way that the stagecraft of Ibsen or Shaw or Arthur Miller do not. This is not to say that Beckett is for this reason greater or more important as a playwright, but it is to suggest that his cultural impact is caught up in different networks of connotation. There is a distinctive matrix of cultural associations and implications that go with the word 'Beckettian'. We approach his work with a host of assumptions and expectations: demanding drama, high-culture, 'deep' theatre, albeit leavened with mordant humour. Audiences may variously be impressed, intimidated or scornful of the aura around the Beckett brand, but they cannot ignore or sidestep it. We could never see Beckett's *Waiting for Godot* as virginal spectators nor capture the initial bemusement and hostility that impelled early attendees to cat-call or to walk out, no more than we can feel the outrage that that greeted Stravinsky's *Rite of Spring* (1913) or the riots after Synge's *The Playboy of the Western World* (1907). For good or ill, Beckett has accrued a fortune of cultural capital since *En attendant Godot* premiered in Paris over sixty years ago.

The first production was directed by Roger Blin in the small Théâtre de Babylone in Paris on 5 January 1953. The play, clearly belonging to a recognisably avant-garde and experimental theatrical style, performed to small and often bemused audiences. It became a talking point, buoyed by the support of esteemed intellectuals and reviewers. In France, Jean Anouilh famously described *En attendant Godot* as a 'music hall sketch of Pascal's *Pensées* as played by the Fratellini clowns', succinctly bringing together the religious, philosophical, vaudeville aspects of the play (1953, 1). Eight productions of *Warten auf Godot* were performed in West Germany over the course of 1953, heralding the deep and abiding affinity Beckett would have with German theatre audiences. For English-speaking audiences, the inaugural moment came with Peter Hall's London premiere in the Arts Theatre on 3 August 1955. Initial notices were poor, audience responses hostile to its 'left-bank' pretension and obscurity. However, the tide turned in London when the more eminent Sunday newspaper reviewers discerned a watershed in the dramatic arts. Kenneth Tynan, reviewer for *The Observer*, proclaimed that *Waiting for Godot* 'forced me to re-examine the rules which have hitherto governed the drama; and, having done so, to pronounce them not elastic enough' (Graver and Federman 1979, 97). These imprimaturs and, in England, much practical support from theatre critic Harold Hobson, helped the play to accrue glamour, respectability, and intellectual and cultural weight, even by those who were not initially well-disposed. Yet it was still capable of evoking bemusement and hostility, especially when the production was badly located and marketed. The first American production, though directed by Alan Schneider, who would go on to be a trusted interpreter of Beckett's stage works, was unwisely put on by the producers in Miami Beach, and billed as 'the laugh hit of two continents'. Audiences, expecting seaside entertainment, walked out in droves (Knowlson 1996, 419–21).

The play travelled around the world quickly, facilitated initially by the formidable international networks of Blin. There are distinct reception histories to be traced in particular countries, each with its own cultural and intellectual milieux and social circumstance (Nixon and Feldman 2009, 1–2). In France, Beckett was associated with the pessimistic philosophy current in the aftermath of the Second World War, the existentialism of Sartre and Camus, and the 'literature of the absurd' (see Esslin 1961). Quite early in its popular and academic reception, buoyed by this context and by the seemingly deracinated quality of the play itself, *Waiting for Godot*'s significance and achievement were ascribed to its universal themes. It seemed to many that the play was saying this is what the human condition (as opposed to particular instances of life, in social and political context) is like: a constant and unfulfilled waiting between cradle and grave; and all we on this blighted earth can do is to distract ourselves with pointless games and futile banter. That the play is mostly shorn of recognisable geographical references has invited many to read it as an archetypal space that can stand in for everywhere or anytime. There are a few scant references to particular places, such as the Eiffel Tower or the River Rhône, which betray the original French in which the play was written. Yet the place and time is not specified. The names of the characters are deliberately transnational. Estragon sounds French, Vladimir Russian. Pozzo's name sounds like an Italian clown's and Lucky's like a household pet. In terms of their dialect, the two tramps speak English with an Irish cadence. So the national cues come from different parts of Europe, a plurality of sourcing that encourages the notion that the stage here is an 'everyplace' and the characters 'everymen'. Vladimir ponders Pozzo's call for assistance when he is prostrate in Act II: 'To all mankind they were addressed, those cries for help still ringing in our ears! But at this place, at this moment of time, all mankind is us, whether we like it or not' (*WFG* 76). Inspired by passages like these, commentators often assume the play is of universal relevance, expressing a pessimistic view of existence that applies to all of us, outside history, politics, or social situation.

As we get further from the play in history, we can see how implicated it is in the cultural context of its composition. However much it changed the course of modern drama, it nonetheless melded the techniques of vaudeville and music with the avant-garde theatre – associated with figures like Antonin Artaud, Jean Anouilh, and Jean Cocteau – that thrived in Paris in the first half of the twentieth century. Equally, for all its seeming deracination, we can see that the play evolves from the pessimism and desolation unleashed by the Second World War, in which Beckett had played a part through his activities for the French Resistance. No cultural document emerges from a vacuum, nor can it signify and survive in an abstract and timeless space. If *Waiting for Godot* has an appeal or meaning that endures, it is not because it speaks directly to an ahistorical human condition, but rather because it can come alive in various contexts and historical moments. The production history of *Godot* attests to the importance of concrete circumstance to lend it meaning. This is one of the fundamental ironies of the play. While its deracinated stage settings seem to transcend the national, it forcefully speaks to particular social or political circumstances – apartheid South Africa, war-torn Sarajevo, and flood-afflicted New Orleans. The value of Beckett is often ascribed to his universal outlook, what he called in an early review 'the issueless predicament of existence' (*Dis* 97). But the productions of Beckett's play remind us forcefully that suffering happens *in situ* – it emerges from social circumstances, in particular concrete instantiations.

This must mean that the play needs to have a chameleonic aspect – it must change its connotations in different situations, places, historical moments. It must be *transnational*, moving across sign systems, but not *transhistorical*, operating above them. This implies a strongly constitutive role for the director or *auteur*, who must bring to the author's text the performative animation which turns the static playscript into a dramatic event in a particular place and time. As time passes, as locations change, these events become more distinct and distinguished. But even early on, the success of the play depends on its ability to accord with the contexts of its production, as the Miami failure attests.

A case in point is the first Irish production of *Waiting for Godot*, in Dublin's Pike Theatre on 28 October 1955, directed by Alan Simpson. It was a great success, enjoying the longest continuous run of any play in Irish history up to that point, belying 'the image of Ireland in the 1950s as an intellectually timid cultural wasteland' (Morash 2002, 206; see also Simpson 1962). One of the reasons that the play found an Irish audience was because the Irish elements, implicit in the English translation, were brought out here. Estragon and Vladimir speak with a Dublin argot – 'Get up till I embrace you'; 'your man' – while Pozzo speaks like an Anglo-Irish landowner – 'Oh I say'; 'my good man' (*WFG* 5, 17, 22, 23). The themes of power and exploitation in the play adopt a particular Irish class configuration with this emphasis that spoke strongly to the Irish audience, familiar with the argot of Synge and O'Casey. If this lends dramatic power for some audiences, and shows how the class differences in the play operate, for other commentators it distorts the play's universal import. Beckett's friend A. J. Leventhal, already familiar with the French première, praised the Pike production but raised misgivings about the Irish emphasis, claiming that 'the author had in mind a universal rather than a regional application of his vision of mankind in perpetual expectation' (1956, 52). This tension between universal and particular in productions of *Godot* has endured in those voices that have been raised against more recent efforts to bring out the Irish dimension in Beckett's work, such as the Dublin Gate Theatre's 1991 Beckett Festival, which was a deliberate attempt to situate Beckett within an Irish dramatic tradition (partly inspired by the absence of an Irish element from the eightieth birthday celebrations in 1986). Michael Colgan was the impresario behind the festival, which toured internationally and would evolve into the Beckett on Film project (2001), a hugely ambitious attempt to bring all nineteen of Beckett's stage plays to the screen (Saunders 2007, 79–96). Both these enterprises had many admirers, but there were others wary that emphasising the Irish aspects of Beckett might draw attention away from his profound indebtedness to European and metropolitan intellectual and cultural currents.

Yet *Waiting for Godot* in performance has tended to perforate the distinctions between universal meanings and particular contexts. This production history of Beckett's great play reveals an abstract work which takes on its significance in concrete situations. It does not do so by forcing allegorical significance into the play through heavily signalled changes to stage directions, dialogue, or costumes. Beckett's play is not, or not yet, like Shakespeare's *Henry V*, which takes on contemporary relevance when overtly brought to bear on contemporary military conflict. The least successful productions have often been those which hammer home the significance in a contemporary setting by experimenting with new dramaturgy or changing the dialogue; the most successful are those which allow the play to resonate in each singular context, without loading down its spare and abstract power with extra dramatic accoutrements designed to telegraph its message (see Kalb 1989; Bradby 2001).

Beckett as Director

Beckett was bemused by the success of *Waiting for Godot*, which occurred relatively late in his writing life, when he was in his late forties. It was based, he felt, 'on a fundamental misunderstanding, that critics and public alike insisted on interpreting in allegorical or symbolic terms a play which was striving all the time to *avoid* definition' (qtd in Graver and Federman 1979, 10; emphasis added). He was dismayed by the attempts of actors, directors, and scholars to find a message or a moral in the play, and chafed against the critical and popular habit of steering his play into a philosophical discourse, away from the domain of art, shape, and structure. When asked by a young producer planning to broadcast readings from *En attendant Godot* on French radio for his ideas about the play, Beckett responded, as he always did, with an insistence on the sufficiency of the words and actions of the characters: 'All that I have been able to understand I have shown. It is not much. But is it enough, and more than enough for me' (*LSB II* 316). Furthermore, the attempt to extract meanings was for him wrong-headed: 'As for wanting to find in all this a wider and loftier meaning to take away after the show, along with the programme and the choc-ice, I am unable to see the point of it. But it must be possible' (316).

The interest in shape above sense, in the artistic effect rather than the philosophical message, marks his practice as a director. Beckett was a scrupulous and fastidious writer, drafting and redrafting his drama and prose works until he found the cadence and effect he needed. This is also manifest in the exactitude of timing and pacing that he sought when he came to directing his own plays in the 1960s and 1970s. He may not have wanted to elaborate on the meanings and themes of his plays, but he was deeply committed to their aesthetic form and design, which explains in part his resistance to directors and actors deviating from his careful end product. His allegiance to form also meant that he tended to reject requests to adapt work into different media, although he was not absolute in his interdictions and could sometimes make exceptions for friends or creative figures whom he trusted.

This close control over other people's productions of his plays means that the results of his own directorial activity, when he did not forebear to make changes to his plays, is of special interest. We are left with an ironic situation. The text is given priority in putting on Beckett's work, not the agency or the creativity of the director and actor, but we can reasonably ask which version of *Waiting for Godot* should be given priority and precedence. Should we go to the first emanation of Beckett's imagination, the playscript of *En attendant Godot*? Or to the English translation, undertaken by Beckett following the success of Blin's original production? The text of *Waiting for Godot* is not simply a faithful translation but also makes numerous subtle changes of emphasis and tone in response to the French production. A key impact of *En attendant Godot* is, therefore, on its own playscript. If his translation into English necessarily involves compromises from this French original, it also allows much of the crucial music hall influence to emerge more fully, since that tradition is more developed in English than in French. It also allows him to inflect his dialogue with Dublin cadences. But the English version, as originally published, also includes the cuts demanded of an appalled Beckett by the Lord Chamberlain, the notorious censor of English theatre at this time – cuts not restored to the Faber edition until 1965.

The text of the play continued to be pruned and refined when Beckett went on to direct his plays. He directed *Godot* in the Schiller Theatre in Berlin in 1975 and supervised a production in the Riverside Theatre in London in 1984. Some suggest, therefore, that the 'most accurate' text of *Waiting for Godot* is to be found in volume I of *The Theatrical Notebooks of Samuel Beckett*, which is based on the revisions to the text that Beckett made during these productions (Ackerley and Gontarski 2004, 620). This edition, indispensable for theatre professionals and academics, does not yet exist in a mass produced version suitable for students or theatre-goers. But against this suggestion, one could argue that any production notebook will inevitably be coloured by the particular circumstance in which it takes place, including the actors and stage spaces in Berlin and London. That is why there are differences in tone and emphasis between the two productions. But whether or not we regard this edition as 'definitive', or even whether it is possible or desirable to have a definitive text for *Godot*, it is surely the case that Beckett's decisions about textual changes to the printed texts, many of which carry over to both productions, demand our attention.

For his Berlin production, Beckett prepared a theatrical notebook, in which he sought to visualise every moment of the play with scrupulous, balletic exactitude. He subsequently amended many of these conceptions, in response to rehearsals, marking the changes in red ink in a second notebook, now published in *The Theatrical Notebooks of Samuel Beckett*. The result is, as James Knowlson puts it, 'a choreography performed to the "music" of the text' (qtd. in Beckett 1993c, xii). We might also add that, complementing this music, is an intensified visual element. Unlike the published edition, which has Estragon on stage at the start and Vladimir entering shortly later, Beckett's revised version begins with a still tableau with both Estragon and Vladimir on stage in an attitude of waiting, reinforcing visually the theme and atmosphere of the play: expectation, underlying stasis, and a silence that is, as Beckett put it, 'pouring into this play like water into a sinking ship' (1993c, xiv). We find words and phrases wrought carefully into repetition and internal patterning. For instance in the San Quentin production, in response to Vladimir's repeated statement 'We're waiting for Godot', Estragon's answer becomes uniform – 'Ah yes' – instead of the variety of answers he gives in the published text: 'Fancy that', 'True', and 'Good idea'.

The effect is to thicken the sense of stasis and also the eerie, automated quality which the play sometimes deploys.

The verbal echoes are reflected in the precision and repetition of movement and gesture that Beckett has added to the stage directions, geared often to the question-and-answer dynamics. Estragon tends to remain more fixed on or around his stone (changed from a 'mound' in the originally published version) while Vladimir moves towards and away from him, adding movement and rhythm to a drama that comes so close to inaction and inertia. These movements, then, compliment the dialogue, often so wrought with repetition, variation, and rhythm.

Beckett's own directorial habits show an obsession with the dramaturgical shape and patterns of the play, rather than a meaning or a message in the rational sense. Indeed, part of the effect of the drama's precision of form is to create an opacity of meaning. Beckett's direction, for all its precision, is aimed at the deliberate cultivation of opacity, confusion, and bewilderment, the avoidance of 'definition'. The effect of the play in Beckett's directorial hands is to help it to achieve this carefully cultivated indefinition – it will not be pinned down or located, a clear meaning will not arrive for us, just as Godot does not arrive for Vladimir and Estragon. They can be confused and uncertain about where they are, where they were, and where they will be, and the audience, by extension, can feel bewildered by the elusive themes of a play which, while orbiting around philosophical and religious issues, tends to keep them at a distance, to keep us in a state of interpretative suspension.

Bewilderment and uncertainty accompany them at every stage. They, and by extension we, cannot be sure when or why they have this appointment, or why things have changed in the second act. Memory is deeply unreliable. Who beat Estragon? Where did he leave his boots and what colour were they? Estragon, who is less certain and less interested in the past than Vladimir, cannot recognise his boots in the middle of the stage. Vladimir is discomfited by the leaves that have appeared on the tree. In his 'Schiller Theater' Notebook, Beckett deliberately registers this aspect of the play with a section titled 'Doubts, confusions', listing, over three pages, moments where the characters are bewildered about where they were the evening before or about details of their appointment. It is partly as an antidote to this bewilderment that they embrace the one guiding principle of which they can be sure: 'What are we doing here, *that* is the question. And we are blessed in this, that we happen to know the answer. Yes, in this immense confusion one thing alone is clear. We are waiting for Godot to come' (*WFG* 76, emphasis in original). But the question of why they wait for Godot, or who Godot is, is never addressed. Throughout the play there are stories that are never completed and questions that are never answered, thwarting those who would want to read clear messages or themes.

This dynamic of confusion and doubt is part of the dramatic effect of the play, a denial of grounding that cannot be reassuringly named, or answered by philosophical scepticism. It is this uncertainty, indefinition, and abstraction which allows *Waiting for Godot* to operate as a sort of skeleton key, opening into various different contexts and situations, connecting around the world and speaking to audiences from disparate cultural, social, and political situations. One effect of the lack of definition, the withholding of a clear meaning, is to shift the attention onto the dramatic qualities of the play rather than the significance of its message, its function rather than its meaning. The withholding of resolution throws our attention onto the play as an event and an experience rather than a philosophical tract, and explains, in part, why Beckett was so resistant to allegorical explanation. Such explanations would stifle this theatrical effect, would give spectators coordinates, even if that meaning was the certainty of unknowability. Based on Beckett's practice, and what we have learned about the play's performances over the past sixty years, the stage directions to the play, its physical movements and pauses, are central to the play's music and effect, to the artwork that constitutes the theatrical event.

Godot in Contexts

Beckett eschewed those who would wish to give to Godot portentous messages. His favoured actors, like Billie Whitelaw or Jack MacGowran, refrained from asking him about meanings or motivations, but focused instead on movement and music. Perhaps for this reason, Beckett had an affinity with those who could relate to Godot viscerally, rather than intellectually, to the inmates in prisons who wrote to him about their experience of the play, feeling affinity with its themes of entrapment and continual waiting, for release, for parole, for a pardon. The most famous such prison encounter occurred when the San Francisco Actors' Workshop took Herbert Blau's production of *Waiting for Godot* into San Quentin's maximum security prison in 1957. Thus began a long and productive relationship between Beckett and the San Quentin drama workshop. Under the directorship of inmate Rick Cluchey, the workshop would put on several of Beckett's plays both inside the prison and, later, as a professional troupe outside it. This included the 1984 production of *Waiting for Godot* in the Riverside studio in London, which, as we have seen, had directorial input from Beckett.

The affinity of the play with conditions of extremity was also manifest in many well-known productions during periods of political or social crisis, when it appeared that confusion, uncertainty, waiting, and hope were pressing with particular and material immediacy. Celebrated examples in the history of *Waiting for Godot*'s staging history include Donald Howarth's 1980 Cape Town production in apartheid South Africa, Ilan Ronen's 1984 Haifa production in Palestine, and Susan Sontag's 1993 Sarajevo production during the Bosnian War. In Howarth's *Godot* black actors played Estragon and Vladimir, white actors Pozzo and Lucky, which activated the play's concern with power relations in the immediate context of the racial conditions in South Africa. Ronen's Haifa production also mobilised the play's surrounding politics, signalling difference and social stratification through language and dialect. In this Arab Israeli version, Estragon and Vladimir spoke colloquial Arabic to each other, but Hebrew to Pozzo; Pozzo spoke Hebrew to Estragon and Vladimir, but bad Arabic to Lucky; and Lucky spoke academic Arabic. Some of these markers of class and social power were embryonic in earlier productions, such as the Dublin première in the Pike theatre, but the transferability of the play to different political contexts is brought out strikingly in these productions. Susan Sontag also sought to activate the relevance and resonance of the play during the siege of Sarajevo. This production was moulded by the difficulty and pressure of the circumstances. Faced with the intense interest of Sarajevo's acting community, Sontag used multiple pairings of Vladimir and Estragon (as well as the original male/male pair, she also placed male/female and female/female ones onstage). She decided to perform only the first act because of pressure on rehearsals and timing. Despite these limitations, Sontag explained her choice to stage *Waiting for Godot* by claiming that 'Beckett's play, written over forty years ago, seems written for and about Sarajevo' (1993, 52).

The fame of the play and its celebrated director (Sontag was one of New York's most famous public intellectuals) no doubt partly explains part of its appeal in Sarajevo, which welcomed high cultural attention when it seemed that the world had forgotten it politically. There is a self-perpetuating cycle at work here: *Godot* comes to peripheral locales swathed in associations of profundity, where it then gains extra dimensions and cultural capital through its instantiation in a new space, especially one of headline grabbing conflict or crisis. One recent production that might be taken as an instance, or perhaps a culmination, of the political productions of *Waiting for Godot* took place in New Orleans in 2007. Harlem's Classical Theater's 2006 production took place in New York but sought to connect the play to the devastation wrought the previous year by Hurricane Katrina in New Orleans, when many of the citizens of that city were left stranded, waiting for a deliverance which often never came. This production, starring New Orleans natives Wendell Pierce and J. Kyle Manzay, made use of a simulated New

Orleans rooftop surrounded by flood waters, a familiar sight on televisual images of the hurricane. In 2007 visual artist and political activist Paul Chan persuaded the director of this show, Christopher McElroen, and the arts organisation Creative Time to take the production to the city itself.

Waiting for Godot in New Orleans has quickly become a landmark moment in the history of this play, perhaps the most significant production of the new century. The *New York Times* listed the project as one of the top ten national art events of 2007 and the archives from the project have been acquired into the permanent collection of The Museum of Modern Art in New York. This production took *Godot* out of its conventional theatrical space and staged it outdoors, free for those who wanted to attend, in the Lower Ninth Ward and Gentilly, communities which had been ravaged by Hurricane Katrina. Part of the attraction of the play in New Orleans, and part of the attention the project received nationally and internationally, stemmed from the attempt to do something original, in such an unlikely setting, to a modern classic, a highpoint of European drama with an unmistakable aura of profundity and cultural capital. But, if that was the initial impetus, the production was able to subvert many of the hieratic and forbidding connotations of the play. It broke down the barrier between mandarin modernist culture and popular street performance, between autonomous art and political activism, between global brand and local event. *Waiting for Godot in New Orleans* emphasised the reality that insofar as theatre is always of its place and time, it involves cross-cultural or transnational movements. Chan and his collaborators spent months seeking to enmesh themselves in the community. They organised social events, discussion groups, and classes in order to consult with locals in an effort to ensure that the play, taking place in the streets of the city, also had an organic connection with its values, perspectives, and problems (see Chan 2010).

It was an intriguing meeting of high modernism and street performance, of art and activism, which nonetheless was a consistent addition to the cultural impact of other productions of Beckett, which use the abstract setting of the play to speak powerfully to highly particular social, historical, and political issues. Alys Moody argues that this potential is deep within the text itself, arguing that the Chan production reveals 'less the universality of *Waiting for Godot* than the way that abstraction can open itself to a cyclical process of decontextualization and recontextualization that reimagines the abstract through the local (and vice versa), and that speaks to the transnational potential of abstraction' (Moody 2013, 539).

Importantly though, the New Orleans production may indicate that what we value about Beckett's play has shifted or expanded. If the earlier critics prized the universal and timeless significance of *Waiting for Godot*, modern scholars tend to find such humanist and essentialist categories ideologically dangerous, eliding the specific and historical conditions that produce so much human suffering. It is not the ability of *Waiting for Godot* to transcend history that is now valued, but rather its capacity to recontextualise vividly in different moments, without sliding into allegory or one-on-one correspondence.

Beckett is inextricably caught up in a globalised culture, branded and consumed around the world. His global success was initially fuelled by the prestige and cultural capital his work – first *Waiting for Godot* and later his other plays and prose works – accrued in the European and American metropolitan centres. Yet at the same time he is hailed for being above the marketplace, for his uncompromising and unmarketable recognition of difficulty and dissatisfaction. There is a contradiction between the Beckett brand – global, instantly identifiable, intellectually chic – and the fractious difficulty and opacity of much of his work. This is a paradox at the heart of the cultural impact of Beckett as a twentieth-century artist. It is a distinct if analogous paradox to that between the discourses of universalism and particularism that marks the critical reception of his work, which ironically his art has always acted to subvert. It subverts it from the beginning by the deep investment of the play in the ordinary, the everyday, and the particular – the boots, carrots, bodily smells and functions – which contribute to the deflation of Pozzo's portentous theatrics or the lofty intellectual rhetoric of Lucky's 'think'. On a metatheatrical level, too, this subversion operates as the play speaks powerfully to both the metropolitan centre and the neglected margins, to the bohemians of Greenwich Village and the vagabonds of New Orleans.

5

EMILIE MORIN

Endgame and Shorter Plays
Religious, Political and Other Readings

'[T]he worst is not / So long as we can say, This is the worst': this fragment from Shakespeare's *King Lear* never ceased to capture Beckett's imagination (Atik 2001, 83). These lines neatly encapsulate the conceptual and imaginative dilemmas that *Endgame* and later stage plays such as *Happy Days*, *Not I*, or *Play* have come to pose to their audiences, readers and critics. This is a theatre of postponements, of frustrated anticipations, of aftermaths; clearly, 'something is taking its course', as Clov puts it in *Endgame*, but the form, nature and temporality of this uncategorised event exceed the conventional limits of theatrical representation and verbalisation (*CDW* 107). Yet if Beckett's characters frequently admit defeat, they are never vanquished: they continue to speak in spite of all, and find solace in the contemplation of an irrevocable and yet elusive ending. The tension that *Endgame* explores between, on the one hand, an unfailing resolution to speak and, on the other, physical fragility and decay has informed many philosophical and critical interpretations of Beckett's singular approach to dramatisation beyond *Endgame*. This chapter considers the ways in which the text of *Endgame* and philosophical interpretations of *Endgame*'s catastrophes – alternately perceived as past, impending or taking their course – provide an appropriate point of departure for identifying important developments in the critical reception of Beckett's plays, from humanist, existentialist and Marxist interpretations to postmodern readings of Beckett's dramatic practice.

Humanist Interpretations

During the 1950s and 1960s, the forms of stasis, atrophy and desolation that *Endgame* keenly explores provided much food for thought to Beckett's contemporaries, who read these facets of his work as expressions of a solipsistic sensibility aligned with French existentialism. The existentialist readings of Beckett's early drama that emerged during this period have left an enduring legacy: perceptions of Beckett's plays have remained, to this day, inflected by prior debates concerning its unremitting pessimism and nihilistic leanings (Kennedy 1989, 63; Gibson 2006, 252). This established line of critical enquiry presents Beckett as a humanist thinker and has given rise to critical approaches that have largely developed, as Peter Boxall observes, under the shadow of 'an Anglo-American brand of liberal humanism' relying on the assumption that 'the literary text preserves universal truths about the human condition in a mystical language and a living, organic form that cannot be translated or even fully understood' (2000, 51, 93). Although early humanist readings indebted to Jean-Paul Sartre's existentialism and Albert Camus's absurdism have now lost the currency they once had, it remains difficult to extricate *Endgame* and its original French-language counterpart, *Fin de partie*, from an absurdist dramatic canon that seemingly provided new verdicts on life, death and the human condition in the wake of the Second World War. Structurally and formally, *Endgame* has much in common with French-language plays of the 1950s such as Sartre's *Huis Clos* (*No Exit*) or Eugène Ionesco's *Les Chaises* (*The Chairs*). Like these plays, *Endgame* summons, parodies and subverts the structure and the conventions of the drawing-room play: some of the dialogues between Hamm and Clov should 'be played as *farcical parody of polite drawing-room* conversation', as Beckett emphasised in the illuminating letters he wrote to the American theatre director Alan Schneider (qtd. in Harmon 1998, 23). The drawing room, the site of bourgeois fantasies of conquest and accumulation, of fears of invasion, demise and decay, becomes laden with barely articulated histories and traumas in *Endgame*: the room's sole ornament, a picture turned against the wall, suggests the bearing of a collective history that can only be articulated in the negative. Existence itself is posited as a permanent absence as suggested by Hamm's remark, 'I was never there [...] Absent, always. It all happened without me. I don't know what's happened' (*CDW* 128).

For early critics of Beckett, particularly those concerned about social and historical change, the affinities between Beckett's early drama, the existentialist philosophies of Sartre and Camus, and the theatrical work of contemporaries such as Ionesco inscribed Beckett's singular approach to dramatisation into a historical and political moment tormented by the realisation that modernity had fostered warfare, genocide and starvation, instead of progress, social equality and peace. During the 1950s, Beckett's representations of destruction and destitution seemed disturbingly topical: *Endgame*, in particular, spoke in powerful ways to Cold War threats of atomic warfare and fears of annihilation, while giving an intuitive form to the anxieties that Sartre and Camus had previously explored from a philosophical perspective. A. Alvarez and Martin Esslin, both early defenders of the theatre of the absurd (a term coined by Esslin in 1961), perceived Beckett's work as leading a sea-change in modern theatre, towards the antiliterary and the antidramatic; both critics, in different ways, inscribed Beckett's early plays (*Waiting for Godot*, *Endgame*, *Happy Days*) into a generic postwar world that did not offer itself to easy interpretation, but rather remained as blatantly illogical as it proved lethal to human life. Beckett's white, middle-class characters, for the most part male and with distinctive European coordinates, were perceived in this particular scenario as representatives of humankind as a whole, facing adversity with enduring resilience. Although readings of the Beckettian dramatic world as postatomic have lost some of their weight, they have paved the way for current interpretations indebted to theories of the posthuman or ecocriticism: in the twenty-first century, the impending 'finish' announced by Clov continues to summon the spectre of ecological disaster, as well as the anxieties of a technologised age that assimilates the human to the mechanic, and in which the organic harbours the inorganic (see Tajiri 2007 and Garrard 2012).

Philosophical and Political Readings

Beckett's plays have a singular status in theatre history for another reason: quite unlike other modern plays, Beckett's texts for the stage – and, later, the television – have received much attention from philosophers of different convictions and formations. The most influential philosophical essays that tackle Beckett's plays are Theodor Adorno's 'Trying to Understand *Endgame*' ('Versuch, das *Endspiel* zu verstehen', dated 1958), Gilles Deleuze's 'The Exhausted' ('L'Épuisé', published with Beckett's television plays in 1992), and, more recently, Alain Badiou's *On Beckett* (*Beckett: L'Increvable désir*, 1995), which has fostered a better understanding of one of the main principles underlying Beckett's writing: the question of intermittency. In all cases, Beckett's perceived affinities with Sartrean existentialism provided the conceptual background which these philosophers sought to interrogate and revisit in their own readings. Like Deleuze, who remained deeply absorbed in Sartre's thought during his formative years, Badiou discovered Beckett when he was, by his own admission, a 'complete and total Sartrean' (Dosse 2007, 117–20; Badiou 2003, 38). Badiou (2003, 39–40) explains that it took him a long time to work his way out of the established 'caricature' of Beckett as expressing despair, nihilism or meaninglessness, and to evolve towards a reading of Beckett 'at his word'. To read Beckett 'at his word', for Badiou, is to account for the work's nuanced expressions of desire, love, nostalgia, beauty or solitude, and to acknowledge the courageous search for exactitude underlying Beckett's labour as a writer. Badiou's reading, as Andrew Gibson points out, also illuminates the capacity of

Endgame and Shorter Plays

Beckett's writing to posit 'a structure of thought that is subject to limits designated with extreme rigour, yet everywhere opened up to astonishing complication and nuance' (2006, 231). For Deleuze also, the immanence of the limit in Beckett's stage and television plays was important; spanning across Beckett's novels, stage and television plays, Deleuze's essay offered an interpretation based on the definition of three distinctive and interconnected 'metalanguages' – linguistic and nonlinguistic iterations consisting of sounds, voices, silences, gaps, object-subject relations and inventories. For Deleuze, the relationship between repetition and nuance in Beckett's dramatic writing should be articulated in the light of Beckett's fiction, in order to account for the capacity of Beckett's œuvre as a whole to invent and utilise different categories of 'metalanguages' whose combination exhausts the field of the possible just as Beckett's individual texts exhaust the means of representation on which they rely across different media.

If Beckett's plays have attracted so much attention from philosophers, this is also due to their capacity to relate to larger philosophical debates. Badiou's appreciation of Beckett is also a reiteration of his own philosophical interests, and Deleuze's work on Beckett is part of a wider exploration of the film image and Bergson's philosophy. Likewise, Adorno's essay on *Endgame* is inscribed in a deeper reflection that Adorno conducted alongside other philosophers of the Frankfurt School on post-Enlightenment relations between modernity, reason, barbarity and technology. The first attempts to conceptualise Beckett's artistic endeavour during the 1950s – by Maurice Blanchot, Georges Bataille, Alain Robbe-Grillet, or Sartre – also developed within a specific intellectual context, in which the growing influence of Heidegger and phenomenology fostered an acute interest in the ontological problems posed by Beckett's drama, by its 'universal pessimism' and its characters who are irremediably present (Robbe-Grillet 1965, 111; Sartre 1976, 128). But there was never a strong consensus around what Beckett's work may diagnose or illustrate, even in the early days; however, there was already – rightly or wrongly – a strong sense of the universal remit of Beckett's theatre, of its ability to speak of all and to all that is human. For humanist thinkers, Beckett's early plays encapsulated a kind of human resilience that warranted their own placing of the human subject at the core of philosophical systems; however, the very ambiguity of the symbolic meanings to be found in Beckett's drama also precluded whole-hearted celebrations of humanist values, and raised troublesome questions about the continuing relevance of those metaphysical questions dear to humanism that had become somewhat tired. Thus Beckett's plays began, in parallel, to provide fodder for antihumanist philosophies that posit forms of reasoning about the human condition as, of necessity, weighted by historical, cultural and politically charged imperatives, and as obfuscating questions of power, history, gender, language, race and ethnicity.

Adorno, attuned to the historical dimension of Beckett's early drama, was the first to draw attention to these problems. His Marxist reading worked against the grain of accepted interpretations of Beckett as the arch Sartrean existentialist, untrammelled by historical, political and societal concerns. His widely influential essay 'Trying to Understand *Endgame*' continues to inspire new readings of the play's historicity (see McCormack 1994; Pearson 2001; Ulin 2006; Blackman 2009; Morin 2009; Lloyd 2010; Kennedy 2012). Breaking away from a budding humanist tradition, Adorno reinscribed Beckett's work into an antihumanist modernist project, and located *Endgame* beyond French existentialism and within a series of symptomatic responses to the Second World War, which ushered, in his view, the demise of realist modes of representation. In a world in which technology, progress and the principles of equality and reason championed by Enlightenment humanism have yielded mass murder, humanism as a historical construct needs to be interrogated carefully, and understanding itself has become a problematic category (witness Adorno's title, suggesting that understanding remains forever tentative, as a ceaseless 'trying' or probing into the unfathomable). For Adorno, it is from this perspective that Beckett's early drama provides a new potential for social critique, exposing objectivity as a sham, just as it exposes the irrationality of realistic social content (1997, 30–1, 249–50).

Endgame, for Adorno, dramatises a 'permanent catastrophe' and connects to a state of civilisation that no longer has a stable or identifiable historical identity, but remains uncategorised, unspeakable, doomed to seek the 'meaning it has itself extinguished' (1982, 148). The play's resistance to interpretation should, for Adorno, be construed as a political phenomenon, and merely reverberates 'the irrationality of bourgeois society on the wane', rendering as absurd all interpretations that pay heed to obsolete principles of intelligibility (122). Adorno's reading paved the way for thinking about *Endgame* as a political play, in which the master-slave relation between Hamm and Clov has economic underpinnings: for Sean Golden, for example, *Endgame* represents the leftovers of an economic system in which there is nothing left to be exploited but 'leftover remnants of the results of exploitation' (1981, 444).

'Extreme Simplicity of Dramatic Situation and Issue'

For Beckett as playwright and director, the play's conceptual ambiguity raised rather different questions, which posed themselves on a dramatic level first and foremost. His letters to Schneider provide precious insights into his vision of the play as being driven by an 'extreme simplicity of dramatic situation and issue' (Harmon 1998, 24). 'Don't seek deep motivation everywhere', he recommended, stressing his own lack of knowledge concerning the characters' background, motives, or any aspects of the play that were not already encoded within the text (qtd. in Harmon 1998, 29). Maintaining ambiguity in terms of location, referent and interpretation was the crux of the matter, and metaphysics was seemingly the least of Beckett's preoccupations. Accounts of rehearsals with Beckett show the degree to which he prioritised minute aspects of gesture, movement, tone and diction, the importance of symmetry, the echoes, symbolism and allusions that should be played against one another with subtlety (Macmillan and Fehsenfeld 1988, 178–85). Some of the indications that Beckett gave to Schneider nonetheless pay heed to the play's dramatisation of an impending catastrophe; he evoked 'the impossibility [...] of the "thing" ever coming to an end' – or, more specifically, a pre- or antiapocalyptic moment concurrent with 'the impossibility of catastrophe': 'Ended at its inception, and at every subsequent instant, it continues, ergo can never end' (Harmon 1998, 24). Wary, perhaps, that such a statement might discourage further efforts, he concluded: 'Don't mention any of this to your actors!' (24) This was a pertinent clue: the 'impossibility of catastrophe' pervades all aspects of the dialogue, beginning with Clov's opening verdict 'Finished, it's finished, nearly finished, it must be nearly finished' (*CDW* 93).

More generally, it was also Beckett's purpose to ensure, as he subsequently put it, that directors eager to give his work a clear-cut meaning would promptly 'lose [their] taste for improving authors' (qtd. in Harmon 1998, 59). History has, however, taken a different turn, and the performance history of *Endgame* is marked with, and greatly enriched by, various disagreements over adaptations and productions that sought to create realistic political and social allegories – so much so that Beckett has become renowned in theatre history for his disputes with the theatre directors he perceived as overly enterprising (Knowlson 1996, 479, 691–2). The 1984 production of *Endgame* by JoAnne Akalaitis was particularly contentious: Akalaitis transformed the play into a work of science fiction, set in a New York City devastated by nuclear war; the mysterious outpost by the sea outlined in the text became an abandoned subway tunnel (Oppenheim 1994, 148–9). For Daniel Albright, such a production was merely an imaginative failure; Akalaitis, he points out, simply 'asked herself in what sort of real world would the behaviour described in *Endgame* make sense', and the production overlooked the play's subtle reflection on theatrical representation (2003, 67). Albright suggests that *Endgame* is, instead, best perceived as 'post-theatrical': it pivots on a 'stage in total decay, instead of a stage that hasn't yet come into being', contrary to its precursor, the 'pre-theatrical' *Waiting for Godot* (61).

Many anecdotes and stories have circulated concerning Beckett's excessive control over productions of his work, but his correspondence and the performance history of his plays show that the reality was much more nuanced, and that his responses to adaptation varied considerably. The indications that Beckett gave to directors and actors centred on the essential need to preserve symbolic ambiguity and sought to ensure that the texts would not be given a clear realistic remit; the author and the director, he explained to Schneider, 'have no elucidations to offer of mysteries that are all of [others'] making' (qtd. in Harmon 1998, 24). He railed against directorial modifications that gave the texts a clear, direct allegorical dimension that they did not support, but as in the case of *Waiting for Godot*, there is a rich seam of performances of *Endgame* that are affixed to specific historical and political circumstances: in and through performance, the power relations explored in the play acquire, of necessity, political inflections that are specific to its performance contexts. While Beckett was unsympathetic to attempts to create a transparency of meaning that he had laboured to curtail, his responses to requests for factual elucidation also point out the capacity of his work to interrogate the workings of theatre as a social practice and institution; when asked to provide some insights into *En attendant Godot* for a French radiophonic audience, he infamously stated that he had nothing to say about theatre in general, let alone his own work, and that his audiences would not find in his play a loftier meaning to take home after the performance (*LSB II* 314–15). This approach finds echoes in his early absurdist drama as well as his later experimental plays, from the actor-less playlet *Breath* to the television play *Quad*: these are texts that raise powerful questions about the nature of representation and of the theatrical event, but do not provide answers.

Reading *Endgame*

Beckett's emphasis on the 'extreme simplicity' of *Endgame* nonetheless provides fruitful clues for close reading and interpretation. The sparse set, structured around two rubbish bins, a chair and two windows (one looking towards the sea, the other towards the earth), suggests that the material reality of the stage takes precedence over the myriad symbolic meanings that the set may evoke but refuses to sustain. There is little difference between the inner and the outer: the walls are as grey as the seascape outside. Green vegetation is nothing but a faint memory; the flora has been reduced to seeds that will not sprout, and the fauna, at least temporarily, to a lone flea and a rat. Clov also catches sight of a small boy, but there is otherwise little to be seen outside. Inside, equally little remains, and the smallest details matter enormously, such as the addition of sand or sawdust to Nagg's and Nell's dustbins, the ownership of a toy dog or the possibility of trading attention against the promise of a sugar plum. Evaluating that which has disappeared (anything from coffins to bicycle wheels to 'painkiller') and that which remains (insecticide, a step ladder or the toy dog) provides the last resort to stave off boredom. The dialogues coalesce in a playful form of self-reflexivity that borrows from the terminology of play-acting: Clov portrays the world as 'corpsed', as both skeletal and failing to deliver a performance; Hamm announces his 'aside' and a 'last soliloquy', and worries that 'complications' or 'an underplot' might be forthcoming; and both recognise that only 'the dialogue' is keeping them 'here' (*CDW* 106, 130, 120–1). The impending end is also deeply and uncompromisingly physical: bodies bleed, itch, smell and ache, and elude any form of control.

Ties of kinship remain elusive: Hamm acknowledges Nagg as his father, but Clov's position as Hamm's servant and his endless, unrewarded labour do not align with blood ties, and the nature of their relationship is further obscured by Hamm's 'chronicle' and Clov's response to it. Yet aspects of the characters' shared history gradually become clear – it emerges, in particular, that Hamm, the head of the family, the landowner, carries responsibility for the death of others. If Clov is to be trusted, Hamm has something to do with the death of Mother Pegg from 'darkness' on the other side of the gulf, a death that prefigures Nell's own gradual disappearance into her dustbin (*CDW* 129). Power relations are gendered and without appeal: this is a patriarchal nucleus in which women do not last long, and are reduced to subaltern roles, merely providing a receptacle for male fantasies, memories and aspirations. The pun underlying the characters' names suggests oppressive power relations that further exclude Nell: notably, 'Nagg' recalls the German word for nail (*Nagel*), 'Clov' the French for nail (*clou*), and 'Hamm' the word 'hammer' (Macmillan and Fehsenfeld 1988, 238). However, Beckett was prompt to temper the views of actors and directors who approached the play as a parable for 'a hammer and three nails', responding to questions such as these with an evasive 'If you like!' (qtd. in Macmillan and Fehsenfeld 1988, 238). These particular tropes are part of a much wider ensemble of allusions to the New Testament and the Resurrection of Christ; the dialogues abound in references to the history of Christianity and its sacred texts, and feature many anticreation motifs (see Lyons 1964). In different contexts, Beckett described the play's dynamics in different ways: as 'fire and ashes', for example, or, in keeping with the more literal indications suggested by the play's title, as the final stage of a game of chess (qtd. in Macmillan and Fehsenfeld 1988, 201; Knowlson and Knowlson 2006, 206). Thinking of the stage as a chess board certainly illuminates the metaphoricity of the stage space. It also brings to the fore the comedy of *Endgame*: for all its acidity and darkness, this is, also, a remarkably funny play.

An Unstable Dramatic Corpus

While philosophical readings have provided important insights into the conceptual intricacies of Beckett's writing, they have also ascribed a solidity of intent to Beckett's texts that the plays themselves rarely support. Indeed, Beckett's intensive labour as a dramatist has generated a remarkably unstable dramatic corpus – in textual and performative as well as linguistic terms. There is no fixed body of work to be found, but a vast and fluid textual realm encompassing French and English versions of each text, translated by Beckett himself for the most part, and, alongside these, the German translations that he closely supervised. There are also different versions of each playscript: the more experience Beckett gained as a director, the more he altered the dialogues and stage directions. His production notebooks reveal his eagerness to make changes of all scales in light of discoveries made during the rehearsal process (see Macmillan 1993). In a type of dramatic writing as pared-down as Beckett's, in which stage directions are so substantial, even minute textual differences matter enormously. *Endgame* illustrates this fluidity of interpretation, text and history: the emendations that Beckett made to the text, particularly to the opening stage directions, were extensive. He suppressed, for instance, the instruction that Clov should have a 'very red face', on the grounds that the initial idea was overly 'far-fetched' (Gontarski 1992, 44, n. 8). Through the changes that Beckett made to *Fin de partie* and *Endgame*, we can trace his evolving dramatic technique: the stage directions are not simply more numerous, more detailed and more precise than in the plays Beckett previously wrote, but also provide measurements and coordinates for a very precise choreography involving four performers and a limited and forever-dwindling number of objects of different sizes. The dedication to Roger Blin, the director of *En attendant Godot* who made the play a success in Paris, bears testament to Beckett's view of *Fin de partie* as a directors' play, which depends on a particular kind of directorial talent.

The translation of *Fin de partie* into English absorbed Beckett's time and energy between May and June 1957, and proved ultimately disappointing; he stressed that the English text did not match the French original (Morin 2009, 94). Beckett's diagnoses and textual interventions, as an author, a director of his own plays and a self-translator, raise the question 'which is the primary or authoritative text' (McDonald 2009, xii), particularly since theatre history has magnified in unforeseen ways some of the divergences between *Fin de partie* and *Endgame*. Due to the difficulty of negotiating a contract with French theatres, the premiere of *Fin de partie* was not staged in France, but in London, at the Royal Court Theatre, which was then seen as a hard-hitting theatre, keen on presenting European innovations to the British public. *Endgame*, in turn, was first performed in New York in January 1958, rather than London, due to a series of escalating incidents with the Office of the Lord Chamberlain. The British stage was at the time submitted to strict scrutiny and censorship: to be licensed, every play had to be reviewed by the Lord Chamberlain's Office. When George Devine, the director of *Fin de partie*, had first applied for a licence to perform in London, the Lord Chamberlain's representative had requested small-scale amendments to the French text but had failed to spot the line that would subsequently unleash fury: Hamm's lament 'The bastard! He doesn't exist!' (*CDW* 119). However, when the English version was submitted for scrutiny in December 1957, the play was deemed 'blasphemous', largely because of this line, and extensive changes to the text were requested (Knowlson 1996, 448). The process of obtaining a licence soon turned into a battle of wills. Eventually, after protracted negotiations, Beckett agreed to settle for 'The swine! He doesn't exist!' for the London performance, a change which the standard published text does not record (Nicholson 2011, 150–5).

Extensive textual changes had, nonetheless, long been integral to the play's composition prior to its publication and rehearsals. The manuscript of *Fin de partie* was completed in 1956, and the genesis of the play was long and protracted. Beckett had been thinking about the play for a long time, and he had been writing similar fragments, and abandoning them, since 1950, working his way through different narratives and structures, searching for brevity and concision (see Van Hulle 2009). Early drafts of *Fin de partie* differ radically from the published text. Beckett initially imagined the play as located in the aftermath of First World War battles: the dialogues evoked a small town in Picardy, in the north of France, and an area close to front lines, 'progressively destroyed in the fall of 1914, the spring of 1918 and the following autumn, under mysterious circumstances' (Gontarski 1985, 33). As Beckett redrafted the play, these historical markers receded, giving way to an unspecified catastrophe that recalls not only the First World War, but also the Second World War, the Great Irish Famine and modern atomic warfare. Interestingly, also, the play's composition history suggests that Beckett had quite a different symbolic system in mind: *Fin de partie* was initially entitled 'Haam', the name of the son of Noah, and an early draft featured a character telling the Biblical story of Noah's Ark. The Biblical curse of Ham or

Haam, among the few survivors of the flood, echoes through the dialogues in the published text (Ackerley 2012, 331–2). While these various indicators confirm that the kind of catastrophe Beckett had in mind had historical as well as Biblical dimensions, the landmarks and allusions featuring in these early drafts should be approached with caution. Reading the composition history of a text as a linear teleological progression, as Dirk Van Hulle has shown, runs counter to what critical rigour would demand; it is more fruitful, instead, to think about the genesis of this play as involving various drafts that 'foreshadow', 'backshadow', and 'sideshadow' one another (see Van Hulle 2009). Different historical landmarks weigh on the portrayal of poverty and starvation presented in the published text, and all of them are residual and necessitate careful historical contextualisation. Most interestingly, Hamm's 'chronicle' about a starving 'pauper' bears similarities with accounts of the Great Famine in colonial Ireland, and the play can be read as a parable of Irish political and colonial history that borrows heavily from Shakespeare's *The Tempest* (see Ulin 2006 and Pearson 2001).

In the Wake of *Endgame*

Other kinds of catastrophes haunt Beckett's later dramatic corpus, from the mime 'Act without Words I', which unfolds in a 'desert', to 'Rough for Theatre I', set at a street corner in the midst of ruins. But, in plays written after *Endgame*, the impending worst also finds self-reflexive representations and integrates a performing body for which movements and utterances remain deeply precarious. *Happy Days*, for example, continues to experiment with the parameters of the drawing-room play, but the stage confines, absorbs and eventually precludes movement. In Act I, Winnie is buried up to her waist in the stage set, a mound covered in scorched grass; in Act II, she is 'embedded up to neck', and the uncertain shadow of catastrophe, both past and impending, bears on each of her lines, smiles and eye movements (*CDW* 160). The stage set, props and technology take on greater dramatic significance in later stage plays, particularly when specific devices are employed to create new variations on the dramatic monologue. *Krapp's Last Tape*, for example, stages a man listening and responding to recordings of his own voice; *Play* presents a confrontation between a spotlight, designated as an 'inquisitor', and three aligned characters who respond to its prompts but cannot see or hear one another (*CDW* 318); *That Time* features a listener breathing to the sound of three layered recordings of his own voice coming from different sides of the stage.

As he began to write regularly for radio and, later, for film and television, Beckett was comforted in his radical approach to dramatisation, and he continued to use body and voice to probe the very limits of dramatic address and figuration. His later plays for stage, radio and television are teeming with severed and suspended heads, mouths and floating voices. But for Beckett there were primordial dramatic differences between stage and radio plays, mostly related to the specific mode of writing demanded by each medium. *Endgame* continued to provide an important frame of reference in Beckett's reflection on other dramatic forms. In a 1957 letter to his American publisher Barney Rosset, Beckett described his first radio play, *All That Fall*, as a 'radio text [...] for voices, not bodies', which 'is no more theatre than End-Game is radio', and he associated the mime 'Act without Words I' with a 'primitive theatre' which 'requires that this last extremity of human meat – or bones – be there, thinking and stumbling and sweating, under our noses, like Clov about Hamm, but gone from refuge' (qtd. in Zilliacus 1976, iv).

Through this unrelenting focus on that which lies at the boundaries of performance and representation, Beckett's later plays also offer a meditation on the nature of watching and problematise the demands made by the spectators' gaze upon the actors' physique and psyche. *Play*, for example, presents three actors who are not able to perform as they should: 'M' suffers from hiccups, as an untrained actor required to speak too quickly may do. *Not I* focuses on a mouth that speaks too much and too fast, but cannot utter that which would enable it to reclaim its own presence: the pronoun 'I'. The later play *Catastrophe*, whose title refers to the Greek term *catastropha*, qualifying a sudden turn or final dénouement, stands as a good example of the ways in which Beckett approached the fundamentals of theatrical spectacle as a reflection on ethics in his later career (Harmon 1998, 429). The play pivots on interactions between a director, an assistant and an unseen technician, who are absorbed in a 'rehearsal' and the 'Final touches to the last scene', shaping the posture of a silent Protagonist named P into a theatrical performance whose details remain undisclosed (*CDW* 457). P's transformation into theatrical spectacle is predicated on the forced abandonment of his own body to the demands of realistic performance; yet the play ends on the promise that his raised head and fixed gaze, directed at the auditorium, might harbour: the sense that his ordeal will end with the spectacle. Familiar Beckettian coordinates remain: the Director, for example, complains virulently about the 'craze for explicitation' which hinders theatrical performance (*CDW* 459). In these moments we can discern a playful proximity to established humanist readings of Beckett's early work, and perhaps a response to the repeated verdicts wielded against the obscurity and difficulty of his plays: the characters are purely identified by their function, but the text refuses to disclose the script that drives their own performance.

Catastrophe is also, uncharacteristically, a realist play, in which the demands of realism reduce the subject, P, to subservience.

The firm limits that Beckett's stage directions impose on the body are central to current scholarship; at present, these issues provide rich avenues for understanding the visual grammar of the Beckettian stage and its dramatisation of sensory perception (Tonning 2007; Maude 2009; McMullan 2010; McTighe 2013). The emergence of new kinds of theatrical and philosophical questions in relation to the body is in many ways indebted to Deleuze's essay on Beckett, which proves most attuned to the capacity of Beckett's dramatic texts to create new kinds of syntax and semantics based on the body, movement and memory. Most significantly perhaps, Deleuze's argument also makes a case for thinking about the interrelations between Beckett's drama and prose. For Deleuze, three different metalanguages coexist within and across Beckett's œuvre: language I, which develops in the novels, is 'a language of names' corresponding to a type of 'combinatorial imagination' in which 'enumeration replaces propositions, and combinatorial relations replace syntactic relations' (1995, 7–8). Language II runs through the novels as well as the radio and stage plays (*Happy Days*, 'Act without Words I' and 'II', *Catastrophe*); it is the language of 'images, sounding, coloring', of voices that 'direct and distribute linguistic corpuscles', of an imagination 'that no longer operates with combinable atoms but with blendable flows' (7–8). Language III traverses Beckett's fiction and stage plays and is fully realised in Beckett's plays for television; it is the language that can 'reunite words and voices with images'; it consists of 'immanent limits that never cease to move about', of 'hiatuses, holes or tears' (8, 10). The peculiar dialogue that Deleuze creates between Beckett's stage and television plays and his fiction also bears testament to the enduring influence of the critical and philosophical readings that have developed around *Endgame*, and conveys the close relations that Beckett's plays have maintained to intellectual history more generally. The ties between Beckett's dramatic imagination and philosophical thought are so rich and diverse that, in the twenty-first century, perceptions of Beckett's plays can rarely be dissociated from philosophical insight.

6

MARK NIXON

Ruptures of the Visual
Beckett as Critic and Poet

'I'm afraid I couldn't write about pictures at all. I used never to be happy with a picture till it was literature, but now that need is gone'. (Beckett to Thomas MacGreevy, 28 November 1936; *LSB I* 388)

'I am no longer capable of writing in any sustained way about Bram or about anything. I am no longer capable of writing *about*'. (Beckett to Georges Duthuit, 9 March 1949; *LSB II* 141)

Introduction

Samuel Beckett's magisterial achievements, plays such as *Waiting for Godot* and *Endgame*, or prose texts such as *Three Novels* or *How It Is*, often overshadow his works in other genres, specifically his criticism and his poetry. The relative critical neglect is undoubtedly also a result of Beckett's disparaging comments on his work in these two modes. Writing to Lawrence Harvey on 20 February 1967, when the scholar was preparing his study *Samuel Beckett: Poet and Critic* (1970), Beckett stated emphatically that he did not think of himself as a poet and even less as a critic. He nevertheless went out of his way to respond to Harvey's queries, and the book surprisingly remains the only full-length study of these two aspects of Beckett's writing. In his introduction, Harvey persuasively argues (xi) that the critical writings develop an aesthetic which informs not only Beckett's poetry, but his entire literary œuvre, and at the same time shows that the poems are worthy of serious scholarly attention.

Beckett's critical and poetic writings have, belatedly, been recently receiving the scholarly attention that they deserve. The publication of the first two volumes of Beckett's correspondence has revealed the way in which Beckett in his letters is consistently acting as a critic, especially in his letters to Thomas MacGreevy and Georges Duthuit. While a comprehensive edition of Beckett's literary and art writings has yet to be published,[1] we now have a meticulously researched critical edition of Beckett's *Collected Poems* (2012), edited by Seán Lawlor and John Pilling.

This essay[2] will give a brief overview of Beckett's critical and poetic output, and will do so by arguing that for the writer, art is necessarily critical.

Already in his lectures on French literature at Trinity College Dublin in 1931, Beckett had praised André Gide for 'refus[ing] to abdicate as a critic' in his novels.³ Six years later, during his journey through Nazi Germany in 1936–7, Beckett similarly praised a painting by Cézanne as 'at last the reassertion of painting as criticism, i.e. art' (GD, 7 February 1937; qtd. in Nixon 2011, 182). Indeed, as this last quotation indicates, Beckett's aesthetic concerns were more often than not formulated through his engagement with the visual arts, and this thinking can subsequently be traced in his poetry and other creative work. At the core of Beckett's aesthetic concerns are questions of perception, the image, the rupture between subject and object, and the related failure of language to adequately give voice to these tensions. At the same time, Beckett repeatedly stated that it is the role of the artist to negotiate this challenge; as he famously wrote in *Three Dialogues with Georges Duthuit*, all art should be the 'expression that there is nothing to express, nothing with which to express, nothing from which to express, no power to express, no desire to express, together with the obligation to express' (*Dis* 139).

Beckett's Early Criticism

Beckett's first ever published piece of writing was a piece of criticism, an essay on Joyce's 'Work in Progress' (later *Finnegans Wake*) entitled 'Dante ... Bruno. Vico ... Joyce', which initially appeared in the book *Our Exagmination Round his Factification for Incamination of Work in Progress* (May 1929) and then in the Parisian magazine *transition* shortly afterward. The subject matter was suggested by Joyce, with the dots between the names designating the centuries that separate the four authors. Beckett spends more than half of the essay discussing Vico before turning briefly to Bruno and then to Dante and Joyce. It is quite obviously the work of a young academic, written while he was on a fellowship teaching at the Ecole Normale Supérieure in Paris. Yet it also shows signs of the tension between the scholarly and the creative which will dominate much of Beckett's criticism of the 1930s. Indeed, on the very first page Beckett declares that 'Literary criticism is not book-keeping' (*Dis* 19), paving the way for a discussion that is saturated with what the poem 'Gnome' (1934) calls the 'loutishness of learning' (*CP* 55). At times Beckett's writing also becomes rather polemical: 'Here form *is* content, content *is* form. You complain that this stuff is not written in English. It is not written at all. It is not to be read – or rather it is not only to be read. It is to be looked at and listened to. [Joyce's] writing is not *about* something; *it is that something itself*' (*Dis* 27). As Ruby Cohn has pointed out, it is statements such as these that 'have been quoted and requoted as keys to Beckett's own work', despite the fact that his 'creative work was barely a gleam in his scholarly eye' (2001, 3). One could argue that Beckett's aesthetics were already formulated – or at least intimated – in his earliest critical pieces on Joyce and the French writer Marcel Proust, as well as in his first novel *Dream of Fair to Middling Women* (written 1931–2, but only published posthumously).

Beckett's 1931 monograph *Proust* in particular contains several aesthetic judgments that anticipate themes that he would subsequently explore within his creative writing. Thus topics that will be central to Beckett's postwar drama and prose are introduced to examine Proust's *À la recherche du temps perdu*: time ('that double-headed monster of damnation and salvation', *PTD* 11), habit ('Habit is the ballast that chains the dog to his vomit. Breathing is habit. Life is habit', 19) and suffering ('the main condition of the artistic experience', 28). Harnessing the pessimism of the philosopher Arthur Schopenhauer, Beckett advocates the renunciation of the will, declaring that 'art is the apotheosis of solitude' (64). Praising Proust for his antirealist and anti-intellectual stance, Beckett is himself at pains to make his study of the French writer as unscholarly as possible, although he is never quite able to remove the erudition that he brings to the task.

Beckett's reluctance to elucidate or explain his subject is evident in the series of book reviews[4] he wrote in the first half of the 1930s, short pieces written mainly for financial reasons or in support of friends' publications. The occasion of these pieces may explain the often vitriolic tone of the reviews; they are self-conscious and satirical, yet not without genuine critical engagement. The most important of these pieces of literary journalism is undoubtedly the review essay 'Recent Irish Poetry', published (under a pseudonym) in *The Bookman* (August 1934). As his earlier critical studies of Joyce and Proust already signposted, Beckett in this essay firmly gives allegiance to European modernism rather than the 'local' Irish literary scene. He separates Irish poets into 'antiquarians' (such as W. B. Yeats) and those who 'evince awareness of the new thing that has happened', the 'breakdown of the object' (*Dis* 70). In its criticism of the Celtic Revival, the essay is a scathing attack on the cultural politics of Ireland, an attack which Beckett broadens out to encompass Irish nationalism and censorship laws in later texts. The first of these is 'Censorship in the Saorstat', an irate and satirical essay written in 1935 but unpublished until 1983, when Ruby Cohn included it in her collection of Beckett's critical writings, *Disjecta*. It is one of Beckett's few overtly political and social texts, although he does criticise his friend Thomas

MacGreevy's study of the painter Jack B. Yeats for narrowly viewing him as a specifically Irish artist.

The most important aspect of the review essay 'Recent Irish Poetry' is its formulation of an aesthetic that would continue to trouble Beckett for several decades. The 'new thing that has happened' is specifically the 'rupture of the lines of communication' between subject and object (*Dis* 70).[5] As such, the contemporary artist needs to be aware of 'the space that intervenes between him and the world of objects', a space that Beckett designates as 'no-man's-land' (70). Over the coming years Beckett approached the question of the subject-object relation specifically through the visual arts. In this context, Beckett's encounter with Paul Cézanne's paintings shortly after writing the 'Recent Irish Poetry' essay proved decisive. Discussing the painting *Montagne Sainte-Victoire* (Tate Gallery) in a letter written to MacGreevy in September 1934, Beckett argued that 'Cézanne seems to have been the first to see landscape & state it as material of a strictly peculiar order, incommensurable with all human expressions whatsoever' (*LSB I* 222). In his next letter, Beckett extended this lack of relation between the artist and the world to encompass the artist's alienation from his own self, arguing that Cézanne 'had the sense of his incommensurability not only with life of such a different order as landscape, but even with life of his own order, even with the life – one feels looking at the self-portrait in the Tate – operative in himself' (227). During his trip through Germany in 1936–7, Beckett continued to be troubled by the issue. As he noted in his diary, he continued to 'talk bilge [...] about relation of subject & object in modern art' (GD, 1 November 1936; qtd. in Nixon 2011, 164).

Looking back at his critical writings of the 1930s, Beckett felt that they were written in an absence of spontaneity and inner need.[6] He levied a similar charge against much of his early poems, dismissing them for being 'facultatif' ('optional') in that they 'did not represent a necessity' (letter to MacGreevy, 18 October 1932; *LSB I* 133).

Beckett's Early Poetry

Beckett's early poems follow a similar trajectory to that of his criticism. They are similarly marked by verbal virtuosity, self-consciousness, learned allusiveness and an attempt to poetically treat the tensions between subject and object. As the editors of the *Collected Poems* point out in explaining their extensive notes to the poems, the 'addition of a commentary seems proper in view of the exceptional difficulty of this most neglected part of Beckett's œuvre' (xvii). One of Beckett's earliest substantial poems, 'Whoroscope', was deemed to be so difficult that upon publication by the Hours Press in

1930 (having won a poetry competition on the topic of 'Time') the editor requested that Beckett append notes (as T. S. Eliot had done for *The Waste Land*). When Beckett in 1962 expressed his amazement that Lawrence Harvey had written nearly 100 pages on 'Whoroscope',[7] he was obviously forgetting that his exhibition of erudition provoked such exegesis. To construct the long poem – a dramatic monologue charting aspects of the life of the philosopher René Descartes – the young poet-scholar Beckett drew from a wealth of secondary material.

Christopher Reid has described Beckett's poetry of these years as 'strident, in-your-face brand of modernism' (Reid 2011), and there is no doubt that Beckett's poetic voice was steeped in European avant-garde verse rather than the mysticism and realism of his native Ireland. One could argue that he served his apprenticeship by translating Rimbaud, Eluard and Apollinaire for various little reviews in Paris, although a lot of his early poetry also relied on recognizably Irish contexts and places.

Beckett only published one collection of poems in the 1930s, a volume entitled *Echo's Bones and Other Precipitates* (Europa Press, 1935), although a further twenty poems exist that either appeared in literary journals or remained unpublished. As David Wheatley has pointed out, the poems of *Echo's Bones* are 'intensely claustrophobic' (2009, xiii), even though the poetic egos embark on various ramblings through the cityscapes of London and Dublin. There is also a distinct sense of absence, of weariness and separation (particularly in the poem 'Malacoda', which deals with the death of Beckett's father in June 1933). Refracted across the particular styles and images adopted in the various pieces is a stark image of decay, of entropy, as in the poem 'Enueg I' (which opens with the lines 'Exeo in a spasm / tired of my darling's red sputum'):

> and the stillborn evening turning a filthy green
> manuring the night fungus
> and the mind annulled
> wrecked in wind. (*CP* 6)

Such imagery is interspersed with 'echoes', intertextual references in particular to literature, art, geography and religion. Indeed, seven of the thirteen poems take their titles from Provençal troubadour genres; thus the three 'Serena' poems refer to the lover's song of anticipation, the 'Enueg' is a 'complaint', whereas the 'Alba' is an aubade, a song to the departing lover at dawn. Several of the poems also circle around the relationship between perception and the creative act, and between the subject and the object. As Beckett stated in his early novel *Dream*, '[p]oetry is not concerned with normal vision, where word and image coincide' (170). Whereas Beckett disavowed much of his writing from the 1930s, he was keen to see *Echo's Bones* remain in print.[8] At the same time, his dismissal of the self-conscious erudition of his early verse is inscribed in the poem 'Casket of Pralinen for the Daughter of a Dissipated Mandarin':

> Oh I am ashamed
> of all clumsy artistry
> I am ashamed of presuming
> to arrange words
> of everything but the ingenuous fibres
> that suffer honestly. (CP 33)

The first poem to reach such a note of authenticity is 'Cascando', a poem of unrequited love written in July 1936. The poem is minimalist and replete with repetition, and as such anticipates Beckett's move to writing in French, which he thought would allow expression 'without style'. Moreover, the poetic voice in 'Cascando' clearly 'suffers' more honestly, in that the feeling of despair is not buried beneath a layer of intertextual allusion.

'The Space that Intervenes' (1936–8)

Having completed the novel *Murphy* in June 1936, Beckett spent the next two years struggling to find a way in which his creative writing was to proceed. During this period it was Beckett's study of the visual arts which enabled him to clarify and shape his aesthetic thinking, and subsequently to find new ways to approach his work. He had at various points in the 1930s viewed art as a viable alternative to his faltering writing career, applying for example for the position of assistant curator at the National Gallery in London in 1933 (Knowlson 1996, 173). From 1936 onward, if not before, Beckett's most succinct aesthetic declarations were made in the context of the visual arts, whether in his personal correspondence, the so-called German Diaries or in published pieces of art criticism.

Central to Beckett's study of the visual arts was his journey through Nazi Germany between October 1936 and April 1937, during which he kept a detailed diary listing and sometimes describing the huge number of paintings that he saw. During his visits to galleries and artists, Beckett continued to be taxed by the question of perception; he thus noted in his diary after a visit to the studio of the Hamburg painter Karl Kluth: 'Gegensatz [contrast] of natural & human. I say his landscape is as though there were no eyes left in the world, Berkleyan Landschaft [landscape]' (qtd. in Bruhns 2007, 98). Beckett had read George Berkeley extensively in the early 1930s – as he did periodically throughout his life – but he had returned to the *Principles and Dialogues* in January 1936, rereading the sections in which the philosopher denied that perception was an act of will. Such a subjective, empirical view of perception also influenced Beckett's continued thinking about the relationship between the painter and the world. Remembering the terms he used in his essay 'Recent Irish Poetry' he commented, after reading texts by the expressionist painter Franz Marc, that it was not simply 'the relation between subject & object' that was under scrutiny, but also 'the alienation (my nomansland)' (GD, 19 November 1936; qtd. in Nixon 2011, 164). Perhaps more important was Beckett's notation of an aphorism by Marc – 'Alles Künstlerische ist alogisch' ['everything artistic is non-logical'] (GD, 19 November 1936, qtd. in Nixon 2011, 177). In many ways Beckett's anti-realist attitude lies at the heart of his poetics, provoking an artistic dilemma which he had already addressed in the early novel *Dream of Fair to Middling Women*: the 'reality of the individual [...] is an incoherent reality and must be expressed incoherently' (101). This in turn leads to the artist being 'skewered on the ferocious dilemma of expression', as Beckett wrote in *Three Dialogues with Georges Duthuit (PTD* 110).

The 1938 review of Denis Devlin's collection of poems, *Intercessions*, for the magazine *transition*, gave Beckett the first opportunity to address the aesthetic and creative questions that had preoccupied him while in Germany. Indeed, there had in fact been so much thinking that Beckett confided to MacGreevy in a 7 July 1937 letter that he was 'look[ing] forward to getting a lot off my chest apropos Denis's poems' (qtd. in Nixon 2011, 182). At the centre of the Devlin review is Beckett's emphatic assertion 'that art has nothing to do with clarity, does not dabble in the clear, and does not make clear' (*Dis* 94). Nevertheless, the artist has a 'need to need' to work, 'whose end is its own end in the end and the source of need' (91–2). As a result, the 'only suggestions therefore that the reviewer may venture without impertinence are such as have reference to this fundamental' need of the artist (92).

The ambiguity of this position, for both the artist and the critic, is further explored in an obscure piece of criticism, entitled 'Les Deux Besoins', written the same year (1938) as the Devlin review.[9] Here again Beckett describes the artistic enterprise, via a geometric figure, as 'Besoin d'avoir besoin (DEF) et besoin dont on a besoin (ABC)' ['the need to have need, and the need of which one has need'] (*Dis* 56). As Ruby Cohn succinctly summarises, the disjunctive images of the piece 'succeed one another in Beckett's plea for an irrational, interrogative art' (173).

Beckett's Postwar Criticism

Between 1945 and 1950 – the prolific period which saw the composition of *Waiting for Godot* and *Endgame*, various pieces of prose as well as the three novels *Molloy, Malone Dies* and *The Unnamable* – Beckett was also deeply engaged in the art world of postwar Paris. During these years, and beyond, Beckett's developing aesthetic theories revolve around particular artists, chief among them the brothers Bram and Geer van Velde, Jack B. Yeats and Henri Hayden, painters who explore the tensions between abstraction and representation, as well as between subject and object.

Beckett's main pieces of art criticism of these years are two essays on the van Velde brothers, 'La Peinture des van Velde ou le monde et le pantalon' (*Cahiers d'Art*, 1945–6) and 'Peintres de l'empêchment' (*Derrière le Miroir*, 1948). Both texts question the very possibility of criticism's capability of discussing art works, and in particular of *evaluating* a painting. Both essays draw on Beckett's aesthetic propositions of the 1930s, and are thus littered, for example, with references to people he had met and paintings he had seen in Germany in 1936–7. And at the heart of both essays is a renewed discussion of the breakdown between subject and object – as such the later essay had originally carried the title 'Le nouvel objet'.

In 'La Peinture des van Velde', Beckett spends the first third of the essay dismissing (or rather, sneering at) professional art criticism, before discussing the two painters in a series of oppositions: 'Bram paints the changed object and Geer the object that changes, the one painting extension and the other sequence' (Cohn 2001, 125–6). Beckett ends by dismissing his own essay, writing 'C'est ça, la littérature', an acknowledgment of the failure of words to capture the visual.

The second essay on the van Velde brothers, 'Peintres de l'empêchment', is more concise, largely devoid of the rhetorical flourishes that characterised the earlier piece. But its aesthetic propositions are largely the same – having once again dismissed the art critical enterprise, Beckett focuses on the way the two painters confront the impossibility of representation. This is the 'impediment' inscribed in the title of the piece and leads him to propose three choices for the modern painter: either he ignores the gulf between subject and object, finds a new relation with the object beyond representation or paints the actual impediment.

Beckett's developing theories on art were heavily influenced by his intellectual exchange with the art critic Georges Duthuit, editor of the resurrected little review *Transition* (now with a capital 'T') which published articles on philosophy, literature, art and politics. It is a well-known fact that Beckett either translated texts or advised on translations for the journal, but as has recently become clear, his role was far more substantial; as John Pilling has stated, 'Beckett, behind Duthuit, is the unmoved mover, the figure hidden in plain view, the largely unacknowledged ghost in the machine of the six postwar issues of *Transition*' (2011, 199).

The public manifestation of Beckett's conversations with Duthuit is the often quoted *Three Dialogues with Georges Duthuit* (published in December 1949 in *Transition*).[10] In these dialogues, 'B' and 'D' discuss in turn the three painters Pierre Tal Coat, André Masson and Bram van Velde. Whereas 'D' supports the first two painters, 'B' sets them against van Velde's 'art of a different order' (*Dis* 142). Once again, Beckett's term of reference is the alienated relationship between subject and object: if the occasion of art 'appears as an unstable term of relation, the artist, who is the other term, is hardly less so' (145). Beckett is here of course revisiting and extending his aesthetic views formulated in the 1930s. In a letter to Duthuit of 2 March 1949 he remembers his 'angry article on modern Irish poets ['Recent Irish Poetry'], in which I set up, as criterion of worthwhile modern poetry, awareness of the vanished object. Already! And talking, as the only terrain to the poet, of the no man's land that he projects round himself' (*LSB II* 131). In *Three Dialogues*, Beckett also returns to the poetics of unknowing he had formulated in the 'German Diaries', stating that 'to be an artist is to fail, as no other dare fail, that failure is his world and the shrink from it desertion, art and craft, good housekeeping, living' (*Dis* 145). It is a view that finds its most succinct expression in a letter to Georges Duthuit dated 9 June 1949: 'Does there exist, can there exist, or not, a painting that is poor, undisguisedly useless, incapable of any image whatever, a painting whose necessity does not seek to justify itself?' (*LSB II* 166).

As is evident from these quotations, the publication of the second volume of Beckett's letters (2011) has shed important new light on the way he shaped his aesthetic concerns. Beckett's correspondence with Duthuit charts the way in which he grappled with the aesthetic propositions that find the light of day in his scattered publications on art.[11] Written in an unguarded manner, with only a personal addressee in mind, these letters express more succinctly the core elements of Beckett's thinking. This is evident for example in a remarkable letter of 9 March 1949, in which Beckett tells Duthuit that Bram van Velde's painting is 'new' because it enacts a 'gran rifiuto':

> it is the first to repudiate relation in all these forms. It is not the relation with this or that order of opposite that it refuses, but the state of being in relation as such, the state of being in front of. We have waited for a long time for an artist who is brave enough, is at ease enough with the great tornadoes of intuition, to grasp that the break with the outside world entails the break with the inside world, that there are no replacement relations for naïve relations, that what are called outside and inside are one and the same. (*LSB II* 140).

As Beckett goes on to say, the very act of his saying this puts Bram van Velde 'back into a relation': it is a vicious circle of expression and failure, and it is one that is evinced by the later homages, catalogue entries and short pieces he wrote on Jack B. Yeats (1954), Henri Hayden (1955 and 1960), Bram van Velde (1961) and Avigdor Arikha (1967).

The ultimate argument that Bram van Velde paints the impossibility of painting is reflected in Beckett's own creative work, in particular in the *Three Novels* written in the second half of the 1940s. Already in his famous letter to Axel Kaun of 9 July 1937, Beckett adumbrated a 'literature of the unword' (*Dis* 173), in which 'language is most efficiently used when it is being most efficiently misused' (171–2). This letter represents a literary aesthetic pronouncement that parallels the 'space that intervenes': 'To bore one hole after another in [language], until what lurks behind it – be it something or nothing – begins to seep through' (172).

Beckett's Postwar Poetry

Beckett's turn to writing in French was undertaken in poetry, after his permanent move to Paris in late 1937. The series of twelve poems written between 1937 and 1939, but only published in November 1946 in *Les Temps modernes* as 'Poèmes 37–39', mark a new direction in Beckett's poetic output. They largely eschew the erudite allusions that marked the earlier English poems, enacting an impersonal statement even when dealing with erotic encounters. Beckett's aesthetic preoccupations of the immediate pre-war years do not appear to have influenced these poems in any overt way, but they do come to the fore in the poems written immediately after World War II. Often grouped as 'Six Poèmes' these poems in French (and partly translated by Beckett into English) address the irredeemable solitude of the poetic voice and separation, evident in the titles of some of the poems ('Mort de A.D.', 'vive morte ma seule saison'). The four-line poem 'je voudrais que mon amour meure' / 'I would like my love to die' encapsulates the nostalgic, elegiac strain:

> I would like my love to die
> and the rain to be raining on the graveyard
> and on me walking the streets
> mourning her who thought she loved me (*CP* 120)

Taken together, these poems are located in a space that is 'between', or what the poem 'my way is in the sand flowing' calls 'shifting thresholds':

> my way is in the sand flowing
> between the shingle and the dune
> the summer rain rains on my life
> on me my life harrying fleeing
> to its beginning to its end (*CP* 118)

The separation of subject and object that predominates Beckett's aesthetic thinking on the visual arts is re-enacted in the later poetry of the 1970s, which performs the struggle of the imagination to enter into dialogue with reality. A good example of this is the poem 'something there' (1975), which opens:

> something there
> where
> out there
> out where
> outside
> what
> the head what else
> something there somewhere outside
> the head (CP 202)

The most extensive series of poems written by Beckett in the latter part of his writing career are the *Mirlitonnades* (published in *Poèmes suivi de mirlitonnades* in 1978), and the related short poems in French and English from the late 1970s and 1980s.[12] Beckett wrote these 'gloomy French doggerel[s]' (qtd. in Harmon 1998, 355) on scraps of paper (envelopes, diary pages, café notepaper, metro tickets and so forth) before transferring them to the so-called 'Sottisier' Notebook (UoR MS2901). As their name suggests, these short *vers de mirliton* are light in manner, condensed witticisms that telescope thematic concerns Beckett was addressing (mainly) in prose. Indeed, these late poems are closely connected to his work in other genres – the so-called *Nohow On* prose trilogy and TV plays such as *Ghost Trio* and ...*but the clouds*....[13] Although the pieces have a throw-away quality, they deal with profound issues – the fleeting nature of life, vain striving, isolation, and the absence of God.

If Beckett's first published piece of writing was a critical essay, his last publication is a poem: 'Comment dire' / 'what is the word'. Written in 1988 and published a year later, the year of Beckett's death, this poem encompasses many of the aesthetic themes that had preoccupied the writer over nearly sixty years of creative endeavour. 'What is the word' performs the failure of expression, the difficulty of perception, the dehiscence of subject and object and – ultimately – the *need* to inscribe these tensions in words, as is evident in this extract:

> folly given all this –
> seeing –
> folly seeing all this –
> this –
> what is the word – (CP 228)

Conclusion

In Beckett's *Waiting for Godot*, Estragon says to Vladimir: 'That's the idea, let's abuse each other' (*CDW* 70). They proceed to exchange insults, which culminates when Estragon exclaims – '*with finality*', as the stage direction tells us – 'Crritic!' (70) The scorn with which Beckett employs this term here sheds retrospective light on his own critical writings, but is more likely directed at the critics who had dismissed his work over the previous three decades. For as we have seen, Beckett advocated an art that was interrogative and ultimately critical. If literature and painting were doomed to fail in the face of that which they cannot explain, Beckett still insisted (in his review of Denis Devlin's *Intercessions*) that 'Art has always been this – pure interrogation, rhetorical question less the rhetoric' (*Dis* 91). Already as a lecturer at Trinity College Dublin in 1931, he had described Gide's creative enterprise as 'interrogative not conclusive' because he 'preserv[ed] integrity of incoherence'.[14] Transforming his aesthetic theory into practice, Beckett's work generates a kind of threshold between what can and what cannot be visualised or represented, or what can be said and what is unsaid. Beckett's criticism and poetry is located within this tympanum, it 'live[s] the space of a door / that opens and shuts' (*CP* 118), and thus rewards the reader's attention.

NOTES

1. A critical edition of Beckett's critical writings is currently being prepared by David Tucker and Mark Nixon for publication by Faber & Faber. At the time of writing, Ruby Cohn's edited collection *Disjecta* remains indispensable, though it contains some errors and also includes letters and the dramatic fragment 'Human Wishes'.
2. I am grateful to Julia Séguier for her help with this essay.
3. Rachel Burrows lecture notes, TCD MIC60, 21r (qtd. in Nixon 2011, 182).
4. These book reviews include pieces on Edward Moerike, J. B. Leishmann's translations of Rainer Maria Rilke, Ezra Pound, Sean O'Casey, Jack B. Yeats and Thomas MacGreevy.
5. Beckett had already hinted at this idea in *Proust*, when he states that 'the observer infects the observed with his own mobility' (*PTD* 7).
6. Letter to Lawrence Harvey, 20 February 1967.
7. Letter to A. J. Leventhal, 4 April 1962.
8. See for example Beckett's letter to his American publisher Barney Rosset in 1956: 'You could put my old ECHO'S BONES on your list if you want to' (*LSB II* 614).
9. See Ackerley (2011) for a good discussion of this difficult text.
10. In a letter to John Fletcher dated 12 December 1962, Beckett stated that he wrote the *Three Dialogues* at Duthuit's request and that they freely summarise their

aesthetic conversations. He also tellingly remarks that he doubts that Duthuit approved of them.
11 The correspondence between Beckett and Duthuit will keep scholars busy for some time to come, although there has already been a wealth of critical attention; see for example Lloyd (2011), Rabaté (2011a) and Uhlmann (2011).
12 For a discussion of Beckett's *Mirlitonnades*, see Wheatley (1995; 2007) and Nixon (2007b), and for Beckett's late poetry in English see Nixon (2007c).
13 Although it is beyond the scope of this paper, it is worth remarking that generic distinctions often break down in Beckett's postwar work. There are exchanges in *Waiting for Godot*, for example, that are distinctively poetic, such as the dialogue commencing 'all the dead voices'. Equally, some of the later shorter prose pieces could be termed prose poems.
14 Rachel Burrows lecture notes, TCD MIC60, 16r (qtd. in Nixon 2011, 182).

PART II
Poetics

7

SHANE WELLER

Beckett and Late Modernism

'Where now? Who now? When now?' The three questions with which Samuel Beckett's *The Unnamable* (1953) opens are, for good reason, generally seen as pertaining to the individual who utters them, that residual figure beyond or beneath the various 'vice-existers', from Belacqua to Malone, who populate Beckett's earlier novels. These questions might no less pertinently be applied, however, to Beckett's œuvre as a whole. Where, if anywhere, does that œuvre belong within modern literary history? Should it be seen as part of European 'high' modernism, alongside the works of Proust, Joyce and Pound, on each of whom Beckett wrote appreciatively in the late 1920s and early 1930s? Or is Beckett's place more properly within the fold of literary postmodernism, alongside writers such as Jorge Luis Borges (with whom he shared the Formentor Group's International Prize in 1961), Vladimir Nabokov and Italo Calvino? Or should one resist the homogenising urge, and instead break down Beckett's œuvre – produced, as it was, over a period of sixty years – into a series of more or less discrete phases? Taking this latter approach, one might, for instance, identify an early, modernist phase, epitomised by Beckett's first, Joyce-indebted novel, *Dream of Fair to Middling Women* (written in 1931–2), and a later, postmodernist phase, initiated in *Watt* and continuing in the postwar novels *Molloy*, *Malone Dies*, *The Unnamable* and the plays, commencing with *Eleutheria* and *Waiting for Godot*.[1] Or are all such attempts to locate Beckett within one or more literary movement not only futile, but in principle wrongheaded? Is his œuvre perhaps best understood as sui generis – as Beckett himself suggests all genuine art must be, when, in his 'Homage to Jack B. Yeats' (1954), he claims that the true artist (who 'stakes his being' in his work) belongs to no tradition, and is quite simply 'from nowhere' (*Dis* 149) – an inexplicable manifestation of the all-too-human need to express?

Those commentators who have addressed the question of Beckett's place within literary history have, for the most part, tended to locate his post-Second World War works, if anywhere, within an emergent postmodernism.

Indeed, as early as 1971, Ihab Hassan is to be found describing Beckett as 'a supreme example of the postmodern artist', the justification for this claim being that Beckett turns 'the malice of language against itself' (210). According to Brian McHale, Beckett moves from modernism to postmodernism between *Molloy* and *The Unnamable*, with the latter work articulating a 'fundamental ontological discontinuity between the fictional and the real' that is characteristic of postmodern literature (1989, 13). For Hassan, Beckett belongs firmly within a tradition of 'antiliterature', alongside writers such as the Marquis de Sade, Stéphane Mallarmé, Franz Kafka and Jean Genet. This is a tradition characterised above all by its commitment to a particular kind of silence: 'the negative echo of language, autodestructive, demonic, nihilist' (Hassan 1971, 248). Seen in this light, the feature of Beckett's œuvre that would render it most obviously postmodern would be its commitment to a form of language scepticism, the philosophical origins of which could be traced back to his reading (in the late 1930s) of the Austrian philosopher Fritz Mauthner's *Beiträge zu einer Kritik der Sprache* (*Contributions to a Critique of Language*, 1901–3).[2]

There is much in Beckett's postwar œuvre to justify this emphasis on his turning of language back against itself in an ostensibly antiliterary manner. To see this as the sign of a postmodern sensibility is, however, no longer as natural a conclusion as Hassan makes it seem. Rather than language scepticism, or acts of (nihilistic) aggression against the means of literary expression or indeed against the literary object as such, postmodernism has come to be seen by more recent theorists of the movement as characterised by a playfully ironic sense of the fabricated nature of that object. Other features of the postmodern would include: the articulation of a representational *mise en abyme* (the ostensibly extratextual referent becoming a product of that function); the conception of both the subject or self and its world as discursively produced; and the reinhabiting of popular genres (especially detective fiction and romance) in a manner that is closer to pastiche than to parody, this generic inhabitation being justified by the sense that the avant-garde notion of the a-generic is a myth. Those who would locate Beckett within literary postmodernism thus often point to his thematising of the act of narration, to the idea explored in *The Unnamable* that the 'I' is a purely linguistic entity – 'I'm in words, made of words' (*Un* 104) – and to the subversion of the representational mode, as, most obviously, at the end of *Molloy* (1951), where the narrator, Moran, declares that, while his narrative may have opened with the seemingly stable constative assertions 'It is midnight. The rain is beating on the windows', in fact (or at least, so we are *told*), 'It was not midnight. It was not raining' (*Mo* 95, 184). In other words, the representational authenticity of Moran's entire narrative is cast into doubt by that narrative, which turns back on itself in such a manner as to leave the reader irretrievably suspended, in no position to determine what is representationally reliable and what is not. The only certainties would therefore be the *potential* unreliability of what is recounted and the awareness that the narrative is itself in no small part *about* the act and reception of narration. The step from Beckett's *Molloy* to Calvino's *If on a Winter's Night a Traveller* (1979) is, it would seem, but a small one.

While an insistence on hard-and-fast principles that would distinguish literary modernism from literary postmodernism will inevitably entail distortions when one seeks literary examples to support one's case, and while there are undoubtedly affinities between Beckett's postwar works and those of writers generally seen as postmodern (Borges and Calvino, for instance), it is nonetheless clear that, on the one hand, in the course of the 1930s Beckett sought to distance himself from the 'high' modernism of Proust and (especially) Joyce, while on the other hand remaining deeply committed to some of the principal tenets of literary modernism. Among those tenets, the most important would be the idea that, as Mallarmé and then T. S. Eliot put it, the writer's task is to 'purify the dialect of the tribe',[3] and that this purification is undertaken in order to achieve a truer presentation – or 'statement', to use one of Beckett's preferred terms – of 'how it is'. In other words, Beckett's art remains committed to the idea that the aim of art is truth, and that, as he puts it in the poem 'something there' (1974), there is undeniably 'something [...] out there' (*CP* 202) – that is, something 'beyond words' – this latter phrase being considered by Beckett as an alternative translation of the title of *L'Innommable* (Van Hulle and Weller 2014, 39). It is very much in line with this modernist commitment to purifying 'the language of the tribe', and with its intrinsic aesthetic elitism, that Beckett should, in each of his works, seek a new form or – one might even go so far as to say of a late work such as *Worstward Ho* (1983) – almost a new language. Given this commitment to a form, a style and a language that would serve, in their radical originality, to capture 'how it is', together with the abiding sense that this struggle is futile, Beckett's postwar œuvre might more accurately be located within neither high modernism nor postmodernism, but rather within that (for Beckett, appropriately liminal and belated) space which has come to be known as *late modernism*.[4]

The concept of late modernism has played an increasingly important role in cultural history and aesthetic theory since its deployment by the architectural historian Charles Jencks (1991). According to Jencks, late modernism in architecture is characterised principally by the persistence of the core tenets of architectural modernism, including utopianism, a purist style and avant-garde moralism. In Jencks's wake, there have been a number of important interventions in the field to determine the historical and aesthetic specificities of late modernism across the arts, and to establish a canon of artists and works that may be defined as distinctly late modernist. Among the most influential of these interventions in the Anglo-American world have been those by Tyrus Miller (1999), Fredric Jameson (2002), J. M. Bernstein (2006) and Edward Said (2006), whose conception of 'late style' is profoundly indebted to Theodor Adorno's 1937 essay on Beethoven. It would be misleading, however, to suggest that there has been any general agreement on the specificities of late modernism (both historically and aesthetically) or on the canon that those specificities would define. Indeed, earlier influential studies of postmodernism such as Hassan's arguably take up late modernist works as examples of the postmodern, thereby obscuring the particularities of the former.

Late modernism has been seen, on the one hand, by Miller, as commencing in the late 1920s and reaching its peak in the 1930s, and, on the other hand, by Jameson, as reaching its height in the postwar works of Beckett and Nabokov, among others. A third approach, taken by Bernstein and Said, has been simply to collapse the distinction between 'high' and 'late' by arguing that modernism as such is always already late, being shaped less by a commitment to 'making it new' (as famously demanded by Ezra Pound) than by a nostalgia for a lost (and no doubt imagined) community. For the most part, the evidence for these historical determinations of late modernism has been drawn from an Anglo-American canon, either within the literary realm or within the visual arts and architecture. For instance, in addition to Beckett, Miller's principal late modernists are Wyndham Lewis, Djuna Barnes and Mina Loy, while Bernstein's (in the sphere of the visual arts) include Jackson Pollock, Cindy Sherman and Frank Stella.

According to Miller, the defining features of late modernism are: the presentation of the world as inauthentic; the absence of any secure position for the authorial subject; an abandonment of the classical literary forms and of the 'symbolic unity' of the work; the reduction of the human body to something grotesque and puppetlike, mechanical rather than natural; and the insistence on a subjectivity that can resort only to 'self-reflexive laughter' or 'play' in the face of its threatened destruction (1999, 63–4). Jameson sees late modernism rather differently (and, unsurprisingly, more politically), its defining features for him being: a reflexive attitude towards the 'status of the artist as modernist', and thus the production of an art that takes artistic creation as its primary subject matter; a sense of the impossibility of art's absolute autonomy; and a recognition of the problems of representation resulting from the failure of artistic modernism to maintain its distance from ideology (2002, 198, 209).

It is not difficult to appreciate how readily Beckett's œuvre seems to exhibit the features of late modernism identified by both Miller and Jameson. Or rather, it is easy enough to see how those features might have been derived from a reading of Beckett. The question of inauthenticity is certainly pervasive in Beckett's œuvre, being explored through the elusive distinction between being and seeming – *Sein* and *Schein* – to the very end: in his last work, 'what is the word' (1988), Beckett places the emphasis heavily on the word 'seem'.[5] As for the authorial subject, Beckett inscribes this figure into the work, in the form of 'Sam' in *Watt*, and then, in *The Unnamable*, through a collapsing of the distinction between the speaking/writing and spoken/written self. In *Watt*, the theory of three kinds of laughter, with the highest being the 'dianoetic', or *risus purus* – that is, 'the laugh laughing at the laugh' (*W* 40) – chimes perfectly with Miller's conception of self-reflexive laughter. Beckett's œuvre reveals an ongoing preoccupation with the finding of new forms – indeed, a new form for each work. In his postwar prose texts, he departs from the 'classical' models of the novel, the novella or the short story, towards something more closely akin to the prose poem (in the tradition of Baudelaire and, especially, Rimbaud, whose poem 'Le Bateau ivre' he translated). This puts him at odds with the majority of postmodern literature, in which these classical models tend to be inhabited, albeit in an ironic manner. One need only compare Beckett with Borges to appreciate how much more closely allied the former remains to the unremittingly antigeneric impulse of the literary avant-garde.

If the presentation of the human body as mechanical or puppetlike is a late modernist trait, then few writers exhibit this more forcefully than Beckett. With Bergson's influential conception of the comic in mind – that is, the comic effect as being produced when that which is living comports itself in a manner that resembles the nonliving – one can connect the incapacitated Beckettian body with that self-reflexive laughter which Beckett effects in part through reimagining the clown as the tragicomic figure par excellence. That said, one should not forget Beckett's late enthusiasm for Kleist's essay on the puppet theatre (Van Hulle and Nixon 2013, 97), and the idea of a gracefulness that can be achieved only through the obliteration of self-consciousness. Beckett's directorial instructions to his actors in the 1970s that they should seek to achieve such gracefulness in their movements sits at odds with his emphasis on the awkward, dysfunctional body in his major postwar prose from *Molloy* to *How It Is*. As for the idea of the human subject as being at play in the face of its own unavoidable (and, indeed, partly desired) extinction, a work such as *Endgame* (1957) immediately comes to mind, even if the play in question is less that of Johan Huizinga's *homo ludens* than that of grimly sadistic beings, informed by Beckett's familiarity with the works of the Marquis de Sade and with Freud's theory of anal-eroticism (see Weller 2010a).

Turning to Jameson's conception of late modernism: here, too, Beckett's œuvre seems to reflect each of the key features. From as early as his first published story, 'Assumption' (1929), Beckett engages directly with the possibility – or, more precisely, the impossibility – of expression and artistic creation. As he puts it (melodramatically but nonetheless seriously) in *Watt*, by way of the figure of Arsene: 'what we know partakes in no small measure of the nature of what has so happily been called the unutterable or ineffable, so that any attempt to utter or eff it is doomed to fail, doomed, doomed to fail' (*W* 51–2). And time and again he places the would-be writer at the centre of his work: Belacqua in *Dream of Fair to Middling Women* is the most obvious example, but the narrators of *Molloy*, *Malone Dies* and *The Unnamable* may all be seen as dark portraits of the artist, while late works such as 'All Strange Away' (1965), *Imagination Dead Imagine* (1966), *Company* (1980), *Worstward Ho* and 'what is the word' thematise the performative act by which a world might be brought into being through its utterance, albeit a shadow-world that never quite materialises, remaining painfully provisional, a weak echo of the divine fiat. As for the sense that art cannot maintain its absolute autonomy, Beckett's comments on other writers and artists suggest, on the one hand, that he believes true art must keep its distance from the world of politics (especially nationalist cultural politics). Beckett's artist is necessarily a solitary figure whose political engagements (and Beckett's life was marked by several, not least his work for the French Resistance during the Second World War) should not be reflected in politically engaged art. It is hardly surprising that Brecht, appalled by Beckett's failure to take advantage of the opportunity, should have thought it necessary to produce an adaptation of *Waiting for Godot* in which the relationships are explicitly rendered as those of class antagonism. On the other hand, as Adorno was among the first to realise, Beckett's postwar work *is* deeply political, albeit in a manner that, for historico-aesthetic reasons, can offer no positive vision of utopia beyond an ever more administered, ever more brutally reified world.[6] It is, however, Jameson's third criterion for late modernism – that it entails a recognition of the problems of representation, resulting, according to Jameson, from the failure of artistic modernism to maintain its distance from ideology – that points most directly to the grounds on which Beckett took his explicit distance from high modernism, while nonetheless remaining within modernism's shadow.[7]

It has often been noted that Beckett's conception of Proust's *A la recherche du temps perdu* (1913–27), as articulated in his 1931 monograph on that work, was strongly influenced by his recent reading of Schopenhauer's

World as Will and Representation (see, for instance, Zurbrugg 1988). No less striking is the fact that Beckett appears to endorse unreservedly the Proustian aesthetic, and indeed takes the opportunity to make a series of statements about art that are presented in such a way as to collapse any potential distinction between Beckett and Proust. And it is precisely on the role of the negative in art that this identification is at its strongest. Beckett asserts, for instance, that 'The artist is active, but negatively' (*PTD* 65). A few years later, in a highly critical review of a book on Proust by Albert Feuillerat, he again endorses Proust's artistic practice, claiming that the latter produces his work 'in dribs and drabs' (*Dis* 65), and that he is never simply the master of his material. As for the other high modernist giant on whom he comments at length at the beginning of his own writing life, Beckett champions Joyce's 'Work in Progress', in his 1929 essay purportedly on the place of Italian thought in Joyce's novel, for achieving a form of 'direct expression' that, Beckett claims, is the very essence of the literary art (*Dis* 26). By 1937, however, Beckett's position has changed radically. In his well-known July 1937 letter to Axel Kaun, an acquaintance made during his 1936–7 trip to Germany, he dramatically sets his own artistic aims in diametrical opposition to Joyce's. In the work that, two years later, would be published under the title *Finnegans Wake* – one of the last major works of European literary high modernism, alongside Hermann Broch's *Death of Virgil* (1945) and Thomas Mann's *Doctor Faustus* (1947) – Joyce achieves what Beckett describes as an 'apotheosis of the word' (*LSB I* 519). In contrast, Beckett declares that he will seek to achieve a 'literature of the unword' (*Literatur des Unworts*). The antithesis on which Beckett wishes to insist here is troubled, however, by the fact that *Finnegans Wake*, like Broch's *Death of Virgil*, captures in its very title a death – the death of high modernism? – that anticipates that of Beckett's Malone, among others. In other words, Beckett chooses as his antithetical touchstone a work that is already *late* high modernism.

In his own later comments on how his aims have come to differ from Joyce's, Beckett distinguishes between the artist as master (namely, Joyce, but also, one might argue, the high modernist artists more generally, such as Rilke, Pound and Eliot, who may in this respect be set alongside nineteenth-century realists such as Balzac and Tolstoy) and the artist of 'impotence' and 'ignorance'.[8] It is to just such an art of impotence and ignorance that Beckett commits himself in his postwar works. Indeed, from 1945 onwards, Beckett's œuvre is governed by an aesthetico-ethical commitment to failure: 'Fail again. Fail better' (*CIWS* 81), as he puts it in *Worstward Ho*. Late modernism is perhaps best understood precisely as such an art of impotence and ignorance, an art that no longer trusts the power of the aesthetic to achieve epiphany, that no longer believes art can, as Heidegger claims in *The Origin of the Work of Art* (1935–6), be the 'setting-itself-to-work of truth' (2002, 49) (although the late modernists never abandon the belief that art is to be judged in terms of its relation to truth), and that sees language as a problem, less a means of disclosure than, in Beckett's metaphor, a veil – akin to the 'veil of Maya' that, for Schopenhauer, hides the monstrous reality of the will. Hence Beckett's commitment to an (impossible) literature of the 'unword'; hence his repeated subversion of the work of art in its very manifestation. And yet, crucially, this deep distrust of the word, this lack of faith in the power of art, leads, in late modernism, neither to a simple abandonment of high modernism's insistence that art alone can save us from ideology, nor to a playful acceptance of the necessary imbrication of art and ideology, which, at its most extreme, can become a celebration of art *as ideology*. Rather than any such step beyond the high modernist problematic, late modernism remains entoiled within it, committed to art as the sole space in which a critical distance from ideology may in principle be achieved, committed, that is, to the (ethical and political) seriousness of art, holding to the belief that, in the face of the worst – totalitarianism, world war, genocide – there is no hope other than in an art which, as Adorno puts it, in some sense faces up to the reality of our dark times. And yet, casting a corrosive shadow across this absolute commitment to art, there remains in late modernism the most acute sense of futility, the sense that (to adapt Kafka) there may be hope in art, indeed infinite hope, but not for the artist. It is the diremptive conjunction of these perspectives that renders Beckett's late modernist work 'anethical', which is to say the enactment of an indecision between nihilism and antinihilism (for a proposed theorisation of the anethical, see Weller 2006, 192–5).

Alongside its residual Enlightenment belief in progress (the ever more insistent, ever more threatened Beckettian 'on'), late modernism is shaped by the belief that art can offer neither transfiguration nor transcendence, any more than it can simply accept the world as it is. Rather, taking up a remark by Beckett on the paintings of Jack B. Yeats in 1945, one could say that late modernist art seeks to 'reduc[e] the dark where there might have been, mathematically at least, a door' (*Dis* 97). Late modernism is thus an art of the shadows, an art of distrust and penury, in which language itself becomes, paradoxically, at once the sole resource and the great obstacle. The major late modernists in Europe – including Beckett, Maurice Blanchot, Paul Celan, Thomas Bernhard and W. G. Sebald – are, in short, writers who create in the shadow of a catastrophic history, and who experience the appalling failure of the Enlightenment project, from which they cannot free themselves, as an unhealable wound.

Late modernism may be understood, then, principally as a post-World War II – and, above all, as a post-Holocaust – phenomenon, and may also be distinguished in its content and its form both from the high modernism of the pre-war era and from the postmodernism with which it is broadly contemporaneous.[9] At the heart of this conception of late modernism is the attitude adopted by the writer towards his or her own means of expression or representation. The late modernist's distrust of language connects this movement with a strand of early modernism that was, in fact, countered in high modernism, namely turn-of-the-century language scepticism, perhaps the best-known literary engagement with this theme being Hugo von Hofmannsthal's 'Ein Brief' (1902), generally known in English as 'The Lord Chandos Letter'. This moment of language scepticism was followed by a commitment to the renewal of language in many of the major high modernists (especially Joyce and Pound), only for this to be followed by a new retreat from the word, or, more precisely, a turning of language against itself, in the late modernism of Beckett and Celan. To understand this late modernist return to language scepticism, one has to take into account the shadow cast by the mid-twentieth-century historical catastrophe. This is not to suggest that late modernism is, in effect, simply another term for 'Holocaust literature', since many of the literary works that address the Holocaust explicitly are decidedly conventional, aesthetically speaking: the novels of Aaron Appelfeld, Elie Wiesel, Arnošt Lustig and Primo Levi are cases in point.[10] Rather, it is to say that the late modernist concern with the limits of language is not simply part of an ongoing reaction to that disenchantment of the world that begins with the birth of modern science and the Enlightenment. While there are those who would argue – as, most famously, does Adorno – that the Holocaust may be seen as a direct consequence of the 'dialectic of Enlightenment', for others it constitutes the great historical caesura or singularity. In order to grasp the distinction between high and late modernism it is necessary to take account of a loss of faith in the power of the word that is intimately bound up with a loss of faith in the human as such.

The language revolution that is so characteristic of the European avant-garde (Futurism, Expressionism, Dada, Surrealism, etc.) and of certain strands of high modernism, especially the later work of Joyce and Pound,[11] stands in dialectical counterpoint to language scepticism, since that revolution is a response to this scepticism, but one that is guided by the conviction that a renewal of expression is possible – hence Beckett's claim that one finds 'direct expression' in Joyce, by which he means an identification of form and content, manner and matter, or the *enactment* of meaning in language.[12] Late modernism, in contrast, returns to this turn-of-the-century language scepticism, haunted by an historically informed sense that it is not the renewal of the word that is required, but rather its negation, a thought that is very much in line with Mauthner's nominalist attack on 'word superstition', his claim that the entire history of Western philosophy is characterised by a mistaking of the word for the reality, that thought has remained metaphorical through and through, and that the only solution lies in the apocalyptic 'Nichtwort' or 'not-word' (1923, I.83), or, less radically (if more feasibly), in an ironic use of language of the kind that, according to Mauthner (as Beckett noted when reading him in the late 1930s), is achieved by Goethe in his autobiographical *Poetry and Truth* (1811–33). Returning to this language-sceptical tradition, late modernism develops forms of linguistic negativism as what it takes to be the only aesthetically and ethically justifiable response to a modernity perceived as both socially and politically catastrophic.

While remaining committed to the high modernist ideal that art must take its critical distance from modernity, the late modernist moment in Europe to which Beckett belongs is characterised by a far more pessimistic view of the power of art to transform society, and of the power of language to communicate either the experience of modernity or the possibility of any alternative to it. High modernism tends to turn to myth in order to make sense of, and to bestow an order or a coherence upon, what T. S. Eliot famously describes (in his 1923 essay on Joyce's *Ulysses*) as 'the immense panorama of futility and anarchy which is contemporary history' (1975, 177). In contrast, late modernism, with its painful awareness of the political uses to which myth was put by the totalitarian regimes of the 1930s and 1940s, has no such faith in any clear alternative to instrumental reason. Instead, late modernism finds itself obliged to take refuge in the negative. In this, it is forcefully anticipated by Kafka, who in what are now generally known as the 'Zürau Aphorisms' (1917–18) asserts that 'To perform the negative is what is still required of us, the positive is already ours' (1994, 8).[13]

Beckett's distancing of himself from high modernism first becomes fully apparent in the late 1930s, after the completion of *Murphy* in 1936. What is perhaps most striking about the timing of this aesthetic shift is that it follows his six-month trip to Nazi Germany and his reading of Mauthner's *Beiträge*. It has often been noted that his next major work, *Watt*, breaks both with the classical structure of the novel in a way that *Murphy* does not, and that, in the celebrated 'pot' episode, it thematises the troubling disparity between word and world. From this point on, Beckett's art will remain deeply engaged with the idea that language, even the most highly crafted aesthetic utterance, will fail to capture the particularity of the real. As Beckett acknowledged, his switch from English to French was owing, in no small measure, to a need to achieve a nominalist impoverishment or weakening of the word – already in the early 1930s, one finds Beckett viewing French, no doubt questionably, as a language in which it is possible to write 'without style' (*Dream* 48). Out of this nominalist sense that language will always be found wanting emerges Beckett's struggle to achieve a 'literature of the unword', that is, a literature in which language is turned back against itself, resulting not in the disappearance of the word (as in the parodic idea that Beckett's last great work would consist of nothing but blank pages), but rather, again and again (and in a striking variety of ways), in works in which forms of unwording are *enacted*. It is in *The Unnamable* that Beckett for the first time achieves such an enactment (rather than the mere thematisation) of unwording. He does so at the micrological level through an extraordinarily intensive reliance on negative affixes (these increasing in the translation drafts), and at the macrological level through a style shaped by almost unremitting epanorthosis, or self-revision (see Clément 1989; Van Hulle and Weller 2014).

The various forms of unwording adopted by Beckett in *The Unnamable* and later works such as *Worstward Ho* are, on the one hand, acts of nominalist aggression against a language (or languages) perceived as having been subjected to reification, and, on the other hand, an attempt to create a linguistic refuge from the coercive force of instrumental reason. It is, then, above all in their commitment to achieving a 'literature of the unword' for reasons that are not simply aesthetic, but also ethical and political, that Beckett's postwar works may be placed alongside those of Blanchot, Celan, Bernhard and Sebald (on Beckettian traces in Sebald, see Weller 2013). In his 1980 work on Alfred Döblin, Sebald comments on Beckett's 'ironic style', arguing that the 'critical meaning' of Beckett's œuvre lies in its revealing that 'regression' is simply the dialectical counterpart of 'progress' (1980, 116). With this in mind, one might suggest that the many incapacitated bodies in Beckett's works are the dark side of the energetic body of Enlightenment-capitalist fantasy. In short, Sebald's Beckett is, like Adorno's, a deeply political writer in the late modernist tradition, committed to a critique of our dark times, but painfully aware that the very idea of critique is no less an Enlightenment myth than is that of progress. If there is hope, then it lies for the late modernist only in modernity's caesurae, its points of weakness, the cracks through which an unimaginable, unthinkable light might be glimpsed: the light of what Adorno repeatedly describes as 'reconciliation' (*Versöhnung*) and Beckett on one occasion as 'happiness', located for the latter in what in *Ill Seen Ill Said* (1981) is described as the 'void' that it would be 'Grace to breathe' (*CIWS* 78). Beckett's signature preposition, 'on' – 'you must go no, I can't go on, I'll go on' (*Un* 134); 'On. Say on. Be said on. Somehow on. Till nohow on. Said nohow on' (*CIWS* 81) – is profoundly late modernist, then, in the sense that it signals at once a critique of, and a commitment to, the Enlightenment's value of values: progress as that which will one day make us free. In this, it is strikingly akin to Blanchot's recurrent 'pas' (step/ not). Crucially, however, there is much to suggest that the progress to which Beckett commits himself is one that would lead not to a purely secular paradise, but rather to an experience that can only be rendered in a language inflected by religious imagery ('grace'; 'unthinkable light'). Like both Walter Benjamin and Theodor Adorno before him, Beckett takes his distance from modernity in such a way as to disrupt any clear alignment of Enlightenment and secularization: in short, the Beckettian 'on' discloses a religious impulse at the heart of the Enlightenment project.

While the late modernist styles of Beckett, Blanchot, Celan, Bernhard and Sebald are certainly distinct, they nonetheless share a number of important features: parataxis, repetition, fragmentation and, above all, linguistic negativism. As soon as one begins to count the negative affixes in these writers' works, one soon realises that their styles are shaped at the deepest level by the sway of the negative, and that this is owing not to some aesthetic game, but to the incessant struggle to speak, as Celan puts it, 'of this / time' (1988, 177); or as Beckett puts it in a text written at the end of the Second World War, of how it is for a 'humanity in ruins' (1995, 278).

Far from having exclusively aesthetic implications, late modernism's response to what it takes to be the catastrophic implications of modernity is highly relevant for any critique of the contemporary world and its institutions, shaped as that world is by the globalisation of the Enlightenment project and the consequent integration of various forms of alterity, at once political, cultural, ethnic and religious. It is no doubt for this reason that Beckett's postwar works continue to strike so many readers as deeply relevant – existentially, politically and affectively – long after many of the most visible European ruins have disappeared. In an irony that underlies the late modernist vision of 'humanity in ruins' that Beckett shares with writers such as Celan, Bernhard and Sebald, the obligation to speak of how it is in such a world becomes all the more necessary when history's literal ruins are no longer visible.

NOTES

1 Another form of dehomogenising reading would be that of Alain Badiou, who argues that Beckett's œuvre falls into two parts, with *How It Is* (1961) marking a shift towards a preoccupation with 'the figure of the Other' (see Badiou 1995, 15–18).
2 For recent analyses of Beckett's reading of Mauthner, see especially Lernout 1994, Feldman 2006b, Van Hulle 1999 and 2011a, and Van Hulle and Nixon 2013.

3 In 'Le Tombeau d'Edgar Poe', Mallarmé (1945) writes of giving 'un sens plus pur aux mots de la tribu' (70). In part II of *Little Gidding*, Eliot (1969) echoes this aesthetic imperative, writing: 'Since our concern was speech, and speech impelled us / To purify the dialect of the tribe' (194).
4 McHale (1989) identifies *Malone Dies* as 'limit modernist' on account of what he takes to be its 'hesitation' between a concern with the epistemological and a concern with the ontological (13). For McHale, such 'limit modernism' is what Alan Wilde (1981) describes as 'late modernism'. Importantly, however, McHale sees this late modernist moment as marking a transition between his earlier modernist phase and his later postmodernist phase.
5 This text builds gropingly towards the line 'folly for to need to seem to glimpse afaint afar away over there what –' (*CIWS* 134).
6 This idea of a 'political Beckett' was later taken up by Terry Eagleton (2006), for whom, as for Adorno before him, Beckett's is an 'art after Auschwitz', a form of realism that serves 'the cause of human emancipation more faithfully than the bright-eyed utopians' (74).
7 Engaging with Jameson's identification of Beckett as late modernist, Conor Carville argues that the latter's work is characterised by an openness or incompletion that has rendered it a touchstone for visual artists seeking to free themselves from a modernism conceived in terms of aesthetic autonomy (see Carville 2011).
8 In conversation with Israel Shenker in 1956, Beckett states: 'With Joyce the difference is that Joyce is a superb manipulator of material – perhaps the greatest. He was making words do the absolute maximum of work. There isn't a syllable that's superfluous. The kind of work I do is one in which I'm not master of my material. The more Joyce knew the more he could. He's tending toward omniscience and omnipotence as an artist. I'm working with impotence, ignorance. [...] I think anyone nowadays who pays the slightest attention to his own experience finds it the experience of a non-knower, a non-can-er' (qtd. in Graver and Federman 1979, 148).
9 It is as an essentially postwar phenomenon that Peter Fifield (2013) understands late modernism in his work on Beckett and Levinas. Taking issue with Tyrus Miller's historical locating of late modernism in the 1930s, Fifield argues – rightly, to my mind – that it is Beckett's postwar work that is preeminently late modernist, 'because it responds to the disaster of the war' and bears witness to an 'historical collapse' that is not only aesthetic. For Fifield, this experience leads the late modernist to question 'the capacity to literature and philosophy to produce a systematic, rigorous, and comprehensive account of the world' (12).
10 This is not to suggest that postmodernism does not engage with the Holocaust, but rather that late modernism entails a very particular engagement with that historical event. An important text for any consideration of the postmodernist engagement with the Holocaust is Eaglestone's *The Holocaust and the Postmodern* (2004). It needs to be borne in mind, however, that while arguing that 'postmodernism in the West begins with thinking about the Holocaust', Eaglestone's definition of postmodernism – namely, 'poststructuralism, a still developing tradition of post-phenomenological philosophy' (2) – is not only distinct from many other, more widely accepted ones, but also limits the movement to philosophy.
11 In 'The Revolution of Language and James Joyce' (1929), Eugene Jolas (1972) claims that 'Modern life with its changed mythos and transmuted concepts of

beauty makes it imperative that words be given new compositions and relationships' (80). This imperative has guided the 'new artist of the word', who has 'recognised the autonomy of language and, aware of the twentieth century's current towards universality, attempts to hammer out a verbal vision that destroys time and space' (79). In addition to Joyce, who 'explod[es] the antique logic of words' (83), other writers identified by Jolas as 'new artists of the word' include Léon-Paul Fargue, Michel Leiris and the other French surrealists, Gertrude Stein and August Stramm.

12 As Beckett famously puts it, in Joyce's 'Work in Progress' 'form *is* content, content *is* form. [...] His writing is not *about* something; *it is that something itself*' (Beckett 1983, 27; emphasis in the original).

13 These aphorisms were formerly known under Max Brod's title for them: 'Reflections on Sin, Suffering, Hope, and the True Way'.

8

ANTHONY UHLMANN

Beckett's Intertexts

There is a good deal of evidence of Samuel Beckett's engagement with other texts, other writers, artists and philosophers, and with whole intellectual traditions such as philosophy, psychology, or mathematics (see Uhlmann 2013). Indeed, the nature of these relations, their extent and significance, has been the major area of critical engagement with Beckett's works since the turn of the century. This upsurge in interest is not accidental, and has been the consequence of the fact that a large amount of primary source archival material related to Beckett has become available to scholars in this period. Various kinds of critical responses have been mobilized to begin to digest these new sources, which have offered genuinely new evidence as to what Beckett read and elements of his response to what he read. We find this in the 'Philosophy notes' and 'Psychology notes' for example (Engelberts, Frost and Maxwell 2006) as well as in the annotations to his extant library (Van Hulle and Nixon 2013) and in the newly published correspondence (*LSB I*; *LSB II*), as well as what he saw in the visual arts and other forms, as detailed in the biographies (Bair 1990; Cronin 1996; Knowlson 1996), and the German diaries (Nixon 2011). So too, over an even longer period work has been and continues to be done on Beckett's manuscripts, with a series of bilingual genetic editions begun by Charles Krance and being continued by Dirk Van Hulle and Mark Nixon in digital form, adding significantly to our knowledge of the genetic development of many of Beckett's works, for example, *Company, Ill Seen Ill Said* and *How It Is* (Beckett 2001; BDMP). It is very clear, then, that Beckett engages with a vast array of other texts within his own, yet many questions remain as to how Beckett uses these other texts. In this essay I touch upon some of these questions in considering aspects of the nature of Beckett's intertextual method.

In the early 2000s Samuel Beckett's 'Philosophy notes' and 'Psychology notes' became available to scholars in the archives at Trinity College Dublin. These materials had been used by James Knowlson in the previous decade when he was working on his authorized biography of Beckett and had been in Beckett's possession before that. While they, in effect, only relate to specific periods of intellectual activity, detailing reading Beckett undertook in the 1930s, they were seized upon as in some sense defining Beckett's relationship to the disciplines of psychology and philosophy. While these are not the only notebooks (see also Beckett 1992b; 1993c; 1993d; 1999b; *DN*) I will take them as my point of departure here. A debate began in the field as to how critics could, or rather, should approach the question of his intertextual relations with other writers. No doubt wishing to provoke, early in his career Matthew Feldman set out an extreme position within this debate, arguing that critics should only claim any intertextual reference if there is clear evidence from primary source archival documents which confirms Beckett's engagement with that text (2006a). It was suggested that this approach was more rigorous and exacting, as it opened itself to tests of falsifiability. The explicit conceptual reference in this essay is to the work of Karl Popper, imported from the sciences and applied to literary criticism. Yet this approach has grave flaws. Firstly, it arbitrarily limits the field of Beckett's reading to what can be verified by surviving source material; for example, Beckett's library does not adequately represent the sum of his reading as Beckett gave away many books and read others in libraries, and as Nixon and Van Hulle point out, interpreting the marginalia itself is highly complex and the 'non-marginalia' in Beckett's works can be as interesting as the marginalia. They show how the adequate interpretation of the marginalia requires reference to passages that appear in the published works (2013, 8). Secondly, this approach in effect requires critics to begin with the necessarily incomplete archives to filter readings of the published texts, when it is clear that the relationship between the two is highly complex and not reducible to a simple line of causation.

Feldman's argument no doubt arose in response to a feeling that too much work has been done that does not attempt to establish any kind of evidentiary link between Beckett's work and those to which it is being compared, yet taken to an extreme an insistence on a certain kind of evidence of relationship would be equally distorting. And this extreme view, in fact, is not one that has been shared by the field, with Feldman himself having moved from insisting on it. Indeed the excellent genetic work that has developed, by Feldman and Chris Ackerley among others, and latterly most impressively by Van Hulle and Nixon, has never attempted to foreclose other approaches, but rather to add depth to them. Any attempt to foreclose readings, had it been adopted universally, would have catastrophically limited our capacity to understand or adequately engage with the challenges offered by Beckett's texts. Moreover, it is difficult to see how it might have led to anything other than the simple and uninteresting affirmation that Beckett did in fact read a certain text. That is, this kind of evidence can only be significant if it in some way adds to our understanding of the published texts of Beckett, and this is indeed true of the best genetic criticism, which can at times be astonishing (such as the BDMP). In short, interpretation that connects the manuscripts and the published texts remains necessary.

Jean-Michel Rabaté (2011b) has argued against the narrow focus implied by the extreme position I have mentioned here, but he has also made use of Beckett's notes on Kant. The notes offer some hints to how Beckett understood Kant's works, but are only so useful. What Rabaté's discussion of Beckett and Kant shows is that work that relates Beckett to Kant and attempts to draw out some of the implications of this relation needs to begin with a sound understanding of Beckett's works, which might then be paired with a sound understanding of Kantian philosophy in order to find valid points of comparison. These points of comparison would have to be justified with reference to evidence drawn from the published works, and any further clues that might be found in manuscripts and in the marginalia in the complete works of Kant, which have been made available in the meantime (Van Hulle and Nixon 2013, 137–43). The manuscripts might, indeed, provide evidence of hidden intertextual relations not apparent in the published texts, but the line of argument revealed by this evidence has to be established through a convincing reading of the published texts.

An example of this kind might be found in the manuscripts to *Worstward Ho*. Here, in an early draft, Beckett uses the words 'all unveiled' (van der Weel and Hisgen 1998, 255). He then excises this word in subsequent drafts replacing 'unveiled' with 'undimmed' (254). Beckett is also known to have read Heidegger and 'unveiling' is a word strongly associated with Heidegger's thought. The link is not definitive, as it does not absolutely guarantee that Beckett is here thinking of Heidegger. It points towards an argument that would have to be made, and that argument could only be made by paying close attention to the published text and showing how it might be said to engage with Heidegger in a meaningful way. This, in turn, if adequately achieved, would bring new light to our reading of one of Beckett's more difficult texts. Equally, intertextual relations might be revealed within the published texts. Chris Ackerley has long done this, discovering references to numerous texts (2010a; 2010b). The readings he develops make use of Beckett's finished work as well as the manuscripts. Clearly, then, rather than being antagonistic, the two approaches necessarily work together.

Yet what is the point of such intertextual readings? How do they add to our understanding, and so to our knowledge of Beckett's works? It might be useful to offer an example of a reading that does not yet exist.

How It Is is one of Beckett's more challenging works and, no doubt as a consequence, it has not yet been fully understood. This in turn means that the current generation of critics are beginning to turn more attention towards it. The work is divided into three parts, 'Before Pim', 'With Pim' and 'After Pim'. In part I, 'Bom' is moving forward through the mud. As the end of this part approaches, no major encounter has taken place as Bom moves forward. There is a sense of impending crisis, however, and mention is made of a cliff or abyss over which the narrator expects to fall. Then all of a sudden something changes: there is a 'swerve' in the line that Bom has taken, which till then had been straight: 'sudden swerve therefore left it's preferable' (*HII* 39). Soon after the swerve Bom encounters Pim, and part II is able to begin.

In the original French version, *Comment c'est*, the word used for 'swerve' is 'écart' (Beckett 1961, 73). In the original manuscript Beckett first writes 'brusque déviation' before changing this to 'brusque écart' (Beckett 2001, 392). He translates this as 'sudden swerve' when he makes his English translation (647). 'Swerve' is the English word and 'écart' is the French word normally used to translate 'clinamen' (which can also be translated as 'déviation' in French). 'Clinamen' is a word that is closely associated with the Roman philosopher Lucretius, who in *De Rerum Natura* describes the philosophical system of the Greek philosopher Epicurus (2007, 42). The clinamen or swerve is that which makes the universe possible. Before the swerve, which is unmotivated and uncaused, atoms are imagined falling uniformly in parallel lines. They fall together and nothing happens, then one atom swerves and collides with another, and from this a network of causal interactions spreads and amplifies, setting off a chain of becoming that develops into the universe we know.

The swerve is one small movement that changes everything. One might argue that in using the word 'swerve' here a clear intertextual reference is being made to the work of Lucretius and through him to Epicurus. The correspondence between the French and English versions of Beckett's texts and the evidence from the manuscripts add further weight. Yet, like the swerve itself, this is only a small movement. It can only become significant if it is shown that this small intertextual movement, this small contact between Beckett's text and another text, has effects within Beckett's texts and opens up the potential for new readings. While I will not attempt such a reading here I would assert that it might be developed: the swerve allows Bom to meet Pim, but it also has implications for the universe evoked by the work where we come to imagine other 'Boms' and 'Pims' moving in parallel, like the parallel falling atoms of Lucretius and Epicurus. It also offers an explanation for change within *How It Is*. In order to develop such a reading, however, one would need to trace these lines more precisely back to both *How It Is* and Lucretius. Yet such a reading does have the potential to change how we see Beckett's text.

Apparently small intertextual exchange can have profound effects on our understandings of Beckett's works as Beckett is aware of the implications of the systems to which he refers and, rather than simply supplying quotations in order to establish his own erudition, is interested in the logic or shape of those systems. The concept of the swerve as it is found in Lucretius is logically compatible with the descriptions of Bom's movements in part I of *How It Is*: it is not an idle reference.

Beckett and Geulincx

These ideas can be clarified by considering Beckett's intertextual relationship with the obscure seventeenth-century Flemish philosopher Arnold Geulincx. Beckett's notes to his reading of Geulincx were among the first made available to scholars through the Trinity Archives in 2001.

At that time only a few critics had attempted to engage with Beckett and Geulincx; the field as a whole had been hampered from doing so because no English language translation of Geulincx's *Ethics* was available. This point itself is no doubt telling with regard to Beckett's use of intertextual material. The work is obscure and only available in Latin, and there is something about obscurity that he finds, at least intuitively, interesting. He writes to Thomas MacGreevy in 1936:

> I have been reading Geulincx in TCD, without knowing why exactly. Perhaps because the text is so hard to come by. But that is rationalization & my instinct is right & the work worth doing, because of its saturation in the conviction that the sub specie aetenitatis [Latin: from the perspective of eternity] vision is the only excuse for remaining alive. He does not put out his eyes on that account, as Heraclites did & Rimbaud began to, nor like the terrified Berkeley repudiate them. One feels them very patiently turned outward, & without Schwärmerei [German: enthusiasm] turned in-ward. (*LSB I* 318–19)

From 2001–6, then, I worked with Han van Ruler (one of the few true experts in Geulincx's works in the world) and Martin Wilson (who had just translated Geulincx's shorter work *Metaphysica Vera*) in producing the first English translation (indeed the first full translation in any living language) of Geulincx's *Ethica*. The resultant book, *Arnold Geulincx' Ethics with Samuel Beckett's Notes*, includes the full text of the *Ethics* along with the full text of Beckett's notes to his reading of the *Ethics*, which were also, originally, in Latin (Geulincx 2006).

While there were many clear indications, even signposts, from Beckett, pointing towards Geulincx, in interviews and letters, it had been difficult for critics to adequately engage with him and consider the nature of the intertextual relation between them before this translation appeared. In *Samuel Beckett and the Philosophical Image* I develop readings drawn from what I found in these works, which I will touch on next. Matthew Feldman was consulting the archives in parallel and working from his own translation (2006b). Since that time David Tucker has developed a book-length reading of the relations between Beckett and Geulincx (2012).

When Beckett's notes to Geulincx themselves are examined it is clear that they are not 'notes' to his reading in the sense we would normally associate with this. He does not, for example, offer insight into his own understanding of what he has read. Nor does he summarize material in his own words in a way that would allow critics to discern the kind of understanding Beckett had developed of Geulincx through his reading of him. Rather, the notes to his reading of Geulincx amount to direct quotations from the original text. This is equally true of the 'Philosophy notes' and the 'Psychology notes'. The former are largely taken from Beckett's notes to the introductory work *A History of Philosophy* by Wilhelm Windelband, while the latter are notes to the works of a number of authors. Beckett's notes are quoted excerpts, so it is possible to see what parts of the text were particularly interesting to him, yet Beckett only very occasionally makes comments that could be taken to offer his own views on what is being said.

The 'Philosophy notes' to Windelband relate to an introductory text, yet it is clear from Beckett's correspondence that he also read many authors separately and in full (such as Kant, Geulincx, Spinoza, Malebranche, Berkeley, Schopenhauer and many others). Rather than talk in general terms about the 'Philosophy Notes', it is worth turning specifically to the notes on Geulincx. The first thing that strikes a reader when examining these notes in the Library at TCD is that three copies have been made. Firstly, there are the remnants of an original manuscript. Secondly, there is a first typed copy of the original manuscript, which is incomplete. Then there is a second typed copy of the first typed copy that includes additional material contained in the original manuscript.

This kind of detailed engagement shows that Beckett was interested in key elements of Geulincx's system. The passages copied are not simple highlights; rather, when read together they allow a reader to understand the key elements of Geulincx's system in summary. The first reader of the notes of course was Beckett himself, whom one might imagine returning to them to refamiliarise himself with Geulincx's system whenever he felt the need over the many years between reading the work at TCD and making use of it in his own works (such as the *Nouvelles*, or *Molloy*, which both came after World War II, or ten years after he first read Geulincx).

Occlusion

A certain kind of occlusion, or obscurity is part of the method Beckett adopts in developing his intertextual references. Writers at times make their references clearly – so that readers can easily pick up the references that are being made so as to follow them up – either by citing the name of the author they are referring to, or citing a fragment from their works in such a way that the reference might be verified. For example, when Faulkner calls a novel *The Sound and the Fury* it is apparent that he is referring to a passage from Shakespeare's *Macbeth*, one indeed that can be directly applied to a reading of Faulkner's novel ("[Life] is a tale/Told by an idiot, full of sound and fury/ Signifying nothing", Act 5, Scene 5, lines 17–28). In contrast, Beckett reveals in *Molloy* that:

> I [...] loved the image of old Geulincx, dead young, who left me free, on the black boat of Ulysses, to crawl toward the East, along the deck. That is a great measure of freedom, for him who has not the pioneering spirit. (*Mo* 50; see also Chapter 12)

While Beckett refers directly to two proper names, Geulincx and Ulysses, the reference remains obscure. So obscure, in fact, that a German translator of *Molloy*, Dr Franzen sought an explanation. Beckett was quick to offer one in a letter of reply:

> This passage is suggested (a) by a passage in the *Ethics* of Geulincx where he compares human freedom to that of a man, on board a boat carrying him irresistibly westward, free to move eastward within the limits of the boat itself, as far as the stern; and (b) by Ulysses' relation in Dante (Inf. 26) of his second voyage (a medieval tradition) to and beyond the Pillars of Hercules, his shipwreck and death [...] I imagine a member of the crew who does not share the adventurous spirit of Ulysses and is at least at liberty to crawl homewards [...] along the brief deck. (Beckett 1984a)

Franzen replied in turn, in dismay, that these were allusions no reader was likely to understand. Such allusions, indeed, require critical interpretation operating at a degree of detail in order to be understood. Whereas there is a direct relation between Faulkner's allusion and the meaning of the short passage from Shakespeare alluded to – one of the narrators, Benji, has the mental age of a small boy and so is 'an idiot', and the question of what things might mean, if they mean anything, is a central concern of the novel – there are steps missing in Beckett's allusions, even when the allusion seems clear and direct. The gaps more or less require us to revisit the text of the original and to know what surrounds the passage alluded to as well as the passage itself.

One way of considering what is at stake in the particular use Beckett makes of intertextual material is to refer back to his own theories of aesthetic method, which are expounded in a number of places in short texts. One of the most famous of these is *Three Dialogues with Georges Duthuit*. In addition there is other material related to this, such as Beckett's other essays on the van Veldes and his letters to Georges Duthuit (see *Dis* and *LSB II*). Taken together these can be read as developing a theory of 'non-relation' in art, or an art in 'the absence of relation'. Whereas art has always worked by leading the reader or viewer to particular relations, Beckett talks about a new art that would refuse to do this. He writes to Duthuit in 1949, while they are working on the *Three Dialogues*:

> For me Bram's painting owes nothing to these feeble consolations. It is new because it is the first to repudiate relation in all these forms. It is not the relation with this or that order of opposite that it refuses, but the state of being in relation as such, the state of being in front of. We have waited a long time for an artist who is brave enough, is at ease enough with the great tornadoes of intuition, to grasp that the break with the outside world entails the break with the inside world, that there are no replacement relations for naive relations, that what are called outside and inside are one and the same. I am not saying that he makes no attempt to reconnect. What matters is that he does not succeed. His painting is, if you will, the impossibility of reconnecting. There is, if you like, refusal and refusal to accept refusal. (*LSB II* 140, see also Gontarski and Uhlmann 2006, 6)

Deliberately leaving gaps between the elements that are related, or between the text and the intertext, then, seems to be part of Beckett's artistic method. This does not mean there is no relation between the text and the intertext, however. Rather, the relation becomes hidden or occluded. It forces the reader to think and to work hard in attempting to leap over the gaps that have been left in the text. This is one explanation for the ongoing power of a text like *Waiting for Godot*. It seems to point towards possible allegorical readings but does not allow us to definitively claim that they are there. Instead it calls on us to question those readings themselves. To offer some banal examples: is Godot God? If so, what is the meaning of waiting? If not, what is the meaning of waiting? Or is Godot simply hope? If so, what is the meaning of waiting? The lines of interpretation, because they are not complete within the text, open out into questions that will differ slightly from reader to reader. The task of the critic is to examine potential readings and establish elements that are being drawn together without being completely related and often this is done by developing sound arguments for intertextual references.

Images of Ideas

There are other possible ways of approaching Beckett's use of intertextual material. One of the most important involves considering how Beckett makes use of 'images' drawn from the works he engages with. James Knowlson, Ruby Cohn and others have established that Beckett would often make use of images drawn from the visual arts within his works. The most famous example of this is a painting by the German Romantic Caspar David Friedrich called 'Two Men Contemplating the Moon'. Beckett told Cohn that he had used this image when he was writing *Waiting for Godot* and that the moon that rises at the end of each act allows him to recreate this image on stage (Knowlson 1996, 256–8).

In *Samuel Beckett and the Philosophical Image* I argue that Beckett adopts a similar approach when working with philosophy. The French philosopher Michèle Le Doeuff has argued that when philosophers come to a gap within their system they tend to cover this gap, or connect the two sides of this gap, by using images or metaphors, which are often borrowed from literature. She gives the example of the 'island of reason', which begins in a twelfth-century Andalusian philosophical novel by Ibn Tufayl called *Riçala* before finding its way into English philosophy through the work of Francis Bacon in the early seventeenth century before returning to literature with Daniel Defoe's *Robinson Crusoe* in the early eighteenth century before in turn being adapted by the German philosopher Immanuel Kant (Le Doeuff 1989, 9–19).

Not only is the image clearly borrowed from one domain and made use of in another, she argues, but crucial elements of the ideas that adhere to the image are also carried across with it. Further, such images are important for Le Doeuff because the relations they convey are unstable or exceed clear links (that is, they are able to be interpreted in various ways), and this lends a measure of flexibility to the philosophical system. Such flexibility is necessary to the survival of such systems that would otherwise be unable to weather serious critique (Le Doeuff 1989, 1–9).

Le Doeuff shows how such images, even when they are used without attribution, carry elements of a problematic that remains common throughout all the works. She then suggests that locating the source of the image is important because it serves to unlock some of the power of the image by adding to our potential to analyse it. So images in philosophy betray gaps, and occlude sources, but are also a source of potential. They carry the potential of deeper understanding once uncovered and interpreted.

This occurs in Beckett's use of Geulincx: the image of 'autology', a term invented by Geulincx, relates to the image of the 'cogito' developed by Descartes, but whereas Descartes imagines a self cut off from all other sensations and reduced to that of which it is certain, an I that thinks, Geulincx imagines a self that is similarly cut off from the world but that is reduced to the sole certainty of an I that does not know, that is ignorant of everything. Such an image of a self that does not know dominates *The Unnamable* but also appears throughout Beckett's postwar works. Rather than 'I think therefore I am' we have 'I think, I do not know'. Other images are also apparent; the rocking chair that recurs in many Beckett works including *Murphy*, *Film*, and *Rockaby* can be traced to Geulincx's image of the cradle in which we are helpless infants, crying so that we might be rocked by the hand of God, though in Geulincx's image the baby crying to be rocked is the would-be suicide who is only able to die because God allows that our will is sometimes in accordance with His (Uhlmann 2006, 64–85).

It is clear in closely reading Beckett that sometimes slight references, or images, if drawn back to their sources (the intertext) can set up a kind of swerve that alters how we read Beckett's text. In short, possessing knowledge of such intertextual references allows us to develop different readings, readings that open out our understanding of Beckett's works.

Many critics have made contributions to our understanding of Beckett's works by convincingly demonstrating that Beckett is making allusions to specific texts. Chris Ackerley's labours of annotation are particularly useful with regard to *Murphy* and *Watt*, and his work with Gontarski is also a valuable reference tool. Ruby Cohn has also provided numerous clues, along with James Knowlson, who like Cohn was often alerted to these clues by Beckett himself. The project of publishing Beckett's letters has added considerably to this, as has the publication of the notes to his library, the description of the 'Philosophy notes' and the 'Psychology notes' and other notebooks such as the *'Dream' Notebook* edited by John Pilling, and the ongoing project, led by Dirk Van Hulle and Mark Nixon, of publishing Beckett's archival material and manuscripts. Such heavy lifting allows others to follow and consider with more precision what references Beckett is making, and what effects those references have on our understanding of the works.

A good deal of work remains to be done, however, as the newly available material provides tools for the critics who follow. An important task for these critics will be to develop new readings based on evidence brought to light by the endeavours of the critics who have preceded them.

Firstly, such new, or deepened lines of connection need to be demonstrated with reference to available material and particular focus on the published texts. Secondly, the critic's task will be to ask to what extent these interactions change, however slightly, what has been seen in the texts before. This involves following the consequences of a worldview or concept. It would amount to a swerve that alters the angle of our approach.

These are not the only ways in which Beckett's works can be approached, of course. Nor are relations to philosophy the only ones that need to be explored. There are any number of other traditions that have been neglected or contain areas that remain underexplored: mathematics and science, politics, the occult, the human sciences, the visual and performing arts and various literary traditions for example. In every case the method of not simply resting within a fragment in order to understand the reference, but of instead following the line of logic being referred to will be important. For example, it is clear that Beckett not only makes reference to mathematics, or geometry, but that the implications of the logic they contain affects those works throughout. The critics who will contribute most to our understanding of these kinds of interactions will attempt to master the fields with which they see Beckett engaging and bring a clearer understanding of the nature of those domains back to the field of Beckett studies.

9

SAM SLOTE

Bilingual Beckett
Beyond the Linguistic Turn

In 1956 Beckett gifted the *Trinity News* with the first publication of *From an Abandoned Work*, which appeared in the 7 June issue. Upon seeing it in print, he was less than happy with their editorial mangling; on 2 July he groused to H. O. White, '*Trinity News* made a great hames of my text with their unspeakable paragraphs and varsity punctuation' (*LSB II* 629). Adding to the newspaper's misrepresentation of Beckett's text, the final paragraph of an accompanying, unsigned biographical article stated that *From an Abandoned Work* is also known as 'Texte pour rien' and 'is Beckett's latest work. Like all his books except *Murphy*, it is in French. French has, in fact, become his native tongue. His writing is illegible in any language' ('The Man Himself', *Trinity News*, 7 June 1956, 5). While Beckett had indeed turned to writing in French after the war (although, apparently unbeknownst to the staff of the *Trinity News*, he had written works beyond *Murphy* in English), *From an Abandoned Work* marked a countervailing turn back to English and is not one of the (plural) *Textes pour rien*, which were written in French. Beckett himself described this work, in a note appended to a fair copy manuscript, as 'the first text written directly in English since *Watt*' (qtd. in Gontarski 1995, xiv). The fact that this was written in English hardly meant that Beckett had abandoned French; rather, it illustrates how Beckett's linguistic turn is more akin to a series of blurry zigzags. A turn, linguistic or otherwise, implies a sense of determined direction, a destination as it were, and Beckett's linguistic turn has anything but; as the narrator of *From an Abandoned Work* states, 'I have never in my life been on my way anywhere, but simply on my way' (*TFN* 57).

In two places *From an Abandoned Work* subtly indicates that it is a text written in English. At one point the narrator ponders the German word *Schimmel*, 'nice word, for an English speaker' (*TFN* 58). And the text ends with the exclamation 'awful English this' (*TFN* 65), a comment that all but invites a metatextual reading. The subsequent French translation – by Ludovic and Agnès Janvier, with Beckett's active collaboration[1] – handles these two moments differently. Apropos the *Schimmel,* the French translation preserves the Anglophone sensibility by noting that the German word is a 'joli mot, pour une oreille anglaise' (Beckett 1972, 13). The idiomatic switch to an 'English ear' as opposed to an 'English speaker' is not without consequence. An Irishman might well be an English speaker, but he would not have an English ear. In distinction, the 'awful English' departs from the Anglosphere in its translation as 'quel français'; this phrase is followed by a further qualification absent from the English, 'j'espère que personne ne le lira' (30). Here, the self-conscious criticism is transposed to the target language but is accompanied by an additional self-denigration, the wish that the text remain unread (if not untranslated). The French translation goes on, on its own way, apart from the English.

The genesis and development of *From an Abandoned Work* is not without complication but might afford a clue to explain Beckett's (incomplete) reversion to English. On 20 January 1954, he writes to Jérôme Lindon that he has a 'false start', distinct from the *Textes pour rien,* that is oxymoronically 'en bonne voie' ['well on the way'] (*LSB II* 446). The following month, Barney Rosset wrote Beckett to encourage him to return to writing in English: 'I have been wondering if you would not get almost the freshness of turning to doing something in English which you must have gotten when you first seriously took to writing in French' (letter of 5 February; qtd. in Gontarski 1995, xiv). Beckett replied: 'I thought myself of trying again in English, but it's only evading the issue like everything else I try. [...] It's hard to go on with everything loathed and repudiated as soon as formulated and in the act of formulation and before formulation' (letter of 11 February; *LSB II* 456–7). The reply suggests that Beckett had already returned to English and that the text 'en bonne voie' referred to in the letter to Lindon is (or would become) *From an Abandoned Work.* This text's existence seems to be confirmed in a letter to Pamela Mitchell of 6 April when he informs her that he has reverted to writing in English to 'pass the time' (qtd. in Pilling 2007, 178). As the narrator of the piece has it, he is not on his way to anywhere in particular, simply still 'on the way'.

In any case, the switch back to English prose was as much an aporia as a fresh new start. It is as if he began *From an Abandoned Work* so that he could abandon English one more time. John Pilling has investigated the varied resonances of forlorn archness announced in the title *From an Abandoned Work.* The text as initially published in the *Trinity News* is an excerpt from a longer piece, in a notebook inscribed 'For Tara MacGowran', and represents about one half of that draft (Pilling 2007, 174). However, after the mangled first publication, Beckett continued to revise it further, with both excisions and additions, as well as undoing the 'varsity punctuation', for its publication by Faber in 1958. Such revisions extended also into the French translation, 'j'espère que personne ne le lira'. 'This extra material testifies to Beckett's commitment to continuance of a text not obviously going anywhere' (175). *From an Abandoned Work* began as one thing and then became another, a false start that temporarily led somewhere else, which is, more or less, exactly what happens with all the individual works across the bilingual œuvre. The problem is, *pace* the editorialising of the *Trinity News*, that Beckett's works are legible, all too legible, across two languages.

Continuing Aporia by Other Means

This small example of translation and progression and aporia in *From an Abandoned Work* indicates a larger point apropos Beckett's bilingual œuvre. Shuttling between and translating across languages allows for a kind of atelic continuation by other means. A stark example of translinguistic continuation comes with the writing, in early 1946, of a story initially entitled 'Suite'. After writing in English for twenty-nine pages, Beckett drew a horizontal line in the manuscript and continued the story in French and then renamed it 'La Fin' (Knowlson 1996, 358). Begun in English, 'Suite' continued in French as an 'end' that let Beckett go on in a different language. In 1954, Richard Seaver, in collaboration with Beckett, translated 'La Fin' (back) into English as 'The End'. In 1960 Beckett, alone, substantially reworked the English version for republication but retained the acknowledgement for Seaver (Dukes 2000, 5).[2]

But this seemingly decisive turn was not without precedence. Prior to 'Suite'/'La Fin' Beckett had already switched to French as the primary language for his poetic composition. On 3 April 1938, he wrote MacGreevy: 'I have the feeling that any poems there may happen to be in the future will be in French' (*LSB I* 614). We see this shift with the sequence 'Poèmes 37–39', which were only published after the war, in *Les Temps modernes*, in November 1946. An English version of one of these poems, 'Dieppe', was published in the *Irish Times* on 9 June 1945, making it the first of these poems to appear in print. Beckett claimed it was first written in French although this claim is impossible to substantiate (2012, 384).

Even before the 'Poèmes 37–39', Beckett wrote poetry in French, with 'Tristesse Janale' (1930) and 'Ce n'est au pélican' as well as other small efforts such as the 'Petit sot' poems (see Knowlson 1996, 294–5) and the essay 'Les Deux besoins'. And, of course, Beckett had worked as a translator, beginning with the translation of Joyce's 'Anna Livia Plurabelle' into French in 1930[3] and translations of Rimbaud and others (see Mooney 2011, 47–73). In her study of the genesis of Beckett's bilingual aesthetic, Chiara

Montini aptly labels Beckett's pre-war work as 'La monolinguisme polyglotte' (2007, 24). Initially, Beckett used foreign languages in his works as a means of enriching them through a broad, even baroque, reservoir of meanings and allusions and styles, but beginning with the 'Poèmes 37–39' and *Murphy*, this polyglot monolingualism evinces a countervailing tendency towards simplification (Montini 2007, 24). Seán Lawlor and John Pilling argue that the 'Poèmes 37–39' 'adopt a deliberate simplification and refinement of means and method' (Beckett 2012, 373). In other words, certain traits and tendencies of the postwar French prose – the attenuation of style – had already begun with the pre-war French poetry.

Many of the terms by which Beckett's bilingual œuvre have been traditionally construed derive from claims made in Beckett's so-called German letter to Axel Kaun of 9 July 1937. The fact that this letter is written in a language other than English is not irrelevant to the larger points that Beckett is striving to make. Beckett expresses to Kaun his frustration with English at precisely the time he has switched to French for his poetry: 'It is indeed getting more and more difficult, even pointless, for me to write in formal English. And more and more my language appears to me like a veil which one has to tear apart in order to get at those things (or the nothingness) lying behind it' (*LSB I* 518). The letter ends with Beckett proclaiming a desire 'to violate a foreign language as involuntarily as, with knowledge and intention, I would like to do against my own language, and – Deo juvante – shall do' (*LSB I* 520). The immediate occasion of the letter is Kaun's request for Beckett to translate some of Joachim Ringelnatz's poetry into English.[4] Beckett begins the letter by stating that Ringelnatz accords with Goethe's dictum that it is '*better to write NOTHING than not to write*' (*LSB I* 517; emphasis in the original).[5] Beckett conflates the desire to violate his native language with the practice of writing nothingness, that is, using language against itself. Perhaps the key line in this letter in terms of the bilingual œuvre comes when Beckett characterises his own provisional attempts to translate his poetry; Beckett mentions the 'co-efficient of deterioration' that is inevitable with translation (*LSB I* 517). Beckett's bilingualism is thus perhaps a means of writing such a coefficient of deterioration *natively*, a means of violating both English and French *à la fois*.

Watt is the key transitional text between Beckett's polyglot monolingualism and his bilingualism. The immediate circumstances for the novel's composition were famously difficult and the manuscript bears traces of its tortuous composition in Roussillon, an enclave suspended between boredom and the madness of war. The manuscript itself is littered with doodles and all manner of erasures, thereby testifying to the difficulty of its strangled composition (see Hayman 1999). As Ann Beer has demonstrated, the manuscript contains some marginal notes in French (1985, 51). Beyond such paratextual matters, the text itself evinces numerous moments of linguistic dissatisfaction and a straining to achieve a coefficient of deterioration. Watt's incessant attempts to rationalise and codify the uncertainties of his tiny world inevitably aggravate that world's madness and uncertainties. Even Watt's uncertainty is itself uncertain: 'As there seemed no measure between what Watt could understand, and what he could not, so there seemed none between what he deemed certain, and what he deemed doubtful' (W 112–13). One means of conveying this uncertainty is the prevalence of French echoes, such as 'facultative stop' (13) (after *arrt facultatif*). Ann Beer has shown that these Gallicisms were predominantly introduced in the later stages of writing and in many cases these revised more conventionally English phrasings (1985, 52).

While sensitive to the differences between the French and English versions of Beckett's texts, Christopher Ricks valorises the English versions as being more amenable for Beckett's purposes: 'As often in Beckett, his original French reads like a highly talented translation of a work of genius, and not the thing itself' (1993, 4).[6] Ricks's phrasing indicates a potential flaw in his argument: following from the Kaun letter, perhaps the way to get at 'the thing itself' is to 'tear apart' (*LSB I* 518) language, that is, to make language foreign. Perhaps the semblance of translation is essential for Beckett's purposes across the bilingual œuvre. Indeed, in many places the stilted and stunted language of *Watt* makes it read like a translation. In *Watt*, Beckett writes in a language that is *not quite* English, an English inflected by French. This opens Beckett up to bilingualism not simply in the sense that he is turning away from English and towards French (that is, his linguistic vector is not straightforward and teleological), but rather, with the tendency towards bilingualism Beckett moves to writing in something that is neither English nor French.

From a Literature of the Unword to Linguistic Atopia

After the war, after 'Suite'/'La Fin', Beckett switches to French, for a time, as the language of composition for his prose. As he wrote George Reavey on 15 December 1946: 'I do not think I shall write very much in English in the future' (*LSB II* 48). Over the years he proffered various explanations, with varying degrees of disingenuousness, for this shift. At one side of the archness scale is the lengthy narrative provided in a contributor's note for *Transition 48*:

> Samuel Beckett is a Dublin poet and novelist who, after long years of residence in France has adopted the French language as his working medium.

Invited to give some account of his reasons for now writing in French, rather than in his native language, he replied that he would be happy to do so and seemed to have some views on the subject. [...] Some considerable time later [...] he confessed at last in a strong or rather weak Dublin accent: '*Pour faire remarquer moi*'. Despite this undoubtedly original syntactical usage of his adopted tongue, Beckett has nevertheless contributed to such French reviews as *Les Temps Modernes, Fontaine,* etc. Any mention here of his English-language writings would, we feel, be out of place despite their indisputably excellent quality. ('Notes about contributors', *Transition* 48.2 [June 1948]: 147)

If anything draws attention to Beckett, it is this extravagant little story, which is itself in English, the better to highlight the imperfect French of the statement '*Pour faire remarquer moi*' (properly, 'Pour me faire remarquer'), itself uttered in a non-English accent. The 'etc.' is more aspirational than actual since, at this time, *Les Temps modernes* and *Fontaine* were the only venues that had published his French work.[7] The 'advertisement for himself' resides in the contributor's note itself, an entirely apposite strategy considering the genre of such notes, and not necessarily in the change of languages.

Beckett's later explanations, while hardly isomorphic, do seem to partake of at least some of the spirit of the letter to Kaun. As Beckett remarked to Israel Shenker, 'It was a different experience from writing in English. It was more exciting for me – writing in French' (qtd. in Knowlson 1996, 357). If French was more exciting, then the turn to that language could also be explained in part by an increasing revulsion towards English; which Beckett described in a letter to Duthuit as a 'Horrible language, which I still know too well' (letter of [?28 June 1949], *LSB II* 170). His most cited explanation, to Niklaus Gessner, 'en français c'est plus facile d'écrire sans style' (1957, 32)[8] can be read as an affront to that particular tradition that champions the *soi-disant* 'génie de la langue française' (see Morin 2009, 59–60). And, indeed, this claim is not entirely true since even if Beckett refrains from a Racinian refinement, his French prose, at least from the 1950s, is highly idiomatic and replete with Parisian slang.

Another explanation, this time to Hans Naumann, more closely reprises certain ideas from the Kaun letter:

> Since 1945 I have written only in French. Why this change? It was not deliberate. It was in order to change, to see, nothing more complicated than that, in appearance at least. [...] I will all the same give you one clue: the need to be ill equipped [le besoin d'être mal armé]. (*LSB II* 462, 464)

Beckett's rationale for changing languages is to impoverish his arsenal of expression, yet by expressing this sentiment in French he allows for a reference to Mallarmé, a poet not unconcerned with tending towards a writing that would 'authentiquer le silence' ('Le Mystère dans les lettres' in Mallarmé 2003, 234).

In the letter to Naumann, Beckett also mentions Fritz Mauthner's *Beiträge zur einer Kritik der Sprache*, which he states had 'greatly impressed me' (*LSB II* 465). He first read this book in the 1930s for Joyce (Van Hulle 1999, 58–9; 2008a, 112–13) and *Sprachskepsis* also informs the Kaun letter, as Dirk Van Hulle has shown (147): 'On the road toward this, for me, very desirable literature of the non-word, some form of nominalistic irony can of course be a necessary phase' (*LSB I* 520). Beckett's desired destination is this 'literature of the unword', an authenticable silence, and the Mallarméan distrust of the word that stains this silence.[9] Mauthner argues that language is utterly incommensurable with the world and is thus insufficient for knowledge: 'Epistemological skepticism is turned into a mysticism of silence. Truth is tautology, the world eludes us, we are left with language alone, and language which cannot grasp a thing, not even itself, is not worth while being spoken anymore' (Weiler 1958, 85). The 'literature of the unword' is a literature that tends towards silence, in whatever language it chooses.

The general trait shared by all Beckett's explanations (or pseudo-explanations) for his move to French is that they involve internal, aesthetic considerations, a desire towards attenuation. Stephen Stacey has provocatively suggested that external, pragmatic considerations are not irrelevant. In 1946, when Beckett switched to French for 'Suite'/'La Fin', there was no market for English-language prose in France. To be sure, such a market did exist in France before the war and it did eventually resurface after the war (such as with the revived *Transition 48*, which was much more centred on Paris than its pre-war counterpart), but in the immediate aftermath it was lacking. Stacey writes: 'By writing in French, however, he changed his prospects markedly, opening up the possibility of publication with one of the French-language reviews whose flourishing was a defining feature of the literary scene in France following Liberation' (see Stacey 2013). Indeed, Beckett's proud listing in his contributor's note for *Transition 48* of the French journals to which he had contributed, and the others *in potentia*, seems to buttress such a possibility.

Even as Beckett turned to French after the war, he did not quite – contrary to his contributor's blurb for *Transition 48* or the editorial in the *Trinity News* or his comments to Reavey – turn his back on English. After the war he continued his work as a professional translator, translating French poetry as well as the UNESCO-funded *Anthology of Mexican Poetry*, which was undertaken in spite of Beckett's less-than-optimal Spanish (see Beckett 2012, 420–1). Already before the war, he began working with Alfred Péron on translating *Murphy* into French (Knowlson 1996, 290). More significantly, his poetry immediately after the war was bilingual; Sinéad Mooney characterises these as 'poems about the condition of being between or athwart languages and culture' (2011, 97). And so the 'frenzy of writing' (Knowlson 1996, 358) that began with the turn to French included within it a frenzy (albeit perhaps initially in a minor key) of translation. Translation was thus already enmeshed within Beckett's horizon as he wrote *Mercier et Camier* and the three novels *Molloy, Malone meurt,* and *L'Innommable*.

If *Watt* signalled Beckett's growing estrangement from English, then *Mercier et Camier* – his first novel in French, begun after 'Suite'/'La Fin' – marks a resistance to a full Francophone assimilation. *Mercier et Camier* seems to occupy a place that is neither quite Ireland nor France, but rather is suffused with elements of both.[10] Irish toponyms are prominent yet Mercier and Camier agonise over the quality of their French. In Mercier and Camier's trek, both Ireland and France are translocated. Indeed, Janvier calls Beckett's language a third term 'qui sert et brise à la fois, l'un par l'autre, l'anglais et le français' ['that simultaneously serves and breaks, the one by the other, English and French'] (1969, 47).

Unsatisfied with *Mercier et Camier*, Beckett withheld publication until 1970 when the pressures of being a recent Nobelist occasioned an imperative for fresh publications (Knowlson 1996, 574–5). Along with the publication of the French, he translated this work into English, a prospect that did not leave him entirely sanguine. Beckett reworked, abbreviated, and excised numerous passages in this translation. 'The omitted material varies from the odd line or phrase to two or three pages at a time, and amounts at a conservative estimate to a loss of about 12% of the material in the French version' (Connor 1989, 28). In terms of style, the translation is considerably sparer than the original, with colloquial expressions largely absent, and is thus somewhat closer to the style of the prose of the early 1970s. The considerable interval between the French composition and the English translation (the largest in Beckett's career) reveals another facet of the bilingual œuvre: across the two languages individual texts can occupy multiple spots within the arc of Beckett's writings.

If *Mercier et Camier*'s entry into the Anglosphere was belated, it was with the translation of *Molloy* into English that Beckett became a bilingual writer, creating a text twice over, in two languages. In translating *Molloy* Beckett began a return, of sorts, to English. With *Molloy* this task was ostensibly collaborative: Beckett enlisted the help of the South African writer Patrick Bowles. Bowles remarked that rather than simply translate, their aim was 'to write a new book in a second language' (1994, 33). However, Beckett extensively revised their joint translation. Starting with *Malone meurt* Beckett performed the work of translation himself, finding it easier than revising someone else's work (Knowlson 1996, 402). Beckett's own attitude towards revisiting his work for translation is less than enthusiastic. In 1953 he wrote to MacGreevy characterising his work with Bowles on *Molloy* as 'an indigestion of old work with all the adventure gone' (letter of 27 September, *LSB II* 407). He later complained to Alan Schneider that working on translations impeded him from doing new work (see Harmon 1998, 131; letter of 11 June 1962). Self-translation exacerbates the frustration of writing; another mode whereby going on and not going on can be coterminous.

Even before Beckett translated the three novels, the spectre of translation and translatability haunts these texts. The so-called Molloy country of Ballyba and environs is recognisably Irish by name and landscape.[11] Malone's hypothetical, exemplary cry 'Up the Republic!' (*MD* 63) - also rendered in English in the French version (Beckett 1951, 102) - suggests a different political resonance for a French reader than for an Irish one (especially considering that Beckett hails from Protestant, Ascendency stock). The three novels and their translations are a kind of linguistic atopia, neither French, nor English, nor Irish.

Leslie Hill remarked apropos Beckett's bilingual œuvre, 'If neither can claim authority over the other, both texts [...] become like versions of something else' (1990, 51). This claim works well over the three novels and their translations since there are numerous incidents across all six texts where each text indicates that it is a translation, even in those texts which were written first. This question of precedence is eminently apposite to the thematic concerns of the two parts of *Molloy*, where Molloy and Moran, in their respective quests, repeat and replay each other in varying ways. Through their repetitions it becomes increasingly difficult to assert unequivocally who, exactly, repeats whom. In a sense, they are all repetitions, each without a clear original.

Examples of the linguistic atopia of the bilingual œuvre exist in texts beyond the three novels. Karine Germoni and Pascale Sardin have demonstrated that, on the one hand, *Fin de partie* consistently exhibits English punctuation style and rhythm, whereas *Endgame* deploys a French sensibility of punctuation (2012, 346). Even if Beckett groused to MacGreevy on 3 July 1957 that in the translation of *Fin de partie* 'all the sharpness [is] gone, and the rhythms' (qtd. in Knowlson 1996, 438), the English does find new rhythms.

The translation of *L'Innommable* into *The Unnamable* culminates this phase of self-translation and aporia. Unsurprisingly, Beckett found translating this work to be much more difficult than the two previous novels.[12] If the Unnamable is trapped in language - 'I'm in words, made of words, others' words' (*Un* 104) - then he is trapped in more than one language. The

Unnamable is thus faced with saying 'it's not I' (*Un* 118, and passim), 'ce n'est pas moi' (Beckett 1953, 188) twice over because he is always already *not* himself in whatever language he might be spoken. The language in which he is spoken is not his and thus *he* – himself – is not his: he is 'othered' by a language that is other. He is other, in a language not his own, twice (see Slote 2011).

As originally published in French in 1953, the final line of *L'Innommable* read: 'il faut continuer, je vais continuer' (Beckett 1953, 213). The novel thus ends with an injunction – remarkably unequivocal for a novel concerned with aporia – to continue. And, indeed, the novel does continue – in a fashion – with its eventual English translation, which adds an additional element to this imperative to continue: 'you must go on, I can't go on. I'll go on' (*Un* 134). The statement of the inability to continue emerges in a continuation of the text in another language. For the 1971 printing of the French version, Beckett added in the Unnamable's ultimate aporia, thereby continuing the Unnamable yet again: 'il faut continuer, je ne peux pas continuer, je vais continuer' (1953, 213; see also *BDMP* 2). The translation into English both carries the Unnamable's progression forward as well as retracts that progression, which is itself a progression that was eventually worked back or retrofitted into the French text.

Self-Traducing, Self-Translation

The extreme involution of the self-conscious contemplation of the phenomenology of consciousness enacted twice over in *L'Innommable/The Unnamable*, in the French and in the English, is something of a dead end. Which is perhaps why, with the exception of some short prose, Beckett turns to the theatre after *The Unnamable* in another example of not going 'on my way anywhere, but simply on my way' (*TFN* 57). After *Fin de partie*, this change of genre entails another shift: with only a few exceptions, English becomes Beckett's predominant language for the stage even as he remains a French writer for most of his prose works after *The Unnamable*. There are examples of stunted theatre in French (the two abandoned *Fragments de théâtre*) and stunted prose in English (the *Texts for Nothing* and *From an Abandoned Work*). Sinéad Mooney posits, in part, a practical explanation for this linguistic bifurcation: although his career as a playwright began in French, his reputation in the Anglophone world led to Anglophone commissions and collaborators. Furthermore, Beckett's frustration with self-translation – as frequently evidenced in his letters to Alan Schneider, his American director – provide a compelling reason to write directly in English for his theatrical works (Mooney 2011, 163–5).

Most of Beckett's translations of his drama from English to French are not much better than serviceable, which is not to say that the issues of translation and self-translation are irrelevant to these works. With his theatre (and, later, his radio and television plays), Beckett begins again, in new genres in English (mostly). However, he eventually winds up in a similar place: Beckett returns to the Unnamable's aporetic involution with *Not I*, a play whose title had been the (English) Unnamable's refrain. In *Not I*, Mouth seems to continue on from the Unnamable, 'what she was trying ... what to try ... no matter ... keep on ...' (*KLT* 93). Mooney likens Mouth's predicament to that of a translator in that both are 'conveyors of other people's words' (2011, 194). Mouth is estranged in a language that is not hers, a language that is other and which reduces her to merely the instrument of speech. And so, if, after the war (if not before), Beckett switched to French for attenuation and diminution, then with the theatre he finds another means and mode of attenuation, an attenuation of the body, rendered (sometimes) in English. Like the turn to French, like the self-translation, the theatre affords Beckett impasse by other means.

The theatre was not Beckett's only mode of continuation past *The Unnamable*. There were spurts of prose for a number of years, including his last novel *Comment c'est/How It Is*. Beckett translated a portion of *Comment c'est* – a section optatively entitled 'From an Unabandoned Work' – even before he had finished drafting that text in French (Beckett 2001, xv). Later prose works evince greater complexity in terms of how Beckett progresses as a bilingual writer. Although initially drafted in English, Beckett began work on the French translation of *Company* soon after its drafting was completed. The French version was published first and so the English version was subsequently revised in light of the French *Compagnie* (Beckett 1993b, xx). Beckett's next work in prose was drafted first in French, *Mal vu mal dit*. Beckett switched back to English for his next work, *Worstward Ho*, a text he was himself unable to translate into French despite some efforts; he granted Edith Fournier permission to translate the text with the condition that it could only be published posthumously (see Slote 2005). While Beckett's final prose work, *Stirrings Still/Soubresauts*, was primarily drafted in English, he did switch between languages during the composition (see *BDMP1*) to such an extent that the claim in the French publication that it is 'Traduit de l'anglais par l'auteur' (Beckett 1989b, 28) is not entirely accurate.[13] For once, at or near the end, 'Oh all to end' (Beckett 1993b, 115), 'Oh tout finir' (Beckett 1989b, 28), translation and composition are cogenetically intertwined: unabandoned, to pass the time, until the time has passed.

NOTES

1 See Ludovic Janvier's account of Beckett's active involvement in the French translation of *Watt* and *From an Abandoned Work* (1990).
2 Seaver recounts his experiences as a translator working alongside Beckett in "Translating Beckett" (Seaver 2006, 104–7).
3 Megan Quigley has shown how Beckett and Alfred Péron's work on the translation of 'Anna Livia Plurabelle' was closer to the final published version (with its unwieldy phalanx of contributors) than has been previously acknowledged.
4 Two days before writing to Kaun, Beckett wrote MacGreevy that his real reason for declining the task of translating Ringelnatz was that he found his poetry 'worse than I thought' (qtd. in Knowlson 1996, 263).
5 From the final sentence of the first chapter of Goethe's *Elective Affinities* (*LSB I* 520 n. 4).
6 Pascale Sardin-Damestoy retorts that Beckett's French would only seem imperfect to a pedantic Anglophone reader (2002, 65).
7 Such aspiration was not misplaced since a year and a half earlier, in October 1946, Beckett had signed a contract with the publisher Bordas for the French *Murphy* and 'all future work in French and English (including translations)' (Knowlson 1996, 362). The dismal sales of the French *Murphy* scuttled this contract, although Beckett's ultimate extrication from Bordas entailed some difficult manoeuvrings (see Weller 2011, 115–17).
8 The German Diaries anticipate this comment: 'I boost the possibility of stylelessness in French, the pure communication' (qtd. in Knowlson 1996, 257).
9 After Beckett's much-cited lament, 'every word is like an unnecessary stain on silence and nothingness', from, of all places, 'Samuel Beckett Talks about Beckett', interview with John Gruen, *Vogue* (December 1969): 210.
10 For an example, see Mooney 2011, 103–4, for a discussion of how the character Monsieur Conaire implicates Padraic O'Conaire, a novelist of Irish exile.
11 'Ballyba itself may have its origins in Ballybetagh, a townland close to Kilternan' (O'Brien 1986, 349 n. 34).
12 On 30 July 1956, in a letter to MacGreevy, Beckett called translating *L'Innommable* 'an impossible job' (*LSB II* 640).
13 Perhaps Beckett claimed the text's primacy in English as a gesture to Barney Rosset, his American publisher and the person to whom the text is dedicated (Knowlson 1996, 699). For more on the bilingual composition of this work, see Van Hulle 2011b.

10

S. E. GONTARSKI

Samuel Beckett and the 'Idea' of Theatre
Performance through Artaud and Deleuze

> 'I should prefer the text not to appear in any form before production and not in book form until I have seen some rehearsals in London. It can't be definitive without actual work in the theatre.'
>
> Samuel Beckett about the text of *Happy Days*, 1961; qtd in Gontarski 2009, 153.

Through Artaud

At the entrance to the smaller, downstairs space of the Théâtre du Rond-Point, two oversized and dominating photographs hung, one of Antonin Artaud, the other of Samuel Beckett. From 1958 the theatre was directed by Jean-Louis Barrault (1910–94), from which post he was dismissed by Gaullist culture minister André Malraux during the student uprising in the spring of 1968, even as the Théâtre du Rond-Point under Barrault's direction was one of the theatres in Paris where the Compagnie Renault-Barrault introduced Parisians to what was then European avant-garde performance, including the plays of Samuel Beckett. The Artaud/Beckett conjunction or contrast was dear to Barrault and formative to his sensibility, but the two influences seemed to represent very different and opposed, if not contrary, strains in the emergence and development of twentieth-century European avant-garde theatre. On the one hand, Artaud advocated a performance-based theatre only loosely respectful of texts, which, he thought, tended to limit or still the dynamics, the motion of performance, advocating instead an infectious theatricality, one that should be uncontained and spread like contamination, like a plague, and feature what he called 'cruelty', intense emotions too often masked by polite, boulevard, or bourgeois theatre. On the other hand, Samuel Beckett, a literary if not lapidary playwright, heir both to Samuel Johnson and James Joyce, protective of his theatrical texts to the point of brooking no deviations from printed or typescript versions. Barrault managed, at least personally, to reconcile such tensions as he did others by working both at the house of Molière, the somewhat staid Comédie Française, and at a trio of more experimental national theatres that not only featured Beckett's work but where Beckett himself would serve something like an apprenticeship and develop into a man of the theatre: Théâtre du Rond-Point, Théâtre Marigny, and Théâtre de l'Odéon. That is, Beckett grew to be a man of the theatre through his interactions with such French avant-garde artists and theatres, to become, finally, a prominent director in his own right who saw in theatre a process of becoming and multiplicity that he had already accepted for his fiction, at least from *Watt* forward, and where the dominant mode of expression was not story per se, not plot, but image. Beckett's primary contact would be through the original director of *En attendant Godot*, Roger Blin, but Blin's influences grew to be Beckett's as well: Artaud, Copeau, and Barrault. As Beckett developed as a theatre artist, theatre would become less a matter of permanent, inviolable texts than a continuous process of movement and flow, and so, finally, of change. And as Beckett grew to be a committed man of theatre himself, such process, such flow came to be associated with the lived feel of existence, of which art was an image, its impact affect. In *What Is Philosophy?*, Gilles Deleuze and Félix Guattari would see such movement in Heraclitus, and then in Spinoza, Nietzsche, and Bergson as a plane of immanence and, further, they found in Artaud's *The Peyote Dance* a link between a 'plane of consciousness' and 'a limitless plane of immanence', which, however, 'also engenders hallucinations, erroneous perceptions, bad feelings' (Deleuze and Guattari 1995, 49). These are Artaud's cruel emotions, based on 'thoughts [...] that begin to exhibit snarls, screams, stammers; it talks in tongues and leads it to create, or to try to' (55). Artaud and finally Deleuze would celebrate such 'hallucinations', such 'snarls, screams', and 'erroneous perceptions' as the work of a madman, an idiot, or even a schizophrenic. For Beckett such fits and stammerings were not simply a gloss on Lucky's speech in *En attendant Godot*, but a way of doing theatre, a line of theatrical development that Deleuze will call immanent, a perspective, an emphasis, or an aesthetics, even, a process of thought and motion that would bring Beckett closer to (but never coeval with) the radical performativity Artaud advocated and find much of its fulfillment in his late plays, stuttering works like *Not I* and *Play*, for example, or 'hallucinatory' works like *What Where*, *That Time*, and *Footfalls*. Barrault's rapport, his rapprochement, his working between these dominant figures was shared with his audiences in the photographs as its members passed between these images into the theatre. The shift is evident in Beckett's own rapprochement with performativity, with an art that hesitates and stutters, and is much in evidence in his communication with publishers since they constitute something of a liminal space between stasis and flow, between literature and performance. He writes to Judith Schmidt of Grove Press about *Happy Days* as early as 18 May 1961 (which he was translating almost simultaneously into German and Italian so that he was juggling at least three versions of the play):

> I should prefer the text not to appear in any form before production and not in book form until I have seen some rehearsals in London [to be directed by Donald McWhinnie, but after Alan Schneider's New York premiere]. It can't be definitive without actual work in the theatre.[1]

But 'definitive' became less transcendent than immanent as he worked more directly in and with theatre; even after the appearance of the 'definitive' text from Grove Press and Faber and Faber, for example, Beckett turned his attention to the work afresh on two subsequent and separate occasions when he approached it as its director: *Glückliche Tage*, the *Happy Days* he directed in German in 1971 at the Werkstatt of Berlin's famed Schiller-Theatre and for which he kept a detailed *Regiebuch*, that is, a director's notebook which amounted to a rewriting, and the more famous production, his 1979 direction of Billie Whitelaw at London's Royal Court Theatre for which he also kept a detailed production notebook that James Knowlson edited and annotated as '*Happy Days*': *The Production Notebook of Samuel Beckett*, which appeared in 1985.

Much of Beckett's transition, a career shift, really, may have been unplanned and came through total theatrical immersion in the 1960s as he found it difficult to escape the demands of performance. He seems to have slipped into a directing career by accident, by default. Although Roger Blin acknowledged Beckett's increased involvement in performance from *En attendant Godot* to *Fin de partie*, the transformational year for Beckett's serious theatre work was post-Blin, probably in or around 1965 as he was preparing with Mariu Karmitz and Jean Ravel a film version of Jean-Marie Serreau's June 1964 version of 'Comédie'. The first of his works for which he received directorial credit was the 1966 Stuttgart telecast of *He, Joe* (broadcast by Süddeutscher Rundfunk, SDR, on his sixtieth birthday, 13 April 1966), after which he was off to London to oversee *Eh Joe*, with Jack MacGowran and Siân Phillips, nominally directed by Alan Gibson but infused with Beckett's Stuttgart experience (BBC 2, 4 July 1966): 'Really pleased with result' (qtd. in Ackerley and Gontarski 2006, 142). He also oversaw two works for solo voice, major vinyl recordings for Claddagh records: *MacGowran Speaking Beckett* (with John Beckett on the harmonium, Edward Beckett on flute, and Samuel Beckett on gong); and *MacGowran Reading Beckett's Poetry*.[2] He then rushed back to Paris to oversee Jean-Marie Serreau's series of one-acts at the Odéon, Théâtre de France, including a reprise of *Comédie*, *Va et vient*, and Beckett's own staging of Robert Pinget's *L'Hypothèse* with Pierre Chabert, originally presented at the Musée d'Art Moderne (18 October 1965). These opened 14 March.

Chabert may have witnessed something like the transformation, a conversion, an epiphanic moment for Beckett as he explains rehearsals for the Pinget play:

> Originally I had agreed to direct *Hypothesis*, a play with a single character. But faced with the daunting problems of this production, Pinget appealed to Beckett to attend rehearsals and to help us. Beckett came to a run-though of *Hypothesis* in the dance studio of the Scola Cantorum. After the run-through he made no comment except that he was willing to work on it, but first he had to find an 'idea' that would make the play more theatrical. In fact his mind was already working on this 'idea', and without another word he left as he had arrived. (1986, 117–18)

What Beckett observed in the rehearsals of *L'Hypothèse* was a character, Mortin, himself rehearsing hypotheses from a text alleged to have been destroyed and in conversation with it or between it and a projected image of some version of himself on a screen. What Beckett saw then was a theatre of dispersed or multiple character images; or character, an actor, the projected series of images, and the textual manifestation of Mortin. Chabert made the inevitable comparison to Beckett's earlier work in which he played the lead under Beckett's direction as well:

> In *Krapp* [*Krapp's Last Tape*], the protagonist, throughout the duration, talks to another version of himself, his recorded voice from thirty years earlier, thanks to a tape recorded. In *Hypothesis*, Mortin encounters, not the ghost of his father, [...], but his own image reflected as in a mirror, an image which never ceases to haunt and invade him – a dialogue made possible thanks to another technical medium, a moving film. (1986, 118)

The text itself, a typescript sitting on a desk, becomes a character in this performance, as it had been implicitly in Hamm's chronicles in *Fin de partie* but which will be featured materially in *Ohio Impromptu*, and becomes thus another mirror, or rather another branching or doubling. And again Chabert phrases this relationship thus:

> The manuscript demonstrates the relationship between Mortin and the writing, Mortin and his work, because without the manuscript, the author is "practically non-existent". Mortin has an umbilical attachment to his work. [...] The relationship between the character and the manuscript is a physical and visceral one. There is a sensual one, even in the contact. [...] The manuscript is an object, *a being*, a relation, *a body*. (1986, 122; emphasis added)

One might quibble some with Chabert's phrasing, which is hierarchical as it focuses on '*the* character' as the primary entity and so subordinates other manifestations as, say, reflections of an original, but, as the sole actor in the performance under Beckett's direction, he can be forgiven for seeing himself as the focal point, as a principal being, in traditional terms a character embodied by a live actor. In performance, however, being itself may finally be elusive, evade confinement and slip into becoming – that is, the movement, flow, or interchange between the live actor, the projected images, and the leaves of the text, which are gradually discarded to cover the stage and are finally burned. This visceral relationship with the text appears to have been 'the idea' that Beckett brought to the production, like that of Krapp with his tapes, and the voice of the projected image, unlike Krapp, Chabert reminds us, is intrusive,

> it breaks into his universe and its presence alone is a form of aggression. [...] It also makes it clear that he is himself the subject, the author about whom he is talking. [...] The form in which the image appears by surprise has a shattering effect in its filmic doubling of the character. (123)

Such an intrusive voice, projected as if exterior, a voice between interior and exterior, would feature in Beckett's own teleplay that he was writing at almost the same moment that he was reconceiving *L'Hypothèse*, *Eh Joe*, begun in earnest at Ussy on 13 April 1965. *The Hypothesis* itself then enacts the devaluing of the text in the performing of it, replaces the material text with its performance, even as its function is raised to that of material character – Artaud, thus, being simultaneously embraced and distanced, if not rejected.

Through Deleuze

If the conjunction between Beckett and Artaud seems, at casual glance, unlikely, another such might be that between Beckett and Gilles Deleuze, whom Beckett doubtless never read, although Deleuze was the apostle, after Nietzsche, of betweenness, which we might define, after Beckett, as a neitherness – that is, neither wholly of one nor of another, but partly of both, which, most simply, is Bergson's definition of the image itself, neither wholly physical nor wholly metaphysical. In his assessment of French cinéaste Jean-Luc Goddard, for instance, Deleuze stresses such in-betweenness, between sound and vision, between television and cinema, between image and text. This is Deleuze's critique of postwar cinema as a 'time image', which offers the perspective of a disinterested, bodiless perceiver and which, at its best, presents the pure flow of time, becoming. Such in-betweenness, admittedly, owes much to what French metaphysician Henri Bergson would call 'durée', and whose formulation of the image Deleuze essentially follows as something between matter and memory, as much material as immanence. As Deleuze reminds us in his essay on Beckett's teleplays, 'The Exhausted', an image is neither representation nor thing, but a process, a constant becoming, which, as it creates affect is the ultimate impact of art, not only in cinema, that is, but in other arts as well. Such process, an emphasis on flow and becoming, a perpetual in-betweenness, between stasis and movement, between text and image, suggests an incipient theory of theatre as well. Certainly, in Samuel Beckett's work – particularly his late work for theatre in which we find a preponderance of spectral figures, ghosts – what appears on stage as a something, a material object, is not always fully present, something not quite wholly material, nor quite immaterial or ethereal either, something in between presence and absence, sound and image, or text and image, between the real and surreal, an image between matter and spirit, Beckett himself is thus an artist in between, neither wholly of his time nor wholly of ours, say, fully neither, even as he is always, if partly, both.

The pacing May of *Footfalls* is a case in point: apparently a physical entity on stage, or at least we perceive an image in motion, she may not be there at all, or not fully there as the final short scene of the stage without her figure suggests. Spirit become light, say, as the assailing voice of *Eh Joe* would have it. Beckett's theatre is thus not about something, not a simulation of a known world; the image or images of the artistic creation are not images of something outside the work; they are *'that something itself'*, as he famously quipped in 1929 in reference to James Joyce's then titled 'Work in Progress' (*Dis* 27; emphasis in the original). Beckett's move into television reemphasized the imagistic nature of performance with bodiless narrators' voices near or contrary to those we see on the screen, offering narrative dislocations. Such a disembodied narrator of *What Where* tells us, for instance, that 'This is Bam', making Bam thus already an object other than the narrating voice of Bam, who apparently is himself plural already, a multiplicity. 'We are the last five', he tells us, the grammar sliding from singular, Bam, to the multiple, a voice that is a 'We' (*KLT* 153). At best, however, images of four characters appear, Bam, Bim, Bom, and Bem, the mysterious fifth, apparently 'Bum' if we follow through on the vowel sequence, only incipient or already dispatched. 'In the present as were we still', the voice continues, the subjunctive tense alerting us to the fact that this statement is contrary to fact (*KLT* 153). These are characters not there, voices from beyond the grave, the pattern of images coming and going, moving to and fro to an off stage fraught with possibility to receive 'the works'.

Such images with their narrative and visual disjunctions disrupt expected continuity and are part of or insight into the pure flow of time, what Deleuze calls the Plane of Immanence, perceptions always on the verge of becoming – that is, becoming other, something else, unsettling the received, that which we expect; they are thus a material bridge that generates affect, an emotional response not always specifiable or describable. Such a world as Beckett achieved is thus a virtual world that includes past and present, material figures, imagination, and memory; off stage or what appears to be empty space is thus a virtual whole, a nothing full of possibilities, including all possible actions and movements. In this regard Beckett's theatre runs contrary to that described by Peter Brook in his famous theatrical treatise, *The Empty Space*; for Beckett the stage is never empty. The fourth scene of *Footfalls* remains full of interpretive possibilities, opens those possibilities even further. It is always replete, full of potential meanings and worlds, of all the possibilities that theatre has to offer since it includes the whole of the past as well as the full potential to create new worlds. The space then is always already full; in short, it contains the process of the virtual, part of what Deleuze will call the Plane of Immanence. Beckett's plays do not represent a world of actuality, a world outside themselves, do not, in fact, represent at all, but offer images that make us feel, in their generated affect, the movement of existence, its flow, becoming, *durée*. Possibilities are not closed off by separating inside from outside, matter from spirit, present from past.

What too often frustrates readers or theatre-goers is precisely this resistance to representation that characterizes Beckett's art since most of us operate on the Plane of Transcendence that produces or alludes to an exterior to the artwork, the world we know and try to represent in art. This is the world of what Beckett calls the classical artist (*PTD* 81). For Deleuze the perceiving mind of a doubting Cartesian subject is a piece of ribbon that separates inside from outside, or is merely a membrane, as Beckett dubs it in *The Unnamable*, where the narrator calls himself a tympanum vibrating and in between, neither, like the ribbon, inside nor out but both in relation to the other. The Plane of Transcendence, or what Foucault has called an 'ethics of knowledge', is the struggle for grounding, a search for ultimate truths, say, that we are driven to obey. Who is Godot? What information is being solicited in *What Where*? What are the secrets being exchanged in *Come and Go*? These are, we might venture, exactly the wrong questions to ask of these works. The right question is to ask how they work, what sorts of affect they are generating, and what possible worlds they have led us into? The series of plateaus, perhaps 1,000, that Deleuze critiques in the book of that name, is an assault against such groundings, the stability of language included, as is Beckett's art. Transcendence is a human disease that

Samuel Beckett and the 'Idea' of Theatre

Deleuze calls 'interpretosis' and what the director of *Catastrophe* calls, 'This craze for explicitation. Every I dotted to death. Little gag. For God's sake!' (*CDW* 459) 'We're not beginning to ... to ... mean something,' asks Hamm. 'Mean something!' responds Clov, 'You and I mean something? Ah, that's a good one' (*E* 22) and they share a communal laugh over the possibility of transcendence, that they might be representative, part of a greater system, or a greater truth beyond images of themselves in performance, in process. The alternative to transcendence is to accept, even to love, simply what is; Deleuze's term like Foucault's is also an ethics, but, after Nietzsche, an 'ethics of the *amor fati*', the love of fate as necessity, or simply of what is.

One anecdote that Hamm tells has often been cited by critics but less than satisfactorily critiqued. The 'madman' that Hamm visits in the asylum is shown the beauty of the exterior, the corn, the herring fleet, from which the madman turns away appalled. Hamm's conclusion is that 'He alone had been spared' (*E* 41). Critics may point out the likely reference here to the visionary poet William Blake, but what or how the 'madman' has been spared is seldom parsed. One possibility is that he has been spared preoccupation with the requirements of a transcendent world, what Deleuze will call the illusion of transcendence, that will close and explain experience. Hamm's 'madman', this 'idiot', is thinking 'other', possible, alternative worlds. It may indeed be those alternative worlds that Hamm keeps asking Clov to find beyond the shelter. In Act II of *Waiting for Godot* the issue is put thus: 'We are all born mad. Some remain so' (*WFG* 77). Perhaps those are the saved, the parallel to the one thief on the cross. Hamm's position is evidently to pull the madman back from the end of the world. Hamm's position, his attitude (yes, seated) would resist the flow of alternatives, becomings, *durée*. Later Hamm concludes the prayer scene with an overt rejection of such transcendence, such 'ethics of knowledge'. Of a transcendental reality, God, he says, 'The bastard. He doesn't exist' (*E* 34). Perhaps Hamm too has been or might be spared, saved.

In his playlet of 1968 that Beckett designated as images of motion, *Come and Go*, we are denied access to information that would, if disclosed, shut down the process of thinking. Without that knowledge the process, the thinking, the generation of possibilities, alternatives, parallels the flow of movement on stage. Language is not so much devalued among the 128 (or so) words in this dramaticule since much of it is elegant and poetic. What is resisted is knowledge that would still movement and flow, freeze it, and end a process that Deleuze calls thinking or philosophy.

When American actress Jessica Tandy complained, first to director Alan Schneider and then, passing him by, directly to Samuel Beckett, that *Not I*'s suggested running time of twenty-three minutes rendered the work unintelligible to audiences, Beckett telegraphed back his now famous but oft misconstrued injunction, 'I'm not unduly concerned with intelligibility. I hope the piece may work on the nerves of the audience, not its intellect' (qtd. in Brater 1974, 200). If we take Beckett at his word and do not simply treat this comment as a dismissal of the actress or an admonition that she listen to her director, through whom, he told her, he would henceforth communicate, he is suggesting a theoretical position, a theory of theatre. Evidence for the latter may be found in his attitude about *Play*, which, similarly, should be staged at incomprehensible speed. Admittedly, many a director, Alan Schneider among them, have resisted. Beckett's instructions to Schneider were that '*Play* was to be played through twice without interruption and at a very fast pace, each time taking no longer than nine minutes' (Schneider 1986, 341); that is, eighteen minutes overall. The producers of the New York premiere, Richard Barr, Clinton Wilder, and, of all people, Edward Albee, threatened to drop the play from the programme if Schneider followed Beckett's instructions. Schneider capitulated, and wrote to Beckett for permission to slow the pace and eliminate the *da capo*:

> For the first and last time in my long relationship with Sam, I did something I despised myself for doing. I wrote to him, asking if we could try having his text spoken only once, more slowly. Instead of telling me to blast off, Sam offered us his reluctant permission. (341)

What then are we to make of such a neural approach to theatre that seems to put the emphasis on what Deleuze, writing *after* Beckett, will call 'pure affect' (Deleuze and Guattari 1995, 96). We can resist Beckett here, as Schneider's producers and, finally, Schneider himself did, or take him at his word; that is, this is how theatre works, not dealing with overall truths, but by demonstrating process and change, life as immanence even as it is materially rooted. 'Make sense who may', Beckett would conclude his final work for the theatre, *What Where*.

In these shorter plays Beckett's most radical artistic vision, his most revolutionary theories of theatre emerge. This brings us, moreover, to one of the most contentious questions in Beckett studies: the degree to which Beckett's work is representational at all, or, on the contrary, whether its persistent preoccupation is with resisting representation, or rather to focus on how slippery and artificial representations are as they are played amid the Plane of Immanence, the perpetual flow of being. That is, Beckett's art on stage or page is not a stand-in for another reality; it is that reality and more often than not 'virtual' in the Deleuzian sense of that term. Beckett's theatre is always a theatre of becoming, a decomposition moving toward recomposition, itself decomposing. It is a theatre of perpetual movement or flow, all comings and goings, a pulse that creates affect. Even as it often appears stationary or static, even amid the famous Beckettian pauses, images dominate, move, flow, become other, not representing a world that we already know, but perpetually creating new worlds. Bergson would call this 'durée', Deleuze 'becoming', Beckett simply art, or theatre. It is a theatre struggling to resist the world as we know it, struggling to resist conceptualizing our world and the condition of being since those are mere snapshots and not the process, becoming.

Praxis

While building her directorial reputation with the Royal Shakespeare Company (RSC), director Katie Mitchell, for one, turned her attention to Beckett, first with *Endgame* at the Donmar Warehouse in 1996 and then to a peripatetic evening of *Beckett Shorts* at the RSC's The Other Place in Stratford-upon-Avon the following year (22 October–13 November 1997): *Not I*, *Footfalls*, *That Time*, *A Piece of Monologue*, *Rockaby*, and, curiously, *Embers*, the 1959 radio play published with *Krapp's Last Tape* by Faber and Faber in 1959 to fill out a slim volume.[3] Of the coupling, the online *Telegraph* in its 'Critic's Choice' column opined that the plays had 'been yoked together to form a production that seems to last for several weeks', and for its European tour the evening was pared to four offerings. Be that as it may, Mitchell's theatrical conception was nothing short of audacious, and the *Telegraph* admitted that the shorts are 'staged in a series of dark rooms through which the promenading audience are shepherded like visitors to the underworld' (Spencer 1997).

Like Deborah Warner before her, American director JoAnne Akalaitis was all but banished to the cold for liberties she took with her 1984 staging of *Endgame* at Harvard University's American Repertory Theatre (ART), in this case Beckett himself shutting her out. She redeemed herself some twenty-four years later with *Beckett Shorts*, a quartet bound to generate attention in New York as much for the actor as either the director or playwright. Celebrated, revered, lionized dancer Mikhail Baryshnikov was featured in all four 'shorts', which opened in December 2007 at the New York Theatre Workshop. The grouping of four included a natural pair, the two mimes, 'Acts without Words I' and 'II', and an unusual linking of 'Rough for Theatre I' and the teleplay *Eh Joe*, now part of the accepted stage repertory with two recent, high profile productions. The two 'Acts without Words' are often paired, and Akalaitis took advantage of Baryshnikov's angelic grace in both, but the pairing of the second half of the evening highlighted the fact that the interrelationship or juxtaposition of the shorts cannot or should not be arbitrary. Beckett wrote to George Reavey on 1 September 1974, for instance: 'Have written a short piece (theatre): *That Time. Not I* family' (Brater 1987, 37). The emphasis in the new short was to be on listening not speaking. In *Not I*, he said, 'she talks'; in *That Time* 'he listens'. Because the later play was 'cut out of the same texture' as *Not I*, he did not want the two on a double bill (Brater 1987, 37). For Beckett at any rate, the image of this silent Listener clashed with that of Mouth's verbal assault in *Not I*, but Katie Mitchell evidently saw much more compatibility in the pairing than Beckett did, as did Akalaitis with hers.

Akalaitis tied her quirky evening of shorts together with a consistent set, but the decision to cover the stage in some six inches of sand made sense only for the first of the four plays. As *The New York Times* theatre critic Ben Brantley noted of Baryshnikov's performance, 'for the rest of the show you can feel good old physics tugging at feet that once took flight like no one else's' (19 December 2007). But more than gravity and age were at work on Baryshnikov who spent the evening trying to dance on a beach, and superb as the high concept desert landscape was for the first 'Act without Words' the sand made stage movement all but impossible for the three subsequent plays, and perhaps this was part of Akalaitis's point, to accent Winnie's observations in *Happy Days*, 'What a curse, mobility!' (*HD* 26). The wheelchair of 'Rough for Theatre I', for example, was immobilized, bogged down in the sand. Moreover, the eponymous Joe of *Eh Joe* could hardly shuffle about his room in his paranoid ballet to shut out prying eyes, real or imagined. But Akalaitis made something of a virtue of that handicap. Joe's movement was filmed and projected as a multiple set of images in a variety of sizes on a series of screens. In fact, this hybrid genre, live theatre, film, and 'live' film, a technique Atom Egoyan had used for his stage adaptation of *Eh Joe* and Beckett himself used for his *Hypothesis* was a central feature to all four plays, used not only to great effect individually but as a thread among the plays: multiple projected images and hence multiple simultaneous perspectives. Less successful was the decision to take the action outside that 'penny farthing hell you call your mind' (*ATF* 115) and to embody Joe's imaginings as a spot-lit woman. Karen Kandel spoke the lines of the text, assailing Joe and recounting the story not of herself but of another. Mercifully, the taunting suicide itself was neither filmed nor reenacted.

Such decisions and the addition of music by Philip Glass were the sort of theatrical latitude that caused such a fuss with her 1984 *Endgame*. But 'Act without Words I' was originally conceived and performed with music by John Beckett, which music was eventually repudiated by the collaborating Becketts. Overall, however, Akalaitis transformed an unlikely collection of short works into a contemporary, multi-imagistic, kaleidoscopic evening that overcame (for the most part) the self-imposed handicap of sand-enhanced gravity. As Brantley (2007) perceptively noted, 'This grounding of a winged dancer poignantly captures the harsh laws of Beckett's universe, where Mother Earth never stops pulling people toward the grave.' But the plays were about more than an aging Baryshnikov. They suggested Akalaitis's returning Beckett to his avant-garde roots with a production more or less traditional and thoroughly new. And of course this is how Beckett approached his own theatre. He invariably reconceived his plays as he began to work with them directly on stage. Writing to critic Ruby Cohn in September 1966 he noted of his slow slide into a full directing career:

> Rehearsing *Comédie* [*Play*] for Théâtre de France with new actors and in absence of director [Jean-Marie] Serreau in the States. Trying a new scenic set-up (spot on stage) to spare rehearsal ennui. Changing also 'Va et vient' ['Come and Go'] to flow. (UoR correspondence with Ruby Cohn, COH/021)

Legendary director Peter Brook was both more overt in his most recent Beckett offering – a sixty-five-minute theatrical evening of five of Beckett short works staged first in French at his Théâtre des Bouffes du Nord in October 2006 and then redirected in English for London's Young Vic in September 2007 – and more off the mark. Brook called his evening 'Fragments', a title that in English suggests a certain incompletion. Brook apparently took his title from his first French offering, *Fragment de Théâtre*, translated as *Rough for Theatre I* by Beckett, but Brook chose the English cognate for his British production as well; but what Brook calls 'Fragments' are of course five complete works: *Rough for Theatre I, Rockaby, Act without Words II, Come and Go*, and the short story that looks to all appearances like a poem on the page but which Beckett insisted was a story, 'neither', treated as a libretto by composer Morton Feldman. 'Pieces' may have maintained more of the spirit of the Beckettian short (as even *En attendant Godot* in its French incarnation is subtitled *un piece de théâtre*), and the term most often used in conjunction with collections of Beckett's short works, *Rockaby and Other Short Pieces*, for example. Nonetheless, Brook's evening of short plays featured talented Complicité (formerly Théâtre de Complicité) performers Marcello Magnim, Jozef Houben, and the versatile, elastic Kathryn Hunter to superb advantage. These are all theatre professionals used to stretching the material with which they work, and Brook and his collaborators stretched Beckett with a cross-gendered *Come and Go* and a *Rockaby* with neither rocking chair nor voice over, which alterations, some might argue, miss the point of both works, or rather adjust the spotlight from what Beckett was doing with these pieces to what Brook and collaborators were doing with them. Kathryn Hunter rocks on a straight-legged chair and speaks the whole text in *Rockaby* and so is more overtly both herself and the ghost of herself (and of her mother) than may at first appear in Beckett's conception. As she leaves the chair to address us and what was her self, she is a multiple, an afterimage of an earlier self. Are such reconceived, reconstituted productions still Beckett, one might ask, and answer quickly, of course they are, Beckett's characters, Beckett's poetry, Beckett's every detail remain. Well, not every detail, but what comes through, finally, is the compelling nature and power of the Beckettian images, the sculpted icons that are the core, the very stuff of Beckett's late, poetic theatre of images.

Beckett spent his creative life chipping away at the inessential in theatre and narrative to expose a pared down, haunting image through which he evoked a sensation. Story itself was often occluded or subverted and so often secondary at best in these short works. We never hear the secrets whispered among the three figures (he almost said women) in *Come and Go*. The story of *Play* is to be run through at such breakneck speed that the rehearsals horrified its original producer, Kenneth Tynan, artistic director of the fledgling National Theatre. Beckett's solution was not to slow the pace but to give the audience a second chance, to repeat the play exactly at nearly the original speed, *da capo*, something of an eternal return, we might add. Beckett's concern was less with the intelligibility of 'story' than with the image created and the affect evoked. As he wrote Schneider to deflect his persistent and wrongheaded questions, 'I no more know where she [Mouth in *Not I*] is or why than she does. All I know is in the text. "She" is purely a stage entity, part of a stage *image* and purveyor of a stage text. The rest is Ibsen' (Harmon 1998, 283; emphasis added). Such comments are not meant to suggest that the author does not know what his own art is about but rather that he has no idea of the significance his images release among audience members or readers. Theatre, at least as Beckett understood it, is not primarily a cerebral experience. Beckett was quite willing to cede such theatre of exposition to the likes of Ibsen, Shaw, and even Brecht in his more didactic works. Even the crafted artifact, W. B. Yeats's 'form as Grecian goldsmiths make / of hammered gold and gold enamelling' (1996, 103), is subservient to the direct expression of the thing, something closer to Eliot's 'heap of broken images' (1971, 135). The result is the least theatricalized, the barest of the Beckett 'shorts', 'Breath': no actors, no story, running time some twenty-three seconds.

This is neither slight nor absurd theatre as major theatrical directors and serious actors of our age continue to discover through performance. Discoveries are made through process, on the boards, in rehearsals, as Beckett himself discovered. This is what Chabert emphasizes as he concludes his essay on Beckett's directing Pinget, 'to relieve some of the tedium,

Beckett, with Pinget's agreement, made substantial cuts in the text. These cuts, which make the play easier to understand, also give a better balance to the different parts of the speech' (1986, 130–1); that is, 'In *Hypothesis* he was searching, experimenting, putting things in, taking them out' (131). In short, Beckett was functioning like a professional director, preoccupied with performance and its impact. The best of contemporary directors function in just this way, following what Chabert calls Beckett's 'perfect direction, combining invention with fidelity' (131). Through their attention to these late, powerfully imagistic works, through their eagerness to offer high profile, international productions of these later plays, major, contemporary directors, like those cited here, attest that these short works, slight as they at times appear, 'unreadable' as they often seem, resistant to paraphrasable meaning as they are, are every bit the measure of the great, more celebrated plays of the 1950s. Production after production has asserted that the Beckett late short works have depth and breadth for actors and audiences to explore and re-explore, and directors and actors are finding, like Beckett himself, 'the idea' of theatricality in them, even as that may swerve from what some might deem a more traditional (if finally static) theatrical 'idea'.

Appendix 10.1

Samuel Beckett, *metteur en scène*

In Paris

Robert Pinget's *L'Hypothèse*, with Pierre Chabert, Musée d'Art Moderne, 18 October 1965

Va et vient and Robert Pinget's *L'Hypothèse*, Odéon Théâtre de France, 28 February 1966 (Beckett uncredited for his own play but credited for the Pinget)

La Dernière bande, Théâtre Récamier, 29 April 1970

La Dernière bande with *Pas moi*, Théâtre d'Orsay (Petite Salle), April 1975

Pas with *Pas moi*, Théâtre d'Orsay, April 1978.

In Berlin at the Schiller-Theatre Werkstatt

Endspiel, 26 September 1967

Das letzte Band, 5 October 1969

Glückliche Tage, 17 September 1971

Warten auf Godot, 8 March 1975

Damals and *Tritte*, 1 October 1976

Spiel, 6 October 1978

Krapp's Last Tape (English), Akademie der Künste with the San Quentin Drama Workshop, rehearsals 10–27 September 1977

In London

Footfalls, Royal Court Theatre, May 1976

Happy Days, Royal Court Theatre, June 1979

Endgame, with the San Quentin Drama Workshop, Riverside Studios, May 1980

Waiting for Godot, with the San Quentin Drama Workshop; rehearsals at the Goodman Theatre, Chicago (November 1983 to January 1984), dir. Walter Asmus; Beckett joined the group at the Riverside Studios, London, (2 February 1984), and rehearsed the actors for ten days. Premiered at the Adelaide Arts Festival (13 March 1984)

Teleplays (all at Süddeutscher Rundfunk, Stuttgart; with date of broadcast)

He, Joe, dir. March 1966 (with Deryk Mendel and Nancy Illig), 13 April 1966

Geistertrio, dir. May–June 1977 (with Klaus Herm and Irmgard Först), 1 November 1977

Nur noch Gewolk, dir. May–June 1977 (with Klaus Herm and Kornelia Bose), 1 November 1977

He, Joe, dir. January 1979 (with Heinz Bennent and Irmgard Först), September 1979

Quadrat, I or II, dir. June 1981 (with Helfrid Foron, Juerg Hummel, Claudia Knupfer, and Suzanne Rehe), 8 October 1981

Nacht und Traüme, dir. October 1982, 19 May 1983

Was Wo, dir. June 1985, 13 April 1986

NOTES

1 Beckett's letter to Grove Press of 18 May 1961 (qtd in Gontarski 2009, 153) opens as follows: 'I shall soon begin to type final text of *Happy Days*. It will go off to you towards end of month. At the same time as to you I shall give copies to McWhinnie, who is to direct London production probably at Royal Court, and to Tophoven for German translation. Copies must also go as soon as possible to Suhrkamp and [Editore] Einaudi. I am not satisfied with it, but cannot bring it any further. I think and hope it is understood that Grove has world rights to this play.' Beckett would 'bring it [...] further' by working directly on stage, and such theatrical testing before publication became his preferred pattern for work written for theatre. For example, he wrote on 24 November 1963 to Barney Rosset: 'I realize I can't establish definitive text of *Play* without a certain number of rehearsals. These should begin with [French director Jean-Marie] Serreau next month. Alan's [Schneider's] text will certainly need correction. Not the lines but the stage directions. London rehearsals begin on March 9th [1964].' In fact, after having read proofs for *Play*, Beckett delayed its American publication so that he could continue to hone the text in rehearsals, as he confirmed to Grove editor Richard Seaver on 29 November 1963: 'I have asked Faber, since correcting

proofs, to hold up production of the book. I realize I can't establish text of *Play*, especially stage directions, till I have worked on rehearsals. I have written to Alan [Schneider] about the problems involved' (Beckett letters cited in "Beckett's *Play*, in extenso," *Modern Drama* 42.3 (fall 1999): 442–55).

2 Both recordings (CCT-03 CD and CCT-22 CD) available now in CD format; MacGowran's stunning reading of 'Enueg II', opening with a soft gong, is also available on the Claddagh Web page: http://claddaghrecords.com/WWW/catalog/product_info.php?products_id=3500.

3 The section on 'Praxis' is partially based on the original, uncut version of the Preface to Samuel Beckett, *Krapp's Last Tape and Other Short Plays*, edited by S. E. Gontarski (London: Faber and Faber, 2009).

PART III
Topics

11

PETER FIFIELD

Samuel Beckett with, in, and around Philosophy

Were it not a critical commonplace, philosophy would seem the most unlikely company for Samuel Beckett's work. The 'love of wisdom' would seem incompatible with Beckett's celebrated advocacy of an art of 'impotence [and] ignorance' (Graver and Federman 1979, 148). Less clear, Beckett's own statements send us in opposing directions. He told Gabriel d'Aubarède in 1961 that 'I never read philosophers [...] I never understand anything they write', and would also tell Lawrence Harvey that 'if he were a critic setting out to write on the works of Beckett (and he thanked heaven he was not), he would start with two quotations, one by Geulincx: "Ubi nihil vales, ibi nihil valis", and one by Democritus: '"Nothing is more real than nothing"' (Harvey 1970, 267–8; Graver and Federman 1979, 217). This apparent oscillation resembles the self-cancelling rhetoric of the trilogy, and sows ambiguity across the range of philosophical readings. These views both discourage and encourage a certain philosophical approach to reading the works, withholding and granting authorial legitimation.

Yet the connection is as firm as it is diverse. Four identifiable – although frequently interwoven – strands are discernable: Beckett's writing is indebted to philosophy consulted prior to and during composition; it is responsive to subsequent interpretation by philosophers and philosophically – inclined critics; it seems to exemplify tenets of certain philosophical systems; and it frequently sports a philosophical feel in its own right. Beckett's œuvre thus stands to embody the product, subject, illustration and practice of philosophy. While this indicates a degree of complexity impossible to trace exhaustively – as testified by the volume of literature addressing these issues – it also speaks powerfully to a striking propinquity. As evident to first-time readers as to long-term devotees, Beckett's work simply seems a good fit with philosophy.

An example from the French philosopher Jean Wahl captures much that is at stake in the relationship between Beckett and philosophy. In the closing speech to the third 'Colloque philosophique de Royaumont', a week-long conference on the work of phenomenologist Edmund Husserl held in 1957, Wahl recorded the delegates' visit to Samuel Beckett's *Fin de partie*, which had had its Paris debut on 26 April, during the conference:

> Et puis ces journées ont été interrompues par l'audition d'une pièce de théâtre. J'ai retenu de cette pièce deux ou trois formules, deux ou trois répliques, que je me permets de vous relire. Je ne sais pas quelle est leur lien exact avec notre sujet: 'Mais qu'est-ce qui se passe qu'est-ce qui se passe – quelque chose qui a son cours'. Et puis un autre personage de la *Fin de Partie* de Beckett: 'Tu m'as posé cette question des milliers de fois, mais j'aime les vieilles questions. Ah! les vieilles questions, les vieilles réponses, il n'y a que cela'. Ainsi ces interruptions n'ont pas été de réelles interruptions. [And then these days were interrupted by the rendition of a piece of theatre. I retained from this piece two or three formulae, two or three retorts, that I will allow myself to reread to you. I do not know what their exact connection is with our subject: 'But what is happening, what is happening – something is taking its course'. And then another character of Beckett's *Endgame*: 'You've asked me this question thousands of times, but I like the old questions. Ah! The old questions, the old answers, there's nothing like them'. As such, these interruptions were not real interruptions.] (Husserl 1957, 131; my translation)

At the earliest historical moment – the very week of the play's opening in the city – Beckett is being watched, discussed, even co-opted by philosophers. While poking fun at the eternal preoccupations of philosophy and its apparent lack of progress Wahl also sees Beckett as a participant in philosophical enquiry. The persistent quality of his work – its repeated return to essential matters and to difficult questions – is something that he has in common with his audience: Beckett both is and is not an interruption from the work of the conference. *Fin de partie* would thus seem not an illustration of a philosophical principle or a scenario demanding a philosophical response, but rather a new philosophical method for a long-running problem: a change of approach if not of subject. If Beckett's work represents, as Enoch Brater suggests, 'a way of thinking' this cannot be wholly separated from the discipline of philosophy (2011, 2).[1] Nevertheless, as revealing as this intimacy is, the complimentary copy of the conference proceedings – entitled *Husserl* – that Jérôme Lindon sent him seems to have gone unread.[2] Where the philosophers were keen viewers of Beckett's drama, Beckett seems to have been a rather less attentive audience.

The secondary literature that this rapport has engendered has long since outstripped adequate summary and perhaps even comprehensive reading. It provides a great deal of detail about the author and his activities, as well as an expanding range of interpretations of the works, which place Beckett everywhere between an exemplary existentialist (see Connor 2009, 56–76)

Samuel Beckett with, in, and around Philosophy

to an evangelist for love (see Badiou 2003). It also reflects changing intellectual trends; long-running critical preoccupations; developments in theatre, publishing and philosophy itself; anniversaries and their attendant public commemorations; and the availability of relevant historical and archival documentation. This richness has driven and been driven by significant methodological issues: How should we read and write on Beckett? What questions ought we ask, and what sort of answers do we consider of value? What sort of critique must criticism itself be subject to? And even what is the object of our study? So essential are these queries that they are not only asked of philosophy in this context, but by it. 'What should we do with Beckett?' is, for readers and audiences, a question so disarmingly direct that it might originate within philosophy itself. As such, the current chapter reflects on writing by and about Beckett, in both of which the role of philosophy is a lively one.

Philosophy and Beckett is not, then, a stable topic, but one with a range of meanings that are subject to ongoing change. Indeed, the academic treatment of the area has moved on even since P. J. Murphy wrote the predecessor of this chapter in 1994, 'Beckett and the Philosophers' (in the first edition of *The New Cambridge Companion to Samuel Beckett*). Murphy judged the significant development to be the transition from the philosophical consideration of human situations depicted by Beckett to a poststructuralist account concerned with the linguistic play that creates and breaks down those characters (1994, 222–40). Beckett studies, perhaps more than any other literary subfield, has been at the forefront of broader shifts in literary-philosophical style. Georges Bataille (1979, 55–64), Maurice Blanchot (1979, 116–21), Theodor Adorno (1982, 119–50) and others met his texts promptly with important philosophical readings; indeed, Shane Weller (2009, 24–39) has identified Beckett's reception in France *as* the treatment of Beckett by the 'philosophes'. As this has continued, developments in literary criticism have not only found Beckett worth discussion, but a precursor to the most recent theories. Accordingly, the third 'Text for Nothing' is quoted at the opening of Michel Foucault's 'What is an Author?' – 'What matter who's speaking?' – as if Beckett himself had dismissed the notion of the author in favour of a more complex author function, which emerges from the text (*TFN* 11). Similarly, the sliding of signifier from signified – for example, 'Looking at a pot [...] it was in vain that Watt said, Pot, pot [...] For it was not a pot, the more he looked' – would anticipate the interests and strategies of deconstruction (*W* 78). Beckett's work is profoundly responsive to philosophical appropriation, but is also the material out of which philosophy seems to emerge.

The publication of James Knowlson's authorised biography *Damned to Fame* in 1996 has been widely seen as having initiated an 'archival turn' in the study of Beckett's work, challenging the authority and prestige of predominantly text-based theoretical readings. The increased availability of archival material has encouraged an approach that returns the author figure to the centre of academic enquiry, allowing study of biographical circumstance, reading habits and writing methods.[3] It has also enriched our understanding of the published works as a phase in a longer process of reading, note-taking, drafting, reshaping, publication, adaptation and revision. Rather than seeing a fixed and stable œuvre as the source for philosophical reflection, much of this work looks at the philosophical sources for Beckett's work, which is returned to a historical framework incorporating ongoing change. Thus it has challenged the polar beliefs that Beckett was either familiar with any philosophical text the critic happens upon, or that, as John Fletcher argued of the pre-Socratic philosophers, 'there is nothing to suggest that his interest has ever gone beyond the anecdotal and superficial' (1965, 43). This can mean a change of subject as well as method: alongside the usual company of Arthur Schopenhauer and Fritz Mauthner, less easily recognised figures such as Wilhelm Windelband and Olga Plümacher emerge.[4]

It is not the case, however, that the philosophical grounding of scholarly work has receded, but rather that its function has altered. For the very methodological debate has emerged within a philosophical frame. Matthew Feldman's agenda-setting article 'Beckett and Popper, or "What Stink of Artifice" (2006a) discerns two divergent interpretative approaches in the field initiated by this 'turn'. One is epitomised by the retrospective application of extrinsic explanatory frameworks, such as those in Richard Lane's collection *Beckett and Philosophy*, and the other by the use of archival material to uncover an existing system of thought within the work. Seeking to avoid the Rorschach element of reading that Beckett's work allows, Feldman presents letters, notebooks and drafts as a substantial ground on which to build a scholarly argument: a cogito moment. His prime criterion, drawn from Karl Popper's falsifiability axiom, is that in order to be considered worthwhile, arguments must be vulnerable to disproof. Such a practice, he asserts, would allow one to approach the most significant problems and make the most interesting assertions, beginning to interpret Beckett from an empirical grounding.[5] Arguments such as many of those advanced in philosophical readings lack explanatory power, he asserts, because they cannot be disputed in this manner. This is not then, a debate between a philosophically literate and an anti-philosophical approach but a conversation conducted squarely within the domain and in the language of philosophy.

The same objection that haunts Popper's thesis necessarily pertains to Feldman's: that the doctrine of falsifiability is not itself falsifiable. That is, to assert that the strongest arguments emerge from adherence to the principle is not something that can be tested, but only asserted as an article of faith. It is not, by its own measure, a strong argument. While Feldman's call to rigour is a salutary one that demands scholars attain a proper standard of research, this objection points up the reason why there has, in reality, been no great methodological schism. As literature does things *other* than make falsifiable statements, so literary critics in turn may choose to respond to a call other than that of Popper. As such, it is worth reframing this debate as a question of purpose. The extent to which criticism addresses issues of a text's current meaning – as opposed to its development, its sources and its basis in biographical events – fosters a continuum in critical work. At one pole is a series of assertions about verifiable events and documents: what the author did, what and how he read, what he saw and wrote. At the other is a set of propositions about the meaning of texts *as they continue to unfold in the present*. Such meaning is contingent and untestable; it flickers into and out of existence with changing fashions in reading and staging, personal knowledge, context and experience. But it is also, critically, the source for the implicit value claims that underpin most readings: *Waiting for Godot* speaks to me; I find *Molloy* touching, and *Endgame* funny. The range of effects a text can have on its audience is the reason it matters to that audience. Indeed, literary œuvres including Beckett's are regularly celebrated because they speak to a broad range of people, whose diverse circumstances often put them at a considerable remove from the author's own.[6] All critical commentary thus negotiates a balance between the demands of a method that is often historical and author-driven, and the values of another that is unstable and reader-oriented. This is a question driven by a combination of factors including individual preference, institutional recognition and cultural value.

At its most basic, Beckett's fitness for philosophical reading is surely a consequence of his works' concern with the same sort of fundamental ideas and experiences addressed by philosophy. *Waiting for Godot* can be read as an examination of existence in a world apparently without meaning: a situation thought universal by existentialism. *How It Is* might be understood to examine the nature of cruelty and suffering, experiences explored at length by Schopenhauer. *Happy Days* poses the question of the tone and value of humour, which Descartes thought not redemptive but characteristic of contempt. This type of reading has taken root in ground indicated by the plays' titles: *Waiting for Godot* is a play about waiting, *Endgame* about ending. This directness suggests that the works are focussed on basic elements of human existence; if they do not provide metaphysical answers they instead offer explorations of certain experiences. In this, then, they resemble a certain kind of philosophical material. These are, of course, among the universal themes of literature: one might consult Dante's *Divine Comedy* for a consideration of cruelty, or Shakespeare's *Much Ado About Nothing* for clues to the value of humour. But Beckett seems to ask these questions particularly insistently, and with a certain philosophical feel. How can we account for this closeness?

We might address the problem via the longest running of philosophical couplings: with René Descartes. Historically as well as critically, this appears a good starting point: a foundation for Beckett's early poem 'Whoroscope', which won Nancy Cunard's competition for the best poem written on the subject of time in 1928, and for influential readings such as Hugh Kenner's 'The Cartesian Centaur' (1961). Beckett's first published novel *Murphy* (1938) also bears the apparent marks of a deep familiarity with Descartes's work. It is the most explicitly philosophical of Beckett's novels, dealing in the concepts and language of philosophical history for plot and person alike. The opening of the work, for example, depicts the eponymous protagonist tied to a rocking chair immersed in meditation, in an appropriately static flight from the world of embodiment: 'it was not until his body was appeased that he could come alive in his mind' (*Mu* 4). Beckett's first great character, then, at first appears to be a card-carrying Cartesian, as he 'felt himself split in two, a body and a mind. They had intercourse apparently, otherwise he could not have known that they had anything in common. But he felt his mind to be bodytight and did not understand through what channel the intercourse was effected nor how the two experiences came to overlap' (*Mu* 70).

Study of Beckett's 'Philosophy notes', written in 1932–3, has allowed us to understand that if *Murphy* owes a debt to Descartes, it is via commentaries and syntheses read by the author, rather than primary texts. Feldman's *Beckett's Books* (2006b) has shown convincingly that Beckett's reading habits were more reliant on digests than the casual reader may suppose. His use of Wilhelm Windelband's *A History of Philosophy* (1893) in particular dominates those notes that fed directly into *Murphy* and other works, so that the terminology of Beckett's Cartesianism is in fact that of his German commentator. For example, Feldman shows that the pineal gland, the mechanism of Murphy's mysterious exchange between body and mind, which is known as the 'conarium' in Beckett's novel, is borrowed not from *Discourse on the Method* or *Meditations on First Philosophy* but from Windelband's rather stolid summary (*Mu* 6). Indeed, after this discovery the novel's broader philosophical debt is revealed as that owed to the early Greek philosophers such as Pythagoras and Democritus, and post-Cartesians such as Nicolas Malebranche and Arnold Geulincx, rather than to Descartes himself. Adequate knowledge of these more obscure sources allows us to see that Murphy's dualism is not a straightforward Cartesianism but something altogether more subtle and more strange. It is cut from the earliest Greek philosophical considerations of the different qualities of the mind and body, the mechanism of their interaction, the return and development of these ideas in seventeenth-century France and Belgium, and, in turn, the subsequent digestion and summary of these ideas in the nineteenth by the German neo-Kantian Windelband.

This research has undoubtedly reshaped academic understandings of Beckett's novel and of his practice as a writer in this period and beyond. Yet its corrective capacity also demands that we reassess what role remains for Descartes. If *Murphy* is not the author's supreme Cartesian novel, is this to be thought an erroneous pairing: a 'pseudocouple' in the strongest sense? Instead, I suggest, we might profitably compare Descartes's writing to the celebrated style of Beckett's postwar writing, where the verbiage of the earlier texts has been peeled away in the belief that 'All true grace is economical' (Brater 2011, 13). This reveals a form of stylistic scepticism in common. Where Descartes subjects experience and knowledge to rigorous doubt in search of a firm grounding, Beckett works to strip away extraneous verbal and formal detail. Rather than a rich depth of character, setting and plot, adopting the conventions of the discipline, Beckett's starting point is a Cartesian 'meremost minimum' (*CIWS* 82). Purged of superfluities and overly complex 'noise', *Endgame*, for example, brings a clarity of purpose and expression to its depiction of obligated care and reliance. This aesthetic intimacy would stand to displace a conceptual debt long established, but now being recalculated – which is to say reduced – with the corrective of the 'Philosophy notes' (see Feldman 2006b). In place of a specifically Cartesian debt – a quotation here or an idea there – stands a broader sense of common atmosphere, with Descartes as an occasional synecdochical figure.

Thus we ought to observe how often Beckett's works read like extended philosophical examples or thought experiments. They make use of significantly reduced means in setting and character, minimizing the range of these steadily throughout the course of the œuvre. Where *More Pricks Than Kicks* (1934) relates Belacqua's wanderings through an assortment of Dublin settings, *Murphy* works its way to the Magdalen Mental Mercyseat, where the core of its action takes place. More quickly still *Watt* (1953) settles into Mr Knott's house; in the trilogy we read stories of traumatic journeys but with an increasing concern for the static situation of the narrator, who is reduced to a room, a bed or a jar; and the later prose seems to take a perverse pleasure in containing its denizens in assorted geometric forms.[7] Similarly, it is notable that the only scene changes in the whole of Beckett's drama are those in the little-loved *Eleutheria*, where we see the same room from different angles and lose a second space between Acts II and III. This concern with reducing and restraining the contents of his fictional worlds implies a certain logic essential to philosophy. The control of variables is central to experimental thought, removing factors that may mask or distort the forces and events under scrutiny. But this practice is also antithetical to broader literary practice, which routinely takes advantage of its ability to summon a broad range of events, people and places. Thus, instead of placing a central character in a range of relationships and places, developing their behaviour and nature via their responses, we are shown one or two protagonists engaged in a particular action and in a specific place. Beckett appears less concerned with creating a convincing narrative of change and development than with posing a certain scenario and holding it near static.

The strange nature of these situations also departs from the realist tradition of aesthetic writing. It does so not by entering a fantastical world of radical difference, but by being slightly off-kilter or even uncanny. All of Beckett's texts depict a scene that resembles an odd limit case: they work in the area between feasibility and actuality. As such, they are not unrealistic but unusual: they appear to be testing a problem, or working through a hypothesis, and to be concerned with the development of significance or the structure of human experience. What would happen if we made a space, and then put a body in it as in 'All Strange Away' (1964)? Would that, as Clov asks in *Endgame*, result in its 'beginning to ... to ... mean something?' (*CDW* 108). How would a human being react? And would the answers to those questions be different if we were to multiply the number of inhabitants, as in *The Lost Ones* (1971)? Other texts would seem to pose perennial questions. What is the value of human life, and is it a function of one's actions? Thus, how would it be to have suicide weighed up by two external agents, as in *Rough for Theatre II*? What would they need to consider, and how?

However, this impression that the works conduct themselves in a philosophical manner would appear to contradict Beckett's own distinction between literary and philosophical styles. His demurral before Heidegger and Sartre, for example, is because 'their language is too philosophical for me', while his remark that his novels would not be necessary if they could have been written philosophically implies a similar distinction (qtd. in Graver and Federman 1979, 219, 217). A further comment when reading Schopenhauer in 1937 that 'it is a pleasure also to find a philosopher that can be read like a poet' suggests a distinction in reading method as well as between the disciplines themselves (qtd. in Knowlson 1996, 268). Confessing an enjoyment of Schopenhauer's writing in this moment, Beckett's statements cut in the other direction as well. They posit the possibility that the boundary between the two subjects can be crossed, and that, more importantly, to do so is a productive and even a pleasurable thing to do. On these grounds we may justifiably enjoy reading Beckett as though he were a philosopher, taking seriously the questions posed and the suggestions given in response.

If the issue of pleasure and satisfaction is a relevant one, the movement between commentary attentive to the author's own interests and a retrospective philosophy-style reflection is not exclusively the result of critical tastes. Shifting between addressing philosophy *in* the texts and conducting philosophy *with* them, we might notice how different works seem to become more and less prominent in critical literature. The directness with which philosophical sources are employed in the early poems, novels and stories has met with abundant accounts of early Greek thought centred on *Murphy*, while it is texts such as *How It Is* and the television plays written in the later part of Beckett's career that have attracted the attentions of Alain Badiou and Gilles Deleuze, respectively.[8] Across the range of Beckett's corpus, philosophical reference appears to become increasingly subtle. A quieter use of philosophy, exercising an apparent allusive restraint, paradoxically makes retrospective philosophical reflection more inviting. What Beckett calls in his 1982 play *Catastrophe* the 'craze for explicitation' is something we might recognise in the author's own early works, while later texts apparently place their philosophical debts under cover (*CDW* 459).

Nevertheless, it remains to be seen whether Beckett's later texts are actually less engaged with his reading in philosophy, or simply that their philosophical debts are yet to be the subject of detailed exposition. As I have observed elsewhere, we can see a direct engagement with philosophical texts in those corners of Beckett's writing assumed to refrain from such allusion (see Fifield 2011). In *The Unnamable*, the narrator's lament that 'I alone am man and all the rest divine' is a direct challenge to Hippocrates' statement transcribed by Beckett in his 'Philosophy notes': 'Nothing is more divine or human than anything else, but all things are alike and all divine.' (*Un* 10; Burnet 1914, 33; qtd. by Beckett in TCD MS10967/8.1). Without addressing this example in detail, it is important to notice that Beckett draws the situation of his novel's protagonist from reading done twenty years – and a World War – previously, while living in London. The fact of this statement having a Hippocratic origin, drawn by Beckett from John Burnet's 1914 overview, *Early Greek Philosophy Part I: Thales to Plato*, is not significant in itself. However, it does allow an understanding of the narrator's torments as a realisation of an ancient debate around the transmigration of souls, Orphicism, and the eschatological function of embodiment. As more of these references are shown to us by scholarship it becomes possible that the major works of Beckett, those that have previously appeared to be characterised by a flight from specificity and allusion, are a tissue of the author's direct engagement with philosophy. If this is the case, the interaction of knowledge claims of different types will continue to be a lively one in the study of Beckett's writing.

If the sense of philosophical debt and interpretative good fit is ever more visible, we must also consider the contrary position. As indicated at the opening of this chapter, Beckett himself made strident rejections of philosophical readings of his work, and, as H. Porter Abbott has explored in 'I am Not a Philosopher', warned strongly against mistaking him for a philosopher (2008, 81–92). This worry is, in Abbott's estimation, born of philosophy's comprehensive remit and its systematising outlook: 'The philosopher's trade, after all, is to make a system with non-contradictory parts' (85). Addressing Francophone criticism Bruno Clément similarly suggests that it is 'a characteristic of the philosophical reading: it must be "without remainder"' (2006, 121). This totalising gesture is undoubtedly a problem for Beckett, whose work is more unruly, and more resistant to a comprehensive and competent metaphysical gesture. But the same would also be true of any worthy literary œuvre. The very richness of a work lies in its exceeding a simple exposition: a work that can be fully accounted for is, one might reasonably assert, one that lacks appropriate depth. This disciplinary or epistemological argument against too vigorous a pairing of Beckett and philosophy is as potent as it is important. But it overlooks a more simple factor: Beckett's personal anxiety about philosophy emerged not when discussing Spinoza, Leibniz or Hippocrates but Sartre, Heidegger and Adorno. The perceived danger of philosophy was at its greatest when it was contemporary and threatened to attach itself to the work at the very moment of its emergence.

This is, history shows us, a legitimate fear for prompt and persuasive interpretations. The influence of Martin Esslin's *The Theatre of the Absurd* (1961), for example, has been so great as to label Beckett's œuvre for the greater part of his audience for half a century. Feldman and Nixon's *International Reception of Samuel Beckett* testifies that the reception of Beckett was in many cases that of *Waiting for Godot* and *The Theatre of the Absurd*, while Michael Y. Bennett (2011) has judged the category sufficiently important to warrant a revitalization. More theoretically challenging readings too, such as that by Maurice Blanchot, have been seen as unduly influential, stifling heterodox interpretations with an unwarranted prestige (see Casanova 2007). As such, Beckett's reluctance to grant Gabriel d'Aubarède's enquiry about contemporary philosophical influence must be seen in the light of another question as to whether existentialism 'may afford a key to your works'. Beckett answered, 'There's no key of problem. I wouldn't have had any reason to write my novels if I could have expressed their subject in philosophic terms' (qtd. in Graver and Federman 1979, 217). As complex as the authorial and disciplinary relationship to philosophy may be, there is a more simple explanation. I suggest that no writer would happily concede that their work was simply an illustration of the latest philosophical or literary fashion.[9] Beckett's proximity to existentialism, published and reviewed in *Les Temps modernes*, compared to Sartre and Camus, and engaged with questions of meaning and its absence, made the danger of mischaracterisation a real one.[10] His enjoyment of Sartre's novel *La Nausée* (1937) in 1938 does not preclude his later dissociation from the ambition, politics, popularity or occasional obscurantism of existentialism.[11] Beckett's general reluctance to join literary groups or schools, as well as his evident desire to forge a singular literary identity during this period, is as good a reason as any epistemological objection to philosophy in general.

This would not, then, suggest that philosophy is seen as an intrinsically overbearing discipline, but rather that it can be deployed as such. The right-minded philosopher, Beckett's practice suggests, is one who knows the limits of the craft, not least the impossibility of a comprehensive account of a literary œuvre. Indeed, Jacques Derrida's well-known half-response to Beckett indicates that the very same proximity that invites engagement is also its deterrent. He says, 'This is an author to whom I feel very close, or to whom I would like to feel myself very close; but also too close. Precisely because of this proximity, it is too hard for me, too easy and too hard' (Derrida 1992, 60). He also accedes to the suggestion that Beckett's work is already so thoroughly deconstructive that there is no opening for deconstruction to produce a response. While this might be thought a problem peculiar to deconstruction, which itself walks that tricky line between philosophy and literature, I suggest that this is more generally applicable to philosophy. The problem of doing philosophy with Beckett is always one of being at once 'too easy and too hard'. The texts are never a neutral ground to which we may bring an objective method; rather, philosophy is already present and at work in them. What we find in Beckett's writing, and in the abundant scholarship that addresses it, is a tumult of references to thinkers across and, notably, beyond the canon. It is also deeply responsive to interpretation based on theories and texts unknown to the author and his works, whether contemporary or historical. While this richness provides innumerable openings for conceptually literate interpretation, it is precisely the fragmentary use and fluctuating sense of these approaches that is central to Beckett's relationship to philosophy. Indeed, it is questionable whether one can make a statement about Beckett and philosophy that is both coherent and accurate. His dealings were almost entirely with philosophers, philosophical texts and philosophical ideas, rather than with a discipline: not generalities but particulars, both demented and otherwise. Thus Beckett would tell MacGreevy 'I am reading

Schopenhauer [...] But I am not reading philosophy, nor caring whether he is right or wrong or a good or a worthless metaphysician' (qtd. in Knowlson 1996, 118). It is the same versatile and powerful tools that philosophy offers to Beckett's readers, including its particular tone, focus and method, which attracted the author himself, both as a young man diligently filling the gaps in his education and as an older figure, whose works became the subject of discussion by some of the most important philosophers of the age. And just as Beckett's patience with and belief in philosophy varied according to context, its value for readers will continue to fluctuate. The central and unanswerable question of philosophy and Beckett will remain, I suggest, one of measure.

NOTES

1. This is a recurring idea, expressed elegantly by Bruno Clément as 'rather than literature and thought constituting two different orders, literature, by itself, thinks' (2006, 122). See also the edited collection *Beckett at 100: Revolving It All* (2008) whose first section gathers essays whose work is 'Thinking through Beckett' as if it were a medium as well as a method (Ben-Zvi and Moorjani 2008).
2. See the series of letters to Barbara Bray in March 1960 for a repeated admission that Beckett had not himself read the book he was recommending.
3. Outstanding examples of this work include Matthew Feldman, *Beckett's Books: A Cultural History of the Interwar Notes* (2006); Mark Nixon, *Samuel Beckett's German Diaries 1936–37* (2006); Anthony Uhlmann, ed. *Samuel Beckett in Context* (2013). The ambitious Beckett Digital Manuscript Project (BDMP), run by Dirk Van Hulle at the Centre for Manuscript Genetics at the University of Antwerp is at the forefront of this kind of study (www.beckettarchive.org).
4. For a survey of Beckett's library and the notes contained in the volume see Dirk Van Hulle and Mark Nixon, *Samuel Beckett's Library* (2013).
5. I have avoided further use of the term 'empirical', which buttresses a shaky distinction. To study a published text with no reference to manuscripts, notes or biographical events, and even to use it to reflect on personal matters is still a project of observation and experiment.
6. See, for example Brater (2011) whose opening chapter covers the range of contexts in which *Godot* has found an audience. *The International Reception of Samuel Beckett*, edited by Mark Nixon and Matthew Feldman (2009), gives a more detailed picture of the global reach of Beckett's work.
7. Curiosities in this respect are *Mercier and Camier* and *The Lost Ones*, which are strangely mobile and populous, respectively. *Film* also draws its narrative from motion, although it depicts the subject in a desperate search for withdrawal and confinement.
8. Some recent examples from a long list of works on Beckett and Greek philosophy include Feldman (2006c); Van Hulle (2008b, 203–16); Weller (2008, 321–33); Fifield (2011, 67–88); for a contrast in method, see Badiou (2003); Deleuze (1995, 3–28).

9 I have argued this point more fully in *Late Modernist Style in Samuel Beckett and Emmanuel Levinas* (2013).
10 For an account of this proximity see Weller (2013, 160–72).
11 Beckett wrote to MacGreevy in May 1938 and passed on his judgment that Sartre's novel was 'extraordinarily good' (*LSB I* 626).

12

JEAN-MICHEL RABATÉ

Love and Lobsters
Beckett's Meta-Ethics

For Beckett, the question of ethics is posed by a voice that displays the author's prerogative, that is absolute power – a power to interrupt his own tale by an intrusive negation, bringing the fiction to an untimely end: a short story, after all, not a novel. This happens at the close of 'Dante and the Lobster': 'She lifted the lobster clear of the table. It had about thirty seconds to live. Well, thought Belacqua, it's a quick death, God help us all. It is not' (*MPTK* 14). Belacqua has fetched a lobster for a dinner to which his aunt has invited him. Believing the 'beast' to be dead, he brings it along as he takes an Italian language lesson with Professor Adriana Ottolenghi, and is surprised when the French teacher's cat tries to catch it. He only discovers that the lobster is alive when he reaches his aunt's kitchen. The extraordinary concision of the ending combines Belacqua's bafflement about Dante's speculation that spots in the moon exemplify divine compassion for Cain and quotidian issues, like: Do we have the right to kill animals in order to eat them? The aunt feels no qualms in boiling a lobster alive and even derides Belacqua's queasiness, knowing that he will devour the lobster once properly cooked and served.

Would the story have been as effective if Belacqua and the aunt had opened and shared a dozen oysters? Probably not, even if one had been reminded that oysters have to be eaten alive. What triggers the ethical shock is the hero's empathic identification with an animal whose struggles he tries to relive: 'In the depths of the sea it had crept into the cruel pot. [...] It had survived the French-woman's cat and his witless clutch. Now it was going alive into scalding water. It had to. Take into the air my quiet breath' (*MPTK* 14). However, the question is not simply whether it is wrong to boil lobsters alive, nor worry about their pain when plunged in boiling water – thus whether it would be humane to kill them before boiling them – but more broadly how to reconcile a grand scheme of things in which we move from God's compassion facing Cain to scenes of sadistic violence in the *Inferno* where we meet damned souls who are plunged in boiling blood, as with the violent souls of the Seventh circle of Hell, with mundane or everyday life concerns.

In *A Beckett Canon*, Ruby Cohn explains that Beckett told her that he wanted to change the ending to: 'Like Hell it is', but preferred to keep three words instead of four (2001, 391, n. 11). The formal determination by linguistic concision was wise: the echo would have been too obvious, mirroring the position of Belacqua halfway between Hell and Heaven, 'stuck' not only in difficult glosses of the moon Canti but also placed in the mediating space defining Purgatory. Yet, we note that even with the rejected change, the negation would not affect 'God help us all'. The fact that such suffering exists and moreover should have a role in a divine scheme is never questioned. Here is the basis of Beckett's ethics: it deploys itself between a religious realm, whether God exists or not, since this is not the question, and the very actuality of a phenomenology of suffering (see Tanaka, Tajiri, and Tsushima 2012).

The interrogation about the function of pain in what may be called a system of divine sadism reappears in 'Text 3', an early poem investigating the complex interaction of pain, pity, and divine justice. It begins with the first word spoken to Virgil by Dante the character: '*Miserere*'. This word is not in Italian but in Latin: '*Miserere* di me' ('Have pity on me', *Inferno*, I, ln. 65) allows us to glimpse Dante's synthetic language, which announces Joyce's experiments. But here it is Proust, not Joyce, who is quoted:

> Proust's cook is in the study,
> she is grieved in a general way for the abstract intestine.
> She is so engrossed that she does not hear the screams of her assistant,
> a sloven she,
> and the dying spit of a Paduan Virtue,
> for alas she has stripped her last asparagus,
> now she is smashed on delivery.
> She rises,
> her heart is full of murder and tears,
> she hunts down the pullet with oaths,
> fiercely she tears his little head off. ('Text 3', *CP* 38)

Proust's famous portrayal of Françoise, a fixture in the family at Combray, is the starting point for a meditation on the juxtaposition of goodness and sadism, on the compound of cruelty and compassion marking all his characters. Françoise has an assistant, a younger kitchen maid who happens to be both sickly and pregnant, and whom Françoise tortures mercilessly, finally forcing her to leave. The narrator's family is surprised to be served asparagus prepared in all possible ways at all their meals: Françoise knows that the kitchen maid is prone to asthma attacks when peeling them (Proust 2002,

127). At another time, the kitchen maid is screaming in pain after her difficult delivery; Françoise grudgingly fetches the book describing her ailment, but never comes back to help the poor woman. She is discovered plunged in the book, full of general compassion for the girl's pain: 'Oh dear, Holy Virgin, it is possible that the good Lord would want a wretched human creature to suffer so?' (125). Yet, just before, the narrator had surprised Françoise in the kitchen; since she was deprived of her usual helper, she had to prepare dinner and kill a recalcitrant chicken. Furious, she cried out repeatedly: 'Vile creature!' (*'Sale bête!'*, 124). Even when the animal was beheaded and its blood collected for appetizing sauces, the oath was repeated. Shocked, the narrator slides away and decides to get her sacked – then considers that without her, he would not get his usual delicacies, and pardons her.

Beckett's poem insists on the gruesome aspects of Françoise's cruelty, whereas Proust makes room for moral laxity given the 'cowardly calculations' we all make in similar circumstances (Proust 1987, 120; 2002, 125). Françoise has to condemn the animal to death in order to perform her menial tasks as a cook. Such inverted ethical impulse (we will kill an animal more easily if we reduce it to the status of a 'dirty beast') was lacking in Belacqua's aunt, which made her bland gesture even more scandalous. Beckett follows Proust's lead when he meditates on affective ambivalence, on the proximity of ethical contraries, and also on the function of moral allegory. The sickly kitchen maid is said to be the 'spit of a Paduan Virtue' ('Text 3', *CP* 38) because Swann, the aesthete, has noted her physical resemblance with Giotto's portrayal of Charity, depicted as a banal looking woman in the Allegories of Virtues and Vices, visible in the Scrovegni chapel of Padua's Arena. The narrator, who keeps a reproduction of the 'Caritas' figure in his room (given to him by Swann) was first surprised by the way Giotto – a contemporary of Dante – presented his Virtues as earthy, stolid, mannish, almost vulgar women. He could not fathom why this 'Charity without charity' (Proust 2002, 83) or the allegory of Justice could be praised by Swann, a disciple of Ruskin in this matter. The latter allegory appeared as 'a Justice whose grayish and meanly regular face was the very same which, in Combray, characterized certain pretty, pious and unfeeling bourgeois ladies I saw at Mass, some of whom had long since been enrolled in the reserve militia of Injustice' (Proust 2002, 83). The narrator later understands how modern allegories are material fragments of a whole whose symbolic meaning can be grafted on the material body. Thus the swollen belly of the kitchen maid evokes painful pregnancy and other visceral aspects of the body in which death is lurking.

The juxtaposition of the figures of Justice and Injustice is a dominant theme in Beckett's works, whose sense of ethics is predicated on an awareness of this baffling reversibility. We can see this theme as late as *How It Is*, a dark novel narrating the progression through mud of a narrator who finds Pim, another quester, whom he tortures mercilessly by carving words on his buttocks with a can opener. Yet, in part III, we are told that their sadistic couplings and subsequent uncouplings obey 'our justice'. A revealing paragraph displays a violent language testifying to metaphysical despair:

> the fuck who suffers who makes us to suffer who cries who to be left in peace in the dark the mud gibbers ten seconds fifteen seconds of sun clouds earth sea patches of blue clear nights and of a creature if not still standing still capable of standing always the same the same imagination spent looking for a hole that he may be seen no more in the middle of this faery who drinks that drop of piss of being and who with his last gasp pisses it to drink the moment it's someone each in his turn as our justice wills and never any end it wills that too dead or none. (*HII* 115)

Jonathan Boulter has interpreted this passage and other references to Justice according to Jacques Derrida's 'Force of Law' as the clash between a Law, which can be deconstructed, and a Justice that cannot be defined or deconstructed (2012, 173–200; see also Cunningham 2008, 21–37). Much as I appreciate Derrida's essay and the subtlety of Boulter's 'post-human' interpretation, Derrida's definition of Justice as a quasi-transcendental aporia or the experience of the impossible is not relevant here. Why is Beckett's Justice calculating, adding up numbers, ensuring that the Same be always repeated identically? The paradox embodied by this passage is that one cannot distinguish Justice from Injustice. Justice means here more a 'Law' of eternal return, blending Nietzsche's concept of time and Louis-Ferdinand Céline's ideology of life as a crawl through mud until death frees us. Both are underpinned by a Dantean vision of excremental Hell (Caselli 2005b, 148–83). In fact, there is no obvious difference between this 'piss of being' ('*cette goutte de pisse d'être*'; Beckett 1961, 159) and the statement that 'we have our being in justice' ('*on est dans la justice*'; *HII* 108; Beckett 1961, 159). The context is clear: 'nothing to be done in any case we have our being in justice I have never heard anything to the contrary' (*HII* 108). The echo of the opening sentence of *Waiting for Godot* signals that 'Justice' does not gesture toward an opening to the incalculable but signals a sad necessity, a mortal and moral fate. The ethical experience proposed by Beckett with a rare rigor – here, the voice uttering something 'to the contrary', the ethical voice, is silent – takes place outside the domain of Justice.

Throughout his work, Beckett's notion of 'Justice' remains indebted to Dante's concept of '*contrapasso*', which formalizes a homology between the types of sins committed on earth and the types of punishment meted out in Hell. Thus, to return to 'Text 3', it is logical to see Dante's allegories relay

Proust's allegories. Both authors taken together have taught Beckett how to overcome an initial reflex of compassion by contemplating 'Justice', knowing fully that it is indistinguishable from 'Injustice'. The souls of the damned speak:

> We are proud in our pain
> our life was not blind.
> Worms breed in the red tears
> as they slouch unnamed
> scorned by the black ferry
> despairing of death
> who shall not scour in swift joy
> the bright hill's girdle
> nor tremble with the dark pride of torture
> and the bitter dignity of an ingenious damnation. (CP 39)

For the eternally damned, there is nothing to expect from death, which is a source of despair but also of pride. This leaves aside the problem of compassion.

> Lo-Ruhama Lo-Ruhama
> pity is quick with death.
> Presumptuous passionate fool come now
> and stand cold
> on the cold moon. (CP 39)

Lo-Ruhama was the daughter Hosea had with a prostitute, symbolizing Israel in Hosea 1:6, because her name means 'not pitied'. This leads to the line that bothered Belacqua: 'Qui vive la pietà quando è ben morta' (*Inferno*, XX, ln. 280). Here, in Hell, pity is only alive when it is fully dead. How can one translate, that is move on by making sense of this brash oxymoron? In 'Dante and the Lobster', Belacqua chews on this magnificent 'pun', unable to translate it. The teacher's superb response 'Do you think, she murmured, it is absolutely necessary to translate it?' (*MPTK* 18) is rigorously parallel to the question Belacqua poses facing Dante the character in his *Commedia*: Why translate? Why keep on moving?

This is Belacqua's question in *Purgatorio*. Dante walking with Virgil hears a voice inviting them to rest. Under a boulder, men sit in the shade. One of them, looking exhausted, his arms around his knees, his head bent down, addresses them. Belacqua's fastidious slowness allows Dante to identify him. When he asks what he is doing, Belacqua answers: 'O brother, what's the use of climbing?' (IV, ln. 121–7). His cheeky '*O frate, andar in sù che porta?*' triggers Dante's 'wan smile', repeatedly invoked by Beckett (as in *Company* or *The Lost Ones*). In fact, Belacqua's predicament derives from laziness: he has waited until the last minute before repenting for his sins, and has to wait in the ante-purgatory a number of years equal to the years spent on earth.

When Beckett chose other alter egos like Murphy or Molloy, they all passed through a moment of regression, experiencing what Murphy calls 'the Belacqua bliss' (*Mu* 71). Like Murphy, then, Belacqua sits in an ante-purgatory, a transitional space between *Inferno* and *Purgatorio*, a limbo for adults who have never been properly born, like Jung's little girl who died because of her immersion in her dream world. Belacqua is a disabused ironist and indolent questioner who, because he is 'stuck' by divine decree, voices critical, wistful, and antiheroic objections to the grand pattern of the quest on which Dante has embarked. Belacqua's exhausted 'What's the point?' is a first adumbration of the ethical voice; it problematizes the teleology of Dante's progression, hence the very notion of 'progress' as such.

Dante attempted to create an 'epic of judgment', as Ezra Pound wrote, an epic of practical or political ethics. Its immense scope required the creation of a new language, which can be compared to Joyce's *Work in Progress*. Beckett's view of Purgatory is modeled on Dante and Joyce, even though the latter is founded on the loss of the absolute: 'In what sense, then, is Mr Joyce's work purgatorial? In the absolute absence of the absolute' ('Dante...Bruno. Vico..Joyce', *Dis* 22). Beckett shared Joyce's antiabsolutism, but not his linguistic optimism. For Joyce, as long as the verbal machine purred on, the process would regenerate itself endlessly, which is why *Finnegans Wake* is a circular text, virtually infinite. For Beckett, however, one should not bypass the ethical moment of questioning, and this manifests itself above all by an interruption of such progress.

In order to bypass the aporia of a Justice looking too much like Injustice, or of a process of purgation revolving too blissfully on itself, Beckett needed a powerful lever. This he found in Arnold Geulincx's *Ethics*, in which he discovered a surprising combination of absolute determinism (everything that happens, including my body's movements, happens because God wills it) and of absolute freedom (I can always will a contrarian gesture). *Molloy* condenses this well: 'I who had loved the image of old Geulincx, dead young, who left me free, on the black boat of Ulysses, to crawl towards the East, along the deck. That is a great measure of freedom, for him who has not the pioneering spirit' (*Mo* 50). Of course, the boat is that of Ulysses by reference to Dante's evocation of the last shipwreck of the hero in *Inferno*, Canto 26, and to Joyce's novel. Even such marginal freedom can perform miracles.

Beckett began to read Geulincx in the 1930s; we find references in the 'Philosophy notes' at Trinity College and in the 'Whoroscope' Notebook. The post-Cartesian Flemish philosopher offered a model of irreducible freedom similar to what Jean-Paul Sartre was elaborating at the same time. We have the text of Beckett's notes in *Arnold Geulincx's Ethics with Samuel Beckett's Notes* (see Van Ruler and Uhlmann 2006). Geulincx's philosophy underpins the narratological development of *Murphy*, once he has settled in the mental hospital. Murphy has leisure to meditate on Geulincx's motto, '*Ubi nihil vales, ibi nihil velis*'. *Murphy* presents a 'negative cogito' first adumbrated by the Occasionalist philosopher whose main verb is '*nescio*' ['I do not know']. '*Ubi nihil vales, nihil velis*' means 'Where you are worth nothing, you will want nothing', even though Anthony Uhlmann, Matthew Feldman, and others have rendered it as 'Where you have no power, you will have no desire'. Such hesitation corresponds to the two meanings of *valeo* in Latin. *Valeo,* the verb at the root of the word 'value', means either 'I am strong, powerful, healthy', or 'I prevail'. The imperative 'Vale!' was a 'Goodbye!' or 'Farewell!'. Beckett found in Geulincx a philosophy that said 'Goodbye' to all previous ethical systems, by displaying the consciousness of a subject who does not know, and the source of a paradoxical moral health reached through negativity and impotence.

Beckett often compared Geulincx's idea of man as a puppet whose very movements are pulled by God with Kleist's meditation on puppets. In both cases, a certain grace or ease comes from the abandonment of one's will. As Thomas Dommange argues, Geulincx is less a philosopher of humility and impotence than a thinker of the permanent miracle: here is a definite mechanization of the ineffable (see Doutey 2012). At least, such a point of view destabilizes certainties, frees us from determinism or the principle of causality. If causality does not regulate the world or our actions, we are free, as Kant and Schopenhauer both observe. The principle of sufficient reason is replaced by a principle of insufficient reason – which leaves room for an unexplained grace. Hence the principle of Unreason is always superior to rational systems of ethics balancing Justice and Injustice.

Beckett transformed Descartes's 'cogito ergo sum', by then a 'received idea' mentioned by Flaubert, into its reversal: 'nescio ergo sum'. The maxim '*Ubi nihil vales, ibi nihil velis*' aims less at restricting will to possible domains of application than at freeing will from having any object. Thus Beckett admired the philosophical pluck displayed by Geulincx, who wrote: 'Are my body and soul pure failures and my intelligence still somewhat valid? Then I shall be a tailor' (qtd. in Doutey 2012, 115). As the old joke of God and the tailor shows in *Endgame*, better to have a good tailor than contemplate the disastrous spectacle of Creation.

If Geulincx brought to Beckett the concept of a thinking of the outside, of a pure determination by the Other, the insight was not accompanied by a mode of writing generated by the philosophy. He discovered this 'other' writing in Marquis de Sade's works. Beckett was to translate de Sade's *120*

Days of Sodom for Jack Kahane in 1938. Discovering the book, he expressed admiration: 'The obscenity of surface is indescribable. Nothing could be less pornographical. It fills me with a kind of metaphysical ecstasy. The composition is extraordinary, as rigorous as Dante's' (*LSB I* 607). The notion that de Sade was a Puritan anticipates theses developed in the 1940s by Pierre Klossowski (1991) and Maurice Blanchot (2004). Beckett insisted that de Sade was not pornographic, for indeed, if de Sade tried to show everything, including whatever exceeds the 'stage', he never attempted to seduce the reader by erotic images. He attempted to convince by a mad reason.

Similarly, Beckett's sadism appears in *Watt* when the narrator and Watt feed their own offspring to rats:

> And then we would sit down in the midst of them, and give them to eat, out of our hands, of a nice fat frog, or a baby thrush, or seizing suddenly a plump young rat, resting in our bosom after its repast, we would feed it to its mother, or its father, or its sister, or to some less fortunate relative. It was on these occasions, we agreed, after an exchange of views, that we came nearest to God. (*W* 133)

Sadean perversity parodies pastoral Rousseauism. Watt and Sam demonstrate that the fundamental law of Nature is crime. The main object of the transgression is parenthood. Like de Sade, Beckett subverts the traditional notion of family as the site of morality. Sam and Watt shift vertiginously from a sham goodness for animals to pure cruelty, then 'reason' about their actions, elaborating a parodic antitheology. Beckett has understood de Sade's wish to emulate an absolutely evil God, a 'supremely-evil-being' as Lacan wrote in 'Kant with Sade' (Lacan 1992; 2006, 652).

For Beckett as for de Sade, the foundation of the cruel fantasy is an inverted theology. De Sade's libertines have such a hatred of religion that in *120 Days of Sodom* the most severely punished violation is to mention God. This point had not been missed by Beckett, who rewrites Pascal's maxim about man who wants to be an angel or god but ends up being a beast. In *Watt*, man is not even able to kill a rat, since rats are curious theological creatures who happen once in a while to eat a consecrated host. Yet, one should not remain stuck in an anthropological discourse:

> For the only way one can speak of nothing is to speak of it as though it were something, just as the only way one can speak of God is to speak of him as though he were a man, which to be sure he was, in a sense, for a time, and as the only way one can speak of man, even our anthropologists have realized that, is to speak of him as though he were a termite. (*W* 64)

Whether God exists or not, in the ethical domain, man is not even a metaphor, he exists only as a catachresis. Watt tries out names on things as if they were old rags found in an attic. Watt can no more say of a pot that it is a 'pot' than of a man that it is a 'man'. His linguistic dereliction calls up the crisis of language experienced by Lord Chandos in Hugo von Hofmannsthal's famous 1902 'Letter'. Sam's and Watt's cruel games produce a tension between an unnamable humanity and an antitheology of cruelty. It is thanks to this tension that an ethics that is not anthropomorphic or theological remains possible.

In *Watt*, Knott embodies Kant's moral law, above all a formalization of what one 'can't do'. Here Beckett's project is comparable to Horkheimer and Adorno's in *Dialectic of Enlightenment* (2002, 63–93), a book coincidentally written at the same time as *Watt* by two exiles from Nazi Germany. Like the refugees from the Frankfurt school, Beckett questions the madness of pure Reason as he explained in an interview: 'The crisis started with the end of the 17th century, after Galileo. The 18th century has been called the century of reason, *le siècle de la Raison*. I've never understood that; they're all mad, *ils sont tous fous, ils déraisonnent*!' (qtd. by Macmillan and Fehsenfeld 1988, 231). Given the loss of faith in Reason on the one hand, and in God on the other, ethics names a space within language in which language struggles against its very limits, as both Hofmannsthal and Wittgenstein knew. What is ethical is therefore inevitably critical, as Adorno knew. In the *Dialectic of Enlightenment*, Horkheimer and Adorno show how Kant's pure Reason has ushered in the calculating madness of a totalitarian order. When the *Critique of Practical Reason* stresses the autonomy and self-determination of the moral subject, so as to define the pure form of ethical action, the philosophy of Enlightenment meets global capitalism with a vengeance. Human concerns have to be ruled out, what matters is merely the conformity of Reason with its own laws. Pure Reason is both abstract and devoid of any object, like the empty compassion of Françoise in Proust's narrative.

As Adorno states, Juliette is more logical than Kant when she draws the conclusion that the order of society justifies crime: crime is regulated by a rationality that regulates human activities and pleasures. And Sadean 'apathy' approximates Kant's 'disinterestedness', both underpinning the brutal efficiency of the bourgeois conquest of the world. The right to enjoyment claimed by de Sade involves the extension of its field up to one's right to enjoy the bodies of others, and to torture them as one likes. The counterpart of this globalized rationality is the systematic mechanization of perverse pleasures in the Sadean orgy. Barthes noted how the orgy functioned as a perfectly oiled mechanism in which everyone had a part to play, since nobody was to remain idle (1989, 152–3).

Watt's eponymous hero calls up the inventor of the steam engine, James Watt, a contemporary of Immanuel Kant and of the Marquis de Sade. His name is synonymous with the inception of the Industrial Revolution in Europe. His main invention was based on a simple interaction of pistons, rods, and cylinders transforming energy into work. It is not such a stretch to see this as a sexual mechanism as well: the steam will easily emblematize bodies whose enjoyment is to be produced in a number or repetitive performances. Watt's name condenses the 'whatness' of technology, an 'essence' which, as Heidegger notes in his writings on technology, has by itself nothing technological, and one of the inventors who paved the way to today's technological revolution.

De Sade points out the dark side of humanitarian ethics when he rephrases man's universality in relation to the unconditionality of the Law, even though it is a caricature. Respect and blasphemy both address the same underpinning of fantasy by the Law of desire, which is presented as the obscene *jouissance* of the divine Other. The transgressive principle described by Lacan, Adorno, and Horkheimer implies a different writing. A transgression that questions the limits of humanity and the law presiding over limits postulates the need for a different writing. This explains the deviant logic and the series of permutations deployed systematically in *Watt*. *Watt* is a Kantian novel staging Sadean tortures of thought because rational knowledge is a machine that barely hides relations of domination, fear, and horror. 'Too fearful to assume himself the onus of a decision, said Mr. Hackett, he refers it to the frigid machinery of a time-space relation' (*W* 15). In a language that stages a repetitive foreclosure, pointing to an elsewhere of ethics, de Sade and Beckett denounce the dark side of universalistic ethics. If man is defined by the unconditionality of his rapport to the Law, then it is a welcome breath of fresh air to let subversion remind us of the reverse of the subject, its determination from behind. The irony is that de Sade's libertines devote their lives to approximating a divine *jouissance* through excess and inflicted pain, and they become slaves to this extreme enjoyment when they believe that they are the masters of the universe. Beckett's solution is different: he postulates an irrational imperative that just states the need to keep on saying, living, and creating.

Beckett's ethical position is shared by Lacan when the latter refuses to take the 'soul' as the seat of negative or positive affects, insisting that one should just pay attention to one's duty of 'saying well' – that is of expressing oneself as best as one can – even facing the most trivial incidents of one's life; as he stated 'sadness' should not be construed as 'a state of the soul', since 'it is simply a moral failing, as Dante, and even Spinoza, said: a sin, which means a moral weakness, which is, ultimately located only in relation to thought, that is, in the duty to speak well, to find one's way in dealing with the unconscious, with the structure.'[1] A Kantian imperative to 'go on', but in style, and this despite all the odds, remains Beckett's enduring ethical testament. In *Watt*, Arsene lists several types of laughter: the bitter laugh laughing at what is not good, the ethical laugh; the laugh laughing at what is not true, the intellectual laugh; and above all, the pure laugh, called 'dianoetic laugh', the laugh laughing at itself (W 40).

After *Watt*, it seems that dianoetic laughter and virtues tend to replace practical virtues in Beckett's works. What count most are virtues like courage, perseverance, wisdom, virtues that seek the truth, placed above practical virtues like honesty, loyalty, goodness, and temperance or compassion, to follow Aristotle's division. This is what Alain Badiou at any rate deduces from Beckett's entire work: an admonition that we should keep the courage to live on, and even find beauty in art and love.[2] If we follow Badiou, Beckett's ethics is truly a meta-ethics. A metaphysical laughter à la Bataille has replaced the earlier exhaustion marked by the pain of having been born, while discovering a concept of the Other.

This analysis can be deduced from *Worstward Ho*, as Badiou has shown (2005, 89–121), but can also have been brought to Beckett by Proust, to whom we need to return. One has often noted the proximity of Beckett's reading of Proust with that of Levinas (see Critchley 2004; Weller 2006; and Fifield 2013) who is often opposed to Badiou, although I would like to connect them. Levinas wrote extensively on Proust during World War II, and then condensed his views in 1947 in his paper 'The Other in Proust' (1989, 160–5). Unlike Sartre, Levinas refused to reduce Proust to psychology; for him, sociology and eroticism were better themes to pursue. Levinas saw *La Recherche* as a philosophical novel whose narrative is constantly cut by digressions offering theories about art, jealousy, homosexuality, music, travels, memory, perception, and so forth. However, those theories do not present theses about ethics, hence one should not read Proust ethically. Proust's investigations explore the spiraling abyss of human perversion. Once Sodom and Gomorrah have been crossed, no ethical system remains intact. For Levinas, no moral value survives unscathed:

> It is curious to note the extent to which Proust's amorality fills his world with the wildest freedom, and confers on definite objects and beings a scintillating sense of possibility undulled by definition. One would have thought that moral laws rid the world of such glittering extravaganzas more rigorously than natural laws and that magic begins, like a witches' Sabbath, where ethics leave off. The change and development in characters, some of them highly unlikely, feel completely natural in a world that has reverted to Sodom and Gomorrah, and relations are established between terms that seemed not to permit them. Everything is giddily possible. (1989, 162)

Proust would rephrase Dostoyevsky's 'God is dead, everything is possible!'. Levinas argues that Proust's amoralism goes beyond the antimorality of de Sade and Nietzsche. The key lies in the lesson brought home to the narrator by Albertine, in the ethical revelation of existence as otherness.

Thus one witnesses a striking convergence between Levinas's and Beckett's readings of an amoral Proust. Writing the first English monograph on Proust in 1931, Beckett highlighted the absence of moral sense in Proust's world: 'Here, as always, Proust is completely detached from all moral considerations. There is no right and wrong in Proust nor in his world' (*PTD* 66). Like Levinas, Beckett offsets this lack of moral concerns by the emergence of a radical otherness embodied by Albertine. The evocation of a plural 'Albertines' establishes a '*pictorial* multiplicity of Albertine that will duly evolve into a *plastic* and moral multiplicity' (47; emphasis in the original). Contradictions in her being are not 'an effect of the observer's angle of approach' but 'a multiplicity in depth, a turmoil of objective and immanent contradictions over which the subject has no control' (47). What the narrator loves in the fickle and lying Albertine is not a disappointing body or a mind that often bores him, but the potential of an infinite otherness it holds. For Levinas, similarly, Proust's fiction acquires exemplary philosophical value in that it achieves a radical break with classical ontology. Proust 'breaks definitively with Parmenides' (Levinas 1989, 165) because he opens the field of an ethics of desire and otherness beyond morality. This new ethics finds an adequate expression in literature, which applies to the whole of Beckett's work.

NOTES

1 Lacan 1990, 22, translation modified. The original has '*devoir de bien dire*' (in Lacan 1974, 39) translated as 'the duty to be well-spoken', which tones down the 'imperative of saying' so crucial for Beckett.
2 I have developed a comparison between Badiou's and Adorno's readings of Beckett, arguing that they assert similar theses in opposite vocabularies: 'Philosophizing with Beckett: Adorno and Badiou' (Rabaté 2010). See also Weller 2010a.

13

ULRIKA MAUDE

Beckett, Body and Mind

Samuel Beckett's writing can be characterised as a literature of the body. There is a striking emphasis on seeing, hearing, smelling, touching, falling, rolling, crawling, limping, ailing and ageing in Beckett's prose and drama, which also dedicates extraordinary attention to everyday physiological processes. Often, this foregrounding of bodily events serves as a rebuttal of philosophical idealism. The narrator of *How It Is* (1964), for instance, makes mention of the bodily functions that will eventually fail him: 'the need to move on the need to shit and vomit and the other great needs all my great categories of being' (*HII* 9). The protagonist of Beckett's first published novel, *Murphy* (1938), strives for a life of the mind, but ends up with his 'body, mind and soul [...] freely distributed over the floor' of a Dublin pub, 'and before another dayspring greyened the earth [Murphy] had been swept away with the sand, the beer, the butts, the glass, the matches, the spits, the vomit' (*Mu* 171). In its remarkable emphasis on embodiment, Beckett's writing distinguishes itself from the Western literary tradition, which has tended to emphasise psychological rather than physiological eventfulness. In Beckett's work, I shall argue, the mind is persistently conditioned by the body and its functions. This emphasis on embodiment developed in response to a number of scientific, medical and philosophical discoveries that took place in the second half of the nineteenth century, but it also had some important literary antecedents.

In or around 1930, Beckett turned his attention to the work of Henri Bergson. He had recently returned from a two-year period (1928–30) as *Lecteur* at the École Normale Supérieure, where he would have had ample exposure to Bergson's ideas.[1] It is unclear whether Beckett would have felt compelled to read Bergson during his residence in Paris, for Bergsonism was just beginning to wane in the period of Beckett's appointment at the École Normale (see Addyman 2012). French literary criticism, however, was predominantly Bergsonian in outlook (see Guerlac 2006), and during his brief period as Lecturer in French at Trinity College Dublin, from 1930–1, Beckett made ample references to Bergson in his undergraduate lectures on French literature, for instance distinguishing 'between Bergson's conception of time and Proust's[,] and between Bergson's attitude to language and Gide's', as the lecture notes of Beckett's former student, Rachel Burrows, in Trinity College Dublin archives reveal (Pilling 1997, 237, n. 25). Furthermore, in October 1930, Beckett wrote to his publisher, Charles Prentice, informing him that he wanted to add some pages to his book on Proust, 'in part to separate Proust's intuitivism from Bergson's'.[2] Beckett's reading notes on Bergson have not been recovered, but I will argue that Bergson's thinking had a lasting influence on Beckett's work. His publisher, John Calder, recalls all-night conversations with Beckett about Bergson from the mid-1950s until his death in 1989 (2001, 109).

One of the books Beckett read around 1930 was Bergson's *Laughter: An Essay on the Meaning of the Comic*, first published in French in 1899. The extended essay was substantially influenced by medical discoveries, and especially the theatrical and often spectacular culture of late-nineteenth-century neurology. In 1862, Jean-Martin Charcot had been appointed head physician at the Salpêtrière Hospital in Paris. Under his directorship, the hospital underwent numerous reforms, including the laicization of its nursing staff, an increase in the number of beds, 'better salaries for ancillary staff, improved bathing facilities, as well as laboratories, a museum, a new lecture hall' and, from 1882, a *Service des hommes* (Harris 1990, xix). By the second half of the 1870s, Charcot's famous Tuesday lectures, which the public flocked in to hear, 'were an essential part of Parisian intellectual life' (xii). At the lectures, Charcot exhibited his patients and developed his case studies before admiring crowds. In 1882, he inaugurated the first neurology clinic in Europe. At his clinic, Charcot and his many eminent students made important discoveries in the understanding of such conditions of the nervous system as Parkinson's disease, epilepsy, Tourette's syndrome and hysteria, which were brought to public attention at the Tuesday lectures and in the many journals founded in the period of the Third Republic, such as *Le Progrès médical*, in which Charcot published a number of his lectures. *La Nouvelle iconographie de la Salpêtrière*, the hospital's own publication, distributed images of epileptics and hysterics and sufferers of other neurological conditions; it ran from 1888 to 1918 and had George Gilles de la Tourette as one of its founders. Knowledge of Charcot's discoveries entered even the popular newspapers and magazines, and a number of Charcot's patients became celebrities in their own right. So pervasive was Charcot's work and so profound its impact on the popular imagination that it rapidly influenced the performance style of the Parisian cabaret and vaudeville 'with a new repertoire of movements, grimaces, tics and gestures', which mimicked the comportment and disposition of the Salpêtrière patients (Gordon 2004, 93). Comedians in particular sported convulsive and marionette-like gaits and movements, and mime troupes and singers followed suit in performances that seemed to cast doubt over received notions of the body's functioning and, by implication, the wider questions of agency and free will. Many cabaret and music hall performers went on to have successful careers in silent film, which adopted the frenetic, convulsive and automatic performance style of vaudeville and cabaret. As Rae Beth Gordon writes: 'There is a continuous line and directing force running from the cabaret and café-concert performances of the last quarter of the nineteenth century, through the films of Méliès and the musicals of Ernst Lubitsch [...]. The uniting element is hysterical gesture and gait' (111). Bergson's *Le Rire* itself was centred around the notion of 'automatic gesture and word', and one can trace a direct genealogy between Charcot's work, the popular culture of the period and Bergson's theory of comedy (109). So fashionable and intriguing did hysteria and neurological disorders prove around the turn of the century that they generated, besides a new performance style, a number of songs and literary works, such as Guy de Maupassant's short story, 'Le Tic' ('The Spasm'), from 1884, or to give an Anglo-American example, T. S. Eliot's poem 'Hysteria', from 1915.

Bergson's *Laughter* was anxiously indebted to neurological discoveries and especially the dyskinesia and the various automatisms that presented in neurological disorders and that figured so prominently in the performance culture of the period. Bergson argued in his book that 'The attitudes, gestures and movements of the human body are laughable in exact proportion as that body reminds us of a mere machine' (1911b, 29). Humour, Bergson reiterated, arises from 'Something mechanical encrusted on the living', for 'a comic character is generally comic in proportion to his ignorance of himself' (37, 16). This makes the subject appear as if deprived of his or her essential freedom:

> The soul imparts a portion of its winged lightness to the body it animates: the immateriality which thus passes into matter is what is called gracefulness. Matter, however, is obstinate and resists. It draws to itself the ever-alert activity of this higher principle, would fain convert it to its own inertia and cause it to revert to mere automatism. It would fain immobilise the intelligently varied movements of the body in stupidly contracted grooves, stereotype in permanent grimaces the fleeting expressions of the face, in short imprint on the whole person such an attitude as to make it appear immersed and absorbed in the materiality of some mechanical occupation instead of ceaselessly renewing its vitality by keeping in touch with a living ideal. Where matter thus succeeds in dulling the outward life of the soul, in petrifying its movements and thwarting

its gracefulness, it achieves, at the expense of the body, an effect that is comic. (28–9)

What neurological conditions such Parkinson's disease, Tourette's syndrome and epilepsy had in common, and what was seen as a source of black humour in cabaret and early cinema, was the body's seemingly mechanical capacity to act outside of the realm of conscious control. Neurological disorders which informed the performance style of music hall, vaudeville, cabaret and film, and as a consequence, Bergson's work, questioned notions of agency and intentionality, and hence cast serious doubt over received notions of subjectivity, suggesting that the mechanical, the automatic and the involuntary were in fact integral to the self. These pathologies, after all, 'raised serious questions about the philosophical viability of the doctrine of free will', something that Charcot and his students suggested was a mere metaphysical construct. Such conclusions doubtless reflect Charcot and his students' anti-clericalism, which permeated not only their political views, but also their research (Harris 1990, xvii, xix).

The question of free will is a central concern in Bergson's work, as the title of his doctoral thesis, and his first published book, *Time and Free Will: An Essay on the Immediate Data of Consciousness*, from 1889, reveals. It is central, for instance, to his notion of duration (*durée*), whose flow is constantly threatened by habit, repetition and automatism. Bergson in fact at times appears overly determined to defend the faculty of free will, to the point where his work frequently unveils a deep-rooted anxiety over its limitations. In his essay *Laughter*, habitual, mechanical, ossified comportment, as we have seen, appears as a source of humour, but it is also a locus of intense anxiety, which persists throughout Bergson's writing. In the essay, laughter is designed to function as 'a bursting out of life and elasticity in the face of the intolerable stiffening of life into automatic or repeated gestures' (Connor 2008, n.p.). However, as Bergson himself often acknowledges, laughter itself can function 'as a kind of machinery', as an involuntary somatic reaction beyond intentional control (Connor 2008, n.p.). Steven Connor writes:

> in laughing at what is inhumanly inelastic, we actually mirror the condition that is said to be comic. This confusion between stimulus and response, or between the laughable and the laugh, runs through Bergson's account. 'Involuntarily I laugh', he writes; and when he asserts that 'it is really a kind of automatism that makes us laugh [une espèce d'automatisme qui nous fait rire]', it is not certain whether he means that we laugh at automatism or that we laugh as an instance of it. (2008, n.p.)

Certain aspects of Beckett's humour, as well as his attitude to language, repetition and compulsion owe much to his reading of Bergson's work. Although

Beckett rejects Bergson's Cartesian division into spirit and matter, his influence can be said to be pervasive, for it is not merely Beckett's humorous works that are infused by Bergsonian ideas.³ The humour, after all, begins to recede from Beckett's writing after *Happy Days* (1961), but Beckett nonetheless retains his interest in the mechanized and ossified structures of comportment, as late plays such as *Footfalls* (1975), *Rockaby* (1980) and *What Where* (1983) so clearly attest. In such plays, Beckett's characters 'sometimes seem to be losing species, regressing to the subhuman, trying to rehearse the figures of instinct but botching the job', as Daniel Albright has put it (2003, 69).

Most pertinent for Beckett's work is perhaps Bergson's machinic notion of language itself, which persists throughout his writing. Language, in its propensity to organise and spatialise, 'violently deforms that temporal quality of living human experience in which "we change without ceasing, and [...] the state itself is nothing but change"' (Salisbury 2012, 173). In *Creative Evolution*, from 1907, Bergson writes:

> Our freedom, in the very movements by which it is affirmed, creates the growing habits that will stifle it if it fails to renew itself by a constant effort: it is dogged by automatism. The most living thought becomes frigid in the formula that expresses it. The word turns against the idea. The letter kills the spirit. (1911a, 127)

Beckett's shift to French in 1946 and the subsequent decision to straddle two languages, may itself have been a magical gesture against the 'rigid, the ready-made, the mechanical' in language, which Beckett's writing manages at once to perform, exemplify and evade (127).

Beckett's reading of Bergson is followed closely in the first half of the 1930s by his study of a number of turn-of-the-century medical books, including Sir William Osler's *The Principles and Practice of Medicine*, Pierre Garnier's *Onanisme Seul et a Deux*, Max Nordau's *Degeneration*, as well as works of psychology and psychoanalysis, among them Robert Woodworth's *Contemporary Schools of Psychology* and Karin Stephen's *Psychoanalysis and Medicine: A Study of the Wish to Fall Ill*. In all of these texts, one can detect an emphasis on and anxiety over chronic or habitual action, which emerges as a source of addiction or compulsion, causing machinic and at times pathological repetitions and actions that are 'amassed in the body' and 'constitute the main office of our nervous system', as Bergson puts it in *Matter and Memory* (1991c, 96). At stake in these medical and psychological studies, as well as in Bergson's writing, is the tension between conceptual and biomechanical models of cognition and behaviour, which is also key to an understanding of Beckett's work.

From the Canadian physician Sir William Osler's highly influential medical textbook, which was first published in 1892 and which was translated into a number of languages and ran into many editions, Beckett draws on the chapter on alcoholism for his short story, 'Echo's Bones' (written 1933; published 2014). Osler (1921, 387–8) describes chronic incoordination, 'unsteadiness of the muscles' and tremor 'best seen in the hands and the tongue' as classic symptoms of alcoholism, and the alcoholic Lord Gall in 'Echo's Bones' is described as 'vibrating from head to foot' (Beckett 2014, 16). As Mark Nixon has observed, Belacqua's 'consideration' for the groundsman Doyle's 'cyanosis' in the story derives from Osler's textbook, where 'a flushed, sometimes slightly cyanosed face' is mentioned as one of the symptoms of acute alcoholism (Osler 1921, 387). The term also finds its way into a number of other Beckett works, including *Dream of Fair to Middling Women*, *Murphy* and 'Love and Lethe' (see Beckett 2014, 103). Addiction, of course, causes mechanical and conditioned behaviour, what Bergson's tutor at the École Normale Supérieure, Félix Ravaisson, refers to as a 'pathological habit' induced by passion and passivity rather than the more positive type of habit, which for Ravaisson involves the will and originates in an intentional act (see Ravaisson 2008). Although Ravaisson acknowledges negative habits, among which he includes chronic illness, he is far more positive than Bergson towards the notion of habit, which he calls a second nature in his book *Of Habit*, from 1838.

From Pierre Garnier's anti-masturbation book, *Onanisme Seul et a Deux*, which Beckett read in Trinity College Dublin library in 1931, in the book's ninth or tenth edition, published in the 1890s, Beckett picks up strands of narrative, curious terminology, and an emphasis on the mechanical nature of sexuality. Hypersexuality, in particular, figures prominently in his early prose works, *Dream of Fair to Middling Women* (completed 1932; published 1992) and *More Pricks Than Kicks* (1934), where the protagonist, Belacqua, is presented as a compulsive masturbator, tormented by his sexuality, which in the narrator's words functions as a 'demented hydraulic that was beyond control' (*Dream* 41). Throughout *Dream of Fair to Middling Women*, as Yoshiki Tajiri has argued, 'pistons, cylinders and switches' function as tropes for masturbation, and even in his mature work, Beckett mostly, with a few exceptions, retains an emphasis on the mechanical rather than erotic nature of sexuality (2002, 195). From Max Nordau's *Degeneration*, which he read in the 1895 translation, Beckett takes notes on Tourette's syndrome and its symptoms of coprolalia (mucktalk) and echolalia. Beckett read the following passage in Nordau's book:

> Gilles de la Tourette has coined the word 'coprolalia' (mucktalk) for obsessional explosions of blasphemies and obscenities which characterize a malady described most exhaustively by M. Catrou, and called by him 'disease

of convulsive tics.' M. Zola is affected by coprolalia to a very high degree. (1986, 499)

He also read Nordau's description of echolalia:

> A perception arouses a representation which summons into consciousness a thousand other associated representations. The healthy mind suppresses the representations which are contradictory to, or not rationally connected with, the first perception. This the weak-minded cannot do. The mere similarity of sound determines the current of his thought. He hears a word, and feels compelled to repeat it, once or oftener, sometimes to the extent of 'Echolalia'; or it calls into his consciousness other words similar to it in sound, but not connected with it in meaning, whereupon he thinks and talks in a series of completely disconnected rhymes; or else words have, besides their similarity of sound, a very remote and weak connection of meaning; this gives rise to punning. (1986, 65)

What is striking about these symptoms of language pathology is their close proximity to poetic language: to polysemy, rhymes, rhythms and punning. Beckett is perhaps the most coprolalic of all the modernist writers, for so-called obscenities figure prominently in his writing, as does the Tourettic notion of language speaking itself, compulsively and convulsively, as in Lucky's speech in *Waiting for Godot* (1953), in *The Unnamable*'s (1958) convulsive prose and in *Not I* (1972).[4] Beckett also acquires from Nordau a knowledge of Charcot's work on male hysteria. He takes a number of notes on the symptoms in his *'Dream' Notebook*, a personal notebook from the early 1930s in which Beckett recorded details of the books he read. A number of the symptoms, such as aboulia (*Molloy*), motor disturbances (*Watt*), delirium (*Malone Dies*), fixed ideas (*Play*), and a range of speech disorders that often characterise the language of hysterics, such as stuttering (*Watt; Ill Seen Ill Said*), telegraphic language (*The Unnamable*), coprolalia (*Krapp's Last Tape*), aphonia and mutism ('The Calmative') are later scattered throughout his writing.[5] Important here is also Beckett's reading of Karin Stephen's *Psychoanalysis and Medicine: A Study on the Wish to Fall Ill* (1933). Beckett made copious notes on this book in the early 1930s (TCD MS 10971/7). Among them figures an annotation on the 'sheer terror of being run away with a bodily function', of the loss of agency in involuntary bodily events. As Laura Salisbury and Chris Code have recently observed,

> The compulsive is not an escape from the mind; rather, it remains contaminated with and indeed driven by feeling, constellating within an affective, affected subject that remains sufficiently conscious to act as its own sometimes amused, sometimes melancholy, witness. (2013, 109)

A case in point is Beckett's play, *Not I*, from 1972, in which Mouth bears witness to her own involuntary logorrhoea. As Beckett wrote to Alan Schneider regarding the play: Mouth's speech is 'a purely buccal phenomenon, without mental control or understanding, only half heard. Function running away with organ' (qtd. in Harmon 1998, 283).

Beckett also takes copious notes on the 1931 edition of Woodworth's *Contemporary Schools of Psychology*, among which are three pages on behaviourism. What John B. Watson's experiments revealed was that much of what had previously been considered intentional human action seemed to be simply a question of mechanical conditioning. In his notes on 'Russian Objectivism' and the 'Conditioned Reflex', Beckett mentions both Bechterev and Pavlov, who worked on motor and secretory reflexes respectively, and goes on to say: 'The conditioned reflex as investigated by Pavlov is one in which response has become attached to some substitute for natural stimulus, as approach of feeder instead of food in mouth, etc' (TCD MS 10971/7, qtd. in Maude 2013a, 86). He adds: 'All behaviour sensorimotor, consisting of stimulus-response units, each of which began with stimulus to a sense organ & terminate in muscular or glandular response. Behaviour might be overt or implicit' (86). What Ivan Pavlov's experiments gave to behaviourism is precisely the conviction that behaviour is acquired through conditioning and learning, in other words through a form of machinic repetition.

One of the most striking examples of a stimulus-response unit in the Beckettian canon is offered in *Play*, from 1963. In this work, three characters, two women and a man caught up in a *ménage à trois*, inhabit urns, which can themselves be seen as analogous to animal cages or pens in a laboratory. The characters appear to be trained to spew out language at the instigation of the beam of a spotlight, conditioned to speak when the light hits them. In an early manuscript draft, entitled 'Before *Play*', this connection is even more explicit, for the three players – Beckett no longer called them characters – are situated in white boxes, 'one yard high' (UoR MS 1227/7/16/6, qtd. in Maude 2013a, 86). *Play* dramatizes the economy of the conditioned reflex: the interlocutor has been substituted by the theatrical spotlight. The stage directions make it clear that '*The response to light is immediate*' as in the reaction to stimuli in Pavlov's experiments (*CDW* 307; italics in original).

Beckett's literature of the body also has important literary antecedents. The most obvious example is James Joyce, but other writers, too, were central. As a student of Romance languages, Beckett was closely acquainted with the grotesque tradition and, specifically, with its master, Rabelais, in whose work the unruly body plays a crucial role. In 1926, on his first trip to France as an undergraduate, Beckett visited Rabelais's birthplace and grave. We also know that in July 1935, Beckett purchased and subsequently read Rabelais's *Pantagruel* in the Génie de France edition. Beckett, furthermore, made copious notes on his reading of Rabelais, now held at Trinity College Dublin, and even wrote a summary of the *Encyclopaedia Britannica* entry on the author. On 31 August of that same year, Beckett wrote to his friend, the Irish poet and critic Thomas MacGreevy, that a 'sign by which [Pantagruel] knew he was getting old, was that he could not put up with inferior wine as well as he used' (TCD MS10402/78, qtd. in Van Hulle and Nixon 2013, 44).

In his major work, *Rabelais and His World*, Mikhail Bakhtin offers his most sustained analysis of the significance of the body in the grotesque tradition. Unlike the more recent 'bodily canon', which features smooth, finished, completed, individualised and 'strictly limited' bodies, the grotesque tradition focuses on the orifices, organs, fluids and other emissions of the body, foregrounding the subject's affinity with the world (1984, 320). The significance of the various orifices of the body, namely mouth, genitals, anus and nose, is precisely that they collapse the confines between the body and its surroundings, facilitating their mutual intermingling. Bakhtin goes on to say: 'Eating, drinking, defecation and other elimination (sweating, blowing of the nose, sneezing), as well as copulation, pregnancy and dismemberment' attest to the collapsing boundary between self, other and world (317). The tradition's stylistic attributes, namely hyperbole, excess, exaggeration and clowning, serve only to heighten these effects, in which the thrust is always downwards, affirming the materiality of the body. Bakhtin adds that 'all that is sacred and exalted is rethought on the level of the material bodily stratum or else combined and mixed with its images' (370–1).

Waiting for Godot, for example, abounds in various images of oozing. Indeed, in the play, as Estragon puts it, 'Everything oozes' (*CDW* 56). Lucky weeps, Gogo bleeds and Didi makes an allusion to semen in his mention of erections and shrieking mandrakes. Gogo's feet stink because they are sweaty. Pozzo '*clears his throat, spits*', while Didi pisses better when Gogo is not around (*CDW* 30; italics in original). Lucky has a 'running sore' on his neck and Estragon a wound that is 'Beginning to fester' (*CDW* 26, 62). Both vomit and excrement are evoked in Estragon's line, 'I've puked my puke of a life away here, I tell you! Here! In the Cackon country!' (*CDW* 57). The grotesque emphasis on various orifices and bodily oozings in the play is striking. It serves to highlight the characters' affinity with the world of matter, which is also a prominent feature of a number of other Beckett works, such as *Play*, in which, as Beckett's stage directions have it, faces are '*so lost to age and aspect as to seem almost part of the urns*' (*CDW* 307; italics in original). In the novella 'The Lost Ones' (1971), the bodies of the vanquished become topographical features of the cylinder which forms their abode.

Bakhtin, furthermore, stresses that in the grotesque tradition, the inner organs of the body, such as 'blood, bowels, heart' acquire extraordinary significance (1984, 318). In *Waiting for Godot*, Pozzo makes mention of his heart, lungs and stomach. Two forms of bacteria, both the cause of a venereal disease, are also mentioned in Estragon's abusive cry, 'Gonococcus! Spirochate!' which perhaps evoke the prostate, for gonococcus causes gonorrhea while spirochates can trigger syphilis (*CDW* 68). Bakhtin also singles out various protrusive body parts as characteristic of the grotesque tradition's penchant for hyperbole and exaggeration. We learn that Estragon's foot is 'Swelling visibly': the tramps discuss the possibility of an erection and the nose is evoked through references to stinking feet, breath and Pozzo's fart (*CDW* 14). Lucky, for his part, has a 'goiter' and eyes 'Goggling out of his head' (*CDW* 26–7). In addition, Bakhtin emphasises the importance of eating, drinking and swallowing in grotesque realism, which, likewise, figure prominently in Beckett's most famous play. The tramps chew and suck on carrots, turnips and radishes. The stage directions, '*Chews, swallows*' are inserted when Estragon chomps at his carrot, and Pozzo, in turn, '*eats his chicken voraciously*' (*CDW* 22, 26; italics in original). The references to religion in *Waiting for Godot* intermingle with profane, embodied allusions. Both Didi and Christ, we learn, go barefoot, with the distinction that, where Christ lived, 'it was warm, it was dry!' and 'they crucified quick' (*CDW* 51). The collapse of the distinction between life and death, a feature Bakhtin defines as crucial to the grotesque tradition, is of course evident in Pozzo's most famous lines in Act II: 'They give birth astride of a grave, the light gleams an instant, then it's night once more' (*CDW* 83). *Breath* (1969), which features no dialogue, only a birth cry which transforms into a death cry in the course of the play's forty-second duration, is one of the many other instances of the blurred boundary between life and death in the Beckettian canon. One thinks, too, of the opening sentences of 'The Calmative': 'I don't know when I died. It always seemed to me I died old, about ninety years old, and what years, and that my body bore it out, from head to foot' (*CSP* 61).

Important, too, was Beckett's reading of Jules Renard's *Journal intime* (1927) in 1931. What particularly impressed Beckett were the close, candid and often meticulous self-observations Renard recorded in his diary. Beckett took a number of notes on the *Journal* in his *'Dream' Notebook*, including one on 'La solitude où l'on peut enfin soigner son nez avec amour' ['the solitude in which you can at last lovingly pick your nose'] (*DN* 32). Details of this and other annotations enter Beckett's first novel, *Dream of*

Fair to Middling Women, as can be seen, for instance, in Belacqua's thought: 'Ah solitude, when a man at last and with love can occupy himself in his nose!' (*Dream* 22). The entry that most impressed Beckett, however, was the final one in Renard's diary, of 6 April 1910: 'Last night I wanted to get up. Dead weight. A leg hangs outside. Then a trickle runs down my leg. I allow it to reach my heel before I make up my mind. It will dry in the sheets' (2008, 300). Bair records Beckett revisiting the passage over and over again (1978, 124), and Anthony Cronin gives an account of Beckett twice reading the passage out loud to his friend, Georges Pelorson (1997, 148). The impact of Renard's diaries can clearly be detected, for instance, in *Malone Dies*, in which the bed-ridden Malone is jotting down aborted narratives and self-observations in his exercise book: 'I have demanded certain movements of my legs and even my feet. I know them well and could feel the effort they made to obey. I have lived with them that little space of time, filled with drama, between the message received and the piteous response' (*MD* 16). The passage problematizes received assumptions about the mind's agency and its superiority over the body, and instead dramatizes their mutual interdependence.

Perhaps the most important influence of all for Beckett's literature of the body, however, was the eighteenth-century writer and lexicographer Samuel Johnson. At the time of Beckett's death, there were more books by and on Johnson in Beckett's library than any other author (Van Hulle and Nixon 2013, 32). Strikingly, however, it was not only Johnson's writing and his famous dictionary that interested Beckett, but the man himself whose life moved the aspiring young writer. From 1936 to 1937, after the completion of his novel *Murphy*, Beckett seems to have become obsessed with Samuel Johnson's life. In a period spanning just over a year, Beckett read more than a dozen books about Dr Johnson for his prospective but never completed play, 'Human Wishes', which took its title from Johnson's most acclaimed poem, 'The Vanity of Human Wishes' (1749), which, like much of Beckett's work, is notable for its uncompromising dramatization of failure. Beckett's intention was to focus on Johnson's frustrated love for Mrs Thrale, but the more he read, the less the amorous plot preoccupied him. Instead, he became increasingly absorbed by Johnson himself, whose many illnesses, eccentricities and physical afflictions captured Beckett's imagination. In his three 'Human Wishes' Notebooks and his correspondence, Beckett comments with great sympathy on Johnson's physical predicament. His notes also reveal his interest in the life of the body and unveil a fertile medical imagination at work.

Beckett's original idea for 'Human Wishes' – his 'Johnson blasphemy', as he called it – may at first glance seem rather conventional: unrequited love is after all the traditional stuff of literature. At the heart of his conception of the play, however, was a specifically *physiological* tragedy, for Beckett hypothesised that Johnson could not consummate his love for Hester Thrale because of his impotence.[6] The first of the three 'Human Wishes' Notebooks is faithful to this idea, although it tellingly contains far more notes on Johnson than on Thrale. By the second notebook, however, Beckett's interest has definitively shifted from the amorous relationship to Johnson himself. Indeed, in his second 'Human Wishes' Notebook, Beckett takes nine pages of notes on Johnson's medical conditions, including his dropsy and its many symptoms such as 'oedema'; 'ascites'; 'hydrothorax' and 'hydorcephalus'; 'tuberculous dermatitis' or 'scrofula'; 'sight of left eye entirely lost'; 'depression'; 'Endocrine disorder'; 'asthma'; 'bad melancholy'; 'Attack of aphasia'; 'sarcocele' (tumour of the testis) and 'urinary crisis'. In addition, Beckett points out, it is 'Possible that he also had myopia' ('Human Wishes' Notebook, UoR MS 3461/2). He also interestingly takes notes on Johnson's nervous disorders, jotting down from James Boswell's acclaimed biography of Johnson that 'Such was the heat and irritability of his blood, that not only did he pare his hands to the quick, but scraped the joints of his fingers with a pen knife [sic.], till they seemed quite red & raw' (UoR MS 3461/2). Most crucially, however, Beckett writes that 'Miss Lucy Porter [Johnson's stepdaughter] mentions his "convulsive starts & odd gesticulations" + Fanny Burney' ('Human Wishes' Notebook, UoR MS 3461/2). Quoting from Fanny Burney's *Letters and Diaries*, Beckett notes:

> In 1777: His mouth is almost constantly opening and shutting as if he were chewing. He has a strange method of frequently twirling his fingers & twisting his hands. His body is in constant agitation, see-sawing up and down; his feet are never a moment quiet, +, in short, his whole person is in perpetual motion. ('Human Wishes' Notebook, UoR MS 3461/2)

Frederik Smith has pointed out that 'the figure of the declining Johnson became for [Beckett] a sort of metaphor of Western man, academic and witty, alone, afraid of dying and yet intrigued by his own physical deterioration' (2002, 111). Johnson's contemporaries comment on the involuntary contortions he suffered, and Boswell suggests in his biography that Johnson's odd gesticulations appeared 'to be of the convulsive kind, and of the nature of that distemper called St. Vitus's dance; and in this opinion I am confirmed by the description which Sydenham gives of that disease' (1980, 150). Beckett makes a note of this passage, observing that Johnson possibly had St. Vitus dance, the popular name for Sydenham's chorea, although twentieth- and twenty-first-century commentators believe that Johnson suffered from Tourette's syndrome, which had also fascinated Beckett, as his notes and his own writing reveal.[7] Johnson's behaviour was also obsessive-compulsive, and Beckett would have read in Boswell's biography the following, rather striking passage, which focuses on the motor and vocal tics for which Johnson was famous:

> while talking or even musing as he sat in his chair, he commonly held his head to one side towards his right shoulder, and shook it in a tremulous manner, moving his body backwards and forwards, and rubbing his left knee in the same direction, with the palm of his hand. In the intervals of articulating he made various sounds with his mouth, sometimes as if ruminating, or what is called chewing the cud, sometimes giving a half whistle, sometimes making his tongue play backwards from the roof of his mouth, as if clucking like a hen, and sometimes protruding it against his upper gums in front, as if pronouncing quickly under his breath, *too, too, too*: all this accompanied sometimes with a thoughtful look, but more frequently with a smile. Generally when he had concluded a period, in the course of a dispute, by which time he was a good deal exhausted by violence and vociferation, he used to blow out his breath like a Whale. (1980, 343; italics in original)

In a letter of 1936, Beckett fantasised 'of a film opening with Johnson dancing home to his den in Fleet Street after the last visit to Mrs Thrale, forgetting a lamppost & hurrying back' (Beckett to Mary Manning Howe, 13 December 1936, *LSB I* 397). Johnson had an obsessive habit of touching each lamppost as he passed and returning to any he missed, and Beckett had clearly taken an interest in this curious behaviour. Even though Beckett never managed to finish his play about Johnson, the influence of Johnson the man can be seen everywhere in Beckett's writing, which repeatedly dramatizes the habit-ridden, eccentric, ageing, decaying and often suffering body. Throughout, his writing resists classical, metaphorical representations of the body whose function is to act as a magical gesture against the fleshly body's decay and inescapable flux. Instead, Beckett's writing, whether for the stage or page, develops a literature of the embodied subject, in which the mind is part and parcel of the body and the body itself is infused with memory and intelligence, as dramatized, for instance in *Krapp's Last Tape* (1958) where Krapp, in the grounds of the hospital 'where mother lay a-dying', is throwing a 'small, old, black, hard, solid rubber ball' to a little white dog (*CDW* 219–20). When the blind goes down in the mother's window and 'all is over and done with, at last', Krapp concludes that he will feel the rubber ball 'in my hand, until my dying day' (*CDW* 220). The centrality of the body for his writing is a conviction Beckett still held in 1979, when Lawrence Shainberg sent him a copy of his newly published book, *The Brain Surgeon* (1979). Beckett read the book and wrote in his thank-you note to Shainberg that

> Mere decay is a paltry affair beside the calamities you describe. It is all I can speak of. And the ever acute awareness of it. And the preposterous conviction

formed long ago, that here in the end is the last & by far best chance for the writer. Gaping into his synaptic chasms.(Beckett to Lawrence Shainberg, Paris, 15 July 79, UoR MS JEK A/2/268)

On 11 July 1937 Beckett had written to Mary Manning:

It isn't Boswell's wit and wisdom machine that means anything to me, but the miseries that [Johnson] never talked of, because unwilling or unable to do so. The horror of annihilation, the horror of madness, the horrified love of Mrs. Thrale... The opium eating [erasure] dreading-to-go-to-bed, preying-for-the-dead, past living, terrified of dying, terrified of deadness, panting on to 75 bag of water, with a hydrocele on his right testis. How jolly. (qtd. in Smith 2002, 115)

Beckett was intrigued by the writers who recorded the helplessness of higher principles in the face of embodied experience, and in this, his reading of Rabelais, Renard and the life of Samuel Johnson were formative. Although Beckett's writing differs from Henri Bergson's Cartesian stance, it simultaneously explores the Bergsonian notion, informed by medicine and experimental psychology, of the limitations of the mind, agency and free will, of 'the deep-seated recalcitrance of matter' (Bergson 1911b, 26), and of the human as always already inflicted by the mechanical. In this, Beckett's writing captures a paradigm shift in our understanding of subjectivity, for since the second half of the nineteenth century, Darwinian thought, neurology, behaviourism and even some aspects of psychoanalysis had pointed to a biomechanical rather than conceptual understanding of the self. If the great question in nineteenth-century literature had been 'Who am I?', Modernist culture characteristically posed the perhaps even more fundamental question of what it means to *be* an 'I', to *have* a self, in the first place. But whereas Bergson and a number of his contemporaries aimed to contest the mechanical, habitual and automatic that threatened to encrust themselves upon the living, in Beckett's writing, the habitual and the automatic become progressively more central, until in the late works, habit and mechanical behaviour constitute a tenuous, fraught and primitive ontology, the residues of an agential self.

NOTES

Extract from Samuel Beckett's 'Human Wishes' Notebook (UoR MS 3461/2, © The Estate of Samuel Beckett) and letter to Lawrence Shainberg of 15 July 1979 (UoR MS JEK A/2/268, © The Estate of Samuel Beckett) reproduced by kind permission of the Estate of Samuel Beckett c/o Rosica Colin Limited, London.

1 Beckett is also likely to have learned about Bergsonian concepts from Alfred Péron, who was the exchange lecturer at TCD from the École Normale (1926–8).

The character of Chas in *Dream of Fair to Middling Women* is partly based on Péron. In the novel, Chas talks to a group of students about Bergson: 'The difference, then I say, between Bergson and Einstein, the essential difference, is the difference between a philosopher and a sociologist .... And if it is the smart thing nowadays to speak of Bergson as a bit of a cod ... it is that the trend of our modern vulgarity is from the object ... and the idea to sense ... and REASON' (*Dream* 212; emphasis in original).

2 On 14 October 1930, Beckett wrote to Prentice: 'Would you let me add 5 or 6 pages to the last 9? Or would that make it too long? I would like to develop the parallel with Dostoievski and separate Proust's intuitivism from Bergson's' (qtd. in Addyman 2012, 77).

3 For an analysis of Beckett as a post-Cartesian writer, see Maude 2009.

4 For a discussion of the relevance of neurolinguistic discoveries on our understanding of Beckett's work, see Maude 2008 and Salisbury 2008.

5 For a fuller discussion, see Maude (2013b, 153–76).

6 Beckett later commented in a letter to Mary Manning Howe, of 2 January 1959, that 'my Thrale theory was all haywire' (qtd. in Pilling 1997, 169).

7 The symptoms of Sydenham's chorea are temporary, but Johnson suffered from verbal and motor tics all his life (see, for instance, Wiltshire 1991, 28–34).

14

SEÁN KENNEDY

'Humanity in Ruins'
Beckett and History

For a long time, critics took Samuel Beckett at his word when he said that he had 'no sense of history' (qtd. in McNaughton 2005, 106), and there was a critical consensus that his imagination functioned almost entirely outside it (Gilman 1988, 83). Having left Ireland, a country with, perhaps, too much history, or, at any rate, an obsessive relationship with the history it had, Beckett was held to have embraced the freedom of the literary scene in Paris, where he wrote profound, placeless works that presented 'a generalized cultural condition' (Boxall 2002, 160). Like Joyce before him, it was argued, Beckett found Ireland inimical to artistic production, modernist art in particular (Kenner 1983, 262–73), preferring 'France in war to Ireland in peace' (Shenker 1956, 147). There, he thought little more about Ireland, focusing rather on the shattered landscapes of postwar Europe. Confronting the new reality of a 'humanity in ruins' (Beckett 1993a, 337), he was drawn ever more towards abstraction and subtraction: twin techniques that brought him as close as any artist to expressing the 'Nothing' that haunted Western thought from its inception. In these circumstances, the artist that mattered, in Beckett's own words, was 'the artist from nowhere' (*Dis* 149).

This picture has changed recently, and changed considerably. New scholarship historicising modernism played an important role, by showing just how various the spaces and times of the modernist project could be (see Stanford-Friedman 2006), while a number of critics, many working from Ireland, demonstrated a more complex relationship between Ireland, modernity and modernist experimentation that troubled the cosmopolitan paradigm (for a representative sample of this work, see Coughlan and Davis 1995; Kiberd 2005; Frazier 2006). In addition, the complexity of Beckett's own position was brought into sharper focus, until it became apparent that he had never merely disavowed history in the first place. New readings of key works such as *Watt* (1953), *Waiting for Godot* (1953), *Endgame* (1958), and the trilogy (1959) revealed Beckett's continuing engagement with historical events, in Ireland and elsewhere (Buning et al. 2005; Bixby 2009; Kennedy and Weiss 2009; Morin 2009; Kennedy 2010a). By way of scholarly attention to Beckett's letters and manuscripts and, in particular, the newly discovered 'German Diaries' of 1936–7, critics showed that he had long been struggling with the relationship between history, politics, art and criticism (see McNaughton 2005; Nixon 2011).

That said there is still an important sense in which his work resists being read historically. Thomas MacGreevy was an important early interlocutor on this subject, and Beckett thought him 'Ireland haunted': trapped in a mode of nationalist criticism that obscured the true originality of artists like Jack B. Yeats (*LSB I* 569). Beckett saw how the struggle for legitimacy in Irish politics had spilled over into debates about the authenticity of this-or-that work of Irish art, and he rejected the entire business: 'To admire painting on other than aesthetic grounds', he said, 'may seem to some uncalled for' (*Dis* 96–7). What mattered, rather, was the manner in which great artists brought 'light' to 'the issueless predicament of existence' (*Dis* 96–7). Read in this light, a philosophical emphasis seemed about right.

It is dangerous, though, to presume complacency on Beckett's part as to the relevance of history to his work. Growing up in the period of the birth of the Irish Free State – a period that encompassed World War I, the 1916 Rising, as well as the Irish War of Independence and the Civil War – Beckett saw how partisan histories were used to bolster competing narratives of Irish identity. He paid close attention to the uses and abuses of art in this context, and incorporated such instances into his work. To take only one example: Oliver Sheppard's statue of Cuchulain at the General Post Office (GPO) in Dublin had only been in situ for a matter of weeks before he attacked it, by way of Neary's head, in the early drafts of his contemporaneous novel, *Murphy* (1938). In unveiling the statue, the Irish Taoiseach Éamon de Valera had described it as a 'creation of Irish genius, symbolizing the dauntless courage and abiding constancy of our people' (Bixby 2010, 78). Beckett loathed this appropriation of art to political ends. He thought art should be 'free to be derided (or not) on its own terms and not those of the politicians' (*Dis* 91).

After completing *Murphy*, Beckett visited Nazi Germany where, as James McNaughton (2005) has shown, he became ever more aware of the danger of terms like 'national destiny' or 'historical necessity'. In terms disconcertingly close to those of De Valera, though with vast differences of intent, Adolf Hitler opened his exhibition of degenerate art in Munich with the call for a 'German Art [...] expressing the life-course of our people' (1998, 561). Against this backdrop, Beckett was defiant:

> I am not interested in a 'unification' of the historical chaos any more than I am in the 'clarification' of the individual chaos, & still less in the anthropomorphisation of the inhuman necessities that provoke the chaos. [...] I say the background and the causes are an inhuman and incomprehensible machinery & venture to wonder what kind of appetite it is that can be appeased by the modern animism that consists in rationalising them [...] I say the expressions 'historical necessity' & 'Germanic destiny' start the vomit moving upwards.
> (qtd. in McNaughton 2005, 107)

In this context, Beckett's claims to having 'no sense of history' might be taken as deliberate, yet disingenuous rejoinders to highly charged debates about nationalist art, especially as they were being conducted in postcolonial Ireland and, in a more sinister vein, Nazi Germany. Beckett knew, however, that one could not simply ignore history in response and so, as McNaughton suggests, he confronted a paradox: any straightforward disavowal of history was inadequate, even dangerous, while rationalising events by way of historical narrative risked complicity with the very nationalist forces he was opposing (2005, 102). In effect, 'history' was both ineffable and ineluctable: it could neither be expressed nor escaped.

Place names offer one way of approaching this complex issue: they recur in Beckett's postwar work, intimating that we might still, in fact, be moving through a conventional historical landscape, without ever settling into a stable frame of reference: Sedan, the Ardennes, the Luneburg Heath, Glasnevin cemetery, Picadilly Circus, Killarney, the list goes on. Places come and go and it is, as Peter Boxall has noted, 'difficult to gain a purchase in the brief space between the acceptance and denial of location' (2002, 160). Yet Boxall rightly insists these works are 'choreographed partly by reference to an Irish and European political geography that will not go away' (162). The Luneburg Heath, for example, was the site of the Nazi surrender in 1945, whilst Glasnevin cemetery is the single most important location for the death cult of Irish nationalism in all its strains (the burial place of Daniel O'Connell and Charles Stewart Parnell among many others). These references gesture towards a historical world, without ever ceding to the demands of historical realism. They haunt the narrative with a history that is, in an important sense, the history of Beckett's own time, but they recur as elements in flux that cannot be pinned down. As David Lloyd reminds us, Beckett's work is 'devoted to the dismantling of the adequacy of both representation and reference in all their dimensions' (2010, 35), and 'history' is just one aspect, albeit a highly significant one, of this project. The point, as Boxall suggests, is to acknowledge the work's 'difficult and ambivalent relationship with a material political geography' without seeking to resolve it in conventional mimetic terms (162). History has not disappeared; it just cannot readily be accounted for.

This tension provides a sort of blueprint for Beckett's treatment of history in the texts written immediately after World War II: the characters rarely express themselves historically, but this does not mean they have escaped history. More often, in fact, it is the manner in which they are ensnared by a history – the content of which they have forgotten (or have tried to forget) – that proves decisive. Time and again, during the 'frenzy of writing' that began in 1946 (Knowlson 1996, 356–87), Beckett situates his characters in ways that both invite and defy historical analysis. The account given of a parasol in *Mercier et Camier/Mercier and Camier* (1946/1974) provides a good example:

> It must have come out about 1900, said Camier. The year I believe of Ladysmith, on the Klip. Remember? Cloudless skies, garden parties daily. Life lay smiling before us. No hope was too high. We played at holding fort. We died like flies. Of hunger. Of cold. Of thirst. Of heat. Pom! Pom! The last rounds. Surrender! Never! We eat our dead. Drink our pee. Pom! Pom! Two more we didn't know we had. But what is that we hear? A clamour from the watch-tower! Dust on the horizon! The column at last! Our tongues are black. Hurrah none the less. Rah! Rah! A craking as of crows. A quartermaster dies of joy. We are saved. The century was two months old.
>
> Look at it now, said Mercier. (*MC* 60)

The Boer War is the obvious reference here, but what exactly is Camier telling us? That he and Mercier are veterans of the siege? That they are, in some way, affiliated politically with those that were? The tone of the passage – mock-heroic – complicates things, but the siege is explicitly associated with an experience of political diminution beginning around the start of the century. Throughout the novel, both characters are haunted by memories of the 'days of innocency, before the flop' (*MC* 89), but as readers we are told little more about it. History intrudes, and then takes us nowhere.

Object Lessons: Beckett and History

What I want to examine here is how the burden of history in Beckett – a burden, we have seen, that can neither be expressed nor escaped – becomes vested in certain objects that encapsulate this double-bind without ever resolving it. Much of the initial shock of Beckett's work after the war stemmed from his radical excision of identifiable social and historical settings. With the move into French, much of what we understand by terms like 'history' and 'society' simply disappeared from view, but I want to suggest that it was condensed and recovered obliquely in some few iconic possessions: 'a good dozen objects at least to put it mildly', says Malone (*MD* 77). These puzzle the reader as recurring, often uninterpretable vestigia of a knowable world, and offer a condensed expression of history in its inexpressibility. As with the parasol, they may provoke personal as well as historical memories, yet they are just as often divested of their history, and cannot easily be read in historical terms. In their stubborn materiality, they intimate the enduring relevance of history even though it cannot be reliably apprehended, embodying the paradox Beckett had confronted in Germany in 1937.

The 'ur-object' in Beckett is the bowler hat. It is the one object 'the history of which', Malone tells us, 'he has never forgotten', and it offers a good example of the dynamic I am trying to identify here (*MD* 79). It appears only once or twice in the work before the war, but becomes ubiquitous in 1946, at the precise moment that conventional settings disappear. It is usually tied to the narrator's greatcoat with string, but 'even lost', Molloy tells us, it would have a place in the 'inventory of [his] possessions' (*WFG* 10). For Hugh Kenner, the bowler hat was 'bequeathed' to the Beckett tramp by Chaplin, but vaudeville is only part of the story (1978, 116–7). In one of the first works written in French in 1946, 'L'Expulsé'/'The Expelled', we are told in more detail of its provenance:

> How describe this hat? And why? When my head had attained I shall not say its definitive but its maximum dimensions, my father said to me, Come, son, we are going to buy your hat, as though it had pre-existed from time immemorial in a pre-established place. He went straight to the hat. I personally had no say in the matter, nor had the hatter. [...] When my father died I could have got rid of this hat, there was nothing more to prevent me, but not I. But how describe it? (*CSP* 48)

Beckett's correspondence of the 1930s confirms the bowler hat as a symbol of his family background, and he uses it as shorthand for the behaviour expected of him by his parents in the 1930s: 'they want me to wear a bowler' (n.d. (1930?) letter to Thomas MacGreevy, TCD MS 10402). Knowlson's biography has dealt in fine detail with the emotional fallout that attended Beckett's decision to quit his teaching post at Trinity College Dublin, when he lamented that he could not be more like his brother Frank, 'with a car and a bowler-hat' (*LSB I* 112). In 'Text for Nothing 8' (1950–2), the narrator confronts a bowler that seems 'a sardonic synthesis of all those that never fitted me', and this ill-fitting bowler is one of a few 'insignia' in the texts that hint at a historical provenance for Beckett's waif (*CSP* 134).

The 1920s and 1930s were a difficult time for Ireland's Protestant minorities as they adjusted to Irish independence (see Bowen 1983), and the bowler had a very specific meaning in Irish politics at this time, where it came to represent the forces (both Irish and Anglo-Irish) that coalesced under the banner of Cumann na nGaedheal to suppress Irish republicanism. Desperate for stability, William Cosgrave built a nonsectarian alliance of what he termed the 'best elements' in Irish society, and he extended a cordial hand to the Protestant minorities in the hope they would contribute capital and political experience to the new State (see Regan 1999). The Anglo-Irish experienced a profound crisis of loyalties in this period (Curtis 1970, 46), and a majority of those that stayed on in Ireland resolved it by way of half-hearted support for Cosgrave's initiative. The bowler hat expressed the shared hopes and ambitions of this new elite, and Beckett spoke unenthusiastically of the Cosgrave enthusiasm of his parents.

In the election campaign of 1932, the opposition, *Fianna Fáil*, fastened on the bowler as a symbol of Cosgrave's betrayal of Ireland's republican aspirations. Playing on anxieties regarding partition and a continuing economic dependence on Britain, they ran cartoons that showed him walking out of step with the rest of the Irish electorate, observed approvingly by Anglo-Irish snobs (Figure 1). De Valera adopted the cloth cap and fedora as more apt symbols of the plain people of Ireland (Keogh 1986, 186; Figure 2), while the Anglo-Irish elements courted by Cosgrave – the Protestant middle classes and residual aristocracy – were shown colluding in their bowlers and top hats to dupe the Irish people (Figure 3). This was a time when the kind of hat one wore said something about the kind of Ireland one hoped for.

As it appears in the postwar writings, the bowler hat condenses all of this history, personal and political, as well as the vaudevillian contexts described by Kenner and others. It reveals that although Beckett left Ireland, he did not ever fully leave it behind. As Hugh Kenner observes, it suggests 'an identity of sorts' for the postwar work (1978, 52). Read historically, it is an apt symbol of Beckett's birth into, later betrayal of, and ongoing 'ontological complicity' with his Protestant Irish background (Bourdieu 2000, 163). When it is subject to knockabout, as in *Waiting for Godot*, it expresses failed (or deliberately frustrated) social mobility in much the same manner as the comedy of Chaplin. The point, though, is that we would struggle to discern any of this from the works themselves. Occasionally, we hear that the waif is 'a member of the reformed church' (*CSP* 85), or he laments the oppressive sexual climate in his native city (Beckett 1946), but these are traces of a social and historical context that has more or less disappeared. The hat condenses what it cannot express and what its owner, all too often, cannot remember.

'Humanity in Ruins'

FIGURE 1. William Cosgrave voting in the 1932 election (Irish Press).

FIGURE 2. The plain people of Ireland suffer under Cumann na nGaedheal's economic policy (Irish Press).

'Humanity in Ruins'

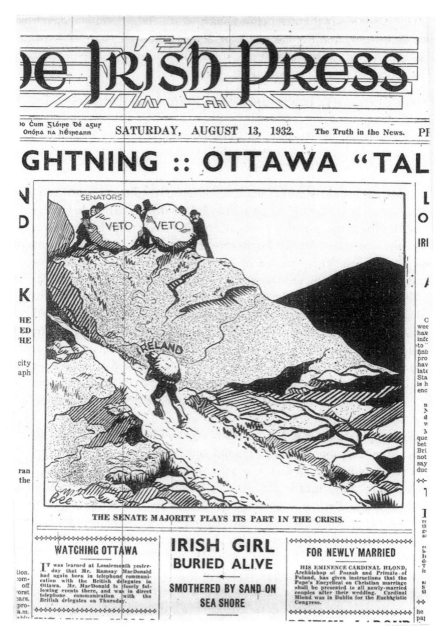

FIGURE 3. Irish Senators frustrate the path of Irish self-sufficiency (Irish press).

This is not to say that the major French works are 'set' in Ireland, at least not exclusively. Another hat, the kepi, demonstrates the complexity of the obscured historical spaces of this period. The narrator of *Premier amour/ First Love* (1946/1974) mentions it:

> Kepis, for example, exist beyond a doubt, indeed there is little hope of their ever disappearing, but personally I never wore a kepi. I wrote somewhere, They gave me... a hat. Now the truth is they never gave me a hat, I have always had my own hat, the one my father gave me, and I have never had any other hat than that hat. (*CSP* 35)

In 1946, the kepi was the common headdress of the French Army, and was indelibly associated with the new French President, Charles de Gaulle. As such, it evokes the complex political situation Beckett returned to in Paris after the war, where De Gaulle oversaw a purge of the residual elements of the pro-German Vichy regime of Marshal Phillipe Pétain. Pétain blamed France's defeat on the weakness of its people. In response, he promulgated a programme for their 'physical development and moral revival' (qtd. in Gibson 2010a, 104), and Andrew Gibson (forthcoming) has shown how Beckett's *Nouvelles* respond specifically to the politics and vocabulary of Vichy. Much of the strange power of these texts, he argues, stems from Beckett's 'violent reaction' to a collaborationist regime that routinely condemned its own people to 'desperation, misery, if not death' (forthcoming). In important ways, then, these are French texts responding to French historical circumstance.

To complicate matters further, many aspects of these works can, in fact, be read in the context of both Ireland and France. In 1929, the Irish government had banned all literature advocating contraception: 'contraceptive practices', it was argued, 'are a contradiction of a nation's life' (Kennedy 2010b, 81). As Beckett knew from research carried out for an unpublished essay of 1934, France had been singled out in Irish parliamentary debates as an example of depopulation due to excessive contraception: 'Is that for the benefit of France', J. J. Byrne had objected, 'Does it make for the production of a better race?' (81). Beckett was unimpressed, and his narrator's outburst to Lulu in 'First Love' – 'Abort! Abort!' – would have shocked almost everybody in Ireland. By 1940, though, France had instigated a ban on abortion that placed it on a par with treason, so Beckett is surely also addressing Pétain's regime (Beckett 1970, 52; see also Gibson forthcoming). At any moment, and this situation persists throughout the work of the great middle period, it is difficult to know whether we are in Ireland or in France, and we may well be in neither. 'It is not my wish to labour these antinomies', the narrator of 'The Calmative' tells us, 'we are needless to say in a skull'

(*CSP* 70; see also Morin 2009). Certain details seem obviously French, others indelibly Irish, while others 'cannot be read historically or even counter-historically' (Gibson forthcoming). In this context, Gibson makes the point that Vichy France, by way of its promotion of agrarianism and pronatalism, bore striking resemblance to postcolonial Ireland (specifically De Valera's vision after 1933), so that many of Beckett's recurring themes – degeneration, social alienation, a general abhorrence of reproduction or any state-sanctioned politics of fertility – resonate in both contexts.

However we want to read all of this, we are some way here from a writer with 'no sense of history'. Rather, finding a way to confront the problem of history was a defining feature of Beckett's artistic method after 1946. By then, he was all too aware of the dangers of the national-historical 'sense' as he had encountered it in Ireland, Nazi Germany and Vichy France. There is a difference, perhaps, between a 'sense of history' and a historical sensibility, and Beckett sought new ways to explore that distinction. As James McNaughton suggests, he knew that aesthetic decisions engaged the same 'narrative challenges presented by shoddy histories and ideological propaganda' (2005, 48), and the question was how to write historically without providing some aesthetic equivalent of the obfuscations of historical narrative. 'One can only speak of what is in front of him' [sic], he told Thomas Driver, 'and that now is simply the mess' (Driver 1961b, 219). A few scattered place names, a few fetishized objects, these are all that remain of conventional historical reality as part of a broader resistance to spurious intelligibility that Beckett cultivated after the war.

Accommodating the Mess: History as Degeneration

Given the way Beckett superimposes these different historical contexts in his writing, is there any way that they might be thought together? Critics have been justly sceptical of attempts to recuperate Beckett's postwar aesthetic as political critique (Lloyd 2010, 36), and there is no one framework that can clarify the postwar œuvre. Nevertheless, one of the objects encountered earlier – the parasol in *Mercier and Camier* – offers a context for further elaboration. The siege of Ladysmith, during the second Boer War of 1899–1902, is now remembered as one of the first events to unsettle Britain's sense of racial superiority as betokened by its glorious Empire. Talk of European degeneration was not new, but in February of 1900 the Boers inflicted a series of heavy losses on British troops in what became known as Black Week. These events shocked the British public and provided seemingly incontrovertible proof that the decline of Western racial stocks – as diagnosed by alarmists like Max Nordau (1895) – had begun in earnest (Eksteins 1985, 20). In the event, it required over 400,000 British troops to quell the Boers, and only after Kitchener implemented a scorched earth policy on the Transvaal. In the circumstances, the imperial idea suffered a loss of moral content, yet, at the same time, a renewed commitment to militarism seemed to offer the only defence against a new 'residuum' of vagrants, degenerates, homosexuals and racialised 'Others' that threatened civilization at home and abroad (Thornton 1966, 103; Nye 1985, 64). Degeneration theory rose to prominence in this period because it provided a way of rationalising Western decline while, more ominously, offering a clear route to salvation: a purge of degenerate elements from the national body (Nye 1985, 65). The discourse of degeneration was, in this sense, one of the more catastrophic examples of a governing historical metaphor – the very thing Beckett would decry later in his 'German Diaries' – and it provided much of the impetus behind the two World Wars. In retrospect, the Boer War of 1900 was 'the imperialist high peak' (Thornton 1966, 99), and what followed was ignominious slaughter, eventuating in the appalling vistas of Auschwitz: 'The century was two months old', says Camier: 'Look at it now' (*MC* 60).

In hindsight, degeneration theory was little more than a rationalization of European insecurities arising out of the profound social changes of the mid- to late nineteenth century. It was anxiety masquerading as history, and Beckett knew it. In 1936–7, he had visited Germany where Hitler vowed to wage 'an unrelenting war of purification against the last elements of putrefaction' in German culture (1998, 562). He had lived through Vichy France, where Pétain sought to reinvigorate the nation by way of a cult of the body that emphasised racial purity and stigmatised non-nationals (such as Beckett himself) (see Gibson forthcoming). In Ireland, degeneration theory had been notably associated with W. B. Yeats, and a dangerous current of nostalgia for Protestant Ascendancy that circulated among the Anglo-Irish after independence (see Kennedy 2014). Yeats interpreted the decline of the ascendancy in stark, eugenic terms: degenerate to a certain extent themselves, they were finally overwhelmed by the dysgenic fecundity of Catholic Ireland (see Howes 1996). In this apocalyptic analysis, survival of the fittest had been replaced by survival of the most fertile, a common trope in degeneration theory (Nye 1985, 65). Yeats may not have been fascist in any straightforward sense, but by *Purgatory* (1939) it is difficult to ignore how a preoccupation with authoritarian government dovetails with a eugenic analysis of the Irish case to sponsor a protofascist synthesis (McCormack 1994, 364). Yeats felt the danger was that 'there would be no war' (2000, 318), yet he died just before war broke out and never got to see quite what he had wished for. In the circumstances, having witnessed the fallout from the death camps, and counting many of his friends among the dead, Beckett felt compelled to respond (Kennedy 2014, 226). Nazism, Vichyism, Ascendancy: these were dubious rationalisations of history and the price paid for such 'clarity' had been unthinkable. 'Tyrants' it has been noted, 'always want language and literature that is easily understood' (Hacker qtd. in Phillips 2013, 291).

This offers one way to contextualise Beckett's treatment of history after the war: 'art has nothing to do with clarity', he suggested on his return from Germany, and 'does not dabble in the clear and does not make clear' (*Dis* 94). Beckett here rejects the view of history, critiqued by Nietzsche, in which 'the meaning of existence' would come 'increasingly to light in the course of its own *process*', insisting, too, that art could play no role in such a process (Nietzsche 1874, 7; emphasis in the original). Art must express the mess of history, not rationalise it. Indeed, to the extent that degeneration is pathologised in the diseased dialectics of Nazism and Yeatsian Ascendancy, I want to suggest, Beckett embraces and even valorises it: he appropriates the terms of the discourse of degeneration but subjects them to an ironic reversal (or transvaluation). In an obvious sense, Beckett's characters are degenerate: vagrants, perverts and the mentally ill were some of the main villains of degeneration theory, and it is precisely these outcasts that dominate his work. In 1895, Nordau suggested such degenerates be 'abandoned to their inexorable fate' (551). Beckett, refusing this logic, acknowledges that his people are 'falling to bits' but insists they embody a 'wretchedness which must be defended to the very end, in one's work and outside it' (Shenker 1956, 148; *LSB II* 25). With its obsessive accounts of regeneration and perfectibility, moreover, degeneration theory was, in an important sense, an attempt to deny entropy: to assert progress in the face of inevitable decline (Chamberlin and Gilman 1985, ix). After the war, entropy becomes the governing dynamic principle of Beckett's work: 'man [...] in spite of the strides of alimentation and defecation', Lucky tells us, 'is seen to waste and pine' (*WFG* 40; see also Gibson 2010b). From now on, there would be no moving away from this stark fact.

Beckett's transvaluation of degeneration theory also played out at the level of artistic form. According to Nordau, the modernist search for new forms was little more than 'hysterical vanity', since forms were 'given by the nature of human thought itself. They would only be able to change', he surmised, 'if the form of our thought itself became changed' (1895, 545). Beckett saw that the forms of human thought were irrational, and that this, too, could no longer be denied. Hence the search for a new artistic form: one that would 'accommodate the mess'. He told Thomas Driver:

> What I am saying does not mean that there will be no form in art. It only means that there will be new form, and that this form will be of such a type

that it admits the chaos and does not try to say that the chaos is something else. The form and the chaos remain separate. (qtd. in Driver 1961b, 219)

Form must accommodate itself to chaos, not chaos to form (for example, in the guise of historical or narrative realism). There is a tension here between accommodation and disintegration: form must not merely surrender to chaos (it would no longer be form), but neither must it seek to domesticate chaos. Rather, it must try, and likely fail, to accommodate chaos: to provide an avenue for its expression. 'Aesthetically', Beckett told Alec Reid in 1956, 'the adventure is that of failed form' (*LSB II* 596). On this basis, he doubted the formal serenity of Kafka's otherwise nightmarish visions: 'I am wary of disasters that let themselves be recorded like a statement of accounts' (*LSB II* 465). This was a new 'attitude of disintegration' that led, finally, to the 'complete disintegration' of *The Unnamable* (1959), and silenced Beckett for many years afterwards (Shenker 1956, 148).

Beckett's decision to embrace degeneration as an aesthetic principle provided one way to contest the monological character of historical narrative, while parodying the logic of degeneration theory. In 1945, when he saw the extent of the damage caused by the Allied bombing of the town of St-Lô, Beckett felt an 'inkling of the terms' in which the human condition would need to be thought again, and this entailed a final rejection of the historical myth of progress, and of the many teleological imperatives – salvation, race fitness, perfectibility, national destiny – that sustained it (Beckett 1993a, 337). By 1945, history might go on, but 'History' was over, and this stark fact provides the backdrop to the 'afterlife all life long' dramatized in Beckett's work (*MC* 86). In a critique of Sartre's existential philosophy, Theodor Adorno suggested Beckett was closer to the truth of history when he presented it as an 'anonymous machinery' (1974, 306), anticipating Beckett's 'German Diaries'. 'The mistake', Beckett told Georges Duthuit, 'is perhaps to want to know what one is talking about' (*LSB II* 98). In this disintegrating world, objects like the bowler hat and the kepi acquire something of the property of symptoms: they insist in the text while resisting interpretation, even as they provide condensed expression of repressed historical materials. Adorno thought Beckett's work dislocated 'to the point of worldlessness' (1974, 314). It is, however, in these occasional objects that a knowable world persists (even as it cannot be read 'historically').

Adorno also asserted that to write poetry after Auschwitz would be 'barbaric' (1967, 34). Yet this was precisely the point at which Beckett's creative powers were finally and fully engaged. In 1944, he outlined a diminished basis for artistic expression: 'The expression that there is nothing to express, nothing with which to express, nothing from which to express, no power to express, no desire to express, together with the obligation to express' (*PTD* 103). When asked why the artist was still 'obliged' to work he answered, characteristically, 'I don't know' (*PTD* 119). Here, rendered in aesthetic terms, is the paradox of history cited at the beginning of this essay: the duty of representation can neither be fulfilled nor forsaken. The obligation to make art persists even as the means to make it have been eliminated: there is 'nothing to paint and nothing to paint with' (*PTD* 120). This is a variation on Clov's predicament in *Endgame* (1958) when he asks 'the words that remain' and 'they have nothing to say' (*E* 48). It is the intractable double-bind of the Unnamable's going on even as he can't go on. Such now was the human condition and, contra Adorno, Beckett felt that the rubble of Western philosophy and letters must be made to speak to it. Man's place in history was inescapable yet inexpressible. Art's new task was to submit, finally, to this 'incoercible absence of relation' (*PTD* 125). If the camps had revealed 'the indifference of each individual life that is the direction of history' (Adorno 2007, 362), it was the eerie accuracy with which Beckett was able to express this, in great works like *Molloy* (1951), *En attendant Godot* (1952) and *Fin de partie* (1957), that secured his reputation.

WORKS CITED

Abbott, H. Porter. 1973. *The Fiction of Samuel Beckett*. Berkeley: University of California Press.
　1996. *Beckett Writing Beckett*. Ithaca, NY: Cornell University Press.
　2008. 'I Am Not a Philosopher'. In *Beckett at 100*, edited by Linda Ben Zvi and Angela Moorjani, 81–92. New York: Oxford University Press.
Abrams, M. H., and Geoffrey Harpham. 2009. *A Glossary of Literary Terms*, 9th edition. Boston: Wadsworth.
Ackerley, C. J. 2010a. *Demented Particulars: The Annotated 'Murphy'*. Edinburgh: Edinburgh University Press.
　2010b. *Obscure Locks, Simple Keys: The Annotated 'Watt'*. Edinburgh: Edinburgh University Press.
　2011. '"Deux Besoins": Samuel Beckett and the Aesthetic Dilemma'. In *The Edinburgh Companion to Samuel Beckett and the Arts*, edited by S. E. Gontarski, 17–24, Edinburgh: Edinburgh University Press.
　2012. 'The Bible'. In *Samuel Beckett in Context*, edited by Anthony Uhlmann, 324–6. Cambridge: Cambridge University Press.
Ackerley, C. J., and S. E. Gontarski, 2004. *The Grove Companion to Samuel Beckett*. New York: Grove Press.
Ackerley, C. J., and S. E. Gontarski. 2006. *The Grove Companion to Samuel Beckett: A Reader's Guide to His Works, Life, and Thought*. London: Faber and Faber.
Addyman, David. 2012. '"Speak of Time, without Flinching ... Treat of Space with the Same Easy Grace": Beckett, Bergson and the Philosophy of Space'. In *Beckett/Philosophy*, edited by Matthew Feldman and Karim Mamdani, 68–88. Sofia: University Press St. Klimrnt Ohridski.
Adelman, Gary. 2004. *Naming Beckett's Unnamable*. Lewisburg: Bucknell University Press.
Adorno, Theodor. 1967. 'Cultural Criticism and Society'. In *Prisms*, translated by Samuel and Sherry Wieber, 17–35. Cambridge, MA: MIT Press.
　1974. 'Commitment'. In *The Essential Frankfurt Reader*, edited by Andrew Arato and Eike Gebhardt, 300–19. New York: Continuum.
　1982. 'Trying to Understand *Endgame*', translated by Michael J. Jones. *New German Critique* 26: 119–50.
　1983. *Prisms*. Cambridge, MA: MIT Press.
　1984. *Aesthetic Theory*, edited by Gretel Adorno and Rolf Tiedemann, translated by C. Lenhardt. London: Routledge & Kegan Paul.

WORKS CITED

1990. *Negative Dialectics*, translated by E. B. Ashton. London: Routledge.
1997. *Aesthetic Theory*, edited by Gretel Adorno and Rolf Tiedemann, translated by Robert Hullot-Kentor. London: Athlone.
2007. *Negative Dialectics*. London: Continuum.
2010a. 'Notes on Beckett.' *Journal of Beckett Studies* 19.2: 157–78.
2010b. 'Notes on *The Unnamable*', translated by Dirk Van Hulle and Shane Weller. *Journal of Beckett Studies* 19.2: 172–8.
Agamben, Giorgio. 2011. *Nudities*, translated by David Kishik and Stefan Pedatella. Stanford, CA: Stanford University Press.
Albright, Daniel. 2003. *Beckett and Aesthetics*. Cambridge: Cambridge University Press.
    2006. 'Beckett's Poems as Plays'. In *Fulcrum: An Annual of Poetry and Aesthetics*, 522–9.
Anouilh, Jean. 1953. *Arts-Spectacles* 400 (27 February–5 March): 1.
Anzieu, Didier. 1983. 'Un Soi disjoint, une voix liante : l'écriture narrative de Samuel Beckett'. *Nouvelle revue de psychanalyse* 28: 71–85.
    1992. *Beckett et le psychanalyste*. Paris: Éditions Mentha Archimbaud.
Atik, Anne. 2001. *How It Was: A Memoir of Samuel Beckett*. London: Faber and Faber.
Badiou, Alain. 1992. *Conditions*. Paris: Seuil.
    1995. *Beckett: l'increvable désir*. Paris: Hachette.
    2003. *On Beckett*, edited by Nina Power and Alberto Toscano. Manchester: Clinamen Press.
    2005. 'Being, Existence, Thought: Prose and Concept'. In *Handbook of Inaesthetics*, translated by Alberto Toscano, 89–121. Stanford, CA: Stanford University Press.
    2012. *The Rebirth of History*, translated by Gregory Elliott. London: Verso.
Bair, Deirdre. 1978. *Samuel Beckett: A Biography*. London: Vintage.
    1990. *Samuel Beckett: A Biography*. New York: Simon & Schuster.
Bakhtin, Mikhail. 1984. *Rabelais and His World*, translated by Hélène Iswolsky. Bloomington: Indiana University Press.
Barry, Elizabeth. 2008. 'Introduction: Beckett, Language and the Mind'. *Journal of Beckett Studies* 17.1–2: 1–8.
Barthes, Roland. 1989. *Sade, Fourier, Loyola*, translated by Richard Miller. Berkeley: University of California Press.
Bataille, Georges. 1951. 'Le silence de *Molloy*'. *Critique* 7: 387–96.
    1979. Review of *Molloy*. In *Samuel Beckett: The Critical Heritage*, edited by Lawrence Graver and Raymond Federman, translated by Jean M. Sommermeyer, 55–64. London: Routledge and Kegan Paul.
Bauman, Zygmunt. 1989. *Modernity and the Holocaust*. Ithaca, NY: Cornell University Press.
Beckett, Samuel. nd. Correspondence with Lawrence Shainberg. JEK MS A/2/268.
    nd. Correspondence with Thomas MacGreevy. TCD MS10402.
    nd. 'Human Wishes Notebook 2'. UoR MS 3461/2.
    1935. *Echo's Bones and Other Precipitates*. Paris: Europa Press.
    1936. Letter to Thomas MacGreevy, 15 April. TCD MS 10402.
    1936–9. '*Whoroscope*' Notebook, Beckett International Foundation. UoR MS 3000.
    1946. 'L'Expulsé'. *Fontaine* 10: 685–708.

WORKS CITED

1951. *Malone meurt*. Paris: Editions de Minuit.
1953. *L'Innommable*. Paris: Editions de Minuit.
1957. Letter to Alan Schneider, 29 December, qtd. in 'Beckett's Letters on *Endgame*'. In *The Village Voice Reader*, edited by Daniel Wolf and Edwin Fancher, 185. Garden City: Doubleday, 1962.
1958. *Nouvelles et Textes pour rien*. Paris: Editions de Minuit.
1960. Letters to Barbara Bray, March. TCD MS 10948/1/72; TCD MS 10948/1/75; TCD MS 10948/1/78.
1961. *Comment c'est*. Paris: Editions de Minuit.
1965. *Proust and Three Dialogues with Georges Duthuit*. London: John Calder.
1967. *Têtes mortes*. Paris: Editions de Minuit.
1970. *Premier amour*. Paris: Editions de Minuit.
1972. 'Dante...Bruno.Vico...Joyce'. In *Our Exagmination Round His Factification for Incamination of Work in Progress*, 1–22. London: Faber and Faber.
1983. *Disjecta: Miscellaneous Writings and a Dramatic Fragment*, edited by Ruby Cohn. London: John Calder.
1984a. Letter to Dr. E. Franzen, 17 February 1954, cited in 'Babel 3, 1984', [magazine]. Ms 2993: The Samuel Beckett Collection, University of Reading, UK. Typescript consulted May 1992.
1984b. 'Peintres de l'empêchement'. *Disjecta*, by Samuel Beckett, 133–7. New York: Grove Press.
1988. *Molloy*. Paris: Editions de Minuit.
1989a. *Le monde et le pantalon*. Paris: Editions de Minuit.
1989b. *Soubresauts*. Paris: Editions de Minuit.
1992a. *Dream of Fair to Middling Women*, edited by Eoin O'Brien and Edith Fournier. Dublin: Black Cat Press.
1992b. *The Theatrical Notebooks of Samuel Beckett, Volume 3: Krapp's Last Tape, with a Revised Text*, edited by James Knowlson. New York: Grove Press.
1993a. 'The Capital of the Ruins'. In *The Beckett Country*, edited by Eoin O'Brien, 337–9. New York: Arcade Publishing.
1993b. *Samuel Beckett's 'Company'/'Compagnie' and 'A Piece of Monologue'/'Solo': A Bilingual Variorum Edition*, edited by Charles Krance. New York: Garland.
1993c. *The Theatrical Notebooks of Samuel Beckett, Volume 1: Waiting for Godot*, edited by Dougald Macmillan and James Knowlson. New York: Grove Press.
1993d. *The Theatrical Notebooks of Samuel Beckett, Volume 2: Endgame, with a Revised Text*, edited by S. E. Gontarski. New York: Grove Press.
1995. *The Complete Short Prose, 1929–1989*, edited by S. E. Gontarski. New York: Grove Press.
1996. *Eleutheria*, translated by Barbara Wright. London: Faber and Faber.
1999a. *As the Story Was Told*. London: John Calder.
1999b. *The Theatrical Notebooks of Samuel Beckett, Volume 4: Shorter Plays*, edited by S. E. Gontarski. New York: Grove Press.
2001. *Samuel Beckett's Comment c'est/How It Is and/et L'image: A Critical-Genetic Edition/Une Edition Critico-Génétique*, edited by Edouard Magessa O'Reilly. London: Routledge.
2006a. *The Grove Centenary Edition*, vol. 2. New York: Grove Press.
2006b. *Malone Dies*. In *The Grove Centenary Edition*, vol. 2, 171–281.
2006c. *Molloy*. In *The Grove Centenary Edition*, vol. 2, 1–170.

2006d. *The Unnamable*. In *The Grove Centenary Edition*, vol. 2, 283–407.
2009a. *Company, Ill Seen Ill Said, Worstward Ho, Stirrings Still*, edited by Dirk Van Hulle. London: Faber and Faber.
2009b. *The Letters of Samuel Beckett, vol. I: 1929–1940*, edited by Martha Dow Fehsenfeld and Lois More Overbeck. Cambridge: Cambridge University Press.
2009c. *Molloy*, edited by Shane Weller. London: Faber and Faber.
2009d. *Watt*, edited by C. J. Ackerley. London: Faber and Faber.
2010. *The Unnamable*, edited by Steven Connor. London: Faber and Faber.
2011. *The Letters of Samuel Beckett, vol. II: 1941–1956*, edited by George Craig, Martha Dow Fehsenfeld, Dan Gunn and Lois More Overbeck. Cambridge: Cambridge University Press.
2012. *The Collected Poems of Samuel Beckett*, edited by Seán Lawlor and John Pilling. London: Faber and Faber.
2014. *Echo's Bones*, edited by Mark Nixon. London: Faber and Faber.
Beer, Ann. 1985. '*Watt*, Knott and Beckett's Bilingualism'. *Journal of Beckett Studies*, old series, 10: 37–75.
Begam, Richard. 1996. *Samuel Beckett and the End of Modernity*. Stanford, CA: Stanford University Press.
Bennett, Michael Y. 2011. *Reassessing the Theatre of the Absurd: Camus, Beckett, Genet and Pinter*. New York: Palgrave.
Ben-Zvi, Linda, and Angela Moorjani, eds. 2008. *Beckett at 100: Revolving It All*. Oxford: Oxford University Press.
Bergson, Henri. 1911a. *Creative Evolution*, translated by Arthur Mitchell. London: Macmillan.
1911b. *Laughter: An Essay on the Meaning of the Comic*, translated by Cloudesley Brereton and Fred Rothwell. New York: Macmillan.
1911c. *Matter and Memory*, translated by Nancy Margaret Paul and W. Scott Palmer. London: Macmillan.
Bernold, André. 1992. *L'Amitié de Beckett, 1979–1989*. Paris: Hermann.
Bernstein, J. M. 2006. *Against Voluptuous Bodies: Late Modernism and the Meaning of Painting*. Stanford, CA: Stanford University Press.
Bixby, Patrick. 2009. *Samuel Beckett and the Postcolonial Novel*. Cambridge: Cambridge University Press.
2010. 'Beckett at the GPO: *Murphy*, Ireland, and the "unhomely"'. In *Beckett and Ireland*, edited by Seán Kennedy, 78–95. Cambridge: Cambridge University Press.
Blackman, Jackie. 2009. 'Beckett's Theatre "After Auschwitz"'. In *Samuel Beckett: History, Memory, Archive*, edited by Seán Kennedy and Katherine Weiss, 71–88. New York: Palgrave Macmillan.
Blanchot, Maurice. 1953. 'Où maintenant? Qui maintenant?' *La Nouvelle Nouvelle Revue Française* 1.10: 678–86.
1979. Review of *L'Innomable*. In *Samuel Beckett: The Critical Heritage*, translated by Richard Howard, edited by Lawrence Graver and Raymond Federman, 116–21. London: Routledge and Kegan Paul.
1995. 'Oh All to End.' In *The Blanchot Reader*, translated by Leslie Hill, edited by Michael Holland, 298–300. Oxford: Blackwell.
1997. *Awaiting Oblivion*, translated by John Gregg. Lincoln, NE and London: University of Nebraska Press.

2001. *Faux pas*, translated by Charlotte Mandell. Stanford, CA: Stanford University Press.
2004. *Lautréamont and Sade*, translated by Stuart Kendall and Michelle Kendall. Stanford, CA: Stanford University Press.
Bolin, John. 2013. *Beckett and the Modern Novel*. Cambridge: Cambridge University Press.
Boswell, James. 1980. *Life of Johnson*, edited by R. W. Chapman. Oxford World's Classics. Oxford: Oxford University Press.
Boulter, Jonathan. 2012. '"We have our being in justice": Samuel Beckett's *How It Is*'. In *Samuel Beckett and Pain*, edited by Mariko Tanaka, Yoshiki Tajiri and Michiko Tsushima, 173–200. Amsterdam and New York: Rodopi.
Bourdieu, Pierre. 2000. *Pascalian Meditations*. Cambridge: Polity Press.
Bowen, Kurt. 1983. *Protestants in a Catholic State: Ireland's Privileged Minority*. Montreal: Queen's University Press.
Bowles, Patrick. 1958. 'How Samuel Beckett Sees the World'. *The Listener* 59: 1011–12.
1994. 'How to Fail: Notes on Talks with Samuel Beckett.' *PN Review* 96 20.4: 24–38.
Boxall, Peter. 2000. *Samuel Beckett: 'Waiting for Godot'/'Endgame': A Reader's Guide to Essential Criticism*. Cambridge: Icon Books.
2002. 'Samuel Beckett: Towards a Political Reading'. *The Irish Studies Review* 10.2: 159–70.
2004. 'Beckett and Homoeroticism'. In *Directing Beckett*, 110–32.
Bradby, David. 2001. *Beckett: 'Waiting for Godot'*. Cambridge: Cambridge University Press.
Brantley, Ben. 'When a Universe Reels, a Baryshnikov May Fall', theater review of 'Beckett Shorts'. *The New York Times*, 19 December 2007. Online at http://www.nytimes.com/2007/12/19/theater/reviews/19beck.html?_r=0.
Brater, Enoch. 1974. 'The "I" in Beckett's *Not I*'. *Twentieth Century Literature* 20 (July): 200.
1987. *Beyond Minimalism: Beckett's Late Style in the Theatre*. Oxford: Oxford University Press.
2011. *Ten Ways of Thinking about Samuel Beckett*. London: Methuen.
Brook, Peter. 1968. *The Empty Space: A Book about Theatre*. New York: Atheneum.
Bruhns, Maike. 2007. 'Ausgegrenzte Avantgarde: Beckett in den Künstlerkreisen der ehemaligen Hamburger Sezession'. In *Das Raubauge in der Stadt: Beckett liest Hamburg*, edited by Michaela Giesing, Gaby Hartel and Carola Veit, 89–101. Göttingen: Wallstein Verlag.
Bryden, Mary. 1998. *Samuel Beckett and the Idea of God*. Houndmills: Macmillan.
ed. 2013. *Beckett and Animals*. Cambridge: Cambridge University Press.
Buning, Marius, Matthijs Engelberts, Sjef Houppermans, Dirk Van Hulle, and Danièle de Ruyter, eds. 2005. *Samuel Beckett Today/Aujourd'hui* 15: *Historicising Beckett/Issues of Performance*.
Burnet, John. 1914. *Greek Philosophy, Part I: Thales to Plato*. London: Macmillan.
Calder, John. 2001. *The Philosophy of Samuel Beckett*. London: John Calder.
Campbell, Julie. 2012. 'Allegories of Clarity and Obscurity'. *Samuel Beckett Today/Aujourd'hui* 24: 89–103.

WORKS CITED

Carville, Conor. 2011. 'Autonomy and the Everyday: Beckett, Late Modernism and Post-War Visual Art.' *Samuel Beckett Today/Aujourd'hui* 23: *Filiations & Connexions/Filiations and Connecting Lines*, 63–78.

Casanova, Pascale. 1997. *Beckett l'abstracteur*. Paris: Seuil.

——— 2007. *Samuel Beckett: Anatomy of a Literary Revolution*, translated by Gregory Elliott, introduction by Terry Eagleton. London: Verso.

Caselli, Daniela. 2005a. *Beckett's Dantes: Intertextuality in the Fiction and Criticism*. Manchester: Manchester University Press.

——— 2005b. 'Staging the *Inferno* in *How It Is*'. In *Beckett's Dantes: Intertextuality in the Fiction and Criticism*, 148–83.

Celan, Paul. 1988. *Poems of Paul Celan*, translated by Michael Hamburger. New York: Persea Books.

Chabert, Pierre. 1986. 'Rehearsing Pinget's *Hypothesis* with Beckett'. In *As no other dare fail: for Samuel Beckett on His 80th Birthday by His Friends and Admirers*, 117–32, translated by John Calder, edited by John Calder. London: John Calder.

Chamberlin, J. Edward, and Sander L. Gilman. 1985. 'Introduction'. In *Degeneration: The Dark Side of Progress*, edited by Edward J. Chamberlin and Sander L. Gilman, ix-xiv. New York: Columbia University Press.

Chan, Paul, ed. 2010. *Waiting for Godot in New Orleans: A Field Guide*. New York: Creative Time.

Chesney, Duncan McColl. 2011. 'Beckett's Silences and Late Modernity.' *National Taiwan University Studies in Language and Literature* 26 (December): 121–36.

Cixous, Hélène. 2007. *Le voisin de zéro*. Paris: Galilée.

Clément, Bruno. 1989. *L'Œuvre sans qualités. Rhétorique de Samuel Beckett*. Paris: Seuil.

——— 2006. 'What the Philosophers Do with Samuel Beckett'. In *Beckett after Beckett*, translated by Anthony Uhlmann, edited by S. E. Gontarski and Anthony Uhlmann, 116–37. Gainesville: University Press of Florida.

Cohn, Ruby. 1962. *Samuel Beckett: The Comic Gamut*. New Brunswick, NJ: Rutgers University Press.

——— 2001. *A Beckett Canon*. Ann Arbor: University of Michigan Press.

Connor, Steven. 1989. 'Traduttore, traditore: Samuel Beckett's Translation of *Mercier et Camier*'. *Journal of Beckett Studies*, old series, 11–12: 27–46.

——— 2007a. 'Beckett's Low Church', lecture presented at the Beyond Belief Symposium. Harvard University. <http://www.stevenconnor.com>. Accessed 27 September 2013.

——— 2007b [1988]. *Samuel Beckett: Repetition, Theory and Text*, revised edition. Aurora, CO: Davies Group.

——— 2008. 'Elan Mortel: Life, Death and Laughter'. <http://www.stevenconnor.com/elanmortel/>. Accessed 30 October 2013.

——— 2009. 'Beckett and Sartre: The Nauseous Character of All Flesh'. In *Beckett and Phenomenology*, edited by Ulrika Maude and Matthew Feldman, 56–76. London: Continuum.

——— 2010. 'Preface' to *The Unnamable*, by Samuel Beckett, vii-xxv.

Coughlan, Patricia. 1995. '"The Poetry is Another Pair of Sleeves": Beckett, Ireland and Modernist Lyric Poetry'. In *Modernism and Ireland: the Poetry of the 1930s*, edited by Patricia Coughlan and Alex Davis, 173–208, Cork: Cork University Press.

WORKS CITED

Coughlan, Patricia, and Alex Davis, eds. 1995. *Modernism and Ireland: The Poetry of the 1930s.* Cork: Cork University Press.

Critchley, Simon. 2004. *Very Little ... Almost Nothing*, 2nd edition. London: Routledge.

Cronin, Anthony. 1996. *Samuel Beckett: The Last Modernist.* London: Harper Collins.

—— 1997. *Samuel Beckett: The Last Modernist.* London: Flamingo.

Cunningham, David. 2008. '"We have our being in justice": Formalism, Abstraction and Beckett's "Ethics"'. In *Beckett and Ethics*, edited by Russell Smith, 21–37. London: Continuum.

Curtis, L. P. 1970. 'The Anglo-Irish Predicament'. *Twentieth Century Studies* 4: 37–63.

Dearlove, J. E. 1982. *Accommodating the Chaos.* Durham, NC: Duke University Press.

Deleuze, Gilles. 1995. 'The Exhausted', translated by Anthony Uhlmann. *SubStance* 24: 3–28.

—— 1998. 'The Exhausted'. In *Essays Critical and Clinical*, by Gilles Deleuze, translated by Daniel W. Smith and Michael A. Greco. London: Verso.

Deleuze, Gilles, and Félix Guattari. 1986. *Kafka: Towards a Minor Literature*, translated by D. Polan. Minneapolis: University of Minnesota Press.

—— 1995. *What Is Philosophy?*, translated by Hugh Tomlinson and Graham Burchell. London: Columbia University Press.

Derrida, Jacques. 1992. *Acts of Literature*, edited by Derek Attridge. New York: Routledge.

—— 2001. 'La veilleuse'. In *James Joyce ou l'écriture matricide*, by Jacques Trilling, 7–32. Belfort: Circé.

Dickens, Charles. 2004. *David Copperfield.* London: Penguin.

Diderot, Denis. 1976. *Rameau's Nephew/D'Alembert's Dream*, translated by Leonard Tancock. London: Penguin Books.

Doherty, Francis. 1992. 'Mahaffy's "Whoroscope"'. *Journal of Beckett Studies*, new series, 2.1: 27–46.

Dosse, François. 2007. *Gilles Deleuze et Félix Guattari: Biographie croisée.* Paris: La Découverte.

Doutey, Nicolas, ed. 2012. *Notes de Beckett sur Geulincx*, with essays by Thomas Dommange, Matthew Feldman, David Tucker, Anthony Uhlmann and Rupert Wood. Besançon: Les Solitaires intempestifs.

Dowd, Garin. 2008. 'Prolegomena to a Critique of Excavatory Reason: Reply to Matthew Feldman'. *Samuel Beckett Today/Aujourd'hui* 20: 375–88.

Driver, Tom F. 1961a. 'Beckett by the Madeleine'. *Columbia University Forum* 4.3: 21–5.

—— 1961b. 'Interview with Samuel Beckett'. In *Samuel Beckett: The Critical Heritage*, edited by Lawrence Graver and Raymond Federman, 217–23. London: Routledge & Kegan Paul, 1979.

Duckworth, Colin. 1996. 'Introduction'. In *En Attendant Godot*, by Samuel Beckett, xlvi. London: Harrap.

Dukes, Gerry. 2000. 'Introduction'. In *First Love and Other Novellas*, by Samuel Beckett, 1–8. London: Penguin.

Eaglestone, Robert. 2004. *The Holocaust and the Postmodern.* Oxford: Oxford University Press.

WORKS CITED

Eagleton, Terry. 2006. 'Political Beckett?' *New Left Review* 40 (July–August): 67–74.
Effinger, Elizabeth. 2011. 'Beckett's Posthuman'. *Samuel Beckett Today/Aujourd'hui* 23: 369–81.
Eksteins, Modris. 1985. 'History of Degeneration: Of Birds and Cages'. In *Degeneration: The Dark Side of Progress*, edited by J. E. Chamberlin and Sander L. Gilman, 1–23. New York: Columbia University Press.
Eliot, George. 2009. *Daniel Deronda*. Oxford: Oxford University Press.
Eliot, T. S. 1969. *The Complete Poems and Plays of T. S. Eliot*. London: Faber and Faber.
    1971. *The Waste Land: A Facsimile and Transcript of the Original Drafts*, edited by Valerie Eliot. San Diego, New York and London: Harcourt Brace.
    1975. 'Ulysses, Order, and Myth.' In *Selected Prose of T. S. Eliot*, edited by Frank Kermode, 175–8. London: Faber and Faber.
Engelberts, Matthijs, Everett Frost, and Jane Maxwell. 2006. *Notes Diverse Holo: Catalogues of Beckett's Reading Notes and Other Manuscripts at Trinity College, Dublin, with Supporting Essays*. Amsterdam: Rodopi.
Esslin, Martin. 1961. *The Theatre of the Absurd*. New York: Doubleday.
Feldman, Matthew. 2006a. 'Beckett and Popper, Or, "What Stink of Artifice": Some Notes on Methodology, Falsifiability, and Criticism in Beckett Studies'. In *Notes Diverse Holo*, 373–91.
    2006b. *Beckett's Books: A Cultural History of Samuel Beckett's 'Interwar Notes'*. London: Continuum.
    2006c. 'Returning to Beckett Returning to the Presocratics, or, "All Their Balls about Being and Existing"'. *Genetic Joyce Studies* 6. <http://www.geneticjoycestudies.org/GJS6/GJS6Feldman.htm>. Accessed 28 May 2014.
    2008. 'In Defence of Empirical Knowledge: Rejoinder to "A Critique of Excavatory Reason"'. *Samuel Beckett Today/Aujourd'hui* 20: 389–99.
Ferrini, Jean-Pierre. 2003. *Dante et Beckett*. Paris: Hermann.
Fifield, Peter. 2008. 'Beckett, Cotard's Syndrome and the Narrative Patient'. *Journal of Beckett Studies* 17.1–2: 169–86.
    2011. '"Of Being – or Remaining?": Beckett and Early Greek Philosophy'. *Sofia Philosophical Review Beckett/Philosophy*, edited by Matthew Feldman, 5.1: 67–88.
    2013. *Late Modernist Style in Samuel Beckett and Emmanuel Levinas*. Basingstoke: Palgrave Macmillan.
Fletcher, John. 1965. 'Samuel Beckett and the Philosophers'. *Comparative Literature* 17.1 (Winter): 43–56.
Frazier, Adrian. 2006. 'Irish Modernisms, 1880–1930'. In *The Cambridge Companion to the Modern Irish Novel*, edited by John Wilson Foster, 113–32. Cambridge: Cambridge University Press.
Frost, Everett, and Jane Maxwell. 2006. 'Catalogues of Beckett's Reading Notes and Other Manuscripts at Trinity College Dublin, with Supporting Essays'. *Samuel Beckett Today/Aujourd'hui* 16: *Notes Diverse Holo*. Amsterdam: Rodopi.
Frost, Everett. 2012. 'Beckett and Geulincx's Ethics: "… my Geulincx could only be a literary fantasia"'. *Samuel Beckett Today / Aujourd'hui* 24: 171–86.
Frye, Northrop. 1957. *Anatomy of Criticism*. Princeton, NJ: Princeton University Press.

1960. 'The Nightmare Life in Death'. *The Hudson Review* 13.3: 442–9.
Garrard, Greg. 2012. '*Endgame*: Beckett's "Ecological Thought"'. *Samuel Beckett Today/Aujourd'hui* 23: 383–97.
Garrison, Alysia E. 2009. 'Faintly Struggling Things'. In *Samuel Beckett: History, Memory, Archive*, edited by Seán Kennedy and Katherine Weiss, 89–109. Houndmills: Palgrave Macmillan.
Germoni, Karine, and Pascale Sardin. 2012. 'Tensions of the In-Between: Rhythm, Tonelessness and Lyricism in *Fin de partie/Endgame*'. *Samuel Beckett Today/Aujourd'hui* 24: 335–50.
Gessner, Niklaus. 1957. *Die Unzulänglichkeit der Sprache*. Zürich: Junis Verlag.
Geulincx, Arnold. 2006. *Arnold Geulincx Ethics: With Samuel Beckett's Notes*, translated by Martin Wilson, edited by Han van Ruler, Anthony Uhlmann and Martin Wilson. Leiden: Brill.
Gibson, Andrew. 1999. *Postmodernity, Ethics and the Novel: From Leavis to Levinas*. London: Routledge.
2002. 'Beckett and Badiou'. In *Beckett and Philosophy*, edited by Richard Lane, 93–107. Houndmills: Palgrave Macmillan.
2006. *Beckett and Badiou: The Pathos of Intermittency*. Oxford: Oxford University Press.
2010a. *Samuel Beckett*. London: Reaktion Books.
2010b. 'The skull, the skull, the skull, the skull in Connemara: Beckett, Ireland and elsewhere'. In *Beckett and Ireland*, edited by Seán Kennedy, 179–203. Cambridge: Cambridge University Press.
2011. Review of *Samuel Beckett: History, Memory, Archive*. *Modernism/Modernity* 18.4 (November 2011): 926–8.
Forthcoming. 'Beckett, Vichy, Maurras and the Body: *Premier amour* and *Nouvelles*'. In *Beckett and Politics*, edited by Seán Kennedy.
Gidal, Peter. 1986. *Understanding Beckett*. Houndmills: Macmillan.
Gilman, Charlotte Perkins. 1981. *The Yellow Wallpaper*. London: Virago.
Gilman, Richard. 1988. '*Endgame*'. In *Samuel Beckett's 'Endgame': Modern Critical Interpretations*, edited by Harold Bloom, 79–86. New York: Chelsea House.
Golden, Sean. 1981. 'Familiars in a Ruinstrewn Land: *Endgame* as Political Allegory'. *Contemporary Literature* 22: 425–55.
Gontarski, S. E. 1985. *The Intent of Undoing in Samuel Beckett's Dramatic Texts*. Bloomington: Indiana University Press.
ed. 1992. *The Theatrical Notebooks of Samuel Beckett, vol. II: Endgame*. London: Faber and Faber.
1995. 'Preface'. In *The Complete Short Prose 1929–1989*. New York: Grove Press, xi–xxxii.
1999. 'Beckett's *Play*, in extenso'. *Modern Drama*. 42.3 (fall): 442–55.
2006. 'Greying the Canon: Beckett in Performance'. In *Beckett After Beckett*, edited by S.E. Gontarski and Anthony Uhlmann, 141–57. Gainesville: University Press of Florida.
2009. 'Revising Himself: Samuel Beckett and the Art of Self-Collaboration'. In *Reflections on Beckett: A Centenary Celebration*, edited by Anna McMullan and S. E. Wilmer, 153–72. Ann Arbor: The University of Michigan Press.
ed. 2010. *A Companion to Samuel Beckett*. Oxford: Wiley-Blackwell.

ed. 2011. *The Edinburgh Companion to Samuel Beckett and the Arts*. Edinburgh: Edinburgh University Press.

Gontarski, S. E., and Anthony Uhlmann. 2006. *Beckett after Beckett*. Gainesville: Florida University Press.

Gordon, Rae Beth. 2004. 'From Charcot to Charlot: Unconscious Imitation and Spectatorship in French Cabaret and Early Cinema'. In *The Mind of Modernism*, edited by Mark S. Micale, 93–124. Stanford, CA: Stanford University Press.

Graver, Lawrence, and Raymond Federman, eds. 1979. *Samuel Beckett: The Critical Heritage*. London: Routledge and Kegan Paul.

Gray, Thomas. 2013. 'Ode on a Distant Prospect of Eton College'. In *Thomas Gray Archive*, edited by Alexander Huber. <www.thomasgray.org>. Accessed 28 August 2014.

Grossman, Evelyne. 1998. *L'esthétique de Beckett*. Paris: Éditions SEDES.

Guerlac, Suzanne. 2006. *Thinking in Time: An Introduction to Henri Bergson*. Ithaca, NY and London: Cornell University Press.

Harmon, Maurice, ed. 1998. *No Author Better Served: The Correspondence of Samuel Beckett and Alan Schneider*. Cambridge, MA: Harvard University Press.

Harris, Ruth. 1990. 'Introduction'. In *Clinical Lectures on Diseases of the Nervous System*, by Jean-Martin Charcot, edited by Ruth Harris, ix-lxvii. London: Tavistock/Routledge.

Harvey, Lawrence E. 1970. *Samuel Beckett: Poet and Critic*. Princeton, NJ: Princeton University Press.

Hassan, Ihab. 1971. *The Dismemberment of Orpheus: Toward a Postmodern Literature*. New York: Oxford University Press.

Hayman, David. 1999. 'Nor Do My Doodles More Sagaciously: Beckett Illustrating Watt'. In *Samuel Beckett and the Arts*, edited by Lois Oppenheim, 199–215. New York: Garland.

Heidegger, Martin. 2002. 'The Origin of the Work of Art'. In *Off the Beaten Track*, edited and translated by Julian Young and Kenneth Haynes, 1–56. Cambridge: Cambridge University Press.

Henning, Sylvie Debevic. 1988. *Beckett's Critical Complicity: Carnival, Contestation, and Tradition*. Lexington: University Press of Kentucky.

Herman, David. 2011. 'Re-Minding Modernism'. In *The Emergence of Mind: Representations of Consciousness in Narrative Discourse in English*, edited by David Herman, 243–71. Lincoln: University of Nebraska Press.

Hesla, David H. 1971. *The Shape of Chaos*. Minneapolis: University of Minnesota Press.

Hill, Leslie. 1990. *Beckett's Fiction in Different Words*. Cambridge: Cambridge University Press.

Hitler, Adolf. 1998. 'From speech inaugurating the "Great Exhibition of Modern Art", Munich 1937'. In *Modernism: an Anthology of Sources and Documents*, edited by Vassiliki Kolocontroni, Jane Goldman and Olga Taxidou, 560–2. Chicago: Chicago University Press.

Hogan, Thomas. 1954. 'The Reversed Metamorphosis'. *Irish Writing* 26: 54–62.

Horkheimer, Max, and Theodor W. Adorno. 2002. *Dialectic of Enlightenment*. Translated by Edmund Jephcott. Stanford, CA: Stanford University Press.

Howes, Marjorie. 1996. *Yeats's Nations: Gender, Class and Irishness*. Cambridge: Cambridge University Press.
Husserl, Edmund. 1957. *Husserl. Cahiers de Royaumont Philosophie No. III*. Paris: Editions de Minuit.
Jacobsen, Josephine, and William R. Mueller. 1964. *The Testament of Samuel Beckett*. New York: Hill and Wang.
Janvier, Ludovic. 1969. *Beckett*. Paris: Seuil.
    1990. 'Au travail avec Beckett'. In *Cahier de l'Herne: Samuel Beckett*, edited by Tom Bishop and Raymond Federman, 103–8. Paris: l'Herne.
Jameson, Fredric. 1994. *The Seeds of Time*. New York: Columbia University Press.
    2002. *A Singular Modernity*. London: Verso.
Jones, David Houston. 2011. *Samuel Beckett and Testimony*. Houndmills: Palgrave Macmillan.
Jolas, Eugene. 1972. 'The Revolution of Language and James Joyce'. In *Our Exagmination Round His Factification for Incamination of Work in Progress*, edited by Samuel Beckett et al., 77–92. New York: New Directions.
Kafka, Franz. 1994. *The Collected Aphorisms*, translated by Malcolm Pasley. London: Syrens.
Kalb, Jonathan. 1989. *Beckett in Performance*. Cambridge: Cambridge University Press.
Katz, Daniel. 1999. *Saying I No More*. Evanston, IL: Northwestern University Press.
Keats, John. 1966. *Selected Poems and Letters of John Keats*, edited by Robert Gittings. London: Heinemann.
    1988. *The Complete Poems*, edited by John Barnard. London: Penguin.
Kelley, Donald R. 1991. *Renaissance Humanism*. Boston: Twayne.
Kennedy, Andrew K. 1989. *Samuel Beckett*. Cambridge: Cambridge University Press.
Kennedy, Seán. 2005. 'Introduction to "Historicising Beckett"'. *Samuel Beckett Today/Aujourd'hui* 15: 21–7.
    2010a. *Beckett and Ireland*. Cambridge: Cambridge University Press.
    2010b. '"First Love": Abortion and Infanticide in Beckett and Yeats'. *Samuel Beckett Today/Aujourd'hui* 22: *Samuel Beckett: Debts and Legacies*, 79–92.
    2012. 'Edmund Spenser, Famine Memory and the Discontents of Humanism in *Endgame*'. *Samuel Beckett Today/Aujourd'hui* 24: 105–21.
    2014. '"Bid us Sigh on from Day to Day": Beckett and the Irish Big House'. In *The Edinburgh Companion to Samuel Beckett and the Arts*, edited by S. E. Gontarski, 222–36. Edinburgh: Edinburgh University Press.
    Forthcoming. *Beckett and Politics*.
Kennedy, Seán, and Katherine Weiss, eds. 2009. *Samuel Beckett: History, Memory, Archive*. New York: Palgrave Macmillan.
Kenner, Hugh. 1961. *Samuel Beckett: A Critical Study*. New York: Grove Press.
    1978. *A Reader's Guide to Samuel Beckett*. London: Thames and Hudson.
    1983. *A Colder Eye: The Modern Irish Writers*. Baltimore, MD: John Hopkins University Press.
Keogh, Dermot. 1986. *The Vatican, the Bishops and Irish Politics, 1919–1939*. Cambridge: Cambridge University Press.
Kiberd, Declan. 1995. *Inventing Ireland*. Cambridge, MA: Harvard University Press.

1996. *Inventing Ireland: The Literature of the Modern Nation.* London: Vintage.
2005. *The Irish Writer and the World.* Cambridge: Cambridge University Press.
Klossowski, Pierre. 1991. *Sade My Neighbor*, translated by Alphonso Lingis. Evanston, IL: Northwestern University Press.
Knowlson, Elizabeth, and James Knowlson, eds. 2006. *Beckett Remembering, Remembering Beckett: A Centenary Celebration.* New York: Arcade.
Knowlson, James. 1996. *Damned to Fame: The Life of Samuel Beckett.* London: Bloomsbury.
Kosters, Onno. 1992. '"Whey of Words": Beckett's Poetry from "Whoroscope" to "What is the Word"'. *Samuel Beckett Today/Aujourd'hui* 1: 93–105.
Lacan, Jacques. 1974. *Television.* Paris: Seuil.
   1990. *Television*, translated by Denis Hollier, Rosalind Krauss and Annette Michelson. New York: Norton.
   1992. *Seminar, Book VII, The Ethics of Psychoanalysis*, translated by Dennis Porter. New York: Norton.
   2006. *Ecrits*, translated by Bruce Fink. New York: Norton.
Le Doeuff, Michèle. 1989. *The Philosophical Imaginary*, translated by Colin Gordon. London: Athlone Press.
Le Juez, Brigitte. 2007. *Beckett avant la lettre.* Paris: Grasset.
Lernout, Geert. 1994. 'James Joyce and Fritz Mauthner and Samuel Beckett'. In *In Principle Beckett Is Joyce*, edited by Friedhelm Rathjen, 21–27. Edinburgh: Split Pea.
Leventhal, A. J. 1956. 'Dramatic Commentary'. *Dublin Magazine* (January–March): 52.
Levinas, Emmanuel. 1989. 'The Other in Proust'. In *The Levinas Reader*, edited by Sean Hand, 160–5. Oxford: Blackwell.
Little, Roger. 1994. 'Beckett's Poems and Verse Translations, or: Beckett and the Limits of Poetry'. In *The Cambridge Companion to Beckett*, edited by John Pilling, 184–95. Cambridge: Cambridge University Press.
Lloyd, David. 2010. 'Frames of Referrance: Samuel Beckett as an Irish Question'. In *Beckett and Ireland*, edited by Seán Kennedy, 31–55. Cambridge: Cambridge University Press.
   2011. 'Beckett's Things: Bram van Velde and the Gaze'. *Modernist Cultures* 6.2: 269–95.
Lucretius. 2007. *The Nature of Things*, translated by Alicia Stallings, introduction by Richard Jenkyns. London: Penguin.
Lyons, Charles R. 1964. 'Beckett's *Endgame*: An Anti–Myth of Creation'. *Modern Drama* 7: 204–9.
Macmillan, Dougald, and James Knowlson, eds. 1993. *The Theatrical Notebooks of Samuel Beckett, vol. I: Waiting for Godot.* London: Faber and Faber.
Macmillan, Dougald, and Martha Fehsenfeld. 1988. *Beckett in the Theatre: The Author as Practical Playwright and Director.* London: John Calder.
Mallarmé, Stéphane. 1945. *Œuvres complètes*, edited by Henri Mondor and G. Jean-Aubry. Paris: Gallimard, Bibliothèque de la Pléiade.
   2003. *Œuvres complètes, vol. II*, edited by Bertrand Marchal. Paris: Gallimard.
Maude, Ulrika. 2008. '"A Stirring Beyond Coming and Going": Beckett and Tourette's'. *Journal of Beckett Studies* 17.1–2: 153–68.
   2011. *Beckett, Technology and the Body.* Cambridge: Cambridge University Press.

2013a. 'Pavlov's Dogs and Other Animals in Samuel Beckett'. In *Beckett and Animals*, edited by Mary Bryden, 82–93. Cambridge: Cambridge University Press.
2013b. 'Somnambulisim, Amnesia and Fugue: Beckett and (Male) Hysteria'. In *Samuel Beckett: Debts and Legacies*, edited by Peter Fifield and David Addyman, 153–76. London: Bloomsbury.
Mauthner, Fritz. 1923. *Beiträge zu einer Kritik der Sprache*, 3 vols. Leipzig: Felix Meiner.
McCormack, W. J. 1994. *From Burke to Beckett: Ascendancy, Tradition and Betrayal in Literary History*, revised ed. Cork: Cork University Press.
McDonald, Rónán. 2009. 'Preface'. In *Endgame*, by Samuel Beckett, vii-xvi. London: Faber and Faber.
McMullan, Anna. 2010. *Performing Embodiment in Samuel Beckett's Drama*. New York: Routledge.
McHale, Brian. 1989. *Postmodernist Fiction*. London and New York: Routledge.
  1992. *Constructing Postmodernism*. London and New York: Routledge.
McNaughton, James. 2005. 'Beckett, German Fascism, and History: The Futility of Protest'. *Samuel Beckett Today/Aujourd'hui* 15: *Historicising Beckett/Issues of Performance*, 101–16.
  2009. 'Beckett's "Brilliant Obscurantics": *Watt* and the Problem of Propaganda'. In *Samuel Beckett: History, Memory, Archive*, 47–69. New York: Palgrave Macmillan.
McTighe, Trish. 2013. *The Haptic Aesthetic in Samuel Beckett's Drama*. Basingstoke: Palgrave.
Mercier, Vivian. 1959. 'The Mathematical Limit'. *The Nation* 14 (February): 144–5.
  1977. *Beckett/Beckett*. Oxford: Oxford University Press.
Migernier, Eric. 2006. *Beckett and French Theory*. New York: Peter Lang.
Miller, Tyrus. 1999. *Late Modernism: Politics, Fiction, and the Arts Between the World Wars*. Berkeley, Los Angeles, and London: University of California Press.
Milne, Drew. 1999. 'The Dissident Imagination: Beckett's Late Prose Fiction'. In *An Introduction to Contemporary Fiction*, edited by Rod Mengham, 93–109. Cambridge: Polity.
Milton, John. 2007. *Paradise Lost*. Harlow: Pearson.
Montini, Chiara. 2007. '*La bataille du soliloque': Genèse de la poétique bilingue de Samuel Beckett*. Amsterdam: Rodopi.
Moody, Alys. 2013. '*Waiting for Godot* in New Orleans: Modernist Autonomy and Transnational Performance in Paul Chan's Beckett'. *Theatre Journal* 65.4: 539.
Mooney, Sinéad. 2011. *A Tongue Not Mine: Beckett and Translation*. Oxford: Oxford University Press.
Mooney, Susan. 2010. '*Malone Dies*: Postmodernist Masculinity'. In *A Companion to Samuel Beckett*, edited by S. E. Gontarski, 275–88. Oxford: Wiley-Blackwell.
Moorjani, Angela. 1982. *Abysmal Games in the Novels of Samuel Beckett*. Chapel Hill: University of North Carolina Press.
  1992. *The Aesthetics of Loss and Lessness*. Houndmills: Macmillan.
  1996. 'Mourning, Schopenhauer, and Beckett's Art of Shadows'. In *Beckett On and On…*, edited by Lois Oppenheim and Marius Buning, 83–101. Madison, NJ: Fairleigh Dickinson University Press.

2004. 'Beckett and Psychoanalysis'. In *Directing Beckett*, edited by Lois Oppenheim, 172–93. Ann Arbor: University of Michigan Press.

2012. 'Beckett's Racinian Fictions: "Racine and the Modern Novel" Revisited'. *Samuel Beckett Today/Aujourd'hui* 24: 41–55.

2013. 'Beckett's *Molloy* in the French Context'. *Samuel Beckett Today/Aujourd'hui* 25: 95–109.

Morash, Christopher. 2002. *A History of Irish Theatre, 1601–2000*. Cambridge: Cambridge University Press.

Morin, Emilie. 2009. *Samuel Beckett and the Problem of Irishness*. Basingstoke: Palgrave Macmillan.

Murphy, P. J. 1994. 'Samuel Beckett and the Philosophers'. In *Cambridge Companion to Beckett*, edited by John Pilling, 222–40. Cambridge: Cambridge University Press.

Nadeau, Maurice. 1952. 'Samuel Beckett ou le droit au silence'. *Les Temps Modernes* 7: 1273–82.

1963. 'En avant vers nulle part'. Reprinted in 'Le dossier de presse de *Molloy*', by Bernard Pingaud, 257–63. Paris: Union d'Éditions.

Nicholson, Steve. 2011. *The Censorship of British Drama, 1900–1968, vol. III: The Fifties*. Exeter: University of Exeter Press.

Nicolayev, Philip, ed. 2007. *Fulcrum: An Annual of Poetry and Aesthetics* 6 (special issue on Samuel Beckett's poetry). New York: Evolution Arts, Inc.

Nietzsche, Friedrich. 1874. 'Uses and Abuses of History', translated by Ian Johnston, 1–65. <https://records.viu.ca/~Johnstoi/nietzsche/history.htm>, accessed on 28 January 2014.

Nixon, Mark. 2007a. '"Text-void": Silent Words in Paul Celan and Samuel Beckett'. In *Beckett's Literary Legacies*, edited by Matthew Feldman and Mark Nixon, 152–68. Newcastle: Cambridge Scholars Publishing.

2007b. '"the remains of a trace": Intra- and Intertextual Transferences in Beckett's *mirlitonnades* manuscripts'. *Journal of Beckett Studies*, new series, 16.1-2: 110–22.

2007c. '"Unutterably Faint": Beckett's Late English Poetry'. In *Fulcrum: An Annual of Poetry and Aesthetics*, 507–21.

2011. *Samuel Beckett's 'German Diaries' 1936–1937*. London: Continuum.

2014. 'Beckett's Unpublished Canon'. In *The Edinburgh Companion to Samuel Beckett and the Arts*, edited by S. E. Gontarski, 282–305. Edinburgh: Edinburgh University Press.

Nixon, Mark, and Matthew Feldman eds. 2009. *The International Reception of Samuel Beckett*. London and New York: Continuum.

Nordau, Max. 1895. *Degeneration*. New York: Appleton and Company.

1986. *Degeneration*, translated by George L. Mosse. Lincoln and London: University of Nebraska Press.

Nye, Robert A. 1985. 'Sociology and Degeneration: The Irony of Progress'. In *Degeneration: The Dark Side of Progress*, edited by Joseph Chamberlin and Sander Gilman, 49–71. New York: Columbia University Press.

O'Brien, Eoin. 1986. *The Beckett Country*. Dublin: Black Cat Press.

Oppenheim, Lois, ed. 1994. *Directing Beckett*. Ann Arbor: U of Michigan P.

2004. *Palgrave Advances in Samuel Beckett Studies*. Houndmills: Palgrave Macmillan.

WORKS CITED

Orwell, George. 2003. *Nineteen Eighty-Four*. London: Penguin.
Osler, William. 1921. *The Principles and Practice of Medicine*. New York and London: D. Appleton.
Pearson, Nels C. 2001. '"Outside of Here It's Death": Co–Dependency and the Ghosts of Decolonization in Beckett's *Endgame*'. *ELH* 68.1: 215–39.
Phillips, Adam. 2013. *One Way and Another: New and Selected Essays*, with an introduction by John Banville. London: Penguin.
Pilling, John. 1969. Interview with Samuel Beckett. Paris. 8 August.
⎯ ed. 1994. *Cambridge Companion to Samuel Beckett*. Cambridge: Cambridge University Press.
⎯ 1997. *Beckett before Godot*. Cambridge: Cambridge University Press.
⎯ 1999. 'Beckett and "the itch to make": the Early Poems in English'. *Samuel Beckett Today/Aujourd'hui* 8: 15–25.
⎯ 2004. 'From the Pointed Ones to the Bones: Beckett's Early Poems'. In *The Irish Book in the Twentieth Century*, edited by Clare Hutton, 68–83. Dublin: Irish Academic Press.
⎯ 2006. *A Samuel Beckett Chronology*. Houndmills: Palgrave Macmillan.
⎯ 2007. '*From an Abandoned Work:* "all the variants of the one"'. *Samuel Beckett Today/Aujourd'hui* 18: 173–83.
⎯ 2011. '"B" and "D" Revisited: a "dialogue" of a Different Kind'. *Journal of Beckett Studies* 20.2: 197–203.
Pilling, John, and James Knowlson 1979. *Frescoes of the Skull: The Later Prose and Drama of Samuel Beckett*. London: John Calder.
Pilling, John, and Seán Lawlor. 2011. 'Beckett in *Transition*'. In *Publishing Samuel Beckett*, edited by Mark Nixon, 83–95. London: The British Library.
Pingaud, Bernard. 1963. 'Le dossier de presse de *Molloy*'. In *Molloy, 'L'expulsé'*, by Samuel Beckett, 255–86. Paris: Union Générale d'Éditions.
Proust, Marcel. 1987. *A la Recherche du Temps Perdu, vol. I*, edited by Jean-Yves Tadié. Paris: Gallimard, Pléiade.
⎯ 2002. *Swann's Way*, translated by Lydia Davis. New York: Viking.
Quigley, Megan M. 2004. 'Justice for the "Illstarred Punster": Samuel Beckett and Alfred Péron's Revisions of "Anna Lyvia Pluratself"'. *James Joyce Quarterly* 41.3: 469–87.
Rabaté, Jean-Michel. 2010. 'Philosophizing with Beckett: Adorno and Badiou'. In *A Companion to Samuel Beckett*, 97–117.
⎯ 2011a. 'Beckett's Masson: From Abstraction to Non-Relation'. In *The Edinburgh Companion to Samuel Beckett and the Arts*, edited by S.E. Gontarski, 131–45. Edinburgh: Edinburgh University Press.
⎯ 2011b. 'Beckett's Three Critiques: Kant's Bathos and the Irish Chandos'. *Modernism/Modernity* 18.4 (November): 699–719.
Ravaisson, Félix. 2008. *Of Habit*, translated by Clare Carlisle and Mark Sinclair. London: Continuum.
Regan, John. 1999. *The Irish Counter-Revolution, 1921–1936*. Dublin: Gill and MacMillan.
Reid, Christopher. 2011. 'The enigmatic Samuel Beckett still thrills: Review of Samuel Beckett's *Collected Poems*'. *New Statesman*, 11 October. http://www.newstatesman.com/culture/culture/2012/10/enigmatic-samuel-beckett-still-thrills.

Renard, Jules. 2008. *The Journal of Jules Renard*, edited and translated by Louise Bogan and Elizabeth Roget. New York: Tin House Books.
   2013. *The Journal of Jules Renard*, edited and translated by Louise Bogan and Elizabeth Roget. Portland, OR: Tin House Books.
Ricks, Christopher. 1993. *Beckett's Dying Words*. Oxford: Clarendon Press.
Robbe-Grillet, Alain. 1965. 'Samuel Beckett, or Presence on the Stage'. In *For a New Novel: Essays on Fiction*, edited by Alain Robbe-Grillet and translated by Richard Howard, 111–25. New York: Grove Press.
Sage, Victor. 1977. 'Dickens and Beckett: Two Uses of Materialism'. *Journal of Beckett Studies* 2: 15–39.
Said, Edward W. 2006. *On Late Style*. London: Bloomsbury.
   2007. *On Late Style: Music and Literature Against the Grain*. London: Bloomsbury.
Salisbury, Laura. 2008. '"What Is the Word": Beckett's Aphasic Modernism'. *Journal of Beckett Studies* 17.1–2: 78–126.
   2012. *Samuel Beckett: Laughing Matters, Comic Timing*. Edinburgh: Edinburgh University Press.
Salisbury, Laura, and Chris Code. 2013. 'Jackson's Parrot: Samuel Beckett, Aphasic Speech Automatisms, and Psychosomatic Language'. In *Literature, Speech Disorders and Disability*, edited by Christopher Eagle, 100–23. London: Routledge.
Sardin-Damestoy, Pascale. 2002. *Samuel Beckett auto-traducteur ou l'art de 'l'empêchement': lecture bilingue et génétique des textes courts auto-traduits (1946–1980)*. Arras: Artois Presses Universitité.
Sartre, Jean-Paul. 1947. 'L'homme ligoté'. In *Situations* 1, 271–88. Paris: Gallimard.
   1976. *Sartre on Theater*, edited by Michel Contat and Michel Rybalka, translated by Frank Jellinek. London: Quartet Books.
Saunders, Graham. 2007. 'Reclaiming Sam for Ireland: The Beckett on Film Project'. In *Irish Theatre in England*, edited by Richard Cave and Ben Levitas, 79–96. Dublin: Carysfort Press.
Sbarbaro, Camillo. 1993. 'Pianissimo'. In *Twentieth-Century Italian Poetry: An Anthology*, edited by John Picchione and Lawrence R. Smith, 169–73. Toronto: University of Toronto Press.
Schneider, Alan. 1986. *Entrances: An American Director's Journey*. New York: Viking Press.
Seaver, Richard. 2006. 'Translating Beckett'. In *Remembering Beckett, Beckett Remembering*, edited by James and Elizabeth Knowlson, 100–7. New York: Arcade.
Sebald, Winfried Georg. 1980. *Der Mythus der Zerstörung im Werk Döblins*. Stuttgart: Ernst Klett.
Shainberg, Lawrence. 1987. 'Exorcising Beckett'. *Paris Review* 104: 100–37.
Shenker, Israel. 1956. 'An Interview with Beckett'. In *Samuel Beckett: The Critical Heritage*, edited by Lawrence Graver and Raymond Federman, 146–9. London: Routledge and Kegan Paul.
   1976. 'Moody Man of Letters: A Portrait of Samuel Beckett'. *New York Times*, 5 May 1956. Reprinted in *Samuel Beckett: The Critical Heritage*, edited by Lawrence Graver and Raymond Federman, 146–69. London: Routledge and Kegan Paul.
Sherzer, Dina. 1976. *Structure de la trilogie de Beckett*. The Hague: Mouton.

Simpson, Alan. 1962. *Beckett and Behan and a Theatre in Dublin*. London: Routledge and Kegan Paul.
Slote, Sam, 2005. 'On *Worstward Ho*'. *Journal of Beckett Studies* 13.2: 188–205.
2011. 'Continuing the End: Variation between Beckett's French and English Prose Works'. In *Publishing Samuel Beckett*, edited by Mark Nixon, 205–18. London: The British Library.
Smith, Frederik N. 2002. *Samuel Beckett's Eighteenth Century*. Basingstoke: Palgrave Macmillan.
Smith, Russell, ed. 2008. *Beckett and Ethics*. London: Continuum.
Sontag, Susan. 1998. 'Godot Comes to Sarajevo'. *New York Review of Books*, 21 October, 52.
Spencer, Charles. 1997. 'Critic's Choice: Theatre: Beckett Shorts'. *The Telegraph*, 8 November. <www.telegraph.co.uk/culture/4710963/Critics-choice-Theatre.html>. Accessed 26 August 2014.
Stacey, Stephen. 2013. 'Translating for Sense: Samuel Beckett's Writing in English, French and English'. Paper presented at Samuel Beckett and the 'State' of Ireland III, University College Dublin, 3 August.
Stanford-Friedman, Susan. 2006. 'Periodizing Modernism: Postcolonial Modernities and the Space/Time Borders of Modernist Studies'. *Modernism/Modernity* 13.3: 425–33.
Szafraniec, Asja. 2007. *Beckett, Derrida, and the Event of Literature*. Stanford, CA: Stanford University Press.
Tajiri, Yoshiki. 2002. 'The Mechanization of Sexuality in Beckett's Early Work'. *Samuel Beckett Today/Aujourd'hui* 12: 193–204.
2007. *Samuel Beckett and the Prosthetic Body*. Houndmills: Palgrave Macmillan.
Tanaka, Mariko Hori, Yoshiki Tajiri, and Michiko Tsushima, eds. 2012. *Beckett and Pain*. Amsterdam: Rodopi.
'The Man Himself'. *Trinity News*, 7 June 1956, 5.
Thornton, A. P. 1966. *The Imperial Idea and its Enemies*. London: Macmillan.
Tonning, Erik. 2007. *Samuel Beckett's Abstract Drama: Works for Stage and Screen 1962–1985*. Oxford: Peter Lang.
Touret, Michèle. 2006. 'Y a-t-il un événement dans le texte?' *Samuel Beckett Today/Aujourd'hui* 17: 15–34.
Trezise, Thomas. 1990. *Into the Breach*. Princeton, NJ: Princeton University Press.
Tucker, David. 2012. *Samuel Beckett and Arnold Geulincx: Tracing 'a Literary Fantasia'*. London: Continuum.
Tynan. Kenneth. 1955. 'Review of *Waiting for Godot* by Samuel Beckett'. *The Observer*, 7 August. Quoted in *Lawrence Graver and Raymond Federman, Samuel Beckett: The Critical Heritage*, 97. London: Routledge Kegan and Paul.
Uhlmann, Anthony. 1999. *Beckett and Poststructuralism*. Cambridge: Cambridge University Press.
2006. *Samuel Beckett and the Philosophical Image*. Cambridge: Cambridge University Press.
2011. 'Beckett, Duthuit and Ongoing Dialogue'. In *The Edinburgh Companion to Samuel Beckett and the Arts*, edited by S.E. Gontarski, 146–52. Edinburgh: Edinburgh University Press.
ed. 2013. *Samuel Beckett in Context*. New York: Cambridge University Press.

Uhlmann, Anthony, et al., eds. 2006. *Arnold Geulincx' Ethics: With Samuel Beckett's Notes*, translated by Martin Wilson. Amsterdam: Brill.
Ulin, Julieann. 2006. 'Famine "Ghost Graves" in Samuel Beckett's *Endgame*'. In *Hungry Words: Images of Famine in the Irish Canon*, edited by George Cusack and Sarah Gross, 197–222. Dublin: Irish Academic Press.
van der Weel, Adriaan, and Ruud Hisgen. 1998. *The Silencing of the Sphinx*. Leiden: Private Edition.
Van Hulle, Dirk. 1999. 'Beckett – Mauthner – Zimmer – Joyce'. *Joyce Studies Annual* 10 (Summer): 143–83.
   2008a. *Manuscript Genetics, Joyce's Know-How, Beckett's Nohow*. Gainesville: University Press of Florida.
   2008b. '"World stuff": Éléments présocratiques dans la genèse de l'œuvre beckettienne'. *Samuel Beckett Today/Aujourd'hui* 20: 203–16.
   2009. 'Writing Relics: Mapping the Composition History of Beckett's *Endgame*'. In *Samuel Beckett: History, Memory, Archive*, edited by Seán Kennedy and Katherine Weiss, 169–82. New York: Palgrave.
   2011a. '"Eff it": Beckett and Language Skepticism'. *Sofia Philosophical Review* 5.1: 201–27.
   2011b. *The Making of Samuel Beckett's 'Stirrings Still'/'Soubresauts' and 'Comment dire'/'what is the word'*. Brussels: University Press Antwerp.
   2012. 'La genèse de *L'Innommable*'. *Littérature* 167: 65–77.
Van Hulle, Dirk, and Mark Nixon. 2013. *Samuel Beckett's Library*. New York: Cambridge University Press.
Van Hulle, Dirk, and Shane Weller. 2014. *The Making of Samuel Beckett's 'L'Innommable'/'The Unnamable'*. Antwerp: University Press Antwerp; London and New York: Bloomsbury Academic.
Vogelweide, Walter von der. 1994. *Werke: Band 1: Spruchlyrik*. Stuttgart: Reclam.
Weiler, Gershon. 1958. 'On Fritz Mauthner's Critique of Language'. *Mind*, new series, 67.265: 80–7.
Weller, Shane. 2005. *A Taste for the Negative*. London: Legenda.
   2006. *Beckett, Literature, and the Ethics of Alterity*. Basingstoke: Palgrave Macmillan.
   2008. '"Gnawing to Be Naught": Beckett and Pre-Socratic Nihilism'. *Samuel Beckett Today/Aujourd'hui* 20: 321–33.
   2009. 'Beckett among the Philosophes: The Reception of Samuel Beckett in France'. In *The International Reception of Samuel Beckett*, edited by Mark Nixon and Matthew Feldman, 24–39. London: Continuum.
   2010a. 'Beckett and Ethics'. In *A Companion to Samuel Beckett*, edited by Stan E. Gontarski, 118–29. Oxford: Wiley-Blackwell.
   2010b. 'Staging Psychoanalysis: *Endgame* and the Freudian Theory of the Anal-Sadistic Phase'. *Samuel Beckett Today/Aujourd'hui* 22: *Samuel Beckett: Debts and Legacies*, 135–47.
   2010c. 'Unwords'. In *Beckett and Nothing*, edited by Daniela Caselli, 107–24. Manchester: Manchester University Press.
   2011. 'Beckett's Last Chance: Les Éditions de Minuit'. In *Publishing Samuel Beckett*, edited by Mark Nixon, 111–30. London: The British Library.
   2013. 'Post-World War Two Paris'. In *Samuel Beckett in Context*, edited by Anthony Uhlmann, 160–72. Cambridge: Cambridge University Press.

Wheatley, David. 1995. 'Samuel Beckett's *Mirlitonnades*: a Manuscript Study'. *Journal of Beckett Studies*, new series, 4.2: 47–75.
  2007. '"Labours Unfinished": Beckett's *mirlitonnades* and the Poetics of Incompletion'. In *Fulcrum: An Annual of Poetry and Aesthetics*, 500–6.
  2009. 'Introduction'. In Samuel Beckett: *Selected Poems 1930–1989*, ix–xix. London: Faber and Faber.
  2013. 'Unquiet Prose: W. G. Sebald and the Writing of the Negative'. In *A Literature of Restitution: Critical Essays on W. G. Sebald*, edited by Jeannette Baxter, Valerie Henetiuk and Ben Hutchinson, 56–73. Manchester: Manchester University Press.
Whitelaw, Billie. 1996. *Billie Whitelaw ... Who He?* New York: St. Martin's Press.
Wilde, Alan. 1981. *Horizons of Assent: Modernism, Postmodernism, and the Ironic Imagination*. Baltimore and London: Johns Hopkins University Press.
Wiltshire, John. 1991. *Samuel Johnson in the Medical World*. Cambridge: Cambridge University Press.
Windelband, Wilhelm. 1958. *A History of Philosophy*, 2 vols., New York: Harper.
Wood, Rupert. 1994. 'An Endgame of Aesthetics: Beckett as essayist'. In *The Cambridge Companion to Beckett*, edited by John Pilling, 1–16. Cambridge: Cambridge University Press.
Yeats, W. B. 1996. *Selected Poems and Four Plays*. New York: Scribner.
  2000. 'On the Boiler'. In *Yeats's Poetry, Drama, and Prose*, edited by James Pethica, 315–6. New York: Norton.
Zilliacus, Clas. 1976. *Beckett and Broadcasting: A Study of the Works of Samuel Beckett for and in Radio and Television*. Åbo: Åbo Akademi.
Zurbrugg, Nicholas. 1988. *Beckett and Proust*. Gerrards Cross: Colin Smythe.

INDEX

Abraham, Nicolas 29
Abbott, H. Porter xxv, 23, 25, 27, 29, 154
Ackerley, C. J. 54, 70, 84, 104, 105, 112, 128
Addyman, David 170, 184
Adelman, Gary 24
Adorno, Theodor xx, xxii, xxiii, 21, 23, 24, 29, 40, 48, 62, 63, 64, 92, 94, 96, 97, 99, 100, 101, 147, 154, 166, 167, 169, 198, 199
Agamben, Giorgio 47
Akalaitis, JoAnne 65, 135, 136, 137
Albee, Edward 134
Albright, Daniel 27, 65, 174
Alvarez, Alfred 61
Anouilh, Jean 49, 51
Anzieu, Didier xxii, 28
Apollinaire 77
Appelfeld, Aaron 97
Arikha, Avigdor 82
Ariosto, Ludovico 16
Aristotle 14, 17, 168
Artaud, Antonin xxi, 51, 126, 127, 130
Asmus, Walter 140
Atik, Anne 60
Aubarède, Gabriel d' 145, 154
Augustine of Hippo 17

Bacon, Francis 111
Badiou, Alain xvii, xxi, xxii, 21, 23, 24, 27, 47, 48, 62, 100, 147, 153, 156, 168, 169
Bair, Deirdre 103, 180
Bakhtin, Mikhail 178, 179
Balzac, Honoré de 95
Barnes, Djuna 92
Barr, Richard 134
Barrault, Jean-Louis 126, 127
Barry, Elizabeth xxvi
Barthes, Roland xxi, 19, 23, 29

Baryshnikov, Mikhail 135, 136, 137
Bataille, Georges 20, 21, 23, 63, 147, 168
Baudelaire, Charles 93
Beauvoir, Simone de 20
Beckett, Edward 128
Beckett, Frank 189
Beckett, John 128, 136
Beckett, Samuel
  'Acte sans paroles I' / 'Act without Words I' 70, 71, 72, 135, 136
  'Acte sans paroles II' / 'Act Without Words II' 135, 137
  'Alba' 10, 16, 17, 77
  'All Strange Away' 94, 152
  All That Fall / Tous ceux qui tombent 71
  A Piece of Monologue 135
  'Assez' 15
  'Assumption' 5, 94
  'Au bout de ces années perdues' xxv
  'A Wet Night' xxv
  'Bare Room' xxv
  'Breath' 66, 138, 179
  ... but the clouds ... 83, 140
  'Cascando' xxiv, 10, 78
  'Casket of Pralinen for the Daughter of a Dissipated Mandarin' 10, 78
  Catastrophe 71, 72, 133, 153
  'Ce n'est au pélican' 116
  'Censorship in the Saorstat' 75
  'Chien anagramme de niche' xxv
  'Come and Go' / 'Va et vient' 128, 132, 133, 137, 138, 139
  Comment c'est / How It Is 34, 41, 46, 73, 93, 100, 103, 106, 107, 124, 149, 153, 161, 170
  'Comment dire' / 'what is the word' 34, 83, 93, 94

Index

Beckett, Samuel (*cont.*)
  Company / Compagnie 34, 43, 46, 94, 103, 124, 162
  'Coups de gong'/ 'Espace souterrain' xxv
  'Dante and the Lobster' xxiv, 6, 7, 158, 162
  'Dante...Bruno.Vico..Joyce' 5, 74, 163
  'Dieppe' 116
  'Ding-Dong' xxv
  Disjecta xxiv, 3, 15, 16, 17, 20, 26, 51, 74, 75, 76, 79, 81, 82, 83, 89, 96, 110, 185, 186, 197
  'Draff' xxv, 8
  'Dream' Notebook 16, 17, 112, 176, 179
  Dream of Fair to Middling Women 3, 4, 6, 9, 12, 14, 15, 16, 17, 23, 36, 37, 39, 75, 77, 79, 89, 94, 99, 175, 179–180, 184
  'Echo's Bones' xxv, 175
  Echo's Bones and Other Precipitates 16, 77, 78, 84
  Eh Joe / Dis Joe 128, 130, 131, 135, 136, 140
  Eleutheria 33, 89, 151
  Embers / Cendres 135
  En attendant Godot / Waiting for Godot xx, 11, 33, 48, 49, 50, 51, 52, 53, 54, 55, 56, 57, 58, 59, 62, 66, 68, 73, 79, 84, 85, 89, 94, 110, 111, 127, 128, 133, 137, 139, 140, 149, 154, 156, 161, 176, 178, 179, 185, 190, 197, 199
  'Enueg I' 5, 7, 14, 16, 77
  'Enueg II' 141
  'Epilogue' xxv
  'Faux départs' xxiv
  Film 112, 156
  'Film-Vidéo Cassette project' xxv
  Fin de partie / Endgame xx, 33, 60, 61, 62, 63, 64, 65, 66, 68, 69, 70, 71, 72, 73, 79, 93, 122, 123, 128, 129, 135, 136, 139, 140, 146, 149, 151, 152, 164, 185, 199
  'Fingal' xxv
  'Fragment de théâtre I' / 'Rough for Theatre I' xxv, 70, 136, 137
  'Fragment de théâtre II' / 'Rough for Theatre II' 152
  From an Abandoned Work 114, 115, 116, 123, 125
  Foirades / Fizzles xxiv
  Footfalls / Pas 127, 131, 132, 135, 139, 140, 174

'German Diaries' xvii, xx, 5, 6, 16, 17, 76, 78, 79, 81, 103, 196, 198
Ghost Trio 83, 140
'Gnome' 74
Happy Days / Oh les beaux jours xxi, 33, 60, 62, 70, 72, 126, 128, 136, 139, 140, 149, 174
'Hommage to Jack B. Yeats' 89
'Hourrah je me suis repris' xxv
'Human Wishes' 84, 180
'Human Wishes' Notebooks 180, 181, 183
'Humanistic Quietism' 6
'Ici personne ne vient jamais' xxv
Imagination Dead Imagine 41, 94
'je voudrais que mon amour meure' / 'I would like my love to die' 82
'J. M. Mime' xxv
Krapp's Last Tape / La dernière bande 3, 33, 70, 129, 135, 139, 176, 182
'La Fin' ('Suite') / 'The End' 118, 120, 121
'La Peinture des van Velde ou le monde et le pantalon' 80
'Last Soliloquy' xxv
'Le Calmant' / 'The Calmative' 176, 179, 194
'Le Concentrisme or Jean du Chas' xxiv, 16
Le Dépeupleur / The Lost Ones 34, 40, 41, 42, 152, 156, 162, 178
'Les Deux Besoins' xxiv, 9, 79, 116
'L'Expulsé' / 'The Expelled' 189
'Lightning Calculation' xxv
L'Innommable / The Unnamable xx, xxi, xxii, xxv, 19, 21, 22, 24, 26, 27, 30, 31, 33, 34, 35, 36, 37, 39, 40, 41, 44, 45, 46, 80, 89, 90, 91, 93, 94, 99, 112, 121, 122, 123, 124, 125, 132, 153, 176, 198
'Long Observation of the Ray' xxv
'Love and Lethe' xxv, 7, 8, 16, 175
'Malacoda' 16, 77
Mal vu mal dit / Ill Seen Ill Said 34, 99, 103, 124, 176
Malone meurt / Malone Dies xx, 19, 22, 27, 32, 33, 80, 89, 94, 101, 121, 176, 180, 189
'Match nul ou L'Amour paisible' xxv
Mercier et Camier / Mercier and Camier 3, 5, 14, 17, 121, 156, 188, 195, 196
'Mime du rêveur A' xxv
Mirlitonnades 83, 85
Molloy xx, 15, 16, 19, 21, 22, 26, 27, 28, 32, 33, 80, 89, 90, 91, 93, 94, 109, 121, 122, 149, 163, 176, 199
'Mongrel Mime' xxv

Index

More Pricks Than Kicks xxv, 16, 33, 151, 175
'Mort de A.D.' 82
Murphy xviii, xix, xx, xxvi, 6, 9, 10, 11, 12, 13, 14, 16, 17, 18, 25, 37, 38, 39, 78, 98, 112, 114, 117, 121, 125, 150, 151, 153, 163, 164, 170, 175, 180, 186
'my way is in the sand flowing' 82
Nacht und Träume 140
'neither' 34, 137
Not I / Pas moi 60, 71, 124, 127, 133, 135, 136, 138, 139, 176, 177
Nouvelles / Stories 33, 39, 109, 194
Ohio Impromptu 18, 46, 129
'On le tortura bien' xxv
'On my way' xxv
Our Exagmination Round His Factification for Incamination of Work in Progress 74
'Peintres de l'empêchement' 26, 80
'Petit Odéon' xxv
'Petit Sot' xxv, 116
'Philosophy notes' 103, 108, 112, 150, 151, 153
Ping 41
Play / Comédie 5, 17, 60, 70, 71, 127, 128, 134, 137, 138, 139, 140, 141, 176, 177, 178
'Poèmes 37–39' 82, 116, 117
Poèmes suivi de mirlitonnades 83
Premier amour / First Love 194
Proust 3, 4, 5, 6, 11, 18, 36, 75, 84
'Psychology notes' 103, 108, 112
Quad 66, 140
Quoi où / What Where 127, 131, 132, 134, 140, 174
'Recent Irish Poetry' 75, 76, 79
Rockaby 112, 135, 137, 138, 174
'Sanies II' 13, 16
'Serena I' 77
'Serena II' 17
'Six Poèmes' 82
'something there' 83
'Sottisier' Notebook 83
Stirring Still / Soubresauts xxv, 33, 34, 36, 40, 41, 45, 124
'Text 3' 159, 160, 161
Textes pour rien / Texts for Nothing xxiv, 15, 33, 34, 40, 41, 45, 114, 115, 123, 147, 189
That Time / Cette fois 13, 70, 127, 135, 136, 139
'The Capital of the Ruins' 14

'The Gloaming' xxv
'The Smeraldina's Billet Doux' xxv
'The Vulture' 7
Three Dialogues with Georges Duthuit 4, 74, 79, 84, 110
'Tristesse Janale' 116
'vive morte ma seule saison' 82
'Walking Out' xxv, 17
Watt xx, 10, 12, 13, 14, 17, 33, 39, 89, 93, 98, 112, 114, 118, 121, 125, 127, 147, 151, 165, 166, 167, 168, 176, 185
'What a Misfortune' xxv, 7, 8
'Whoroscope' 18, 76, 77, 150
'Whoroscope' Notebook 163
Worstward Ho xxv, 34, 41, 43, 46, 91, 94, 95, 99, 105, 124, 168
'Yellow' xxv, 7, 8
Beer, Ann 117, 118
Begam, Richard 32
Benjamin, Walter 100
Bennent, Heinz 140
Bennett, Michael Y. 154
Ben-Zvi, Linda 156
Bergson, Henri 63, 93, 127, 130, 131, 135, 170, 171, 172, 173, 174, 175, 183, 184
Berkeley, George 78, 107, 108
Bernhard, Thomas 96, 99, 100
Bernstein, J. M. 92
Bion, Wilfred 28, 29
Bixby, Patrick 25, 32, 186
Blackman, Jackie 64
Blake, William 133
Blanchot, Maurice 20, 22, 23, 24, 31, 63, 96, 99, 100, 147, 154, 165
Blau, Herbert 56
Blin, Roger 49, 50, 53, 68, 127, 128
Bolin, John 17
Bordas, Pierre 125
Borges, Jorge Luis 89, 91, 93
Bose, Kornelia 140
Boswell, James 181, 182, 183
Boulter, Jonathan 161
Bourdieu, Pierre 190
Bowen, Kurt 190
Bowles, Patrick 29, 121, 122
Boxall, Peter xx, xxiii, 31, 33, 61, 185, 187, 188
Bradby, David 52
Brantley, Ben 136, 137
Brater, Enoch 134, 136, 146, 151, 156
Bray, Barbara 156

Index

Brecht, Bertolt 94, 138
Broch, Hermann 95
Brod, Max 102
Brook, Peter 132, 137
Brueghel, Pieter (the Elder) 5
Bruhns, Maike 78
Bruno, Giordano 74, 163
Bryden, Mary 31, 32
Buning, Marius 186
Burnet, John 153
Burney, Fanny 181
Burrows, Rachel 84, 85, 171
Burton, Robert 6
Byrne, J. J. 194

Calder, John 171
Calvino, Italo 89, 91
Campbell, Julie 32
Camus, Albert 20, 50, 61, 155
Carville, Conor 101
Casanova, Pascale xviii, 23, 32, 154
Caselli, Daniela xvii, xxv, 161
Catrou, Jacques 175
Cavell, Stanley 23
Celan, Paul 96, 97, 99, 100
Céline, Louis-Ferdinand 20, 29, 161
Cervantes, Miguel de 15, 18
Cézanne, Paul 74, 75, 76
Chabert, Pierre 129, 130, 138, 139
Chamberlin, J. Edward 197
Chan, Paul 58
Chaplin, Charles Spencer 189, 190
Charcot, Jean-Martin 171, 172, 173, 176
Cixous, Hélène xviii, 23
Clément, Bruno 23, 27, 99, 154, 156
Cluchey, Rick 56
Cocteau, Jean 51
Code, Chris 176
Cohn, Ruby xxiii, xxv, 21, 27, 29, 74, 75, 79, 80, 84, 111, 112, 137, 159
Colgan, Michael 52
Connor, Steven xxi, 32, 121, 146, 173
Copeau, Jacques 127
Cosgrave, William 190, 191
Coughlan, Patricia 185
Critchley, Simon xxii, 19, 22, 23, 24, 168
Cronin, Anthony xx, 103, 180
Cunard, Nancy 150
Cunningham David 161
Curtis, L. P. 190

Dante xvii, xxi, xxiii, 16, 17, 38, 74, 109, 150, 158, 159, 160, 161, 162, 163, 165, 167
Davis, Alex 185
Dearlove, J. E. 32
Defoe, Daniel 111
Deleuze, Gilles xvii, xx, xxi, xxii, 23, 41, 45, 62, 63, 72, 126, 127, 130, 131, 132, 133, 134, 135, 153, 156
Democritus of Abdera 145, 150
Derrida, Jacques xviii, 23, 27, 155, 161
Descartes, René 31, 32, 77, 112, 150, 151, 164
De Valera, Éamon 186, 190, 195
Devine, George 69
Devlin, Denis 9, 14, 79, 84
Dickens, Charles 38, 39
Diderot, Denis 4
Döblin, Alfred 99
Dommange, Thomas 164
Dosse, François 62
Dostoyevsky, Fyodor 169, 184
Dou, Gerard 17
Doutey, Nicolas 164
Driver, Thomas 26, 195, 197, 198
Duchamp, Marcel 16
Dukes, Gerry 116
Duthuit, Georges xx, 4, 26, 73, 80, 81, 84, 85, 110, 119, 198

Eaglestone, Robert 101
Eagleton, Terry 101
Effinger, Elizabeth 30
Egoyan, Atom 136
Einstein, Albert 184
Eksteins, Modris 195
Eliot, George 39, 40, 47
Eliot, T. S. 77, 91, 95, 98, 101, 138, 172
Eluard, Paul 77
Engelberts, Matthijs 103
Epicurus 106
Esslin, Martin 50, 61, 154

Fargue, Léon-Paul 102
Faulkner, William 109
Federman, Raymond 23, 29, 49, 53, 101, 145, 152, 154
Fehsenfeld, Martha 65, 67, 68, 166
Feldman, Matthew xvii, 50, 100, 104, 108, 148, 149, 150, 151, 154, 156, 164
Feldman, Morton 137
Ferrini, Jean-Pierre xvii

Index

Feuillerat, Albert 95
Fifield, Peter xxii, xxv, xxvi, 32, 101, 145, 153, 156, 168
Flaubert, Gustave 164
Fletcher, John 84, 148
Foerst, Irmgard 140
Foron, Helfig 140
Foucault, Michel xviii, 23, 132, 133, 147
Fournier, Edith 124
Franzen, Erich 109
Frazier, Adrian 185
Freud, Sigmund 27, 94
Friedrich, Caspar David 111
Frost, Everett xvii, 103
Frye, Northrop 28

Galileo Galilei 166
Garnier, Pierre 174, 175
Garrard, Greg 62
Garrison, Alysia E. 24
Gaulle, Charles de 194
Genet, Jean 20, 90
Germoni, Karine 122
Gessner, Niklaus 119
Geulincx, Arnold xvii, xviii, xxii, 107, 108, 109, 112, 145, 150, 163, 164
Gibson, Alan 128
Gibson, Andrew xxii, xxiii, 24, 32, 46, 61, 62, 194, 195, 196, 197
Gidal, Peter 24
Gide, André 74, 84, 171
Gilman, Richard 185, 197
Giotto di Bondone 160
Glass, Philip 136
Goddard, Jean-Luc 130
Goebbels, Joseph 13
Goethe, Johann Wolfgang von 98, 117, 125
Golden, Sean 64
Goldoni, Carlo 16
Gontarski, S. E. xvii, xxi, 54, 68, 69, 110, 112, 114, 115, 126, 128, 140, 141
Gordon, Rae Beth 172
Graver, Lawrence 23, 29, 49, 53, 101, 145, 152, 154
Gray, Thomas xxi
Grossman, Evelyne 30
Gruen, John 125
Guattari, Félix 127, 134
Guerlac, Suzanne 170

Hacker, Theodor 197
Hall, Peter 49

Harmon, Maurice 7, 61, 65, 66, 71, 83, 122, 138, 177
Harris, Ruth 171, 173
Harvey, Lawrence E. xx, 3, 16, 73, 77, 84, 145
Hassan, Ihab 90, 92
Havel, Václav 48
Hayden, Henri 80, 82
Hayman, David 117
Heidegger, Martin 63, 96, 105, 152, 154
Heraclites 107, 127
Herm, Klaus 140
Herman, David xix
Hesla, David H. 26, 27, 31, 32
Hill, Leslie 27, 30, 32, 122
Hippocrates 153, 154
Hisgen, Ruud 105
Hitler, Adolf 186, 196
Hobson, Harold 49
Hogan, Thomas 25
Horkheimer, Max 166, 167
Houben, Jozef 137
Howarth, Donald 57
Howes, Marjorie 196
Huizinga, Johan 93
Hummel, Juerg 140
Hunter, Kathryn 137
Husserl, Edmund 146

Ibn Tufayl 111
Ibsen, Henrik 49, 138
Illig, Nancy 140
Inge, W.R. 16
Ionesco, Eugène 61

Jacobsen, Josephine 32
Jameson, Fredric 41, 92, 93, 94, 101
Janvier, Agnes and Ludovic 114, 125
Jencks, Charles 91
Johnson, Samuel xxii, 180, 181, 182, 183, 184
Jolas, Eugene 101, 102
Jones, David Houston 24
Joyce, James 20, 28, 40, 74, 75, 89, 91, 95, 97, 98, 101, 102, 116, 120, 126, 131, 159, 163, 177, 185
Jung, Carl Gustav 163

Kafka, Franz 20, 28, 90, 98, 198
Kahane, Jack 165
Kalb, Jonathan 52
Kandel, Karen 136

Index

Kant, Immanuel 105, 108, 111, 164, 165, 166
Karmitz, Mariu 128
Katz, Daniel 32
Kaun, Axel 82, 95, 117, 118, 119, 120, 125
Keats, John xxiii, 40
Kennedy, Seán xxii, xxiii, 24, 36, 61, 64, 185, 186, 194, 196, 197
Kenner, Hugh 26, 31, 150, 185, 189, 190
Keogh, Dermot 190
Kermode, Frank 29
Kiberd, Declan 25, 36, 185
Kitchener, Herbert Horatio 196
Kleist, Heinrich von 93, 164
Klossowski, Pierre 165
Kluth, Karl 78
Knowlson, James xvii, xxiv, 17, 18, 32, 50, 54, 65, 69, 78, 103, 111, 112, 116, 119, 121, 122, 125, 128, 147, 152, 154, 156, 188, 189
Knupfer, Claudia 140
Krance, Charles 103
Kristeva, Julia xviii, 29, 30

Lacan, Jacques xviii, 29, 165, 167, 169
Laloy, Louis 17
Lane, Richard 148
Lawlor, Seán 73, 117
Leibniz, Gottfried 154
Leiris, Michel 102
Leishmann, J. B. 84
Le Juez, Brigitte xvii
Le Doeuff, Michèle 111
Lernout, Geert 100
Leventhal, A. J. 22, 52, 84
Levi, Primo 97
Levinas, Emmanuel 23, 24, 101, 157, 168, 169
Lewis, Wyndham 92
Lindon, Jérôme 20, 115, 146
Lloyd, David 64, 85, 187, 195
Loy, Mina 92
Lubitsch, Ernst 172
Lucretius 106, 107
Lustig, Arnošt 97
Lyons, Charles R. 67

MacGowran, Jack 56, 128, 141
MacGowran, Tara 115
MacGreevy, Thomas 9, 10, 16, 17, 73, 75, 76, 79, 84, 107, 116, 122, 125, 155, 157, 178, 186, 189

Macmillan, Dougald 65, 67, 68, 166
Magnim, Marcello 137
Malebranche, Nicolas 108, 150
Mallarmé, Stéphane 90, 91, 101, 120
Malraux, André 116
Mann, Thomas 95
Manning Howe, Mary 182, 183, 184
Manzay, J. Kyle 57
Marc, Franz 79
Masson, André 81
Maude, Ulrika xxii, xxvi, 32, 72, 170, 177, 184
Maupassant, Guy de 172
Mauthner, Fritz xxi, 90, 98, 100, 120, 148
Maxwell, Jane xvii, 103
Mays, J. C. C. xxv
McCormack, W. J. 64, 196
McDonald, Rónán xix, xx, 48, 69
McElroen, Christopher 58
McHale, Brian xx, 90, 101
McMullan, Anna 72
McNaughton, James xxii, 185, 186, 187, 195
McTighe, Trish 72
McWhinnie, Donald 128, 140
Méliès, Georges 172
Mendel, Deryk 140
Mercier, Vivian 24, 26, 32
Messina, Antonello da 26
Migernier, Eric 32
Miller, Arthur 49
Miller, Tyrus 92, 93, 101
Milne, Drew 34, 35, 44
Milton, John 38, 43
Mitchell, Katie 135, 136
Mitchell, Pamela 115
Moerike, Edward 84
Molière 126
Montini, Chiara xxi, 116–117
Moody, Alys 58
Mooney, Susan 31, 32
Mooney, Sinéad xxi, 32, 116, 121, 123, 125
Moorjani, Angela xx, 19, 22, 23, 26, 27, 28, 31, 32, 156
Moorjani, Kishin 26
Morash, Christopher 51
Morin, Emilie xx, 60, 64, 68, 119, 186, 195
Mueller, William R. 32
Murphy, P. J. 147

Nabokov, Vladimir 89, 92
Nadeau, Maurice 21, 22, 23

Index

Naumann, Hans 119, 120
Nicholson, Steve 69
Nietzsche, Friedrich 127, 130, 133, 161, 169, 197
Nixon, Mark xvii, xx, xxii, xxv, xxv, 5, 16, 50, 73, 74, 76, 79, 84, 85, 93, 100, 103, 104, 105, 112, 154, 156, 175, 178, 180, 186
Nordau, Max 174, 175, 176, 195, 197
Nussbaum, Martha xxii
Nye, Robert A. 196

O'Brien, Eoin 125
O'Casey, Sean 52, 84
O'Conaire, Padraic 125
O'Connell, Daniel 187
Oppenheim, Lois 65
Orwell, George 46
Osler, Sir William 174, 175
O'Toole, Fintan xix, xxv
Ovid 6, 16

Parmenides 169
Parnell, Charles Stewart 187
Pascal, Blaise 49, 165
Pavlov, Ivan 177
Pearson, Nels C. 64, 70
Pelorson, Georges 180
Perkins Gilman, Charlotte 37
Péron, Alfred 120, 125, 183, 184
Pétain, Philippe 194, 196
Phillips, Siân 128, 197
Picon, Gaëtan 20
Pierce, Wendell 57
Piette, Adam xxv
Pilling, John xvii, xviii, xix, xxiv, 3, 42, 73, 80, 112, 115, 117, 171, 184
Pingaud, Bernard 21
Pinget, Robert 129, 138, 139
Pinter, Harold 48
Plato 153
Plümacher, Olga 148
Poe, Edgar Allan 101
Pollock, Jackson 92
Popper, Karl 104, 148, 149
Porter, Lucy 181
Pound, Ezra 84, 89, 92, 95, 97, 163
Prentice, Charles 171, 184
Proust, Marcel 20, 75, 89, 91, 94, 95, 159, 160, 162, 166, 168, 169, 171, 184
Pythagoras 150

Quigley, Megan 125

Rabaté, Jean-Michel xviii, xxii, 85, 105, 158, 169
Rabelais, François 177, 178, 183
Racine, Jean xxi
Ravaisson, Félix 175
Ravel, Jean 128
Reavey, George 13, 118, 120
Regan, John 190
Rehe, Suzanne 140
Reid, Alec 198
Reid, Christopher 77
Reid, Thomas xxii
Renard, Jules 17, 179, 180, 183
Ricks, Christopher 118
Rilke, Rainer Maria 84, 95
Rimbaud, Arthur 12, 77, 93, 107, 116
Ringelnatz, Joachim 117, 125
Robbe-Grillet, Alain 63
Ronen, Ilan 57
Ronsard, Pierre de 8
Rosset, Barney 71, 84, 115, 125, 140
Ruskin, John 160

Sade, Marquis de 90, 94, 164, 165, 167, 169
Sage, Victor 38
Said, Edward 45, 92
Salisbury, Laura xxvi, 21, 24, 32, 176, 184
Sardin, Pascale xxi, 122, 125
Sartre, Jean-Paul 20, 27, 50, 61, 62, 63, 152, 154, 155, 157, 163, 168, 198
Sbarbaro, Camillo 4
Schmidt, Judith 127
Schneider, Alan 50, 61, 65, 122, 123, 128, 133, 134, 140, 141, 177
Schopenhauer, Arthur 22, 29, 75, 94, 96, 108, 148, 149, 152, 154, 164
Seaver, Richard 116, 125, 140
Sebald, W. G. 96, 99, 100
Séguier, Julia 84
Serreau, Jean-Marie 128, 140
Shainberg, Lawrence 182, 183
Shakespeare, William xxi, 52, 60, 70, 109, 150
Shaw, George Bernard 49, 138
Shenker, Israel 101, 119, 185, 197, 198
Sheppard, Oliver 186
Sherman, Cindy 92
Sherzer, Dina 32
Simpson, Alan 51
Slote, Sam xxi, 114, 123, 124
Smith, Frederik 181
Sontag, Susan 57
Spinoza, Baruch xxii, 108, 127, 154, 167

Index

Stacey, Stephen 120
Stanford-Friedman, Susan 185
Stein, Gertrude 102
Stella, Frank 92
Stendhal 15
Stephen, Karin 174, 176
Stoppard, Tom 48
Stramm, August 102
Stravinsky, Igor 49
Synge, J. M. 29, 49, 52
Szafraniec, Asja 32

Tajiri, Yoshiki 31, 32, 62, 159, 175
Tal Coat, Pierre 81
Tanaka, Mariko Hori 32, 159
Tandy, Jessica 133
Thales 153
Thornton, A. P. 196
Thrale, Hester 180, 181, 182, 183, 184
Tolstoy, Leo 95
Tonning, Erik 72
Torok, Maria 29
Touret, Michèle 32
Tourette, Georges Gilles de la 171, 175
Trezise, Thomas 23, 32
Tsushima, Michiko 32, 159
Tucker, David xvii, 84, 108
Tynan, Kenneth 49, 138

Uhlmann, Anthony xvii, xviii, xxi, 27, 32, 85, 103, 110, 112, 156, 164
Ulin, Julieann 64, 70

Valéry, Paul 16
van der Weel, Adriaan 105
Van Hulle, Dirk xxii, xxv, 30, 69, 70, 91, 93, 99, 100, 103, 104, 105, 112, 120, 125, 156, 178, 180

van Ruler, Han 107, 164
van Velde, Bram and Geer 15, 19, 80, 81, 82, 110
van Velde, Jacoba xxiii
Verhulst, Pim xxxii
Vico, Giambattista 74, 163
Virgil 159, 162
von der Vogelweide, Walther xix
von Hofmannsthal, Hugo 97, 166

Wahl, Jean 145, 146
Warner, Deborah 135
Watson, John B. 177
Watt, James 166
Weiler, Gershon 120
Weiss, Katherine 186
Weller, Shane xx, 22, 23, 89, 91, 94, 96, 99, 125, 147, 156, 157, 168, 169
Wheatley, David 77, 85
White, H. O. 114
Whitelaw, Billie 56, 128
Wiesel, Elie 97
Wilde, Alan 101
Wilder, Clinton 134
Wilson, Martin 107
Wiltshire, John 184
Windelband, Wilhelm 108, 148, 150, 151
Wittgenstein, Ludwig 166
Woodworth, Robert 174, 176

Yeats, Jack B. 16, 76, 80, 82, 84, 89, 96, 186
Yeats, W. B. 75, 138, 196

Zilliacus, Clas 71
Zola, Emile 176
Zurbrugg, Nicholas 95

Cambridge Companions to...

AUTHORS

Edward Albee edited by Stephen J. Bottoms
Margaret Atwood edited by Coral Ann Howells
W. H. Auden edited by Stan Smith
Jane Austen edited by Edward Copeland and Juliet McMaster (second edition)
Beckett edited by John Pilling
Bede edited by Scott DeGregorio
Aphra Behn edited by Derek Hughes and Janet Todd
Walter Benjamin edited by David S. Ferris
William Blake edited by Morris Eaves
Jorge Luis Borges edited by Edwin Williamson
Brecht edited by Peter Thomson and Glendyr Sacks (second edition)
The Brontës edited by Heather Glen
Bunyan edited by Anne Dunan-Page
Frances Burney edited by Peter Sabor
Byron edited by Drummond Bone
Albert Camus edited by Edward J. Hughes
Willa Cather edited by Marilee Lindemann
Cervantes edited by Anthony J. Cascardi
Chaucer edited by Piero Boitani and Jill Mann (second edition)
Chekhov edited by Vera Gottlieb and Paul Allain
Kate Chopin edited by Janet Beer
Caryl Churchill edited by Elaine Aston and Elin Diamond
Cicero edited by Catherine Steel
Coleridge edited by Lucy Newlyn
Wilkie Collins edited by Jenny Bourne Taylor
Joseph Conrad edited by J. H. Stape
H. D. edited by Nephie J. Christodoulides and Polina Mackay
Dante edited by Rachel Jacoff (second edition)
Daniel Defoe edited by John Richetti
Don DeLillo edited by John N. Duvall
Charles Dickens edited by John O. Jordan
Emily Dickinson edited by Wendy Martin
John Donne edited by Achsah Guibbory
Dostoevskii edited by W. J. Leatherbarrow
Theodore Dreiser edited by Leonard Cassuto and Claire Virginia Eby

John Dryden edited by Steven N. Zwicker
W. E. B. Du Bois edited by Shamoon Zamir
George Eliot edited by George Levine
T. S. Eliot edited by A. David Moody
Ralph Ellison edited by Ross Posnock
Ralph Waldo Emerson edited by Joel Porte and Saundra Morris
William Faulkner edited by Philip M. Weinstein
Henry Fielding edited by Claude Rawson
F. Scott Fitzgerald edited by Ruth Prigozy
Flaubert edited by Timothy Unwin
E. M. Forster edited by David Bradshaw
Benjamin Franklin edited by Carla Mulford
Brian Friel edited by Anthony Roche
Robert Frost edited by Robert Faggen
Gabriel García Márquez edited by Philip Swanson
Elizabeth Gaskell edited by Jill L. Matus
Goethe edited by Lesley Sharpe
Günter Grass edited by Stuart Taberner
Thomas Hardy edited by Dale Kramer
David Hare edited by Richard Boon
Nathaniel Hawthorne edited by Richard Millington
Seamus Heaney edited by Bernard O'Donoghue
Ernest Hemingway edited by Scott Donaldson
Homer edited by Robert Fowler
Horace edited by Stephen Harrison
Ted Hughes edited by Terry Gifford
Ibsen edited by James McFarlane
Henry James edited by Jonathan Freedman
Samuel Johnson edited by Greg Clingham
Ben Jonson edited by Richard Harp and Stanley Stewart
James Joyce edited by Derek Attridge (second edition)
Kafka edited by Julian Preece
Keats edited by Susan J. Wolfson
Rudyard Kipling edited by Howard J. Booth
Lacan edited by Jean-Michel Rabaté
D. H. Lawrence edited by Anne Fernihough
Primo Levi edited by Robert Gordon

Lucretius edited by Stuart Gillespie and Philip Hardie
Machiavelli edited by John M. Najemy
David Mamet edited by Christopher Bigsby
Thomas Mann edited by Ritchie Robertson
Christopher Marlowe edited by Patrick Cheney
Andrew Marvell edited by Derek Hirst and Steven N. Zwicker
Herman Melville edited by Robert S. Levine
Arthur Miller edited by Christopher Bigsby (second edition)
Milton edited by Dennis Danielson (second edition)
Molière edited by David Bradby and Andrew Calder
Toni Morrison edited by Justine Tally
Nabokov edited by Julian W. Connolly
Nelson Mandela edited by Rita Barnard
Eugene O'Neill edited by Michael Manheim
George Orwell edited by John Rodden
Ovid edited by Philip Hardie
Harold Pinter edited by Peter Raby (second edition)
Sylvia Plath edited by Jo Gill
Edgar Allan Poe edited by Kevin J. Hayes
Alexander Pope edited by Pat Rogers
Ezra Pound edited by Ira B. Nadel
Proust edited by Richard Bales
Pushkin edited by Andrew Kahn
Rabelais edited by John O'Brien
Rilke edited by Karen Leeder and Robert Vilain
Philip Roth edited by Timothy Parrish
Salman Rushdie edited by Abdulrazak Gurnah
Shakespeare edited by Margareta de Grazia and Stanley Wells (second edition)
Shakespearean Comedy edited by Alexander Leggatt
Shakespeare and Contemporary Dramatists edited by Ton Hoenselaars
Shakespeare and Popular Culture edited by Robert Shaughnessy
Shakespearean Tragedy edited by Claire McEachern (second edition)
Shakespeare on Film edited by Russell Jackson (second edition)
Shakespeare on Stage edited by Stanley Wells and Sarah Stanton

Shakespeare's History Plays edited by Michael Hattaway
Shakespeare's Last Plays edited by Catherine M. S. Alexander
Shakespeare's Poetry edited by Patrick Cheney
George Bernard Shaw edited by Christopher Innes
Shelley edited by Timothy Morton
Mary Shelley edited by Esther Schor
Sam Shepard edited by Matthew C. Roudané
Spenser edited by Andrew Hadfield
Laurence Sterne edited by Thomas Keymer
Wallace Stevens edited by John N. Serio
Tom Stoppard edited by Katherine E. Kelly
Harriet Beecher Stowe edited by Cindy Weinstein
August Strindberg edited by Michael Robinson
Jonathan Swift edited by Christopher Fox
J. M. Synge edited by P. J. Mathews
Tacitus edited by A. J. Woodman
Henry David Thoreau edited by Joel Myerson
Tolstoy edited by Donna Tussing Orwin
Anthony Trollope edited by Carolyn Dever and Lisa Niles
Mark Twain edited by Forrest G. Robinson
John Updike edited by Stacey Olster
Mario Vargas Llosa edited by Efrain Kristal and John King
Virgil edited by Charles Martindale
Voltaire edited by Nicholas Cronk
Edith Wharton edited by Millicent Bell
Walt Whitman edited by Ezra Greenspan
Oscar Wilde edited by Peter Raby
Tennessee Williams edited by Matthew C. Roudané
August Wilson edited by Christopher Bigsby
Mary Wollstonecraft edited by Claudia L. Johnson
Virginia Woolf edited by Susan Sellers (second edition)
Wordsworth edited by Stephen Gill
W. B. Yeats edited by Marjorie Howes and John Kelly
Zola edited by Brian Nelson

TOPICS

The Actress edited by Maggie B. Gale and John Stokes

The African American Novel edited by Maryemma Graham

The African American Slave Narrative edited by Audrey A. Fisch

Theatre History by David Wiles and Christine Dymkowski

African American Theatre by Harvey Young

Allegory edited by Rita Copeland and Peter Struck

American Crime Fiction edited by Catherine Ross Nickerson

American Modernism edited by Walter Kalaidjian

American Poetry Since 1945 edited by Jennifer Ashton

American Realism and Naturalism edited by Donald Pizer

American Travel Writing edited by Alfred Bendixen and Judith Hamera

American Women Playwrights edited by Brenda Murphy

Ancient Rhetoric edited by Erik Gunderson

Arthurian Legend edited by Elizabeth Archibald and Ad Putter

Australian Literature edited by Elizabeth Webby

Autobiography edited by Maria DiBattista and Emily Wittman

British Literature of the French Revolution edited by Pamela Clemit

British Romanticism edited by Stuart Curran (second edition)

British Romantic Poetry edited by James Chandler and Maureen N. McLane

British Theatre, 1730–1830, edited by Jane Moody and Daniel O'Quinn

Canadian Literature edited by Eva-Marie Kröller

Children's Literature edited by M. O. Grenby and Andrea Immel

The Classic Russian Novel edited by Malcolm V. Jones and Robin Feuer Miller

Contemporary Irish Poetry edited by Matthew Campbell

Creative Writing edited by David Morley and Philip Neilsen

Crime Fiction edited by Martin Priestman

Early Modern Women's Writing edited by Laura Lunger Knoppers

The Eighteenth-Century Novel edited by John Richetti

Eighteenth-Century Poetry edited by John Sitter

English Literature, 1500–1600 edited by Arthur F. Kinney

English Literature, 1650–1740 edited by Steven N. Zwicker

English Literature, 1740–1830 edited by Thomas Keymer and Jon Mee

English Literature, 1830–1914 edited by Joanne Shattock

English Novelists edited by Adrian Poole

English Poetry, Donne to Marvell edited by Thomas N. Corns

English Poets edited by Claude Rawson

English Renaissance Drama, second edition edited by A. R. Braunmuller and Michael Hattaway

English Renaissance Tragedy edited by Emma Smith and Garrett A. Sullivan Jr.

English Restoration Theatre edited by Deborah C. Payne Fisk

The Epic edited by Catherine Bates

European Modernism edited by Pericles Lewis

European Novelists edited by Michael Bell

Fairy Tales edited by Maria Tatar

Fantasy Literature edited by Edward James and Farah Mendlesohn

Feminist Literary Theory edited by Ellen Rooney

Fiction in the Romantic Period edited by Richard Maxwell and Katie Trumpener

The Fin de Siècle edited by Gail Marshall

The French Enlightenment edited by Daniel Brewer

The French Novel: from 1800 to the Present edited by Timothy Unwin

Gay and Lesbian Writing edited by Hugh Stevens

German Romanticism edited by Nicholas Saul

Gothic Fiction edited by Jerrold E. Hogle

The Greek and Roman Novel edited by Tim Whitmarsh

Greek and Roman Theatre edited by Marianne McDonald and J. Michael Walton

Greek Comedy edited by Martin Revermann

Greek Lyric edited by Felix Budelmann

Greek Mythology edited by Roger D. Woodard

Greek Tragedy edited by P. E. Easterling

The Harlem Renaissance edited by George Hutchinson

The History of the Book edited by
Leslie Howsam

The Irish Novel edited by John Wilson Foster

The Italian Novel edited by Peter Bondanella
and Andrea Ciccarelli

The Italian Renaissance edited by
Michael Wyatt

Jewish American Literature edited by Hana
Wirth-Nesher and Michael P. Kramer

The Latin American Novel edited by
Efraín Kristal

The Literature of the First World War edited by
Vincent Sherry

The Literature of London edited by
Lawrence Manley

The Literature of Los Angeles edited by
Kevin R. McNamara

The Literature of New York edited by
Cyrus Patell and Bryan Waterman

The Literature of Paris edited by
Anna-Louise Milne

The Literature of World War II edited by
Marina MacKay

Literature on Screen edited by
Deborah Cartmell and Imelda Whelehan

Medieval English Culture edited by
Andrew Galloway

Medieval English Literature edited by
Larry Scanlon

Medieval English Mysticism edited by
Samuel Fanous and Vincent Gillespie

Medieval English Theatre edited by Richard
Beadle and Alan J. Fletcher (second edition)

Medieval French Literature edited by
Simon Gaunt and Sarah Kay

Medieval Romance edited by
Roberta L. Krueger

Medieval Women's Writing edited by
Carolyn Dinshaw and David Wallace

Modern American Culture edited by
Christopher Bigsby

Modern British Women Playwrights edited by
Elaine Aston and Janelle Reinelt

Modern French Culture edited by
Nicholas Hewitt

Modern German Culture edited by
Eva Kolinsky and Wilfried van der Will

The Modern German Novel edited by
Graham Bartram

The Modern Gothic edited by Jerrold E. Hogle

Modern Irish Culture edited by Joe Cleary and
Claire Connolly

Modern Italian Culture edited by
Zygmunt G. Baranski and Rebecca J. West

Modern Latin American Culture edited by
John King

Modern Russian Culture edited by
Nicholas Rzhevsky

Modern Spanish Culture edited by
David T. Gies

Modernism edited by Michael Levenson
(second edition)

The Modernist Novel edited by Morag Shiach

Modernist Poetry edited by Alex Davis and
Lee M. Jenkins

Modernist Women Writers edited by
Maren Tova Linett

Narrative edited by David Herman

Native American Literature edited by
Joy Porter and Kenneth M. Roemer

Nineteenth-Century American Women's Writing
edited by Dale M. Bauer and Philip Gould

Old English Literature edited by
Malcolm Godden and Michael Lapidge
(second edition)

Paradise Lost edited by Louis Schwartz

Performance Studies edited by Tracy C. Davis

Piers Plowman by Andrew Cole and
Andrew Galloway

The Poetry of the First World War edited by
Santanu Das

Popular Fiction edited by David Glover and
Scott McCracken

Postcolonial Literary Studies edited by
Neil Lazarus

Postmodernism edited by Steven Connor

The Pre-Raphaelites edited by
Elizabeth Prettejohn

Pride and Prejudice edited by Janet Todd

Renaissance Humanism edited by Jill Kraye

The Roman Historians edited by
Andrew Feldherr

Roman Satire edited by Kirk Freudenburg

Science Fiction edited by Edward James and
Farah Mendlesohn

Scottish Literature edited by Gerald Carruthers
and Liam McIlvanney

Sensation Fiction edited by Andrew Mangham

The Sonnet edited by A. D. Cousins and
Peter Howarth

The Spanish Novel: from 1600 to the Present
edited by Harriet Turner and Adelaida López
de Martínez

Textual Scholarship edited by Neil Fraistat and Julia Flanders

Travel Writing edited by Peter Hulme and Tim Youngs

Twentieth-Century British and Irish Women's Poetry edited by Jane Dowson

The Twentieth-Century English Novel edited by Robert L. Caserio

Twentieth-Century English Poetry edited by Neil Corcoran

Twentieth-Century Irish Drama edited by Shaun Richards

Twentieth-Century Russian Literature edited by Marina Balina and Evgeny Dobrenko

Utopian Literature edited by Gregory Claeys

Victorian and Edwardian Theatre edited by Kerry Powell

The Victorian Novel edited by Deirdre David (second edition)

Victorian Poetry edited by Joseph Bristow

War Writing edited by Kate McLoughlin

Writing of the English Revolution edited by N. H. Keeble